"Cezanne made a living out of a teacup, or rather in a teacup he realized the existence of something alive. He raised still life to such a point that it ceased to be inanimate. He painted these things as human beings, because he was endowed with the gift of divining the inner life in everything. His colour and line are alike suitable to the spiritual harmony. A man, a tree, an apple – all were used by Cezanne in the creation of something that is called a "picture", and which is a piece of true inward and artistic harmony."

– Wassily Kandinsky

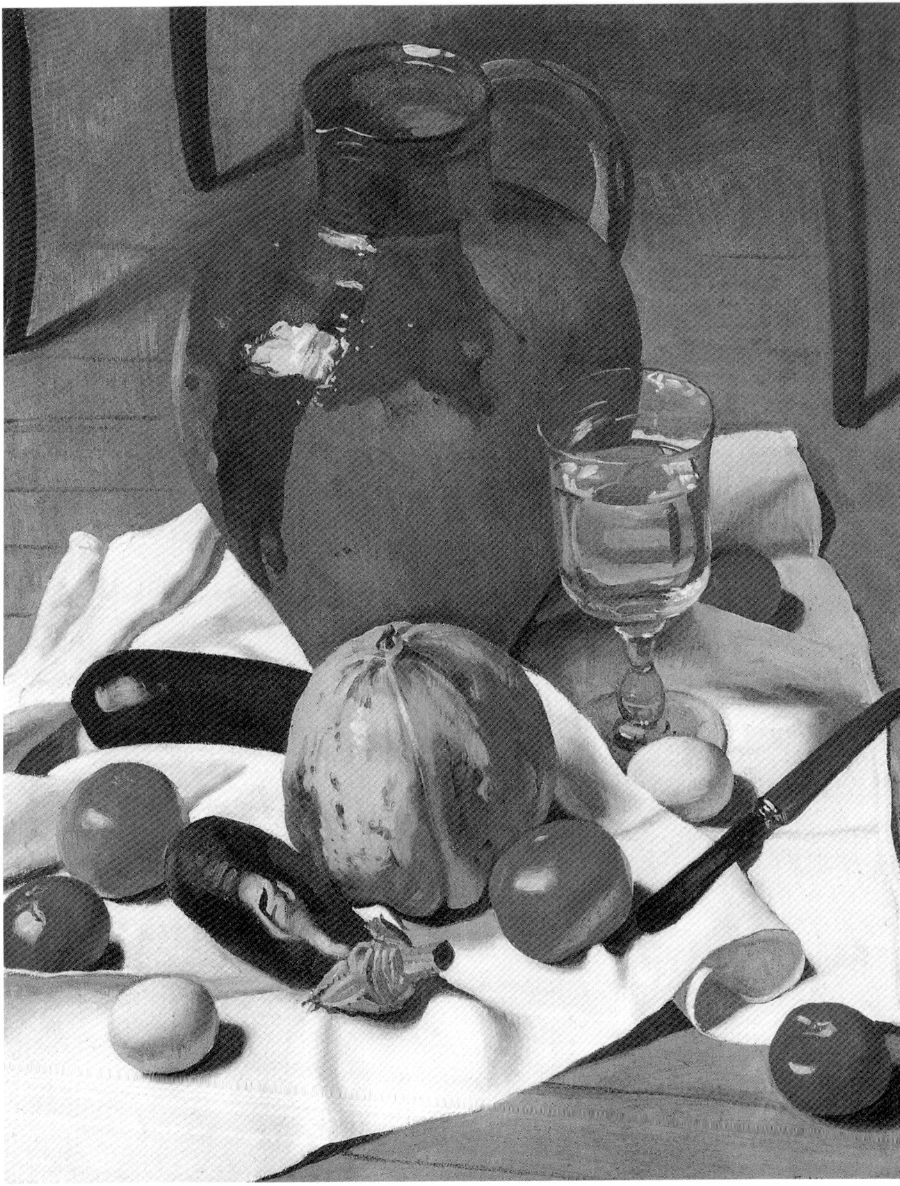

Contents

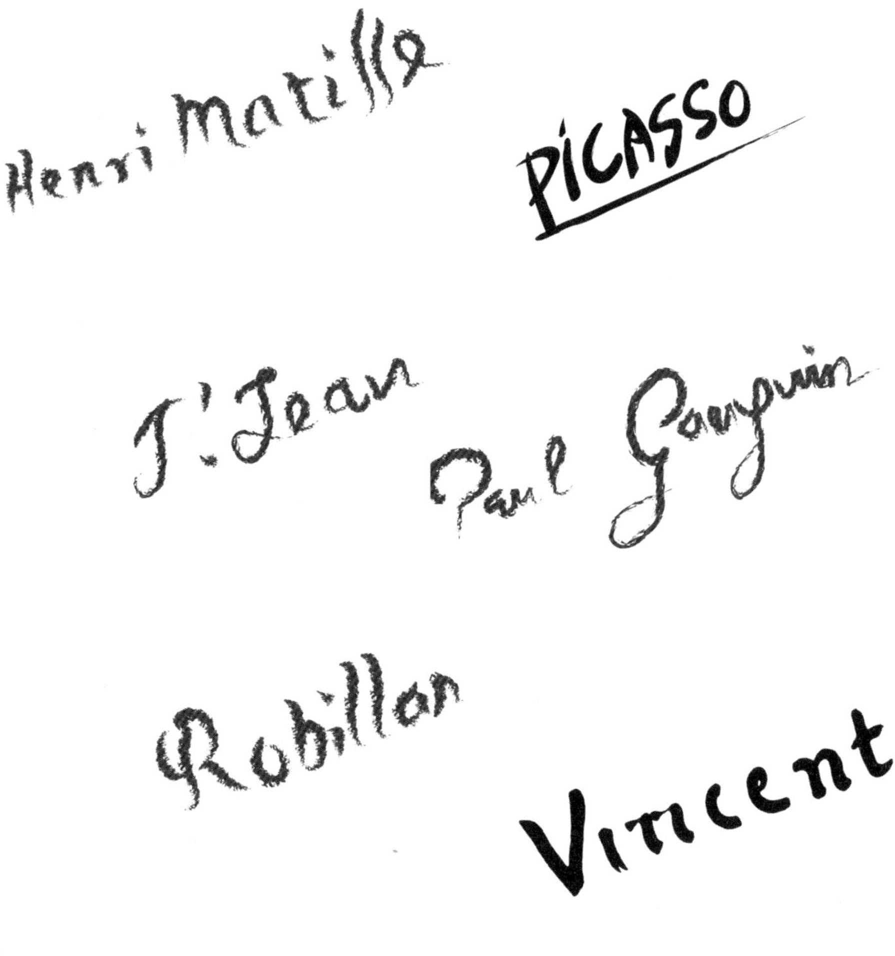
Henri Matisse
PICASSO
Paul Gauguin
Robillon
Vincent

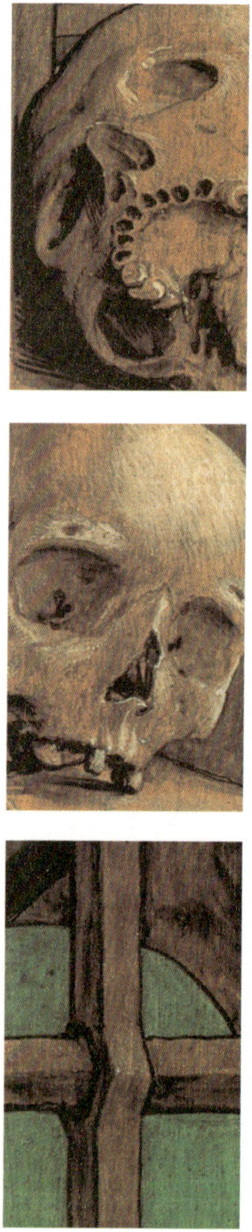

One should treat with doubt the extremely widespread conviction that the still life has been in art since time immemorial. We know of a large number of "still lifes" from the art of the antiquity, but it cannot serve as the sole criterion for today's definition of still life in art history.

Two Skulls on the Embrasure of a Window

Hans Holbein the Younger
tempera varnished on wood; 33 x 25 cm
Public collection, Art Museum, Basel

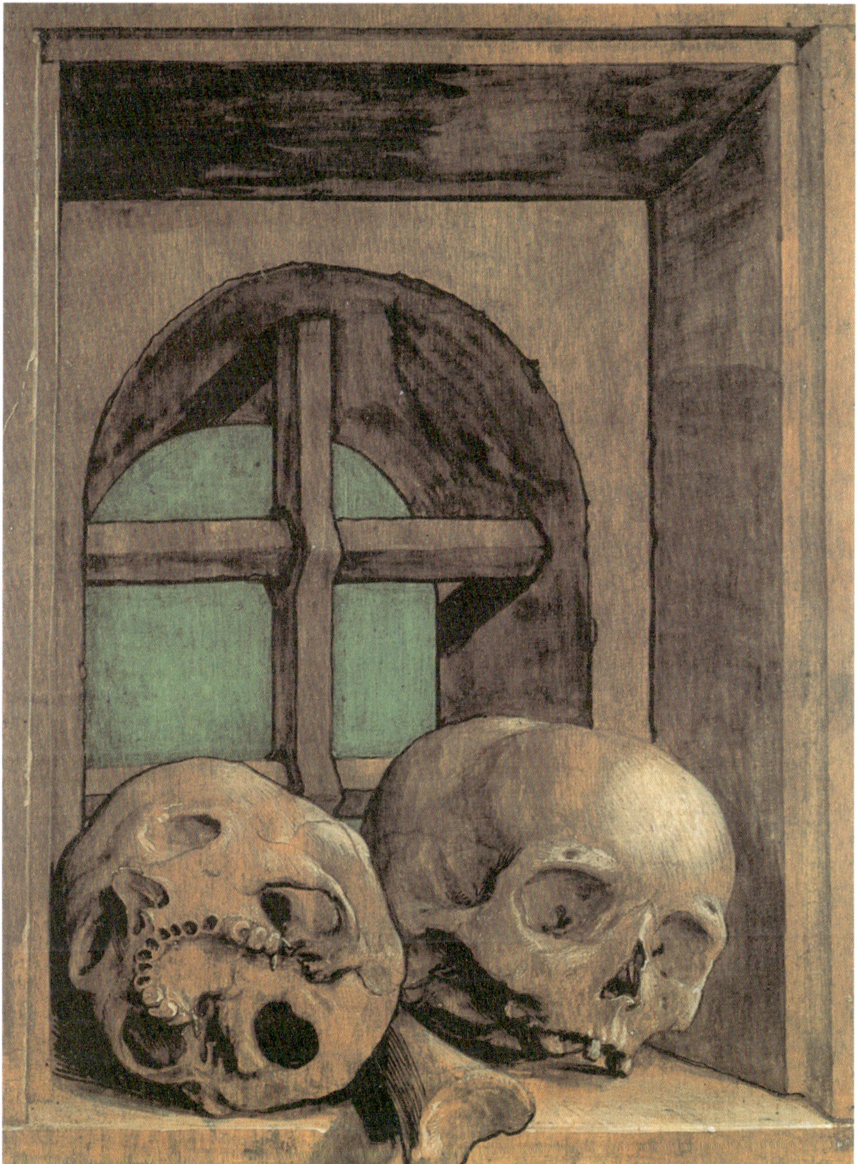

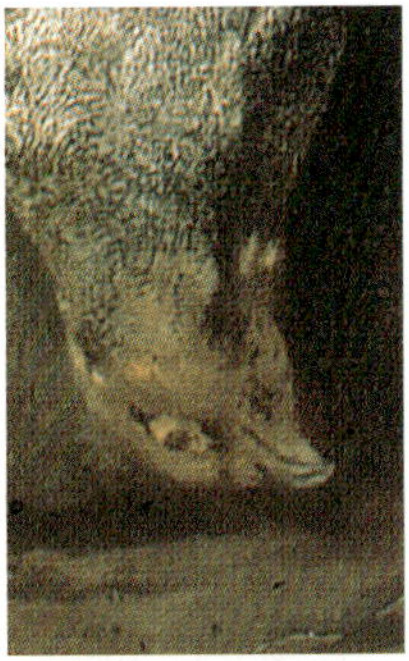

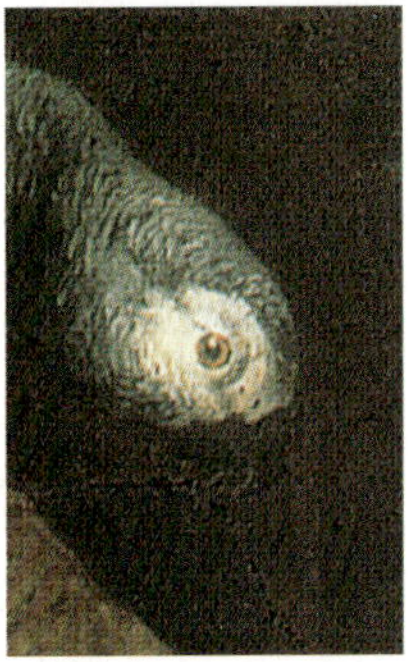

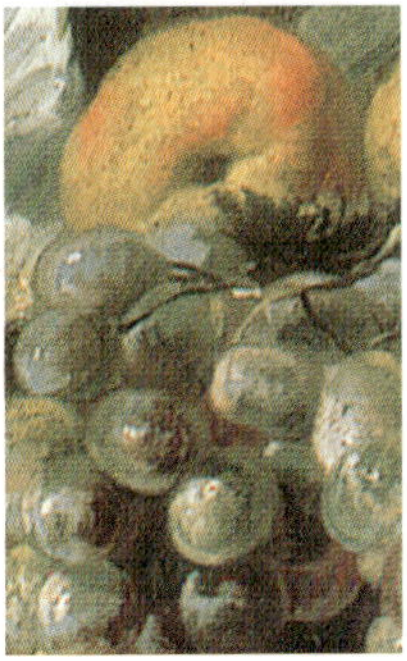

We should therefore avoid a confusion of the genre's history with its pre-history. It seems that the researchers link the history of the still life with the easel painting, "where its laws manifest themselves most distinctly and have direct parallels with the emergence of other genres within painting."

Game and Fruits

Peter Boel
Oil on canvas, 61.5 x 81 cm
Museum of Western and Oriental Art, Odessa

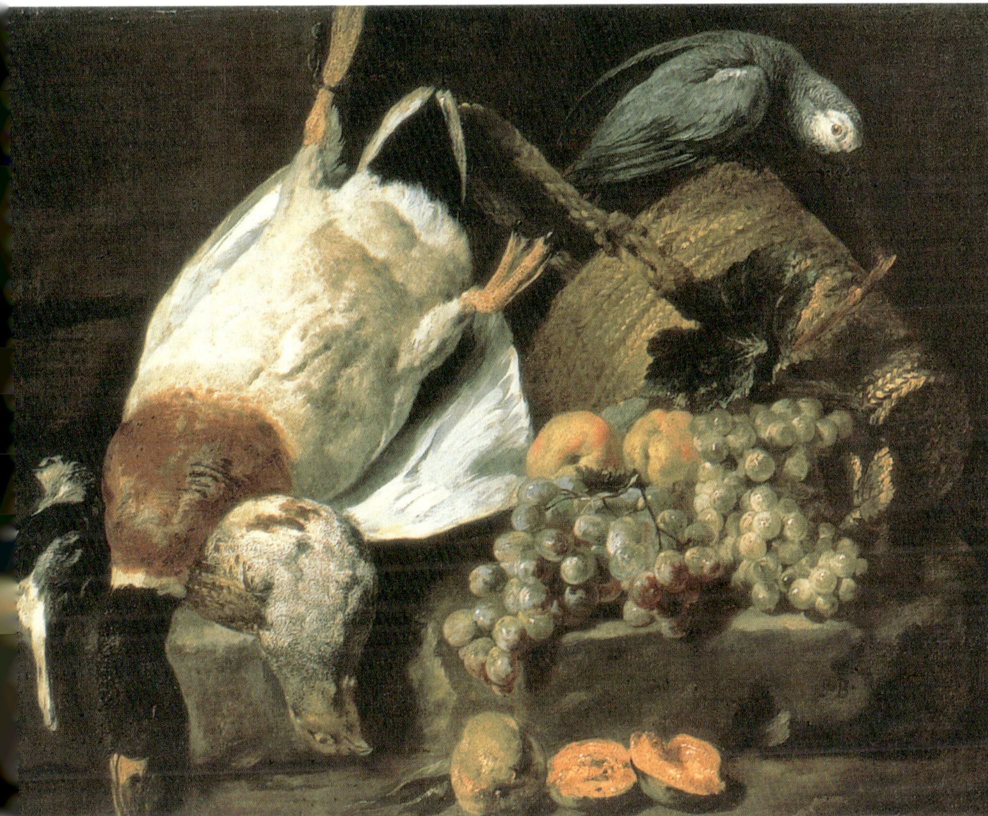

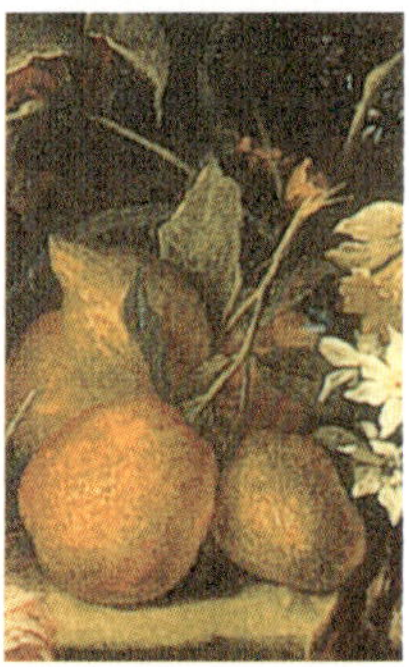

The Dutch term "stilleven" ("the quiet life"), first recorded in the year 1650, came into general use only towards the end of the seventeenth century. Later still, it was taken up by the English and German languages, and only then

Flowers and Fruit

Jean-Baptiste Monnoyer
Oil on canvas, 74.5 x 122 cm
The Hermitage, Saint Petersburg

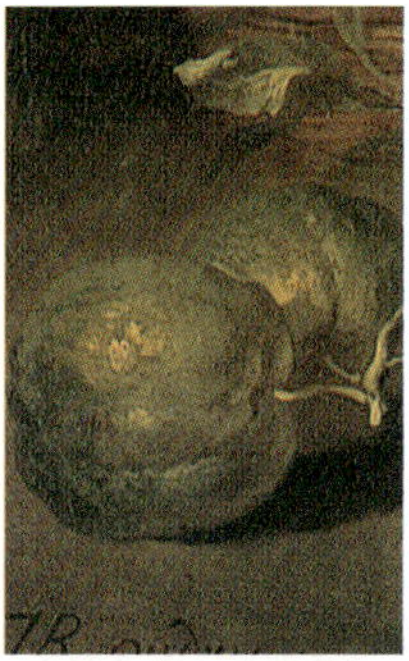

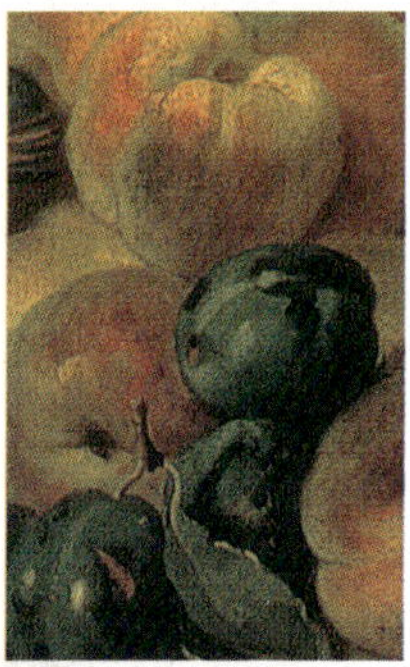

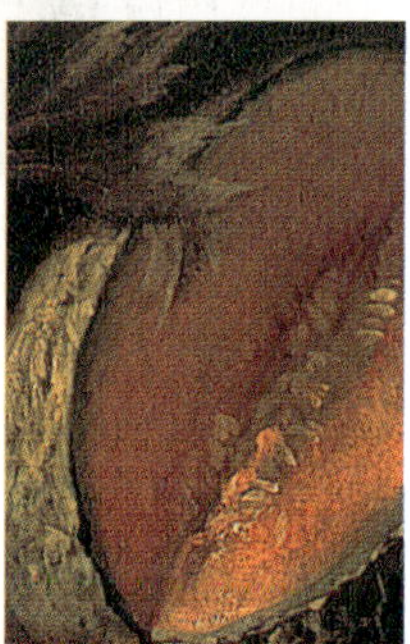

was its meaning inherited by the French term "nature morte," which shows however some degree of narrowing down, if compared with the original connotation. The fate of the still life proved completely different from that of the majority of genres in painting.

Fruits

Jean-Baptiste Oudry, 1721
Oil on canvas, 74 x 92 cm
Pushkin Museum of Fine Arts, Moscow

JB. oudry
1721

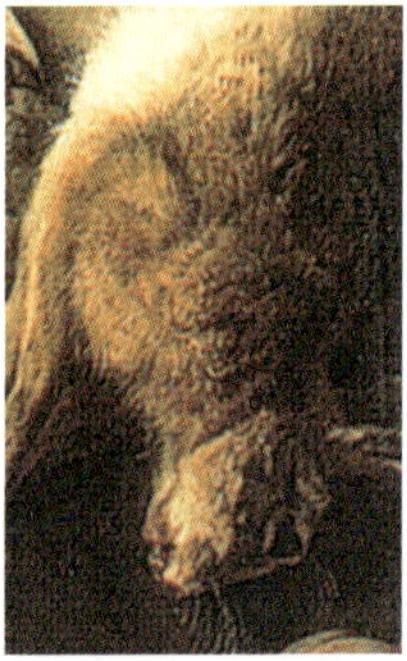

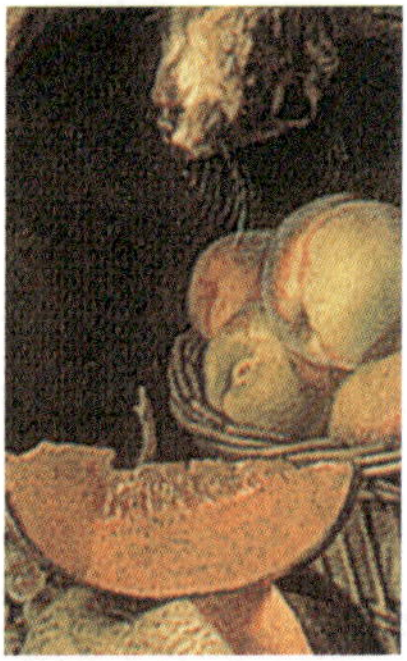

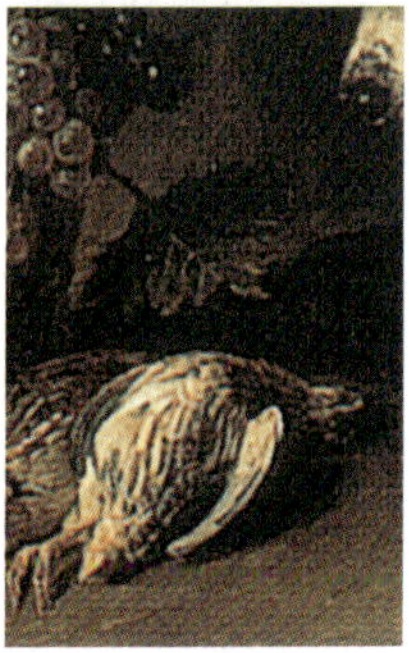

Alexandre-François Desportes, the noted still-life artist, "painter of the royal hunts", was still entirely in the thrall of the Flemish school, as can be seen from *Still Life with a Hare* and *Fruit and Still Life with Game and Vegetables* (both in the Hermitage).

Still-Life with a Hare and Fruits

François Desportes, 1711
Oil on canvas, 115 x 199 cm
The Hermitage, Saint Petersburg

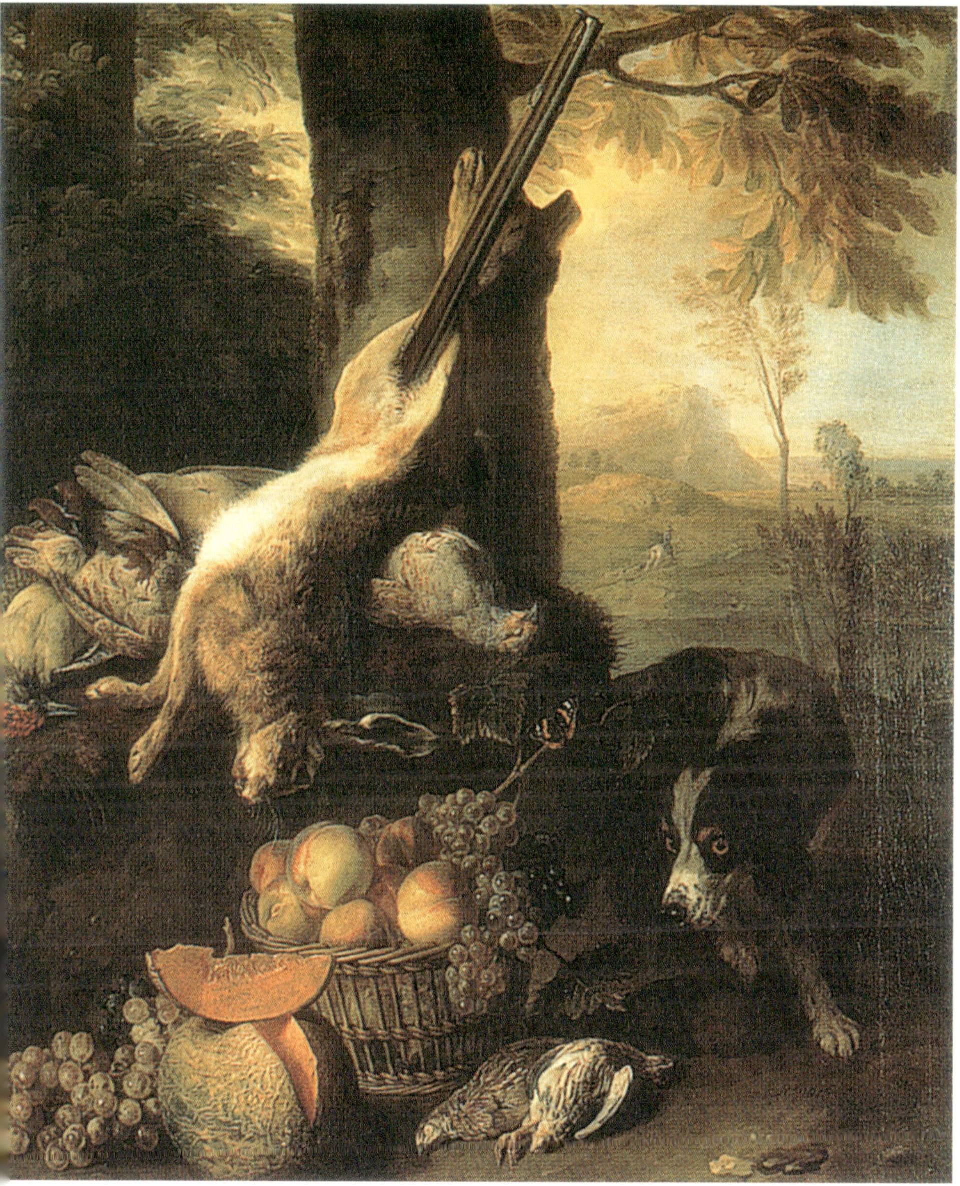

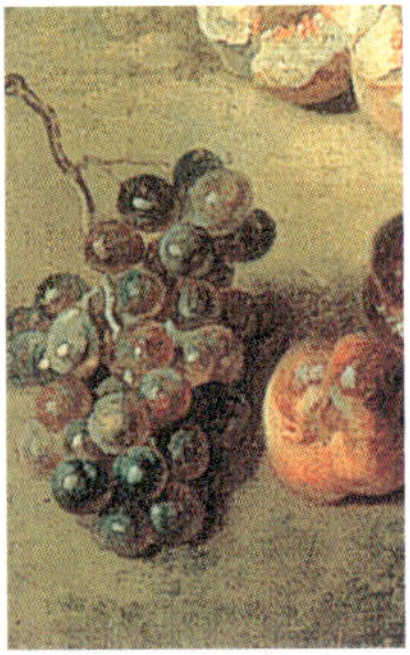

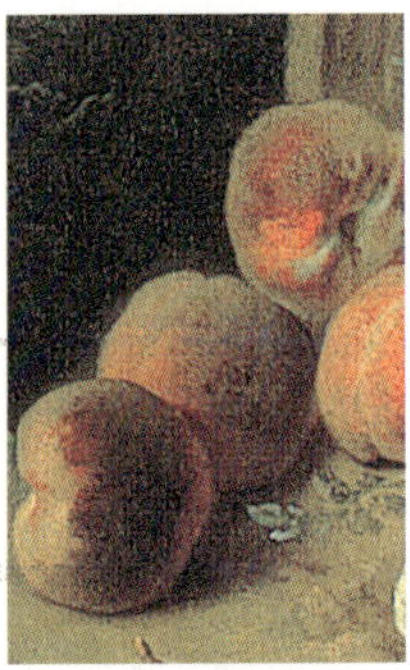

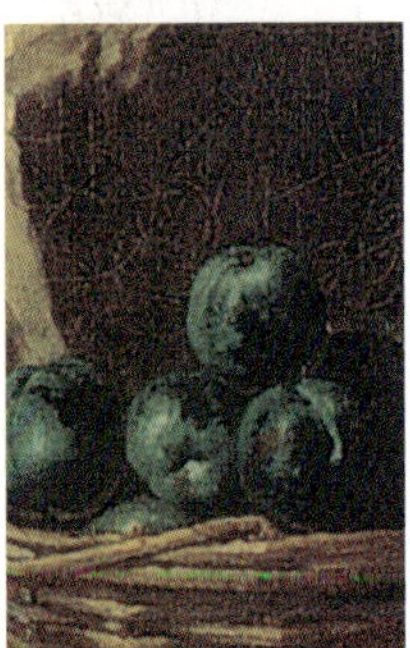

He displays the same refined naturalism in the juxtaposition of different textures to create his effect – foliage, fruit, stone, wood, feathers, wool, fur, and so on. His still lives might also include works of art such as, say,

Still-Life with Fruits

Jean-Baptiste Oudry, 1721
Oil on canvas, 74 x 92 cm
The Hermitage, Saint Petersburg

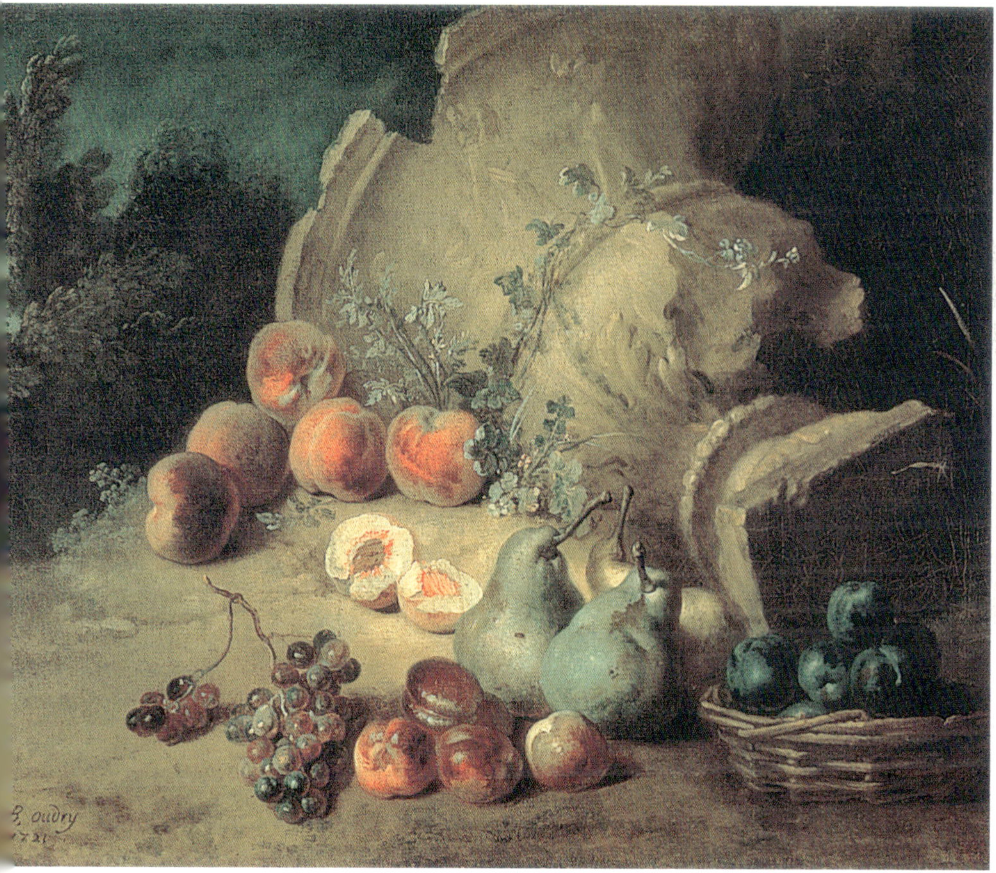

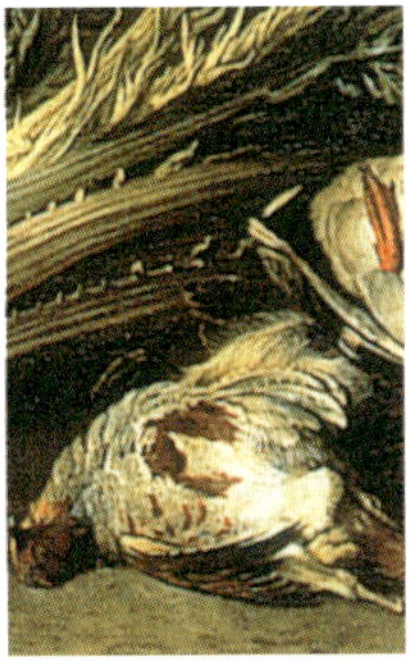

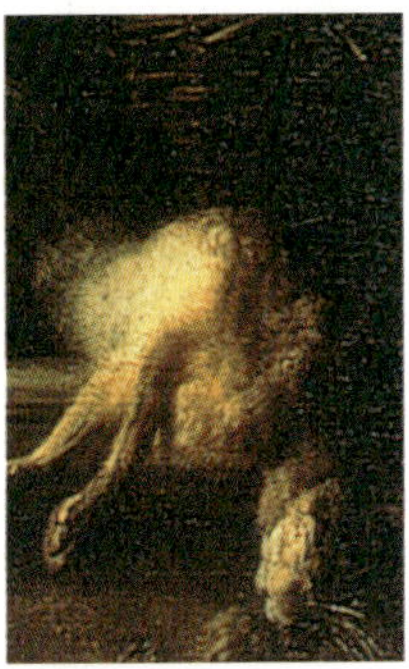

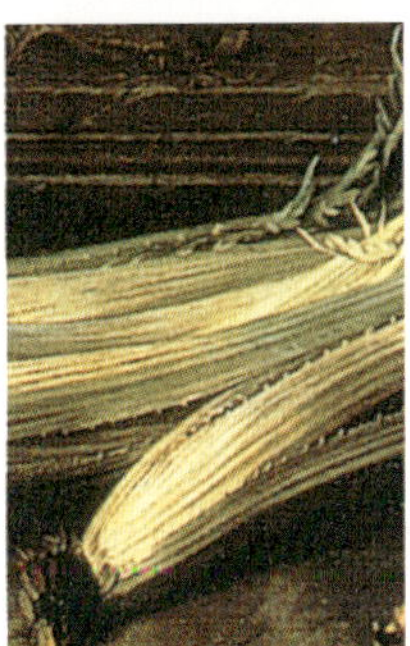

the relief by Duquesnoy included in *Still Life with Dead Game and Vegetables* – one of the highly fashionable "quotations" found in French painting from that time (and one more proof of close Franco-Flemish links in art).

Still-Life with Game and Vegetables

François Desportes, c. 1700
Oil on canvas, 121 x 135 cm
The Hermitage, Saint Petersburg

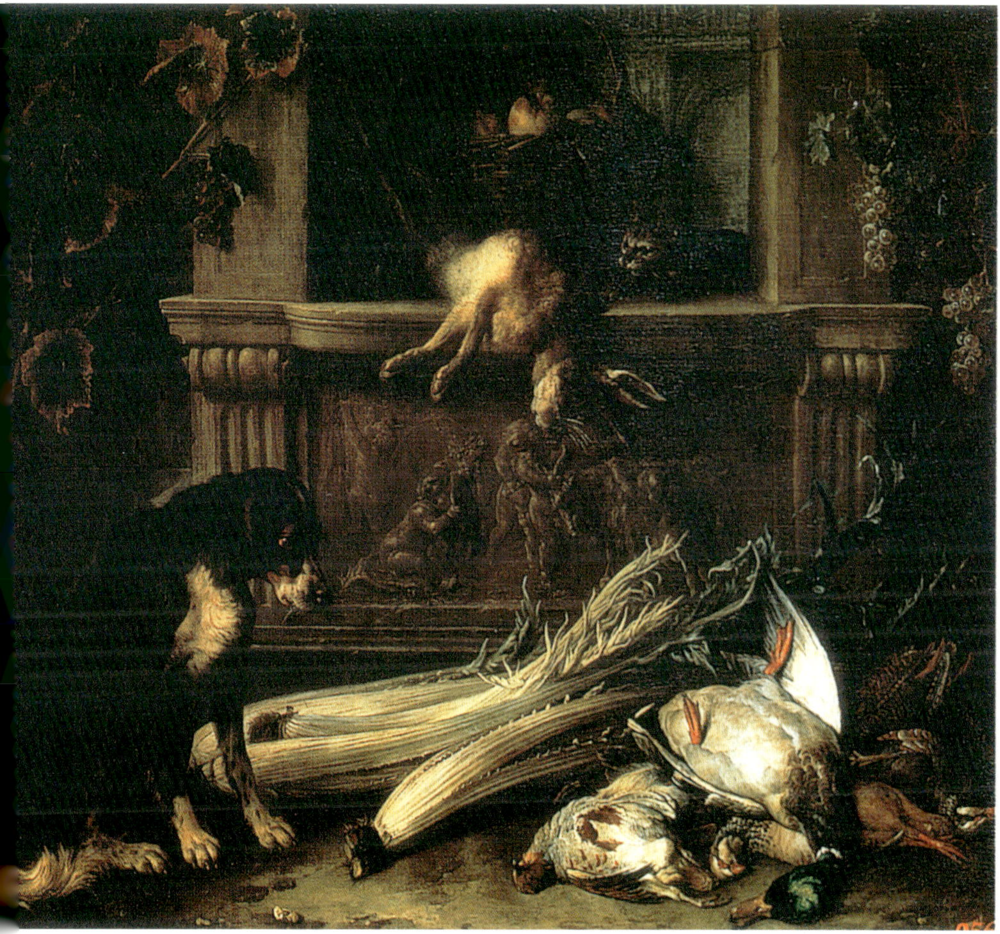

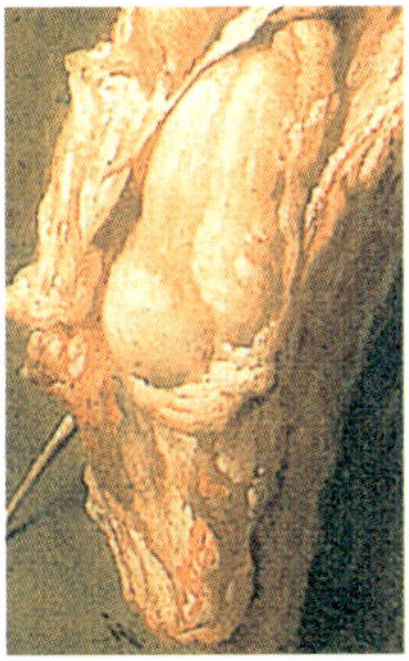
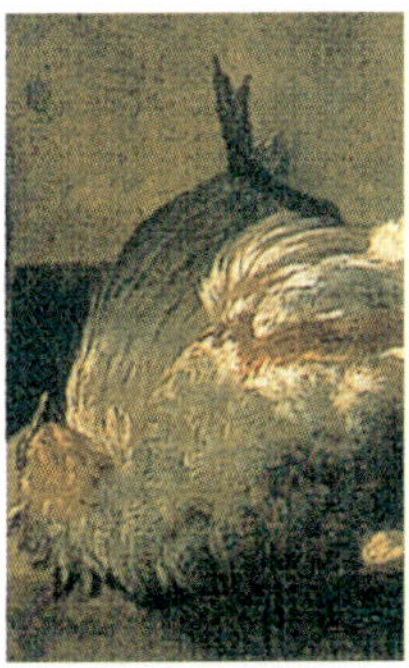
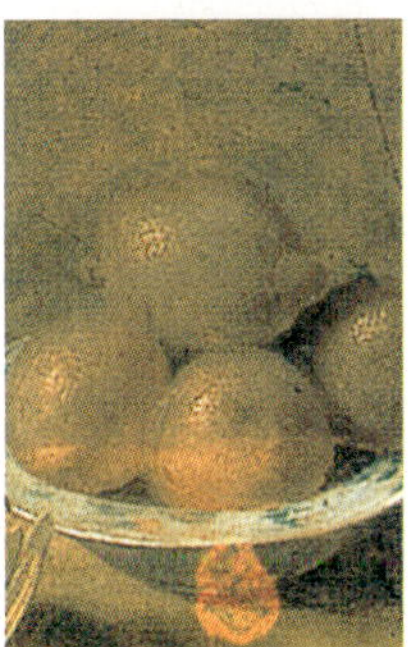

In short, in this modification the genre demonstrates what Boris Vipper termed a striving "to turn the still life into a living nature". Diderot notes in 1765 that it is to Chardin that we owe the fact that things, which had till then

Still-Life with a Leg of Veal

Jean-Baptiste Oudry, c. 1720
Oil on canvas, 98 x 74 cm
The Hermitage, Saint Petersburg

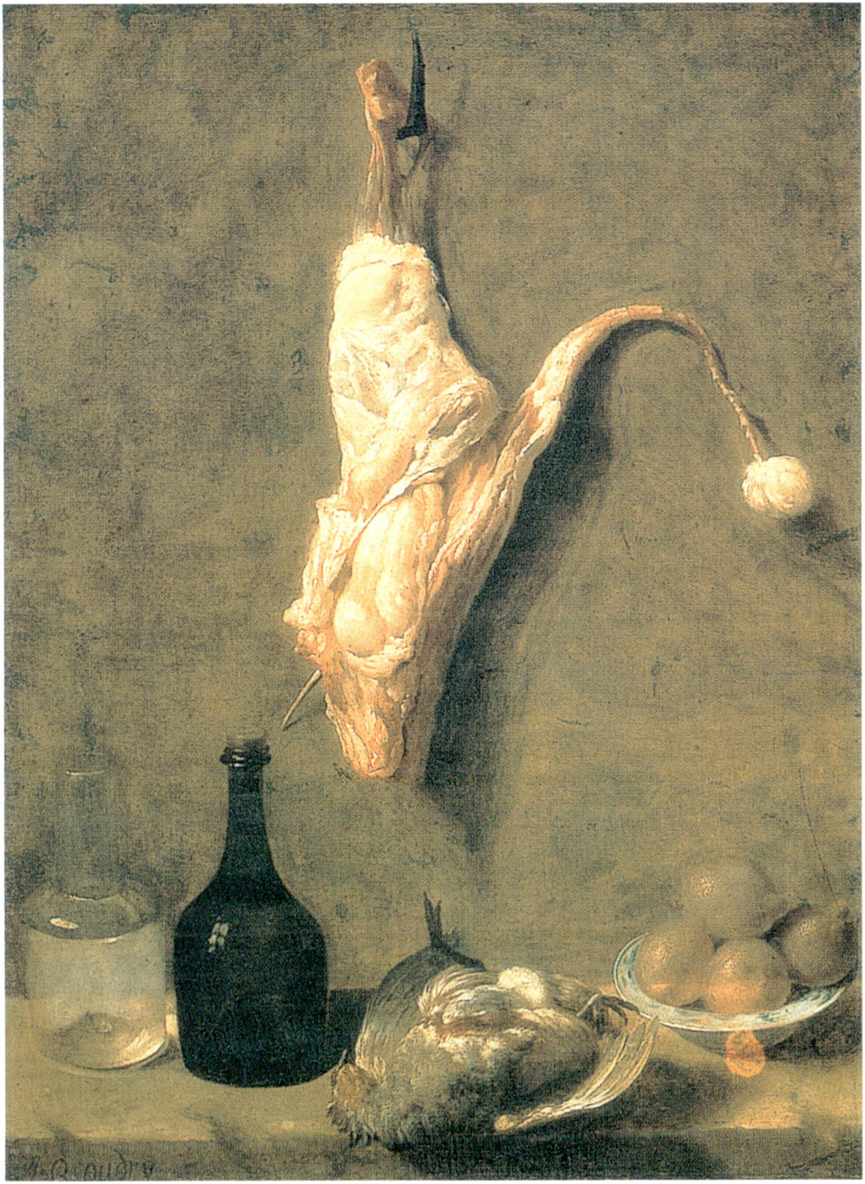

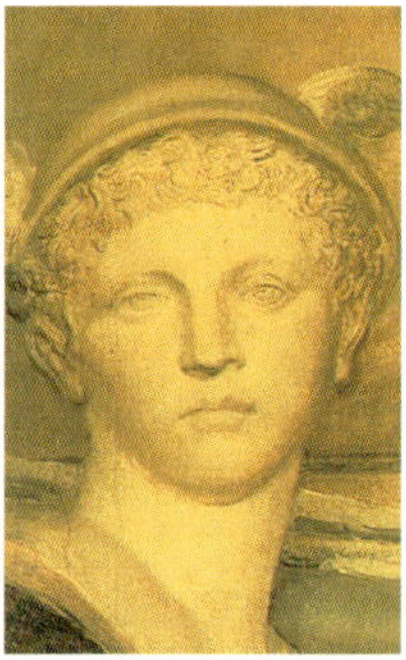

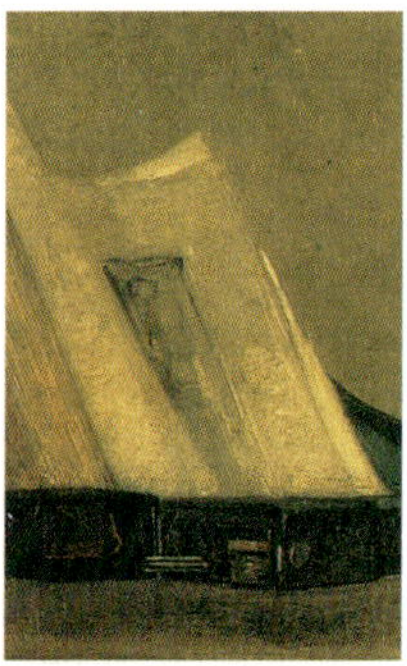

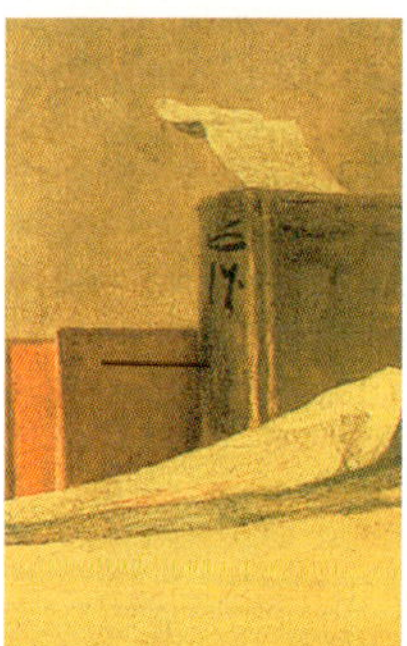

imitated perhaps beautiful, but nonetheless alien prototypes, those "silent creations" finally began to speak in French. Chardin recreated the genre, as it were, on the basis of the national artistic tradition.

Still Life with the Attributes of the Arts

Jean-Baptiste-Siméon Chardin, 1760s
Oil on canvas, 53 x 110 cm
Pushkin Museum of Fine Arts, Moscow

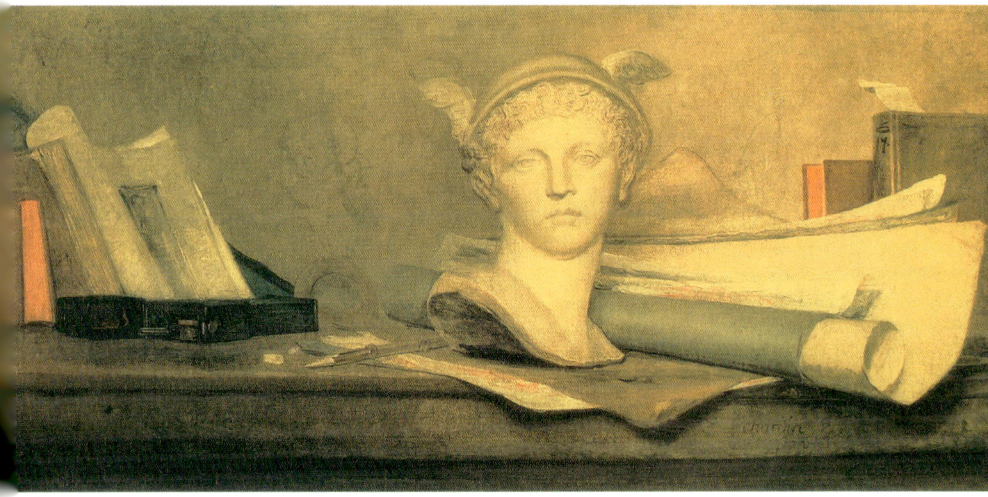

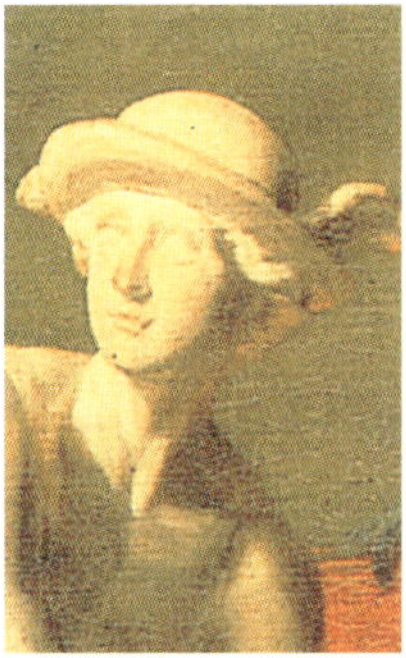

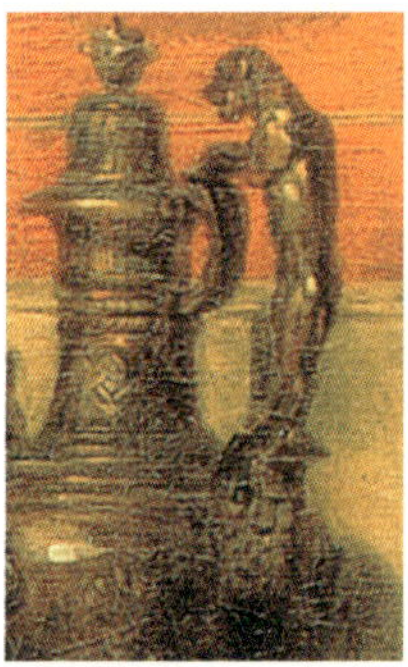

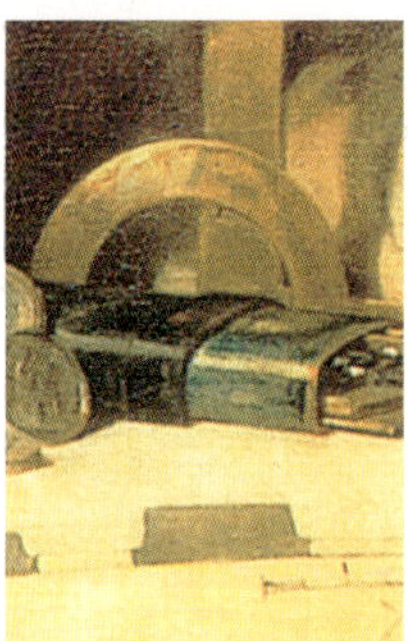

It is important to bear in mind that the system of genres is anthropocentric: even if the human being is not shown directly in a work, the human element forms the basis of any genre orientation.

Still Life with the Attributes of the Arts

Jean-Baptiste-Siméon Chardin, 1760s
Oil on canvas, 112 x 140.5 cm
The Hermitage, Saint Petersburg

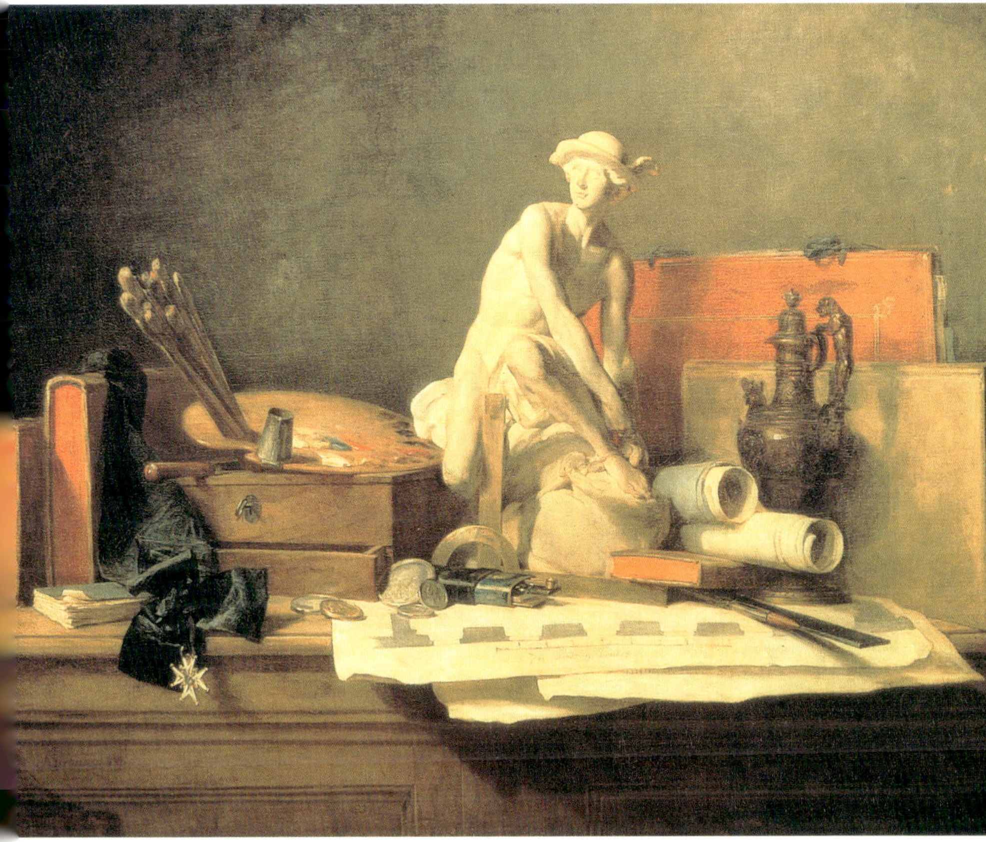

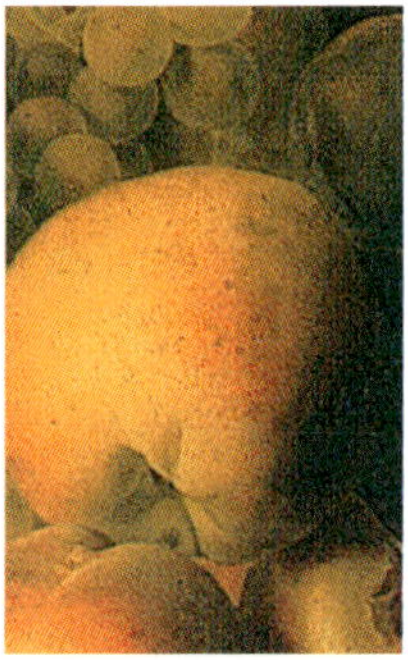

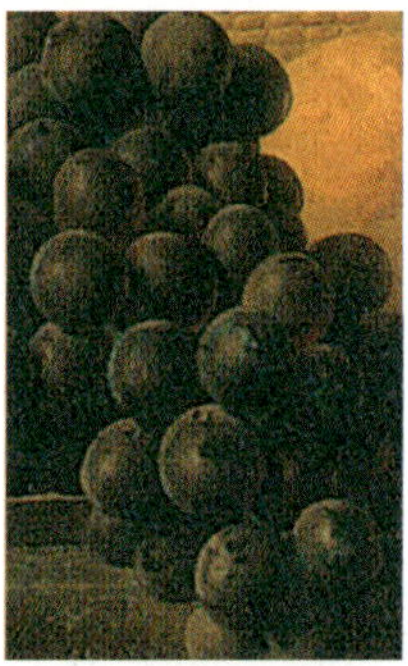

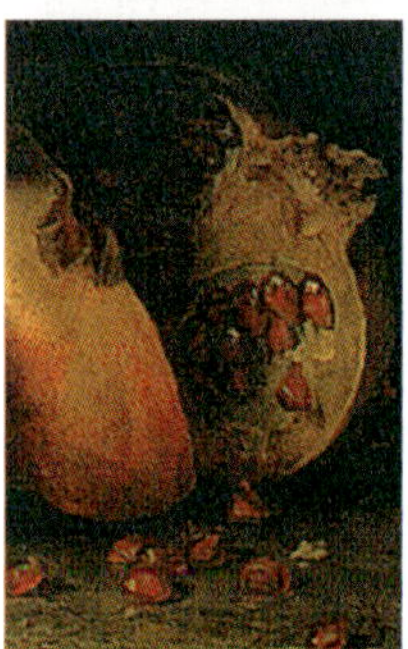

That means that objects arranged to make something independent, forming something whole, do not supplant, but only mask the human subject expressing in a new manner its aim with regard to the world as a whole.

Fruits

Jean-François van Dael, 1808
oil on wood, 56 x 45 cm
Pushkin Museum of Fine Art, Moscow

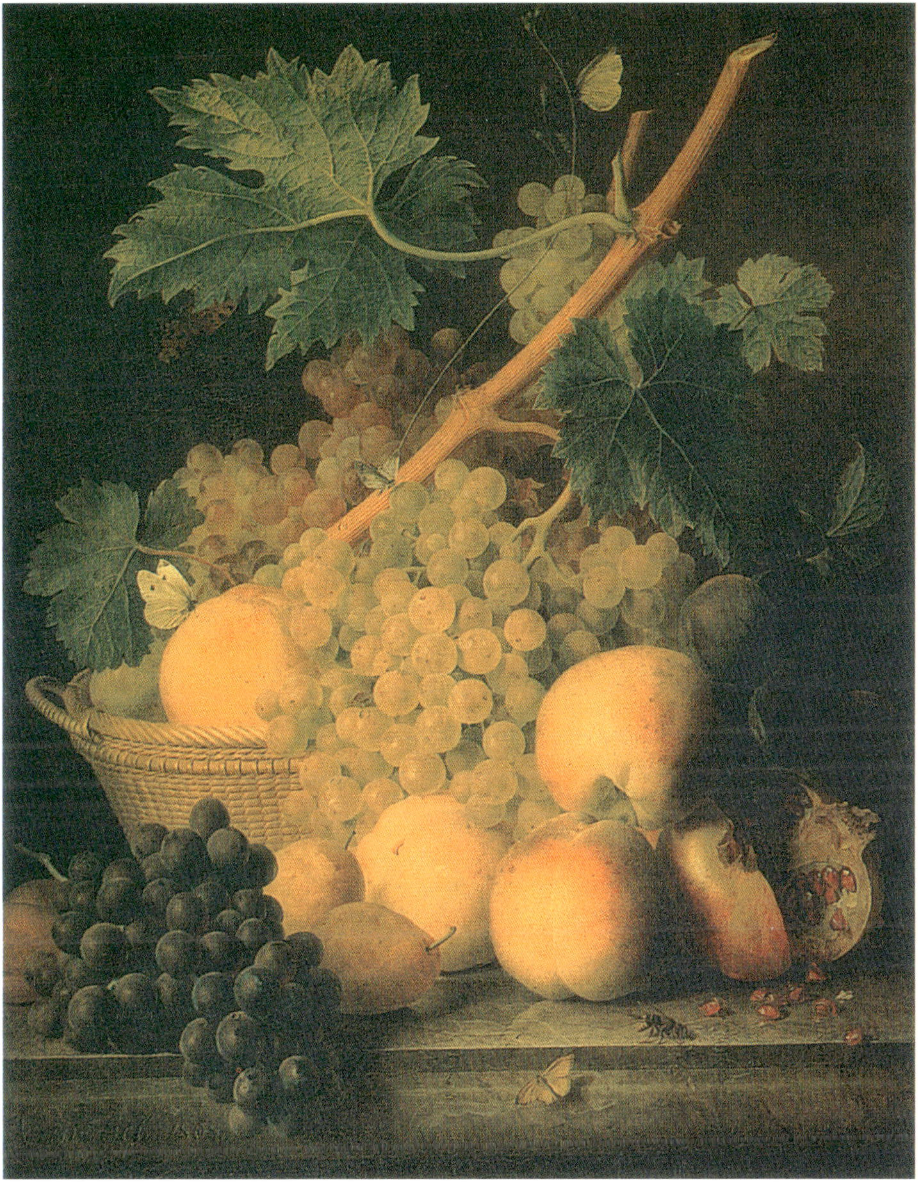

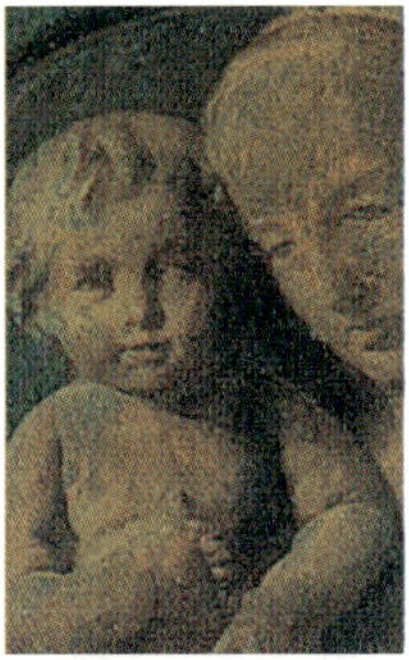

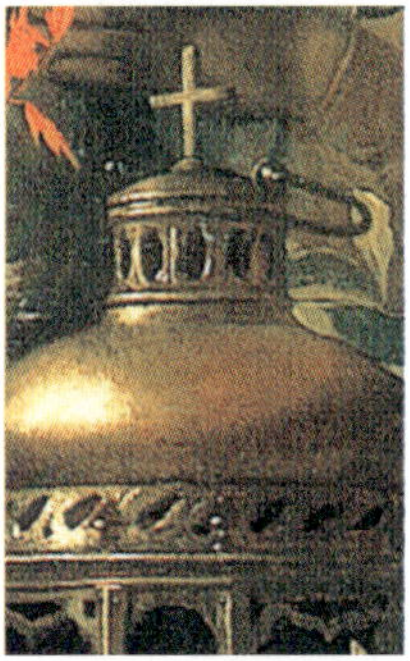

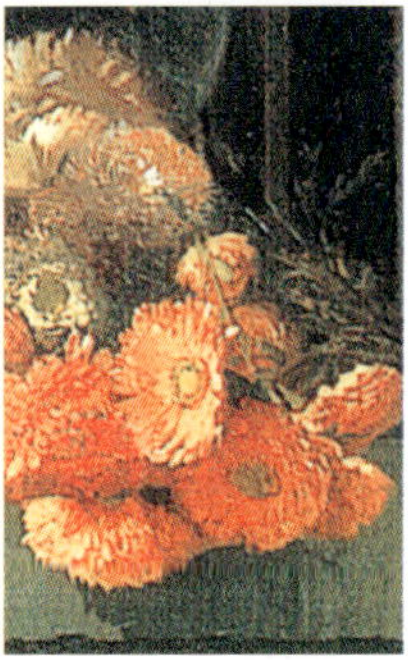

In Chardin's painting "inanimate objects" (the usual description of the genre at the time) blended together, as it were, to express in their own way the character of the national perception of the world.

Still Life

Unknown artist, first half of the 19th century
Oil on canvas, 115 x 92 cm
Art Museum, Sebastopol

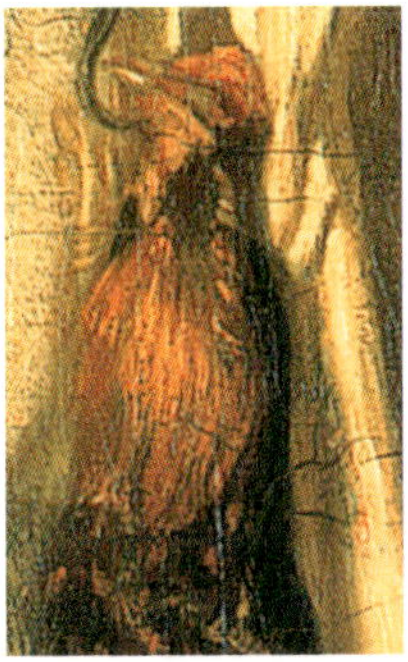

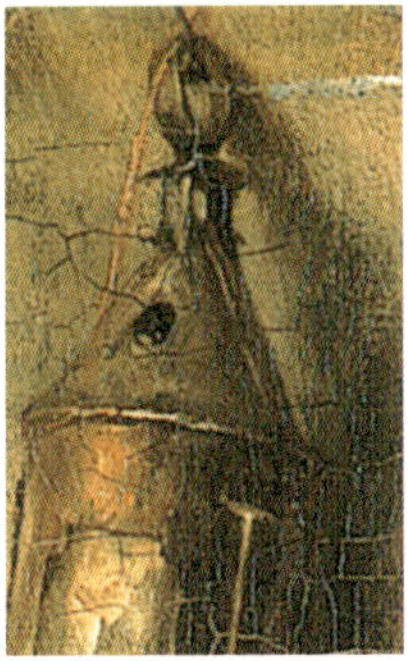

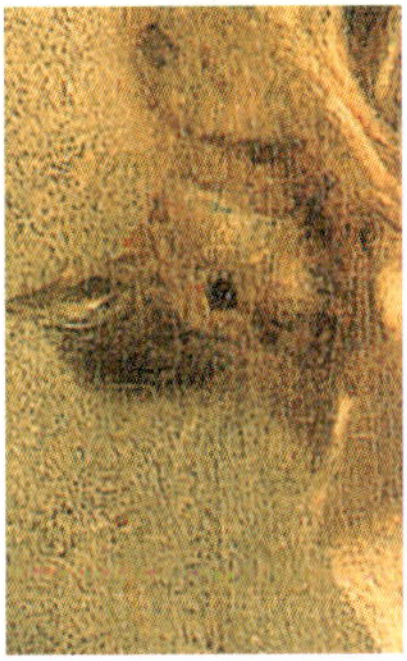

While in his early still lifes Chardin paid tribute to the Dutch and Flemish traditions, his mature work marks the establishment of a new set of stylistics for the genre. Without himself being aware of it, Chardin resolved within the sphere of a little genre a task of almost state magnitude.

Still Life

Alexandre Gabriel Decamps
oil on panel, 28 x 24 cm
The Hermitage, Saint Petersburg

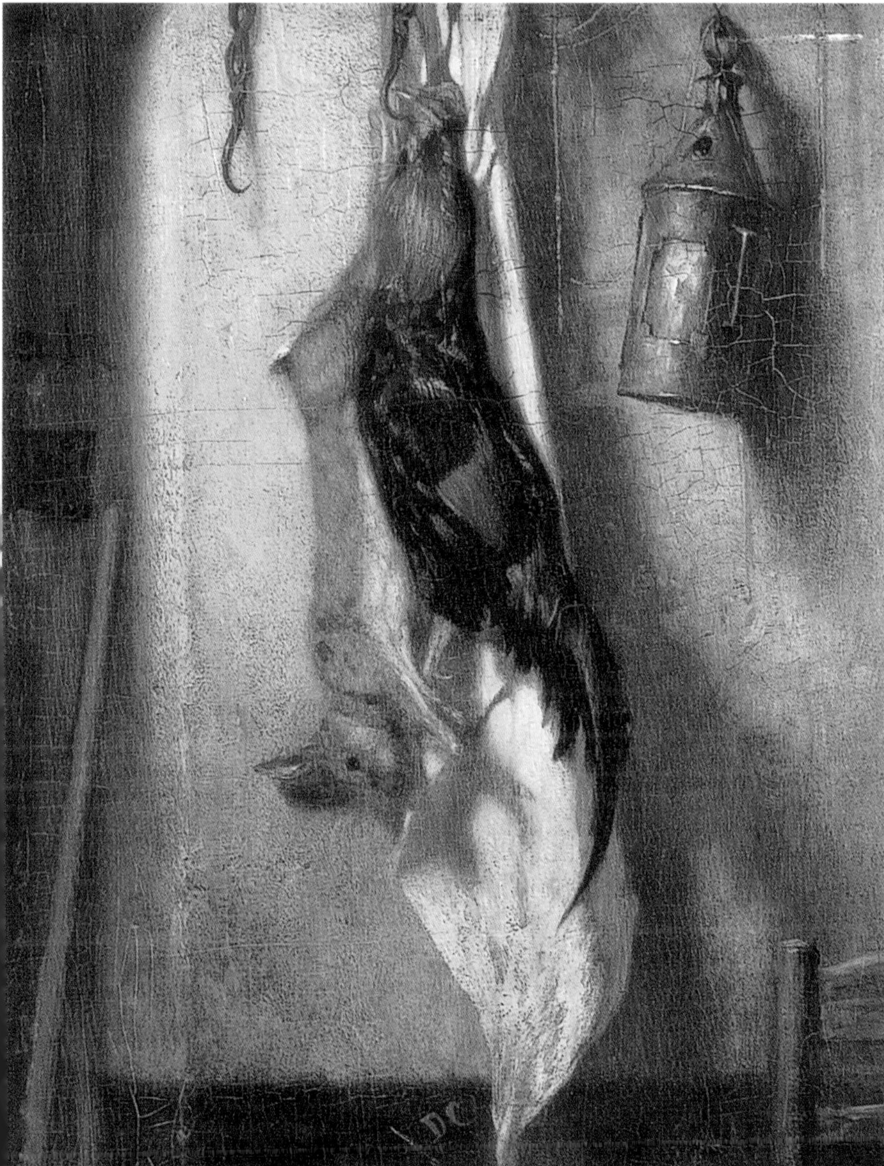

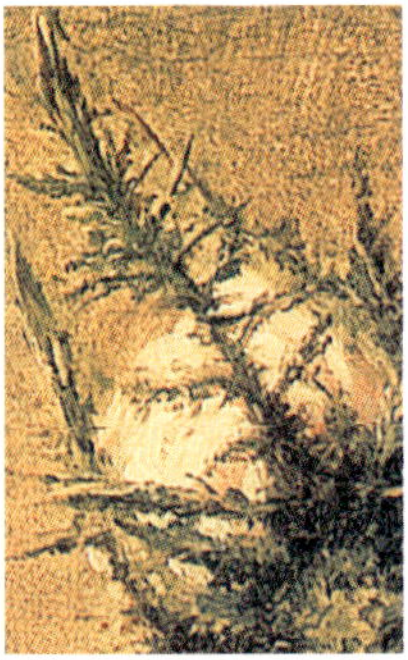

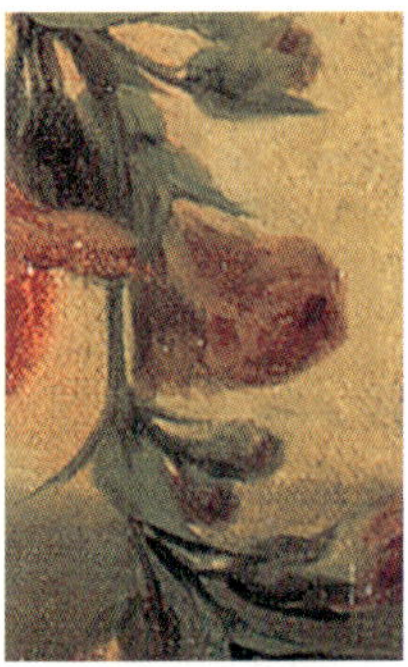

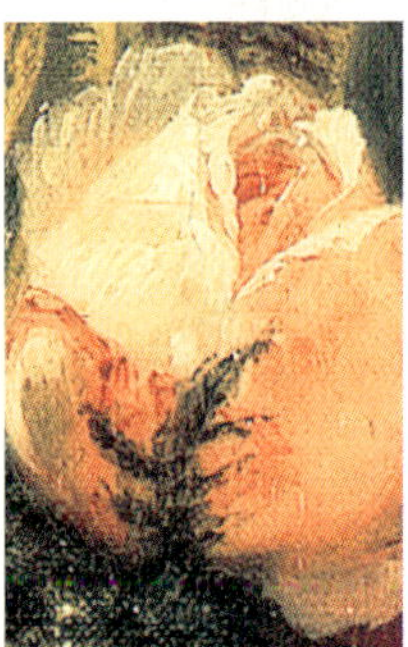

And then came Cézanne. To a certain extent he drew the balance of European easel painting, the application of the still-life formula specifically to the landscape, the portrait and the composition with figures.

Bouquet of Flowers in a Vase

Simon Saint-Jean, 1856
Oil on canvas, 47 x 38 cm
The Hermitage, Saint Petersburg

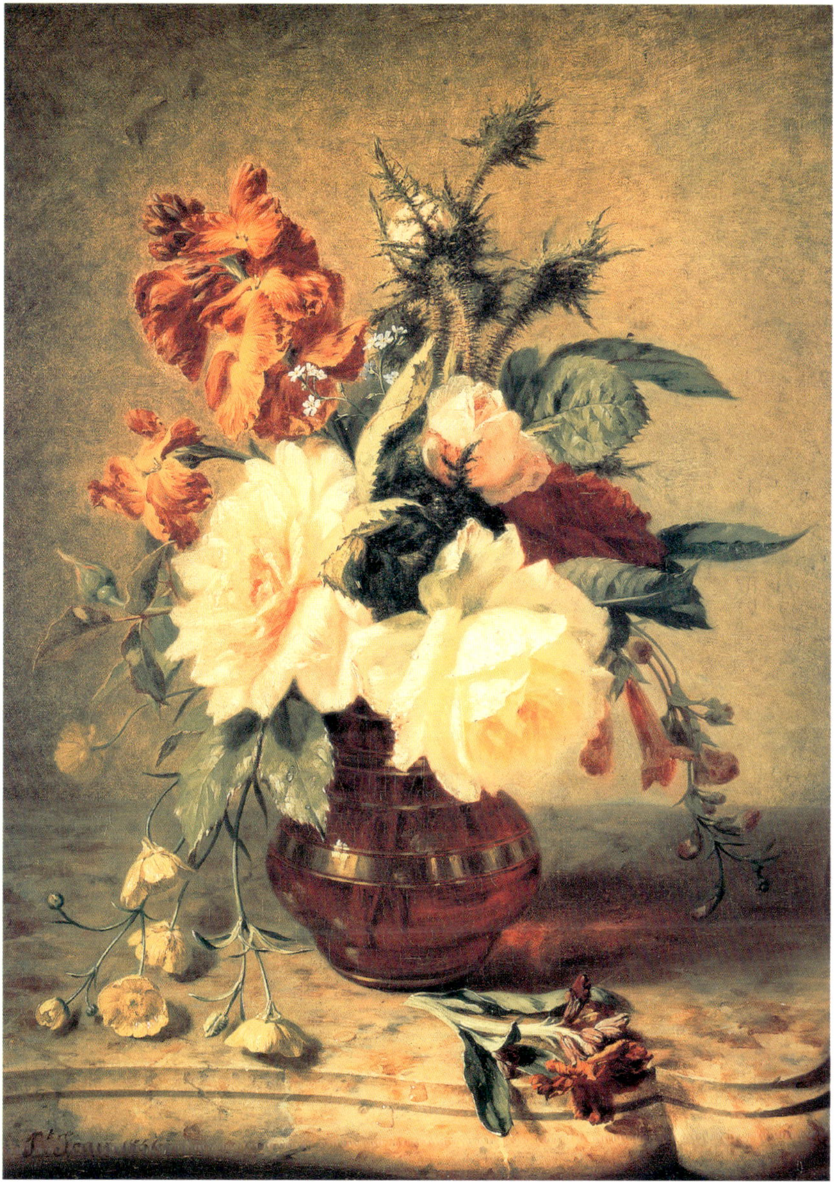

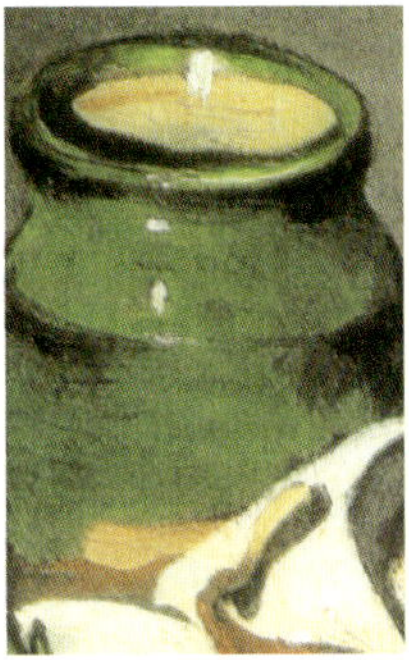

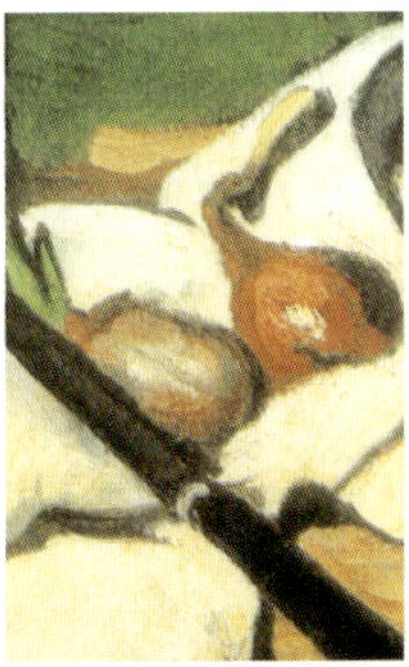

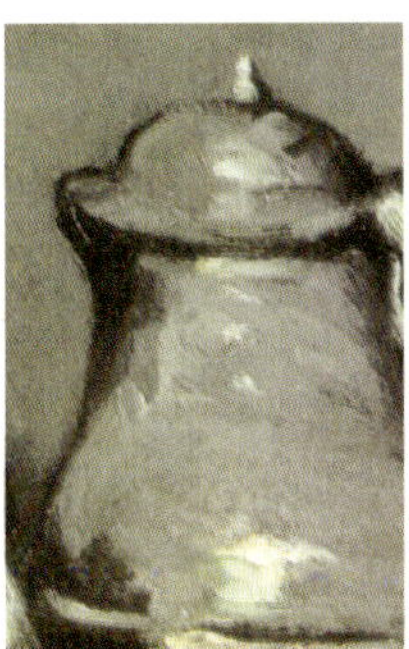

Now it required no effort of the imagination to see that the folds of drapes and the folds of a mountain, a person's head and an apple are identified in a paintwork visual whole. Cézanne's painting is devoid of isolated shapes and colours, just as it does not

Still Life. Green Pot and Tin Kettle

Paul Cézanne, c. 1869
Oil on canvas, 64.5 x 81 cm
Musée d'Orsay, Paris

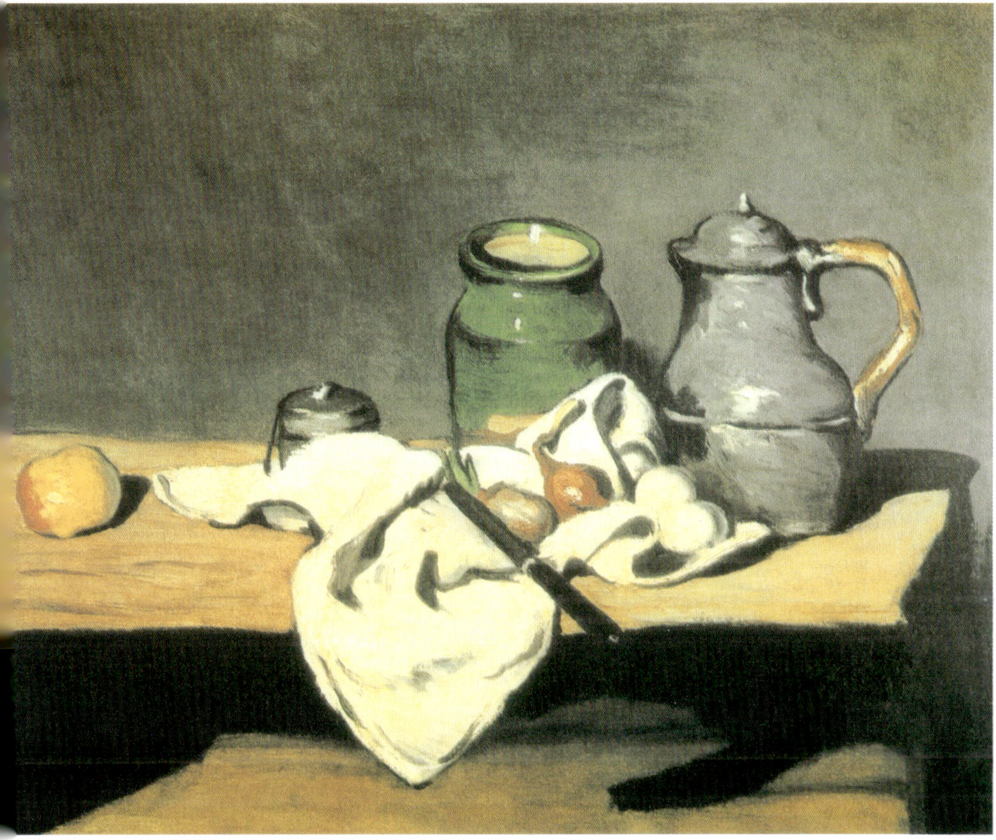

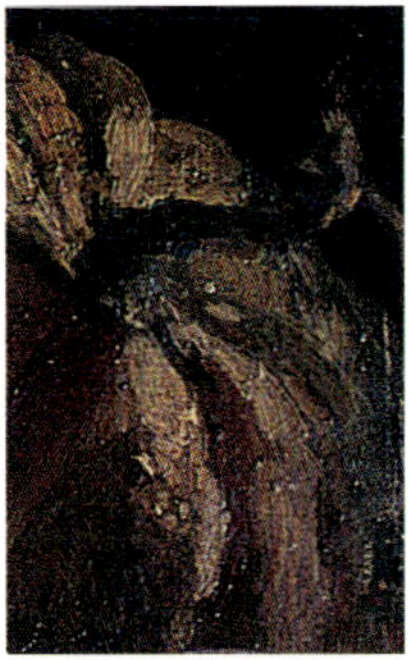

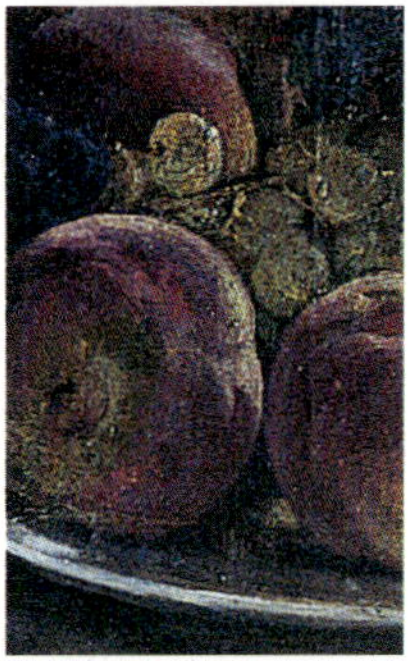

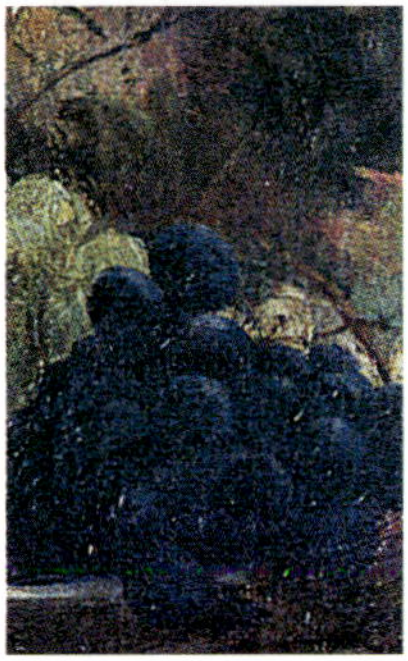

recognize the dichotomy of line and colour. According to the painter and critic Emile Bernard who recorded Cézanne's thinking on art, the painter asserted that neither lines nor shapes exist – there are only contrasts.

Still Life with Fruits

Nicolae Grigorescu, 1869
Oil on canvas glued on wood, 38 x 71 cm
Location unknown

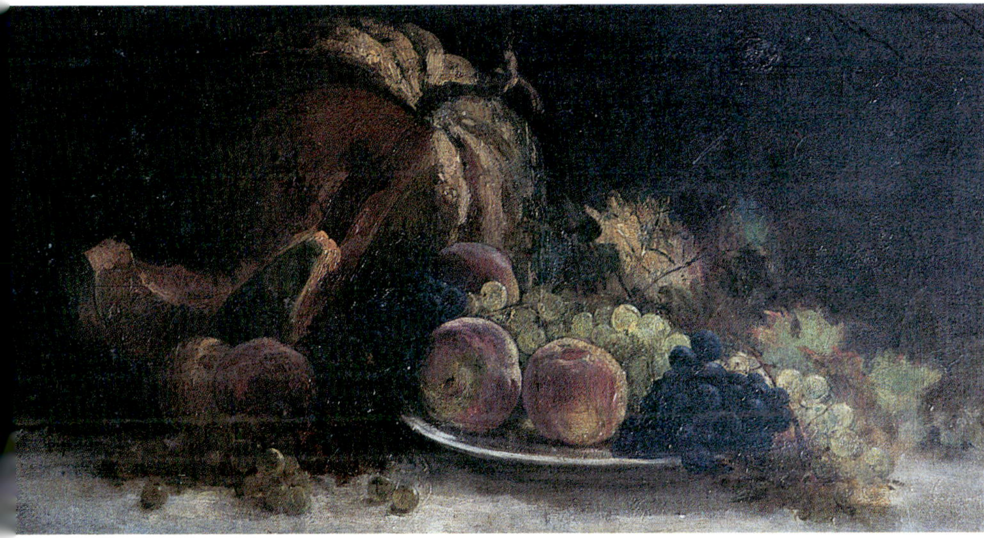

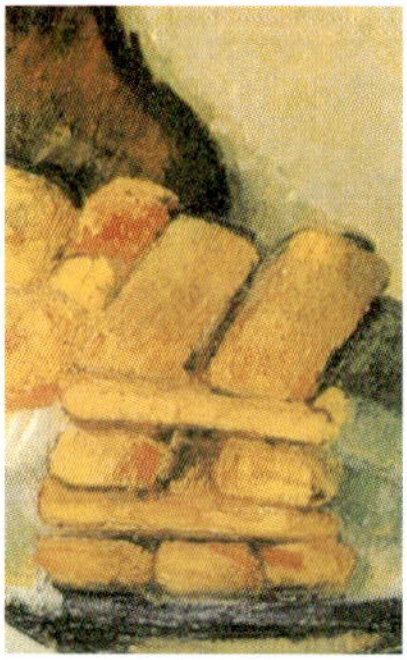

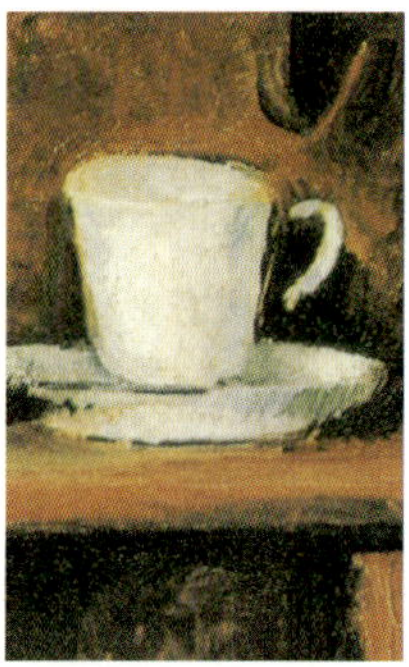

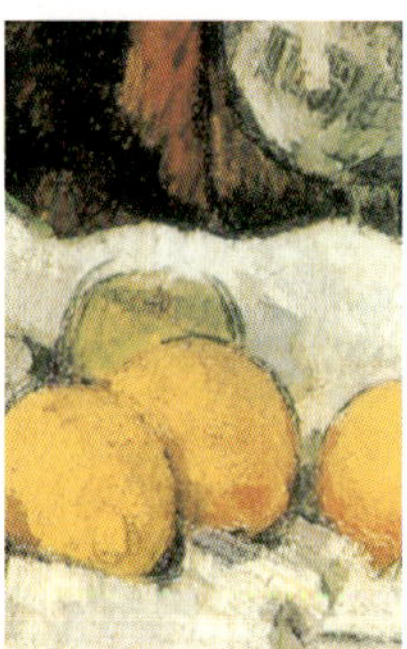

Shape is created by a precise interrelationship of tones, and if they are harmoniously juxtaposed, then the painting creates itself. For that reason the verb "model" should be replaced in the painter's vocabulary by the word "modulate".

The Buffet

Paul Cézanne, 1873-1877
Oil on canvas, 65 x 81 cm
Szépmüvészeti Muzeum, Budapest

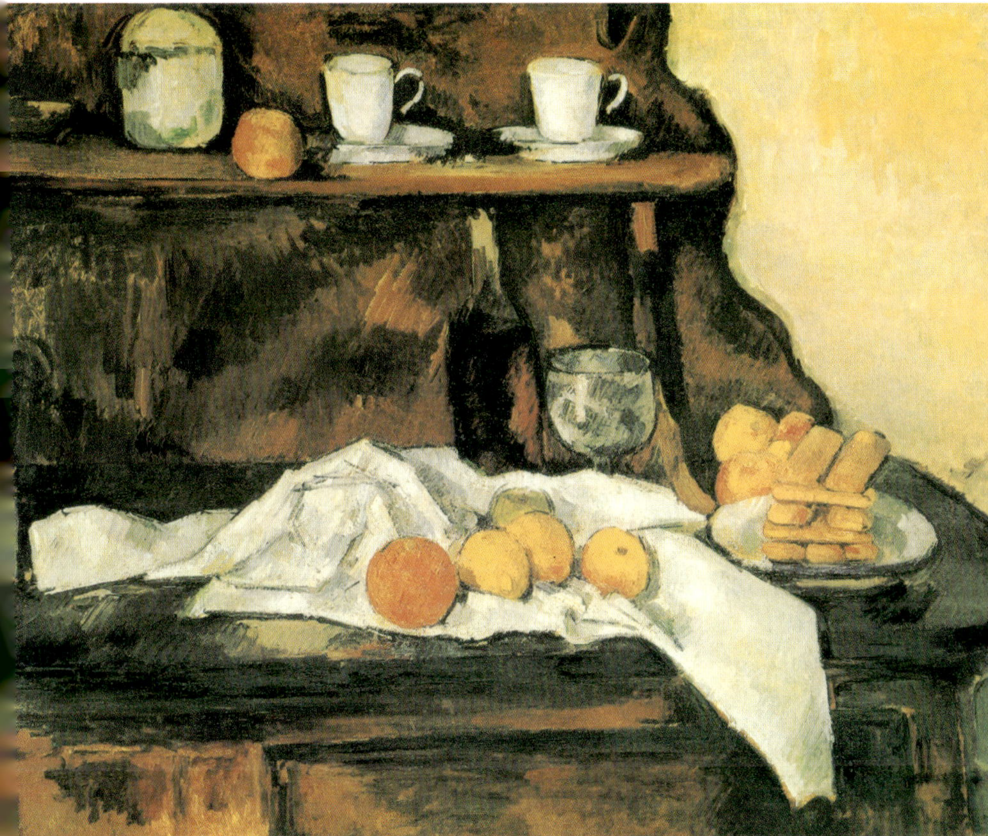

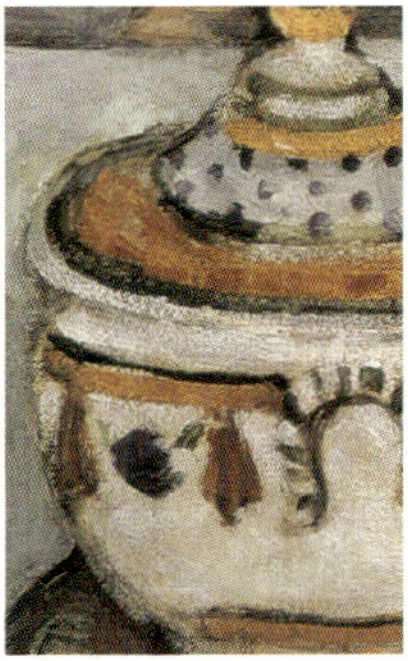

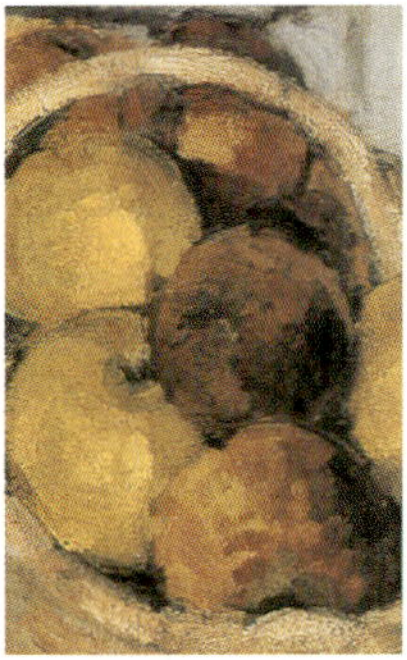

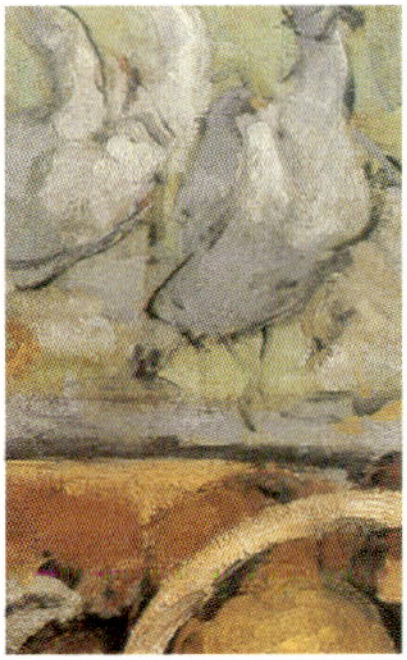

In seeking out the fundamentals of expressivity, Cézanne did not draw sharp boundaries between genres. The objects on his table, be it a jug, cup or apple, are of no less significance than the figures in some painted "story".

Still Life with a Soup Tureen

Paul Cézanne, c. 1877
Oil on canvas, 82 x 65 cm
Musée d'Orsay, Paris

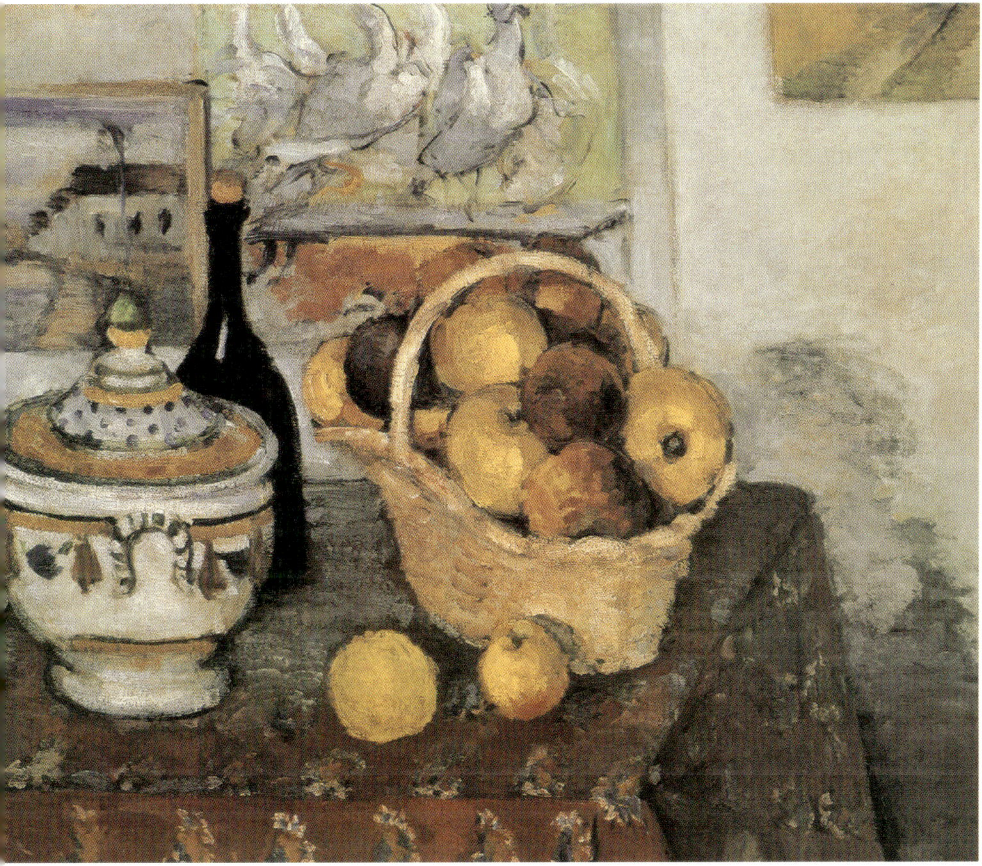

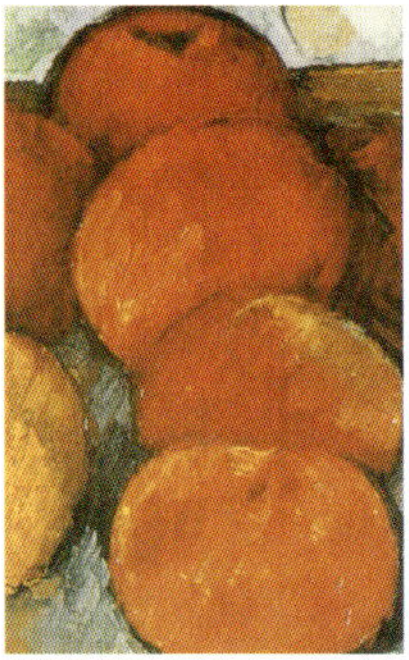

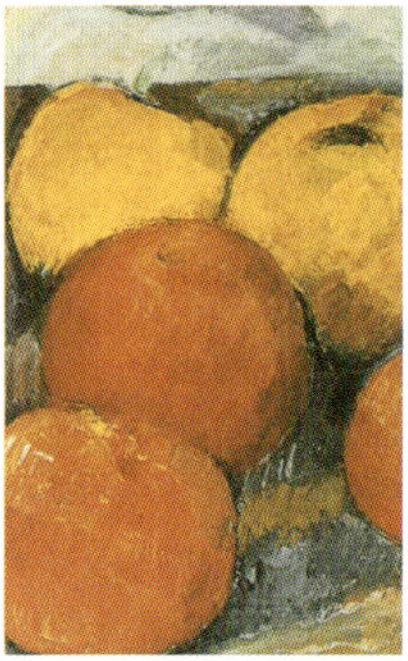

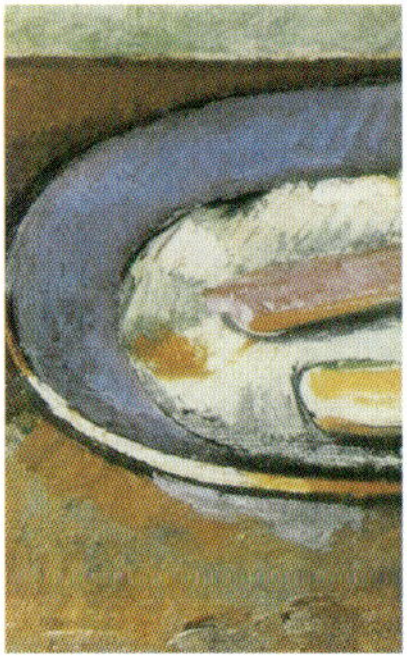

He had a profound respect for the Old Masters, regarding them as intermediaries between art and nature. And since the study of the great variety of nature comprises the hardest part of a painter's studies, a few objects gathered together can become a subject of universal significance.

Apples and Biscuits

Paul Cézanne, 1879-1882
Oil on canvas, 45 x 55 cm
Musée de l'Orangerie, Paris

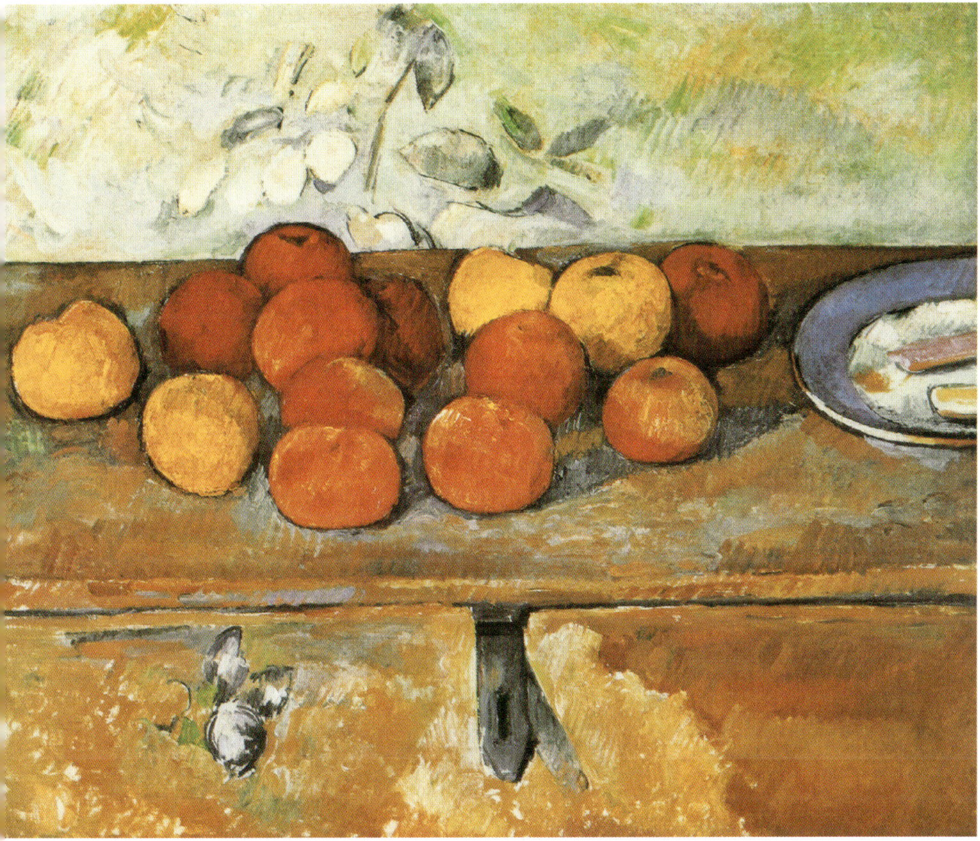

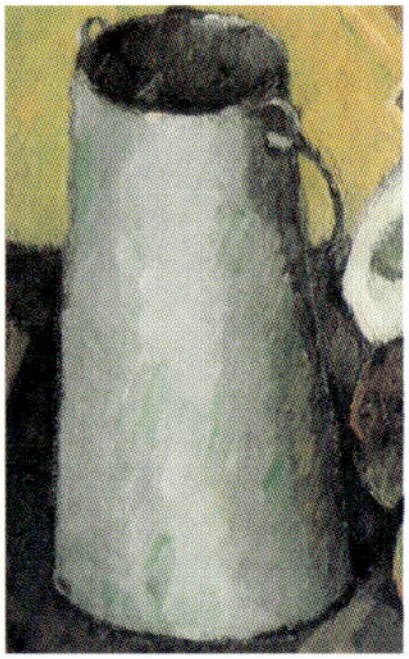

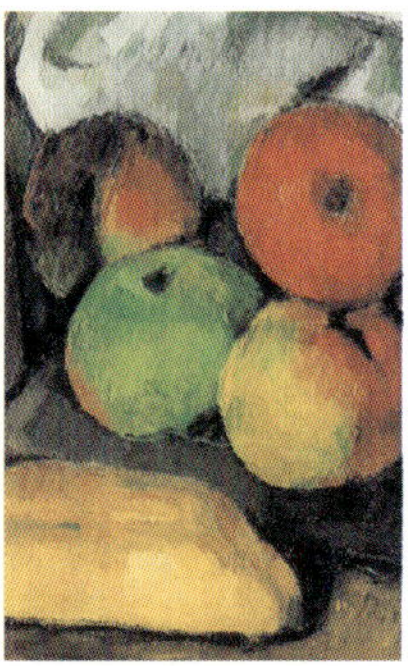

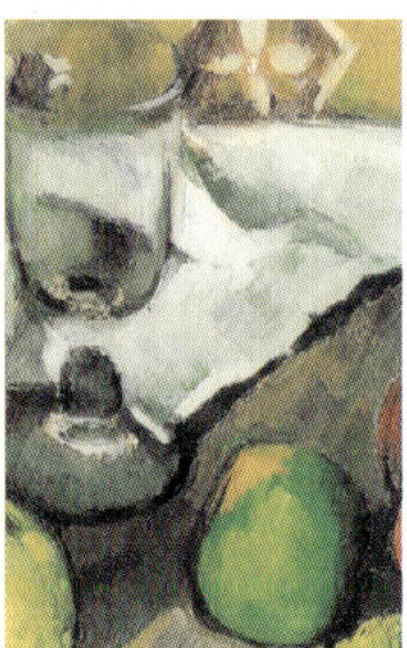

Not without Chardin's influence, still life became a privileged genre in painting (although the very concept of genre was no longer as important as it had been). Many of the greatest painters of Cézanne's era were indebted to him, including Gauguin, who overtly imitated Cézanne, by intensifying the decorative, rhythmic aspect to the detriment of an integral understanding of the paintwork element.

Still Life. Pitcher, Fruits and Tablecloth

Paul Cézanne, 1879-1882
Oil on canvas, 60 x 73 cm
Musée de l'Orangerie, Paris

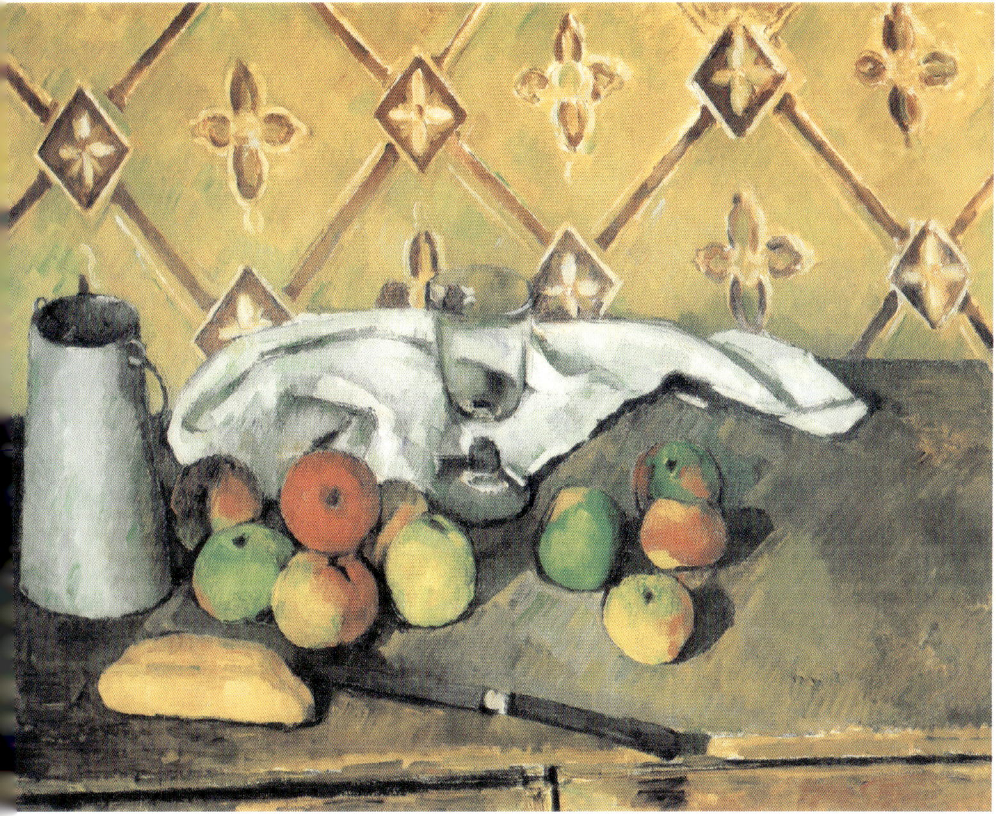

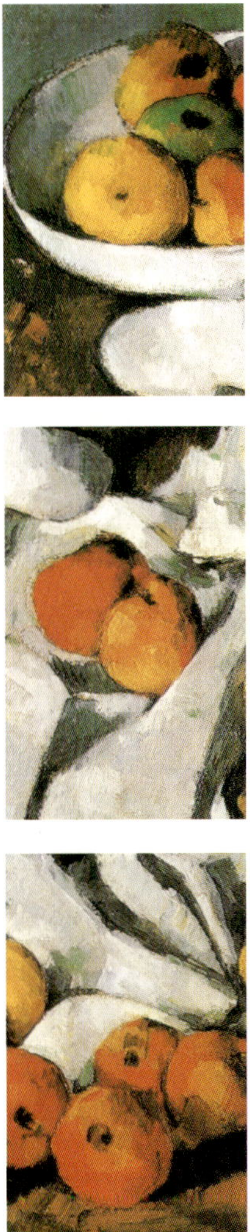

Generally speaking, the impression emerges that Cézanne's work served as a "key junction" in which the paths of European painting came together before diverging once again. It has become a cliché to speak about the link of inheritance between Cubism and Cézanne, although on closer examination the situation proves much more complex than supposed.

Dish of Apples

Paul Cézanne, 1879-1882
Oil on canvas, 55 x 74.5 cm
Collection Oskar Reinhart, Winterthur

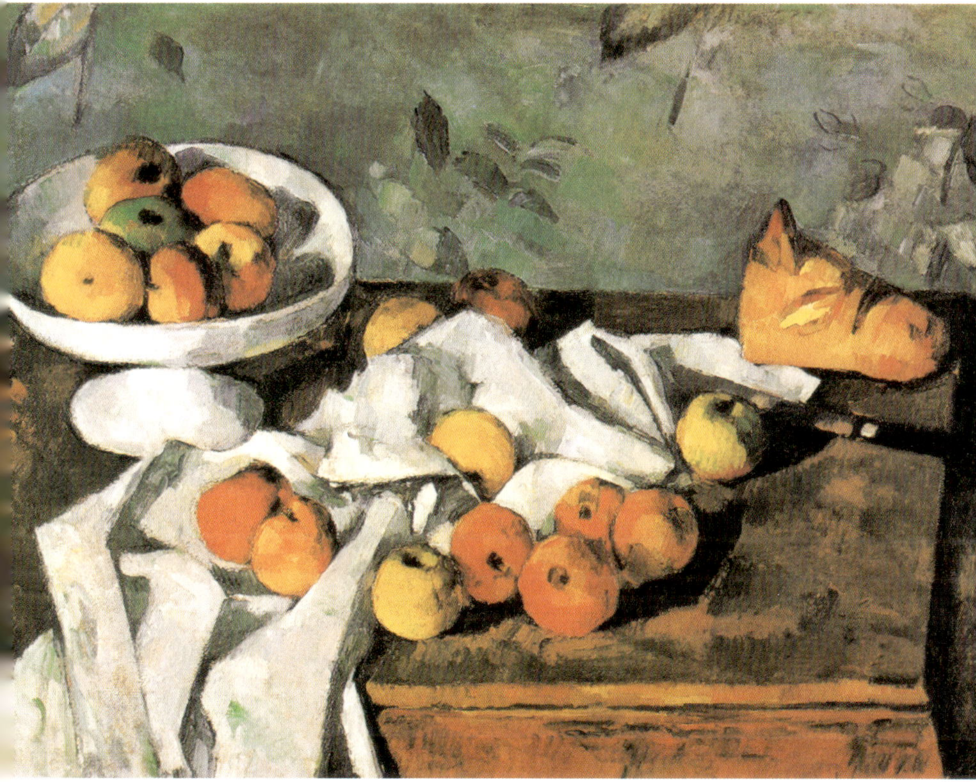

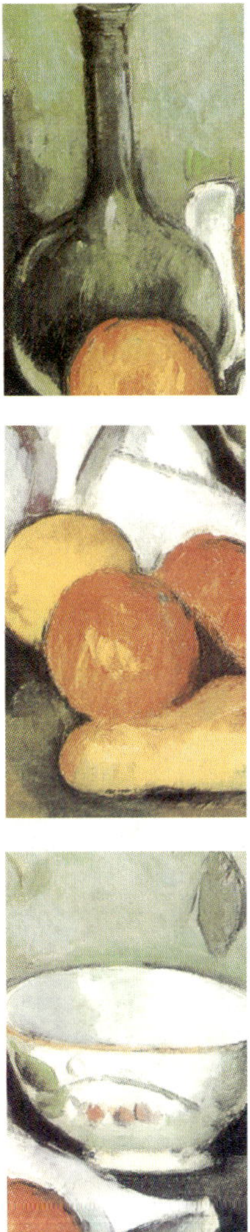

One way or another this link does exist and clearly proclaims its existence in the powerful lapidary forms of the early Cubist paintings, in which still life will play an essential role as an experimental genre. The astonishing pace with which the language of objects changed in Picasso's painting is eloquently demonstrated by the still lives of 1906-1908.

Still Life with Fruits

Paul Cézanne, 1879-1880
Oil on canvas, 45 x 54 cm
The Hermitage, Saint Petersburg

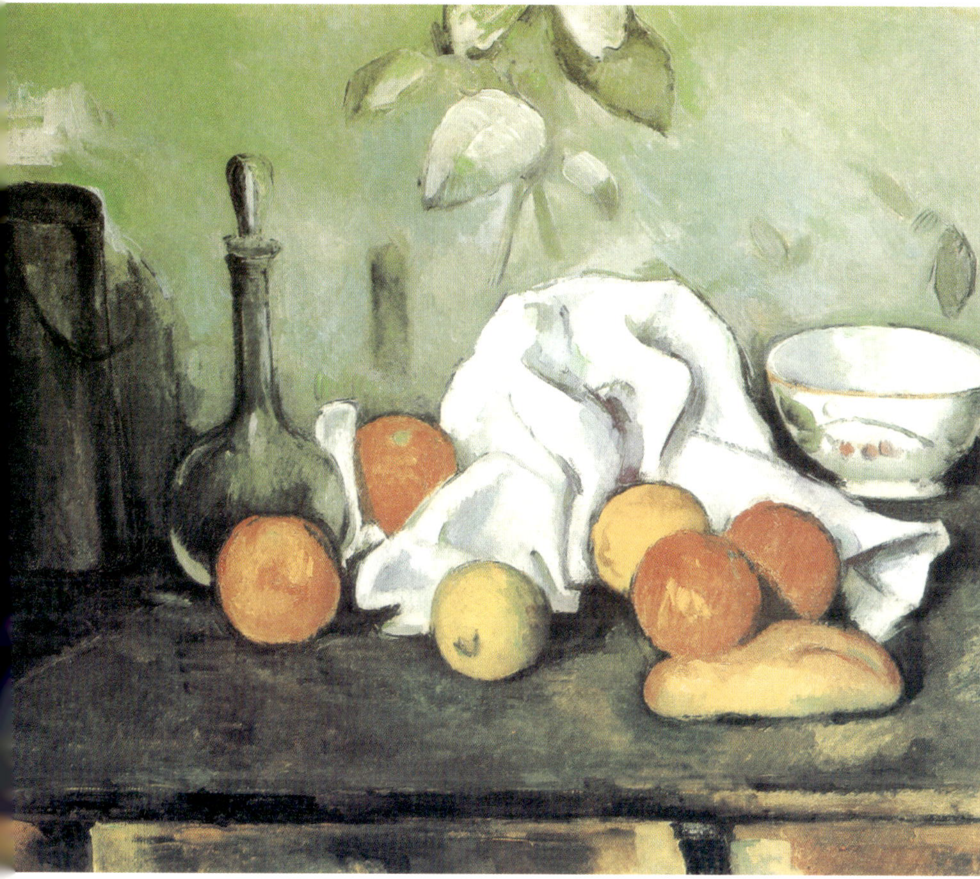

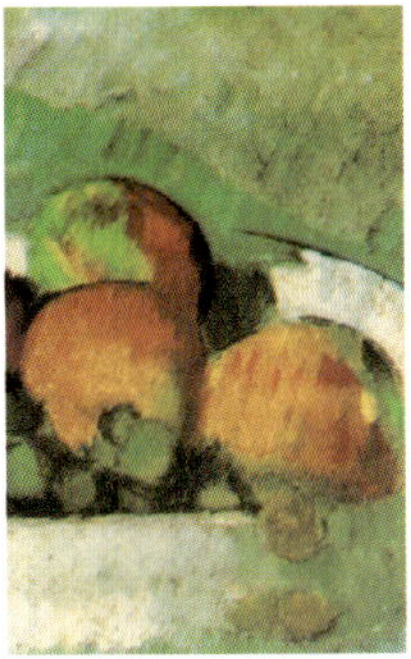

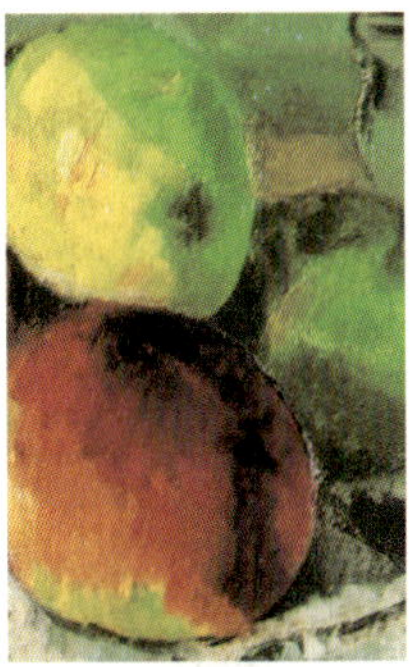

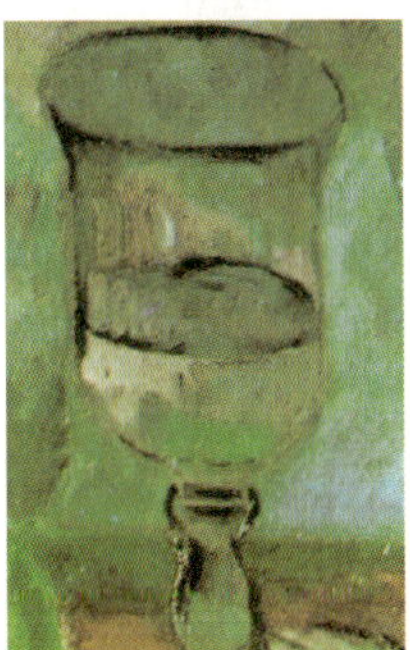

If there is anything that most closely expresses Cézanne's celebrated behest, it is the still lives which Picasso produced on the threshold of Cubism. The objects in them appear as symbols of "object-ness" itself, as if the artist intended to carve out in the thickness of paint graven images of minor deities – the patrons of form and substance.

Still Life with Dish, Glass and Apples

Paul Cézanne, 1879-1880
Oil on canvas, 46 x 55 cm
Private collection, Paris

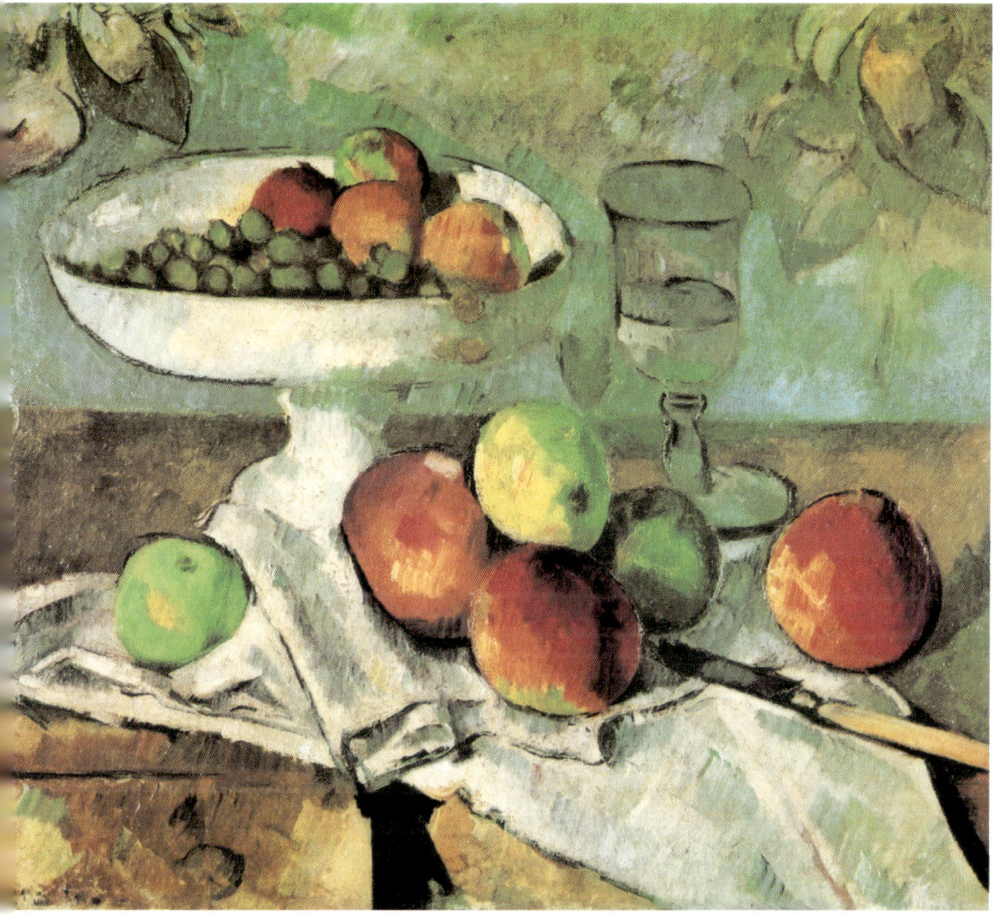

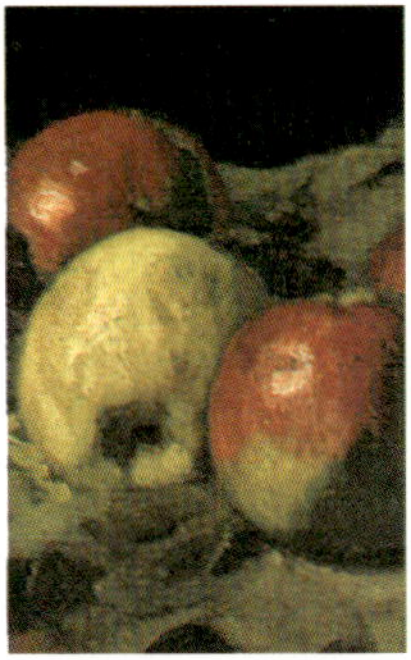

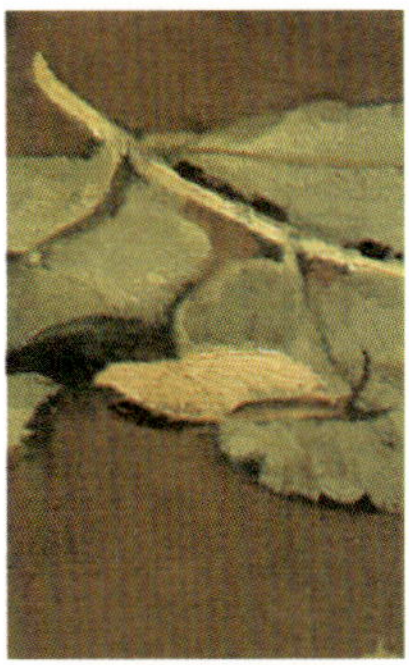

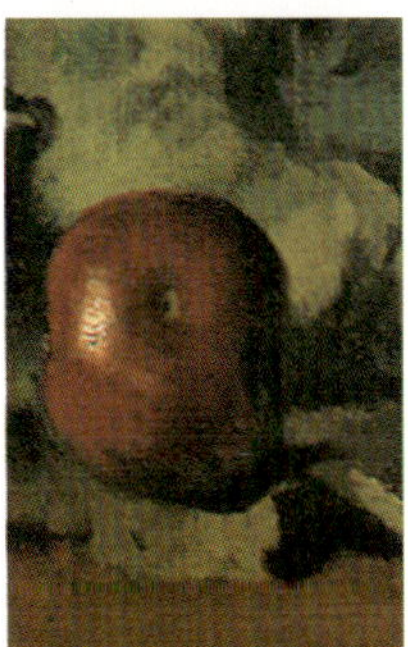

The principle of "reverse perspective" together with dense texture creates the impression of a palpable density of space, which the founders of Cubism attempted to "tame" (to somewhat distort Braque's words).

Apples and Leaves

Ilya Repin, 1879
Oil on canvas, 64 x 75.5 cm
Russian Museum, Saint Petersburg

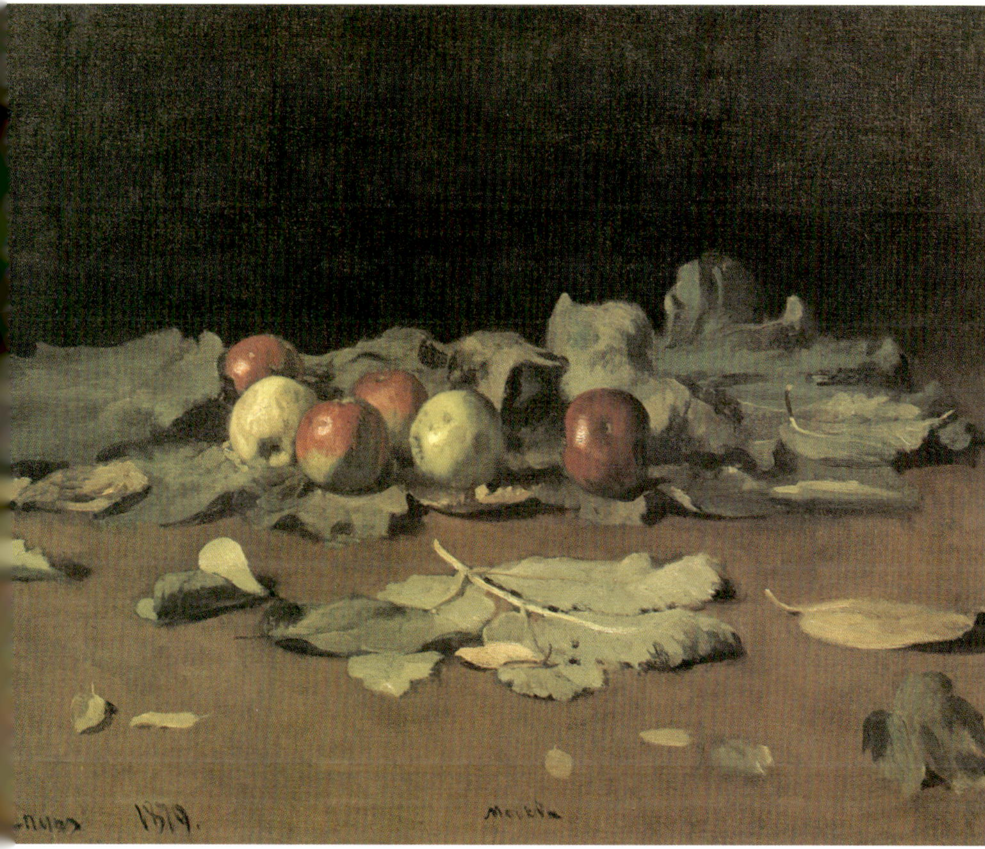

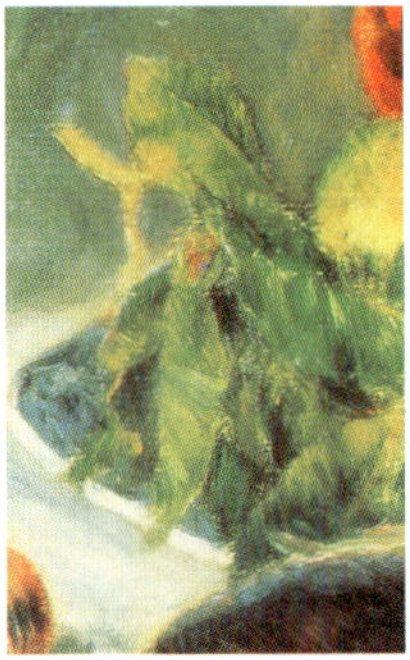

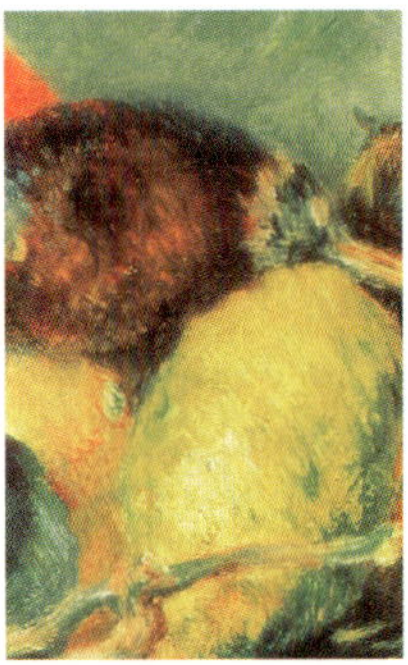

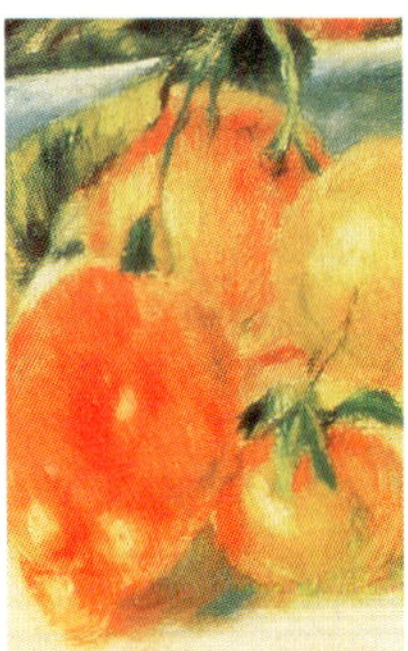

Picasso never became hung up on the realization of abstract ideas and moved by inner impulses, continued to change rapidly. Henri Matisse understood the language of things and the very tradition of the genre in a totally different way.

Fruits from the Midi

Auguste Renoir, 1881
Oil on canvas, 51 x 68 cm
The Art Institute, Chicago

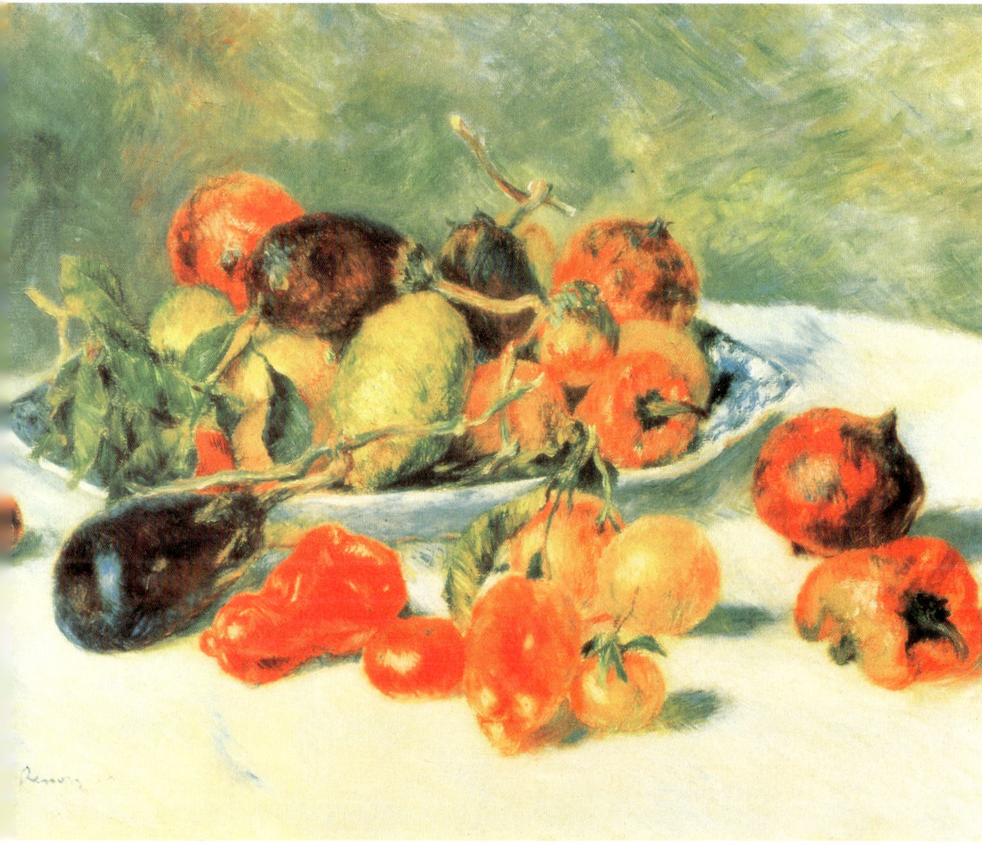

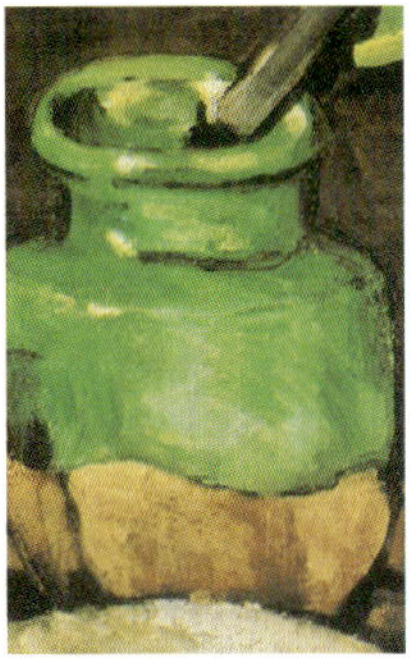

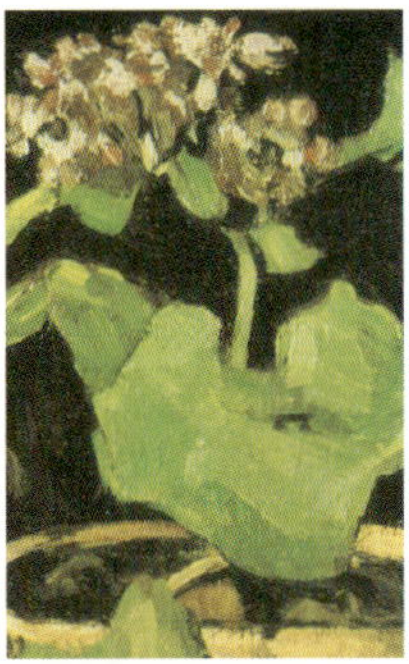

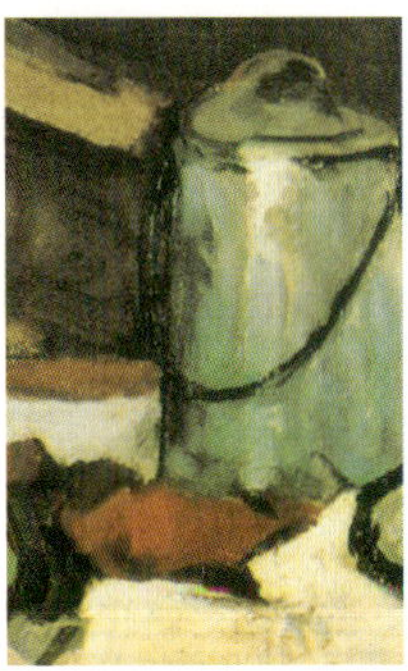

He did long studies of artistic tradition and made many copies of Old Masters. At the same time, Matisse had an affection for the Primitives and children's drawings which was fully in keeping with his pursuit of pure expressivity.

Vase of Flowers on a Table

Paul Cézanne, 1882-1887
Oil on canvas, 60 x 73 cm
Private collection, Paris

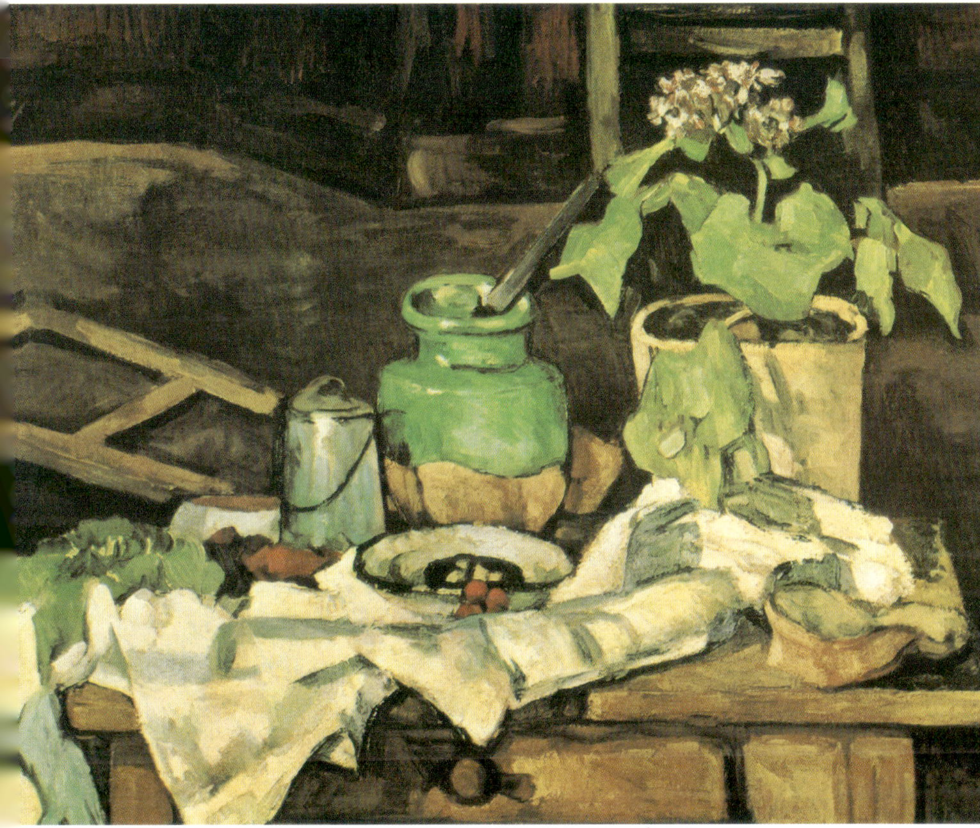

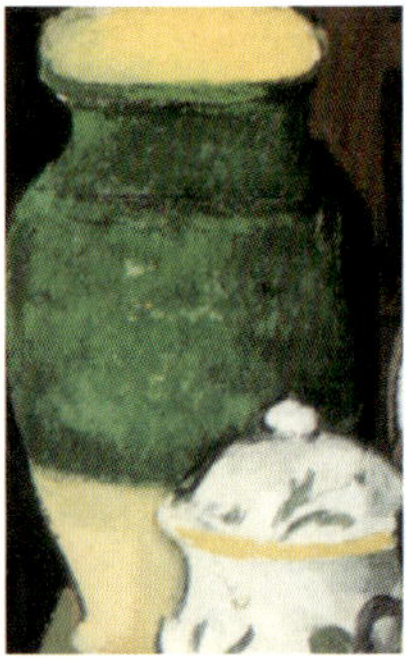

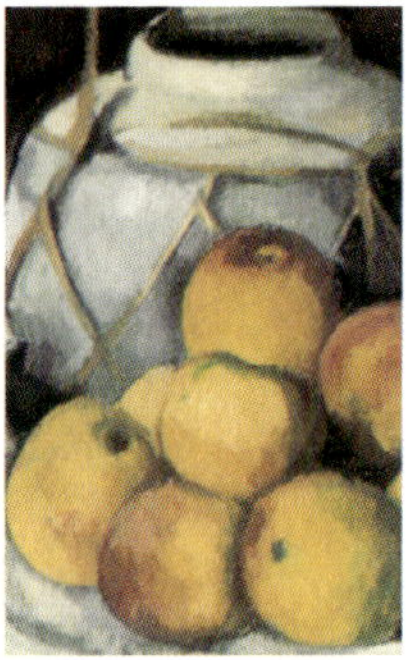

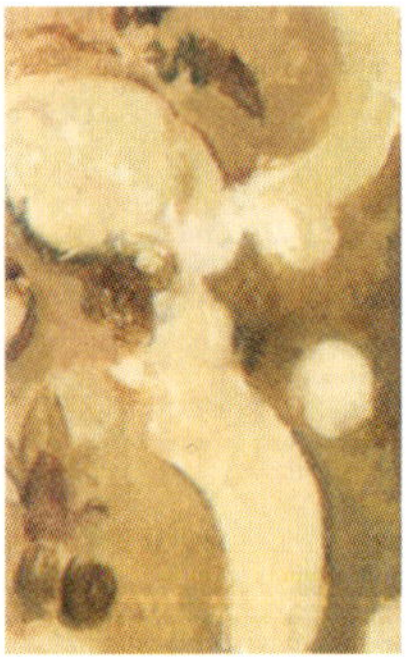

His still lifes reflect various stages in the cleansing of the palette and change of techniques used to apply paint. In the mid-1910s Matisse's painterly hand gained assurance and his colour a saturated intensity.

Still Life with a Chest of Drawers

Paul Cézanne, 1883-1887
Oil on canvas, 73.3 x 90.2 cm
Bayerische Staatsgemäldesammlungen
Neue Pinakothek, Munich

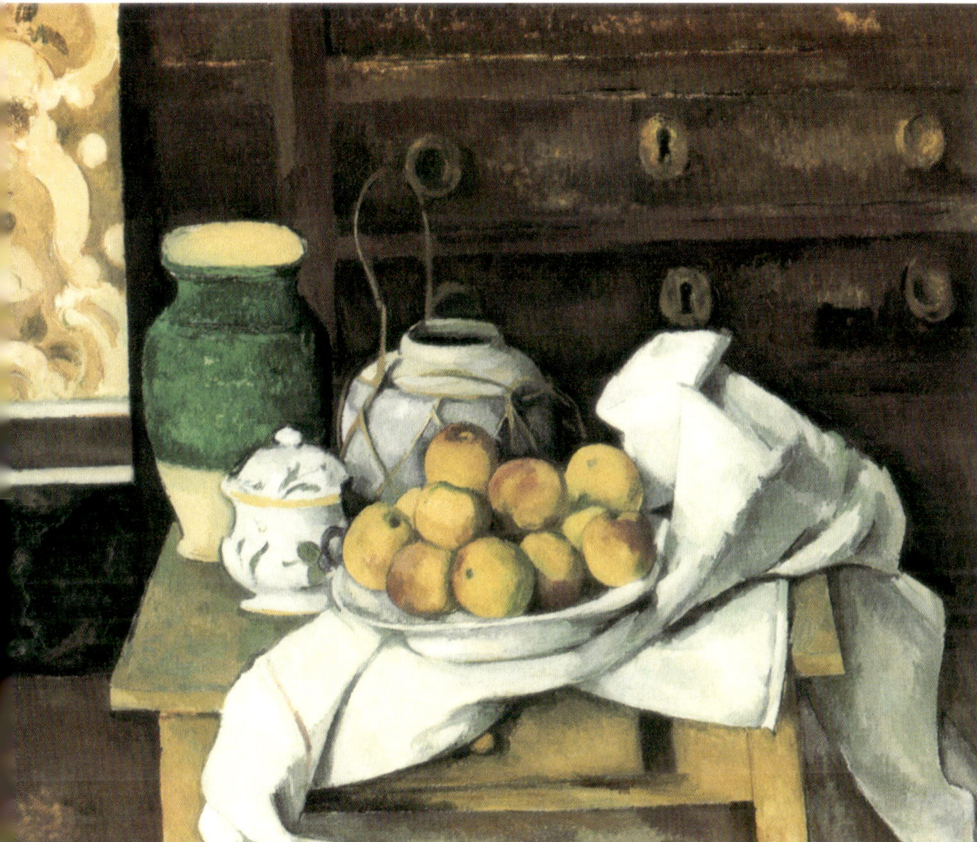

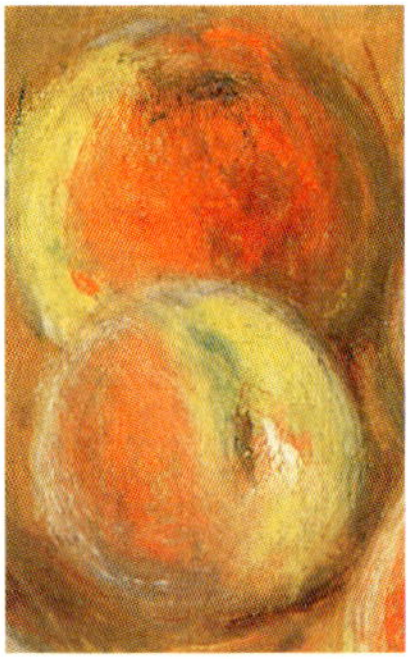

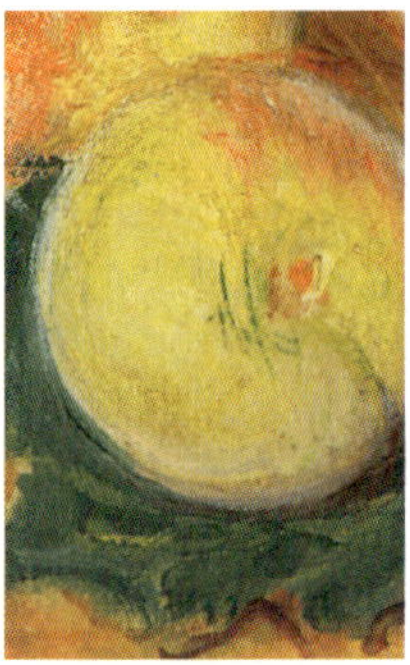

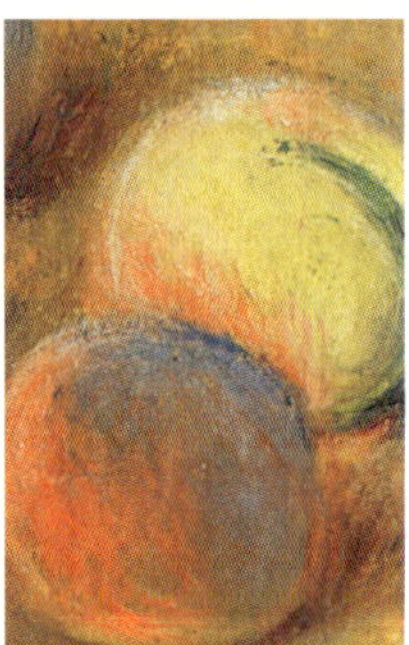

He freed himself completely from the compromise of halftones and revealed the limits of pure expressivity inherent in line and colour, yet he did not break with the material world. His further path is clear and consisted in bringing the principles he had discovered to perfection.

Peaches
(in the door of the Salon Durand-Ruel)

Claude Monet, 1883
Oil on canvas, 50.5 x 37 cm
Private collection

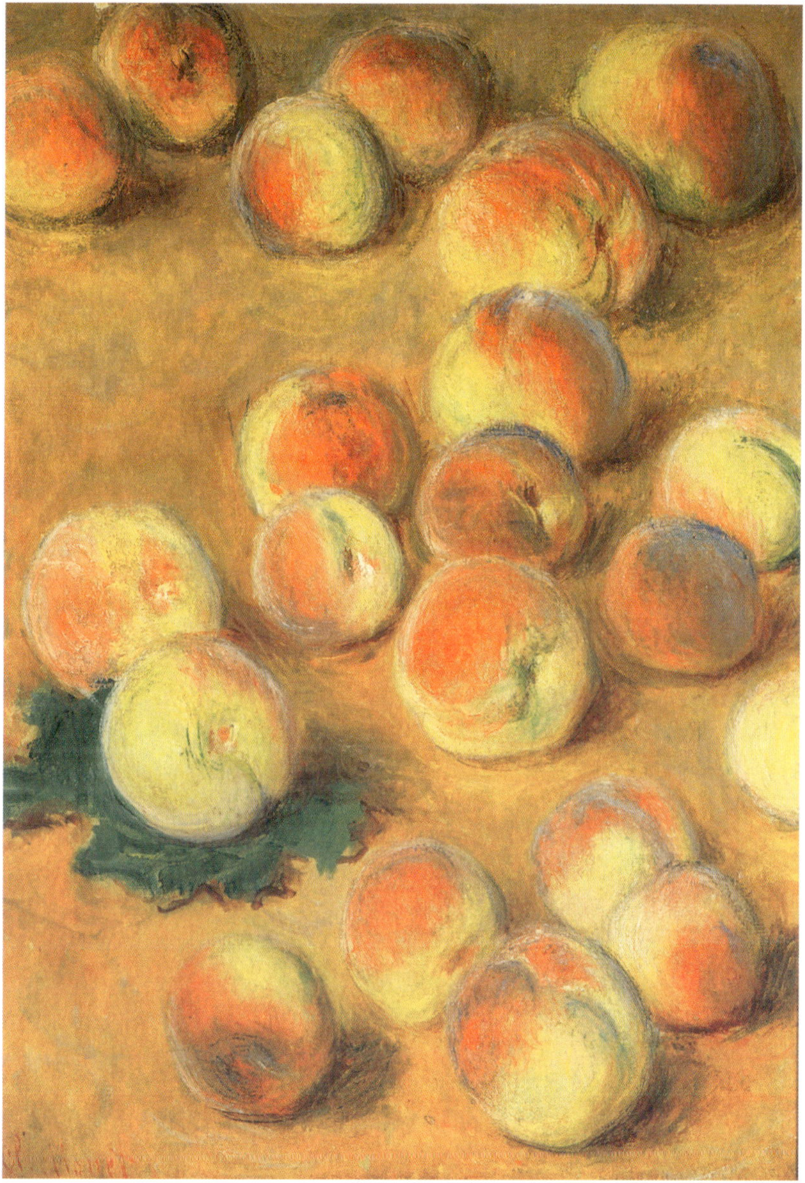

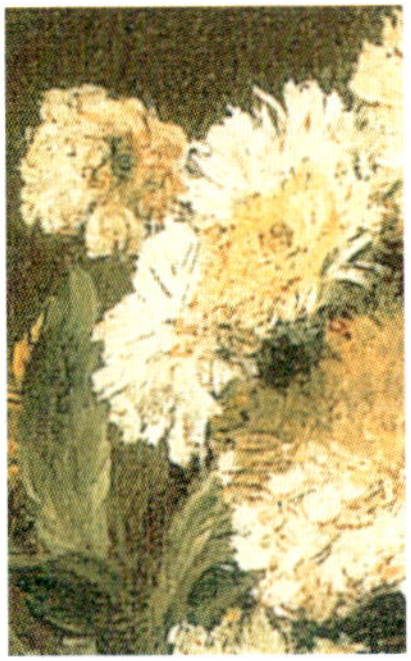

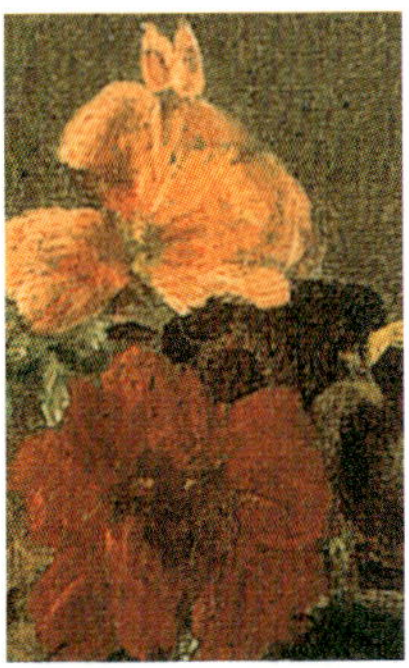

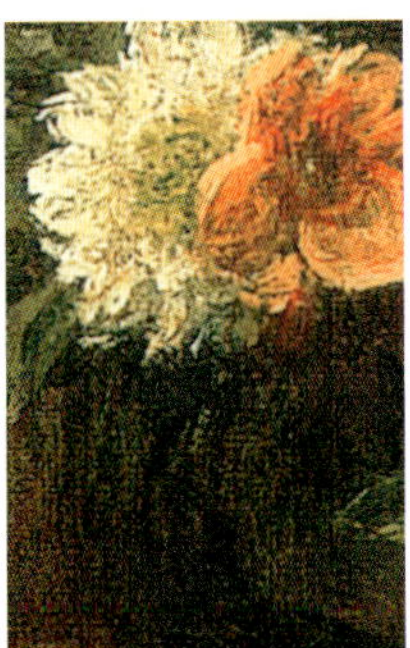

André Derain evolved from "Fauvism" to "Cubism", while retaining his relative independence. His painting represents an intermediate link between Matisse and Picasso, as he strove to avoid extremes to the benefit of a certain eclecticism.

Flowers in an Earthenware Vase

Henri Fantin-Latour, 1883
Oil on canvas, 22.5 x 29 cm
The Hermitage, Saint Petersburg

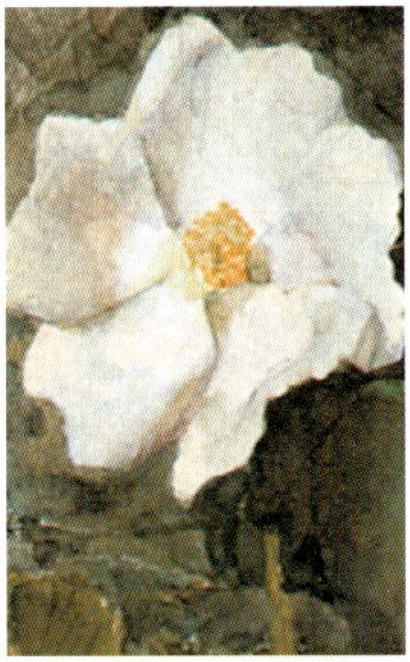

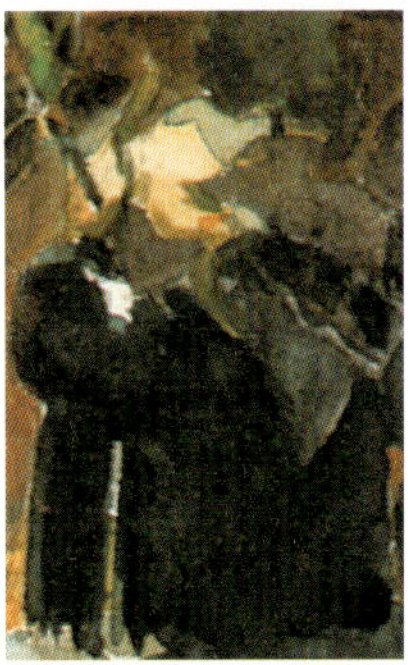

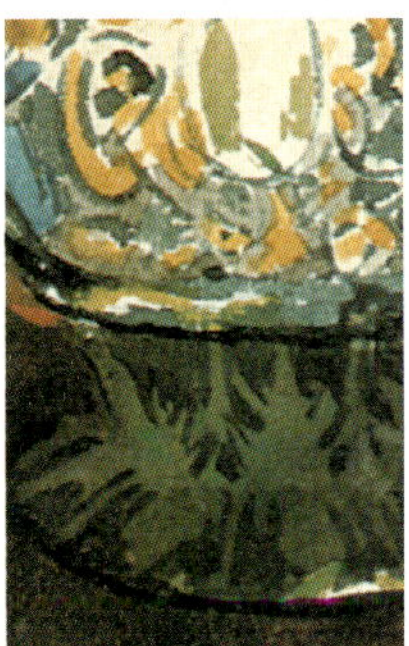

"Neo-Primitivism" is a term which corresponds to this period, to the extent that it really does capture something essential in the artistic searches of Derain, Matisse and Picasso as well as other leading figures of this period.

Dogrose

Mikhail Vrubel, 1884
water-colour on paper, 24.5 x 19.5 cm
Private collection, Kiev

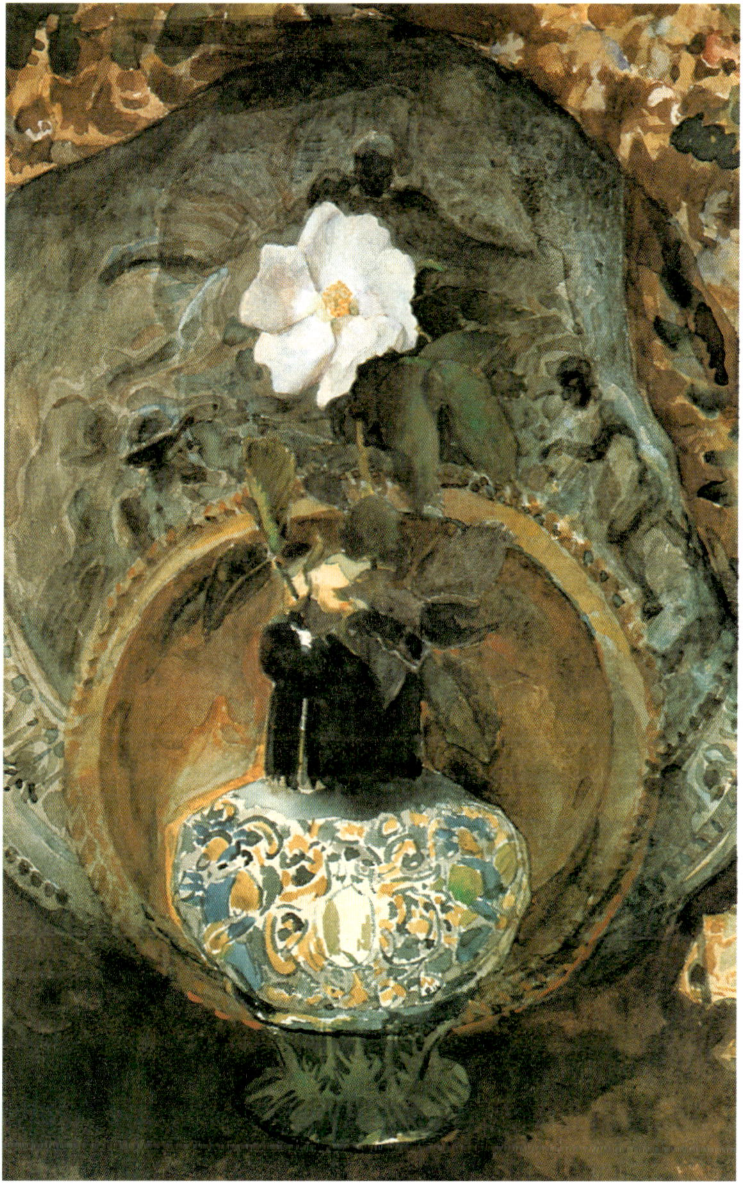

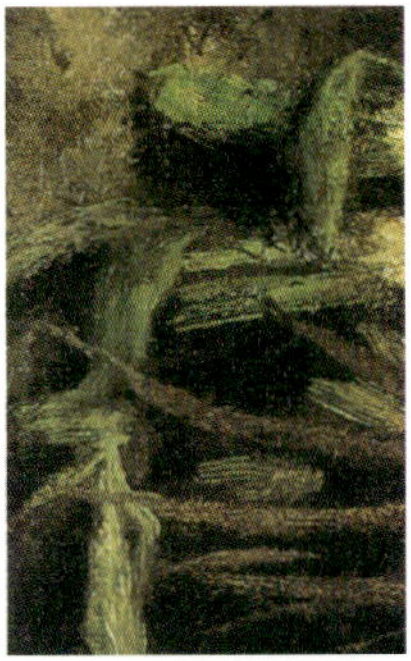

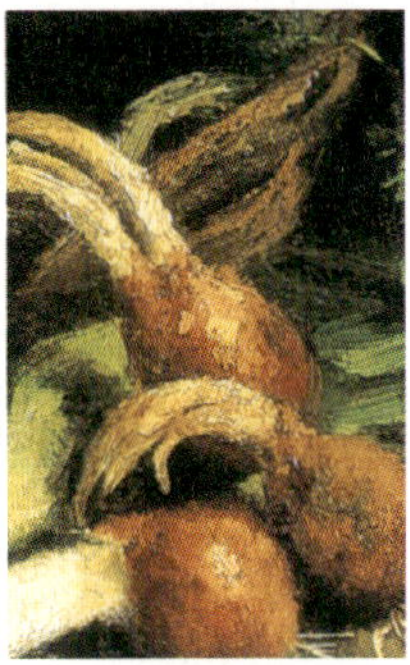

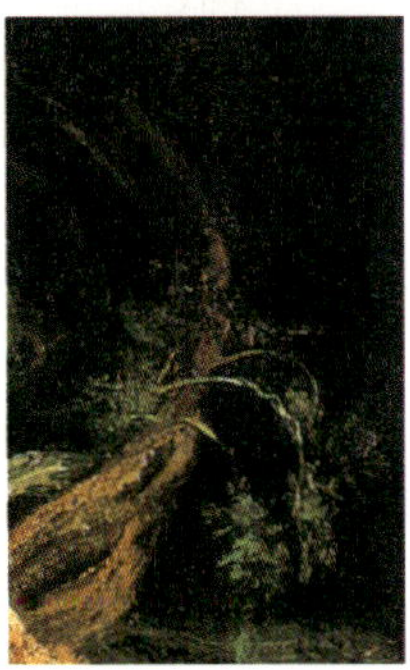

Indeed, until that time there were relatively few painters who devoted their energies primarily to still life. Decorative pictures of fruit and vegetables were influenced by the Dutch and Italian still life and served as models for the nineteenth century painters.

Still Life with a Basket of Vegetables

Vincent van Gogh, 1885
Oil on canvas, 35.5 x 45 cm
collection Anneliese Brand
Landsberg/Lech (Germany)

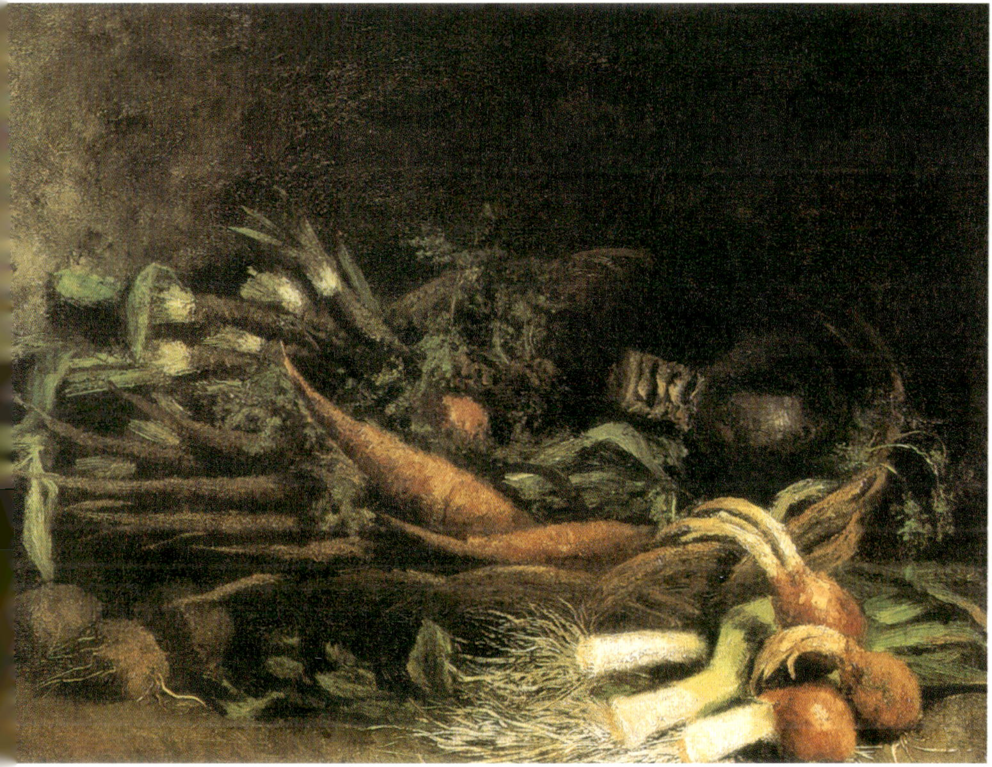

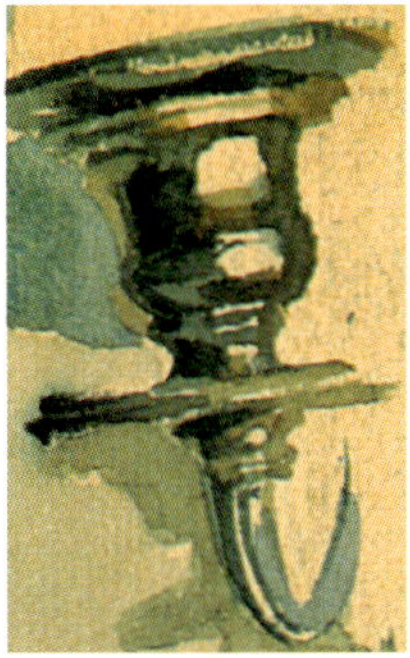
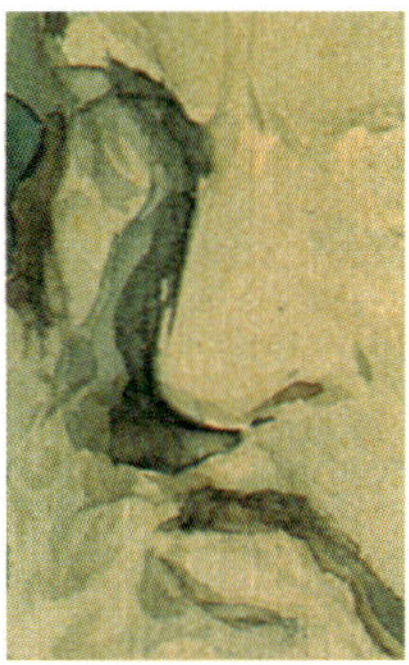
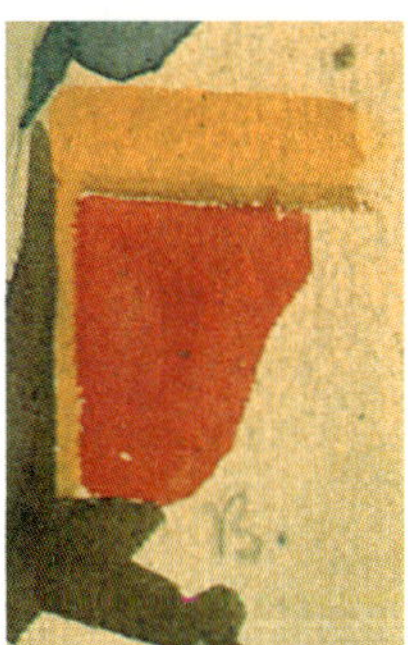

One or two of them departed from the norm by substituting indigenous vegetables, such as onions, carrots, mushrooms and parsley, in place of the hothouse fruits typically included in the Dutch and Italian compositions.

Still Life with Plaster Mask and Sconce

Mikhail Vrubel, 1885, unfinished
water-colour on paper, 18.5 x 11.7 cm
Museum of Russian Art, Kiev

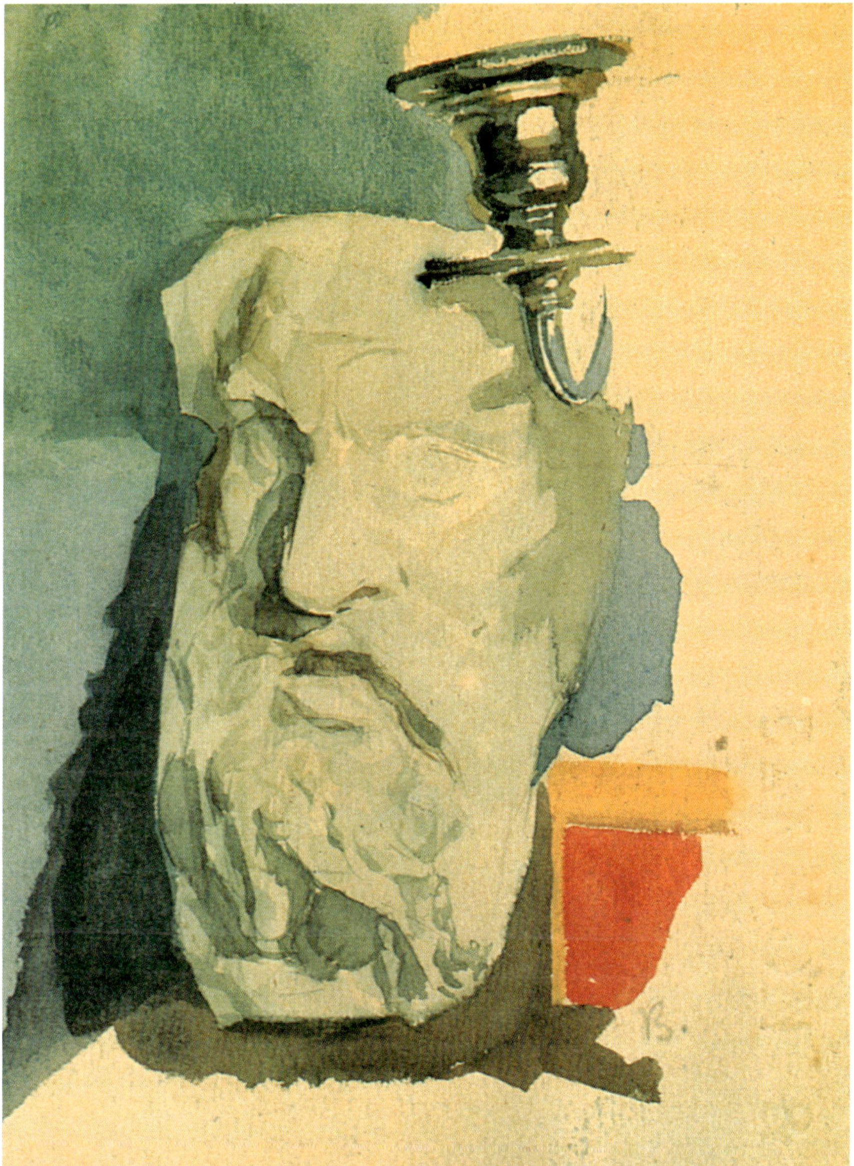

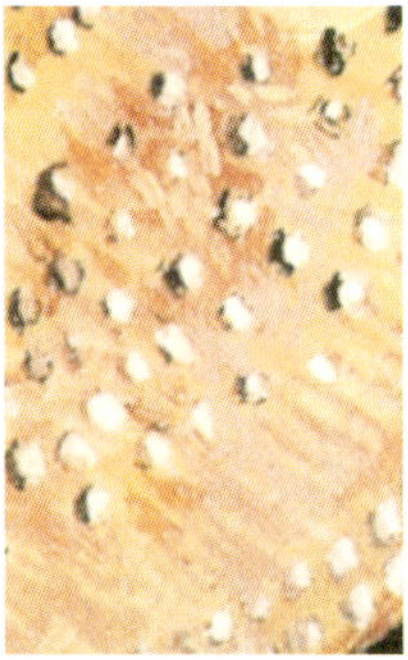

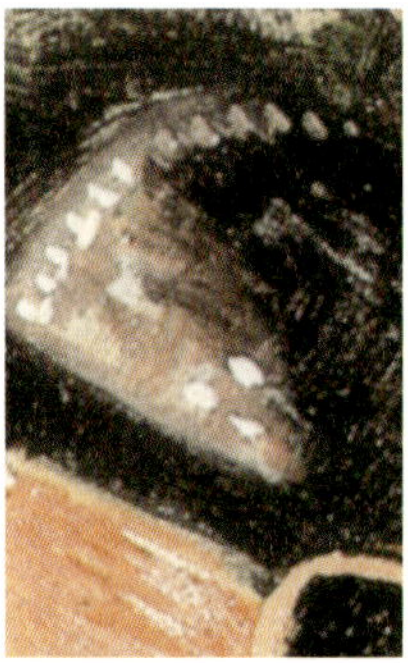

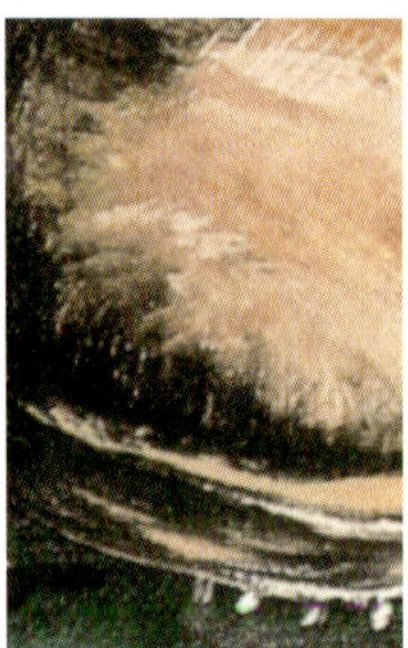

Still-life elements also frequently figure in portraits. During the first few decades of the twentieth century still-life painting was one of the most inventive art forms, both in terms of technique and subject matter and imaginative treatment.

A Pair of Shoes

Vincent van Gogh, 1887
Oil on canvas, 34 x 41.5 cm
The Cone Collection
The Baltimore Museum of Art, Baltimore
the 4th Marquess of Hertford

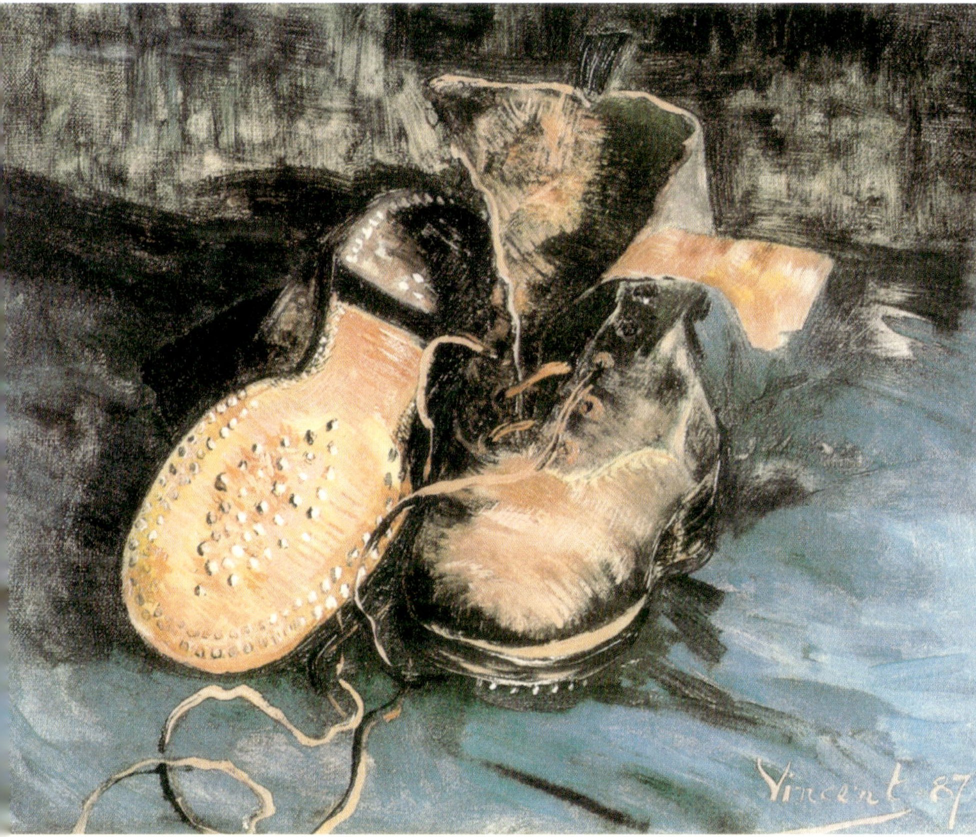
Vincent 87

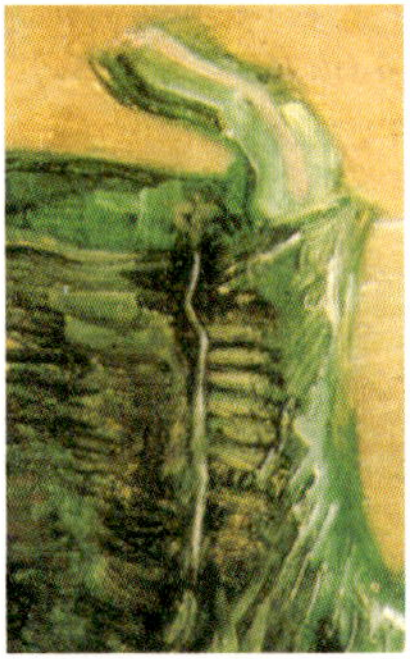

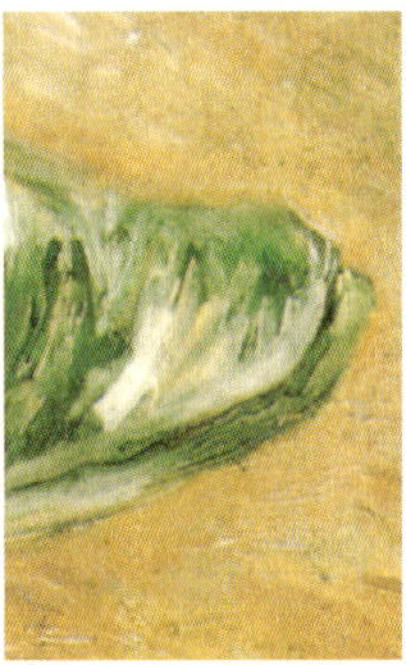

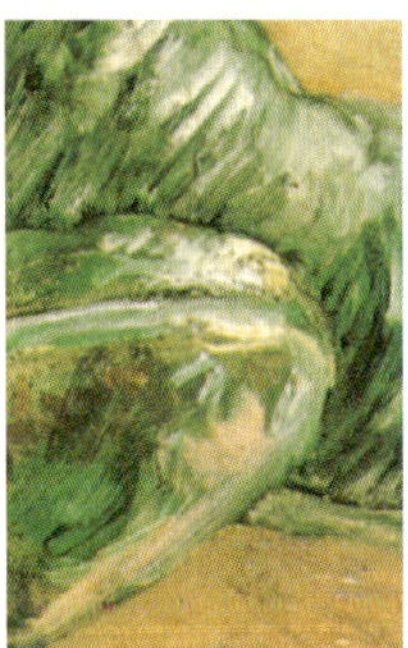

One reason was that it was a natural vehicle not only for the decorative and aesthetic philosophy of the World of Art movement but also for the Impressionist's and Post-Impressionist's experiments with colour and the avant-garde's experiment with form.

A Pair of Shoes

Vincent van Gogh, 1887
oil on cardboard, 33 x 41 cm
Rijksmuseum Vincent van Gogh
Amsterdam, Foundation Vincent van Gogh

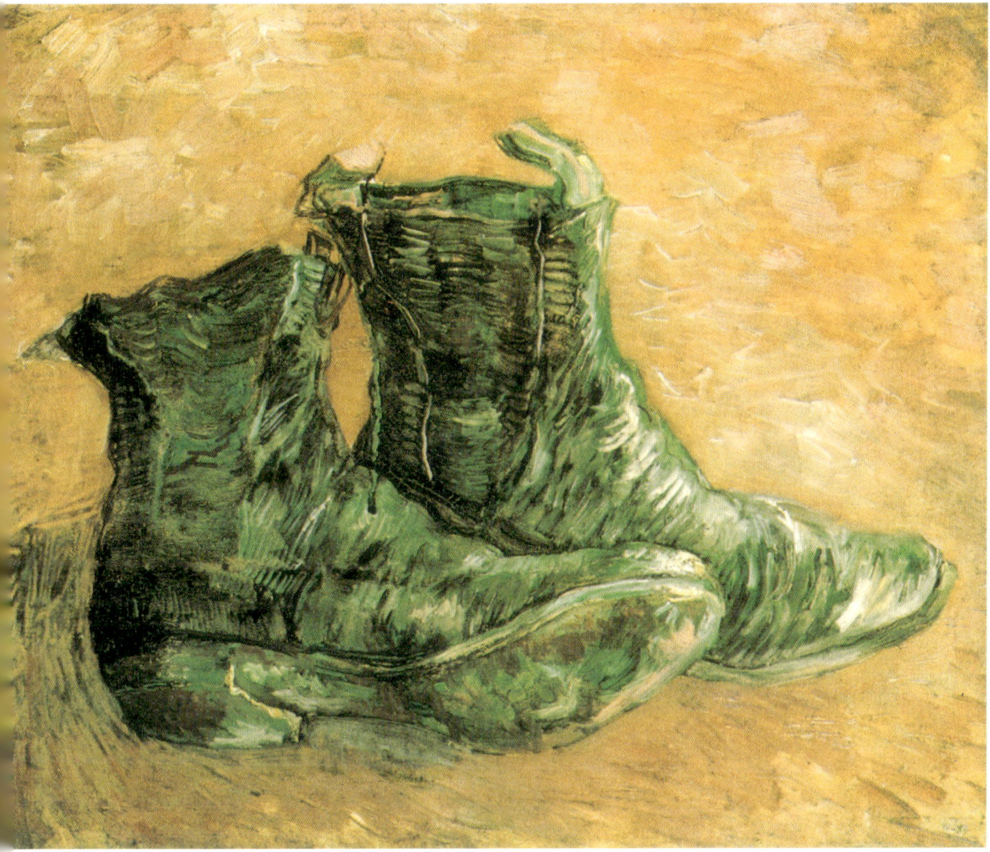

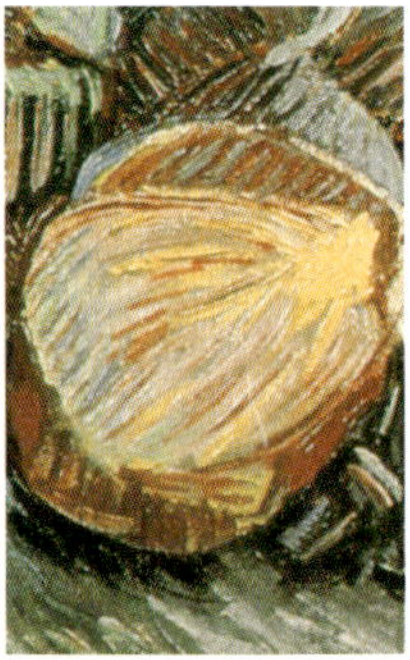

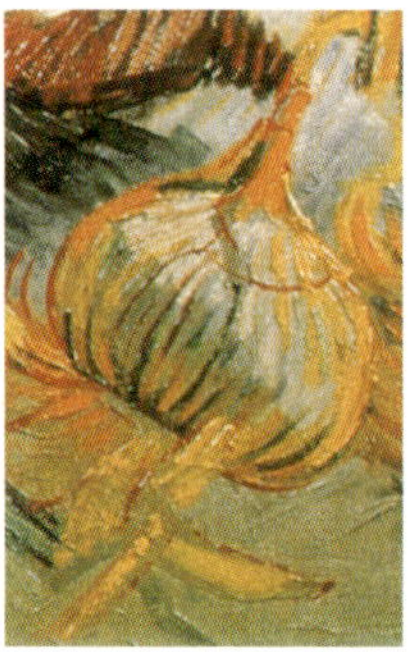

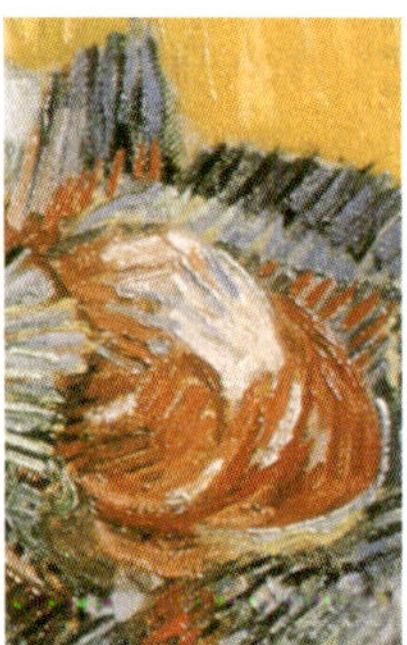

The Artists:

Pieter Boel (1622-1674)

Flemish painter born in 1626 in Antwerp. He probably went to Italy between 1650 and 1651 and then became a master of the Guild of Antwerp. Whilst working for Charles Le Brun at his Parisian tapestry workshop he was also a court painter. He is famous for his vanitas still lifes. Pieter Boel died in 1674 in Paris.

Still Life with Red Cabbages and Onions

Vincent van Gogh, 1887
Oil on canvas, 50 x 64.5 cm
Rijksmuseum Vincent van Gogh
Amsterdam, Foundation Vincent van Gogh

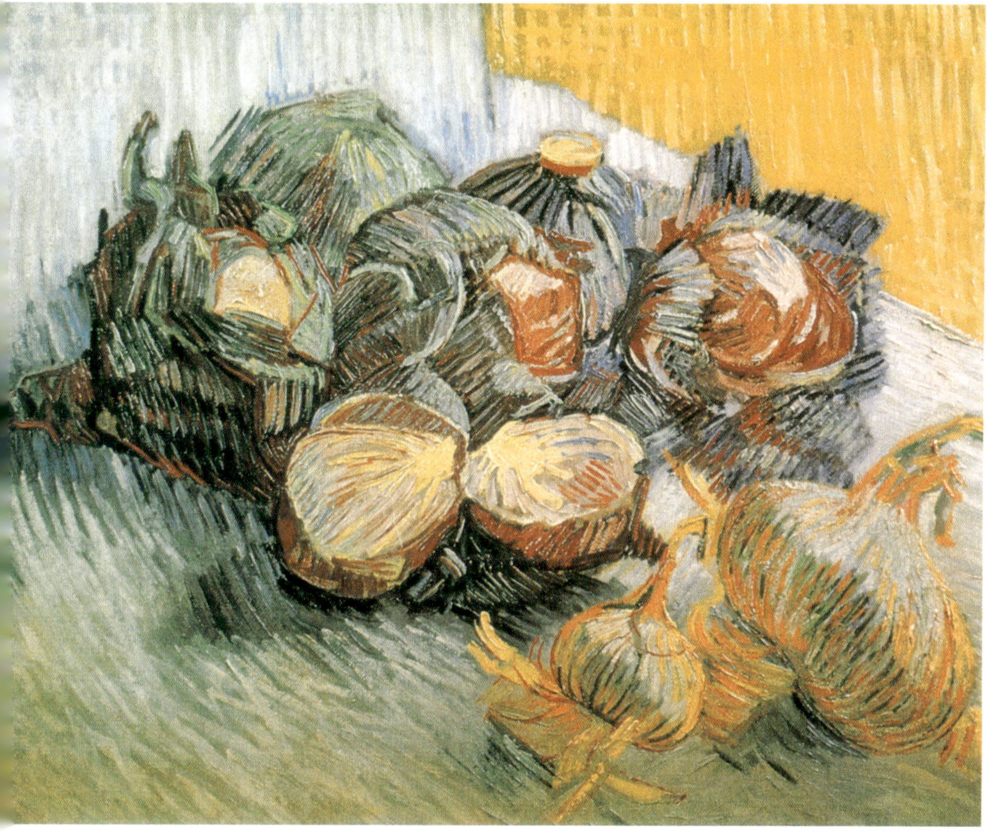

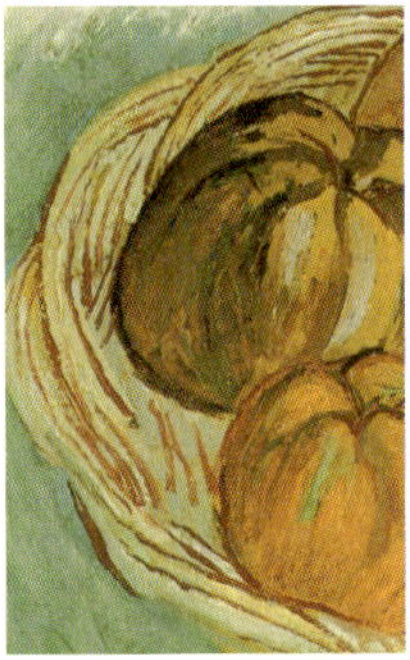

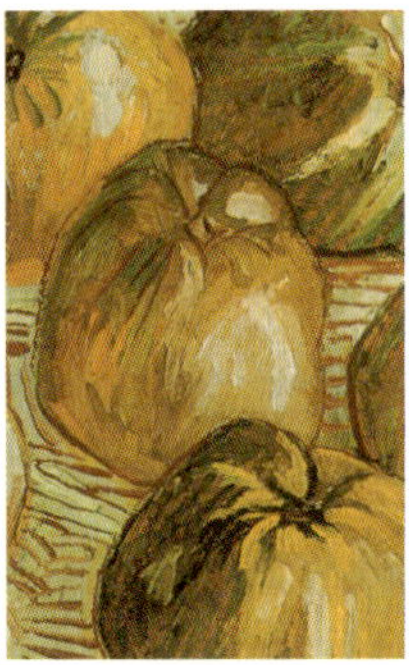

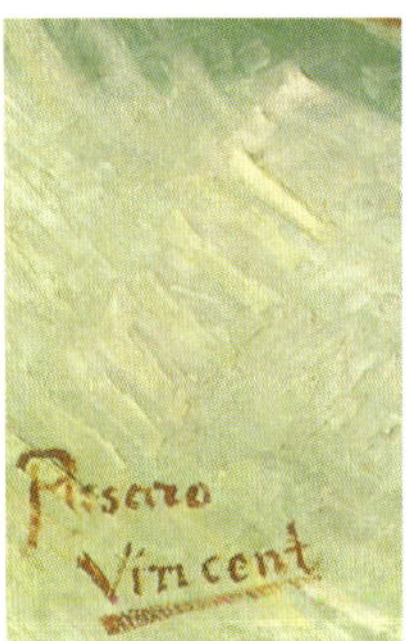

Jean-Baptiste Monnoyer (1634-1699)

Born in 1634 in Lille, and died in 1699 in London. Trained in Antwerp, Monnoyer was a Franco-Flemish flowers-painter. He worked for Louis XIV for a certain time but in a fit of pique he left the French court and worked for the Duke of Montague in London until his death. He is famous for his splendid paintings of flowers.

Still Life with Basket of Apples
(to Lucien Pissarro)

Vincent van Gogh, 1887
Oil on canvas, 50 x 61 cm
Rijksmuseum Kröller-Müller, Otterlo

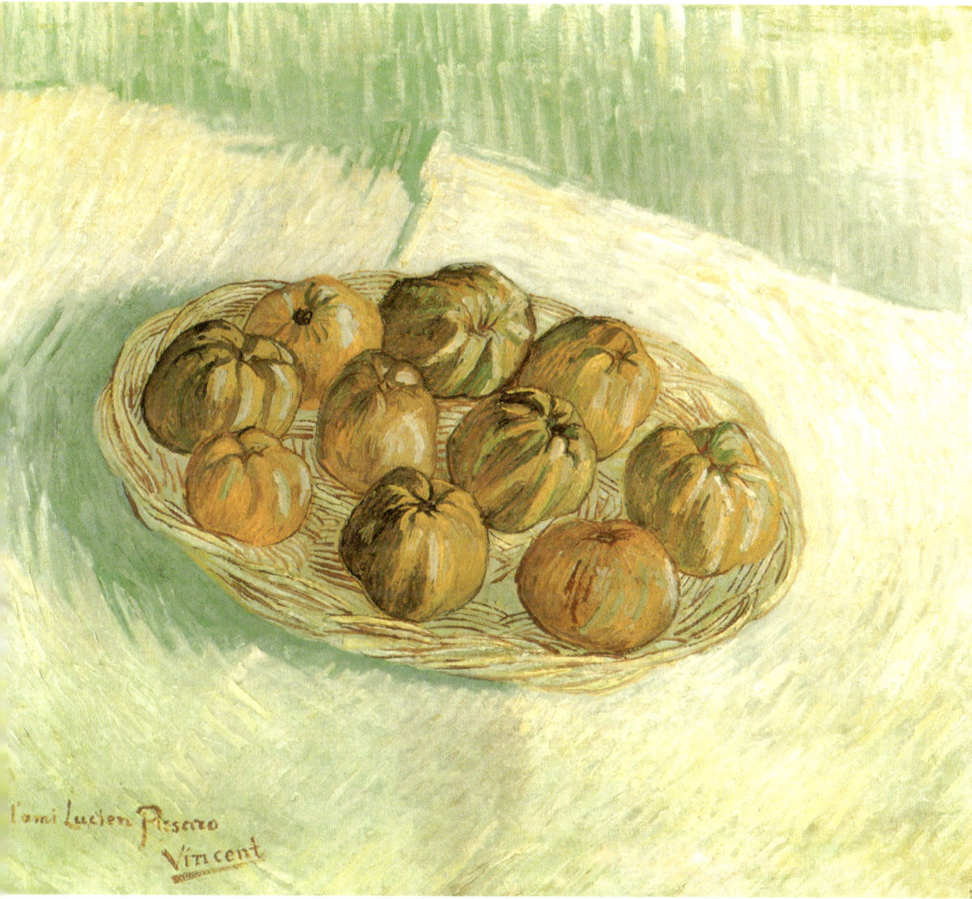
l'ami Lucien Pissaro
Vincent

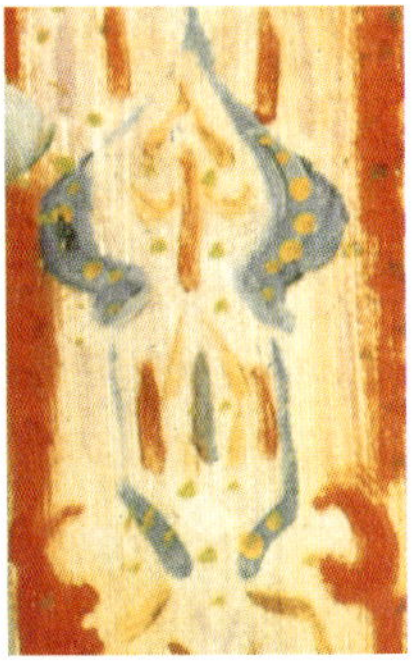

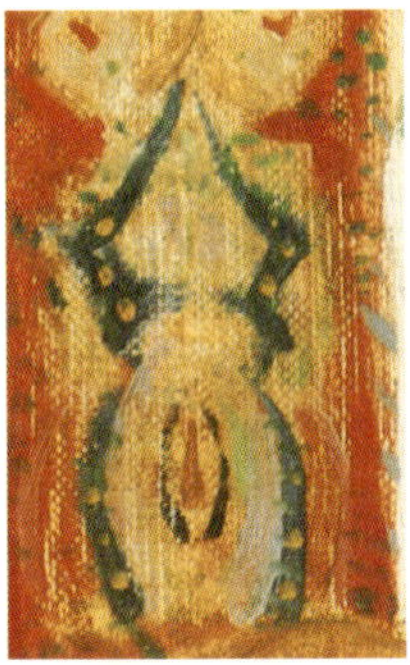

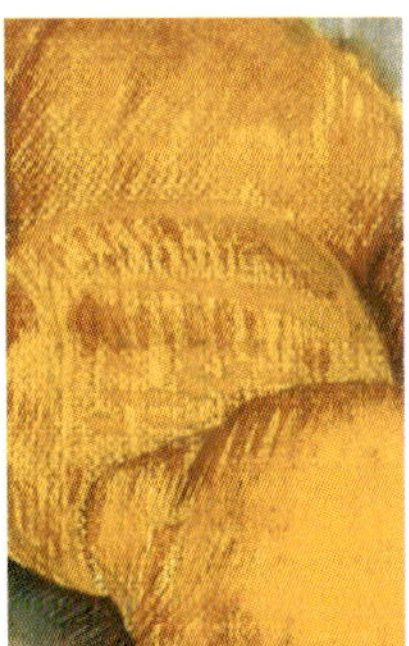

Alexandre-François Desportes

(1661-1743)

Born in 1661 in Champigneulles, France, Desportes was a painter of dogs, game, hunting scenes, and flowers. After a short stay at the court of John III in Poland, he returned to France and took up hunting subjects. He also travelled to England in 1712 where he was well received. He became the favorite painter of both Louis XIV and Louis XV. Desportes died in 1743 in Paris.

Still Life with Decanter
and Lemons on a Plate

Vincent van Gogh, 1887
Oil on canvas, 46.5 x 38.5 cm
Rijksmuseum Vincent van Gogh
Amsterdam, Foundation Vincent van Gogh

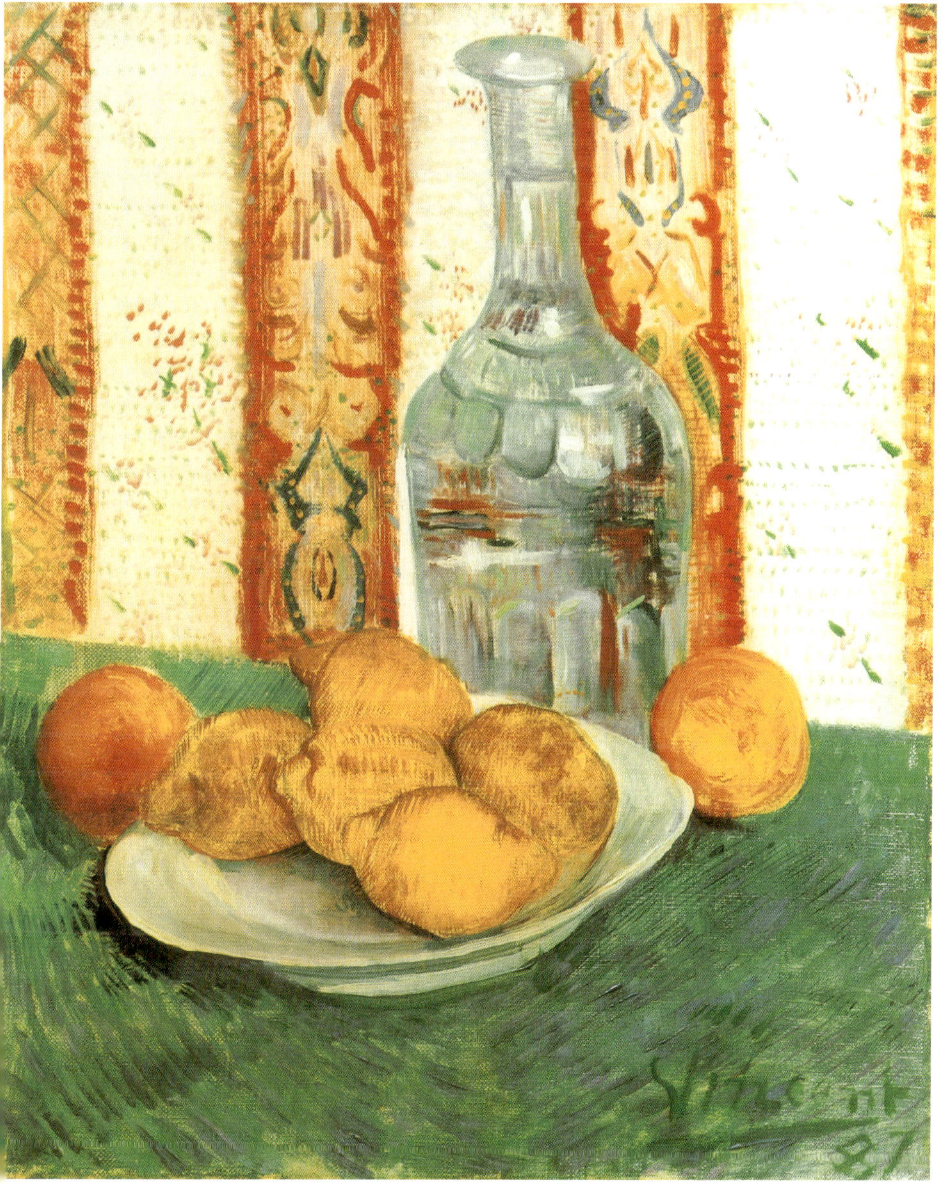
Vincent
87

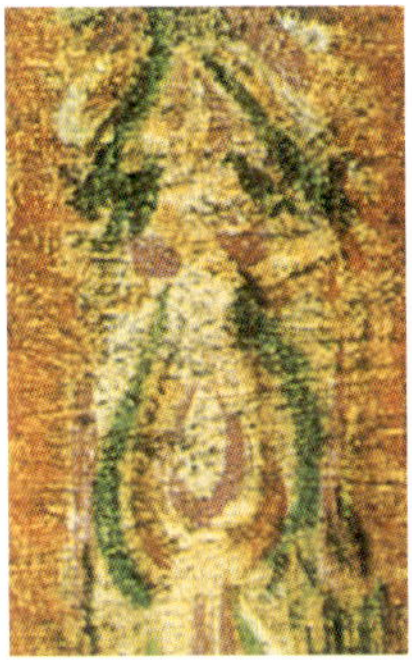

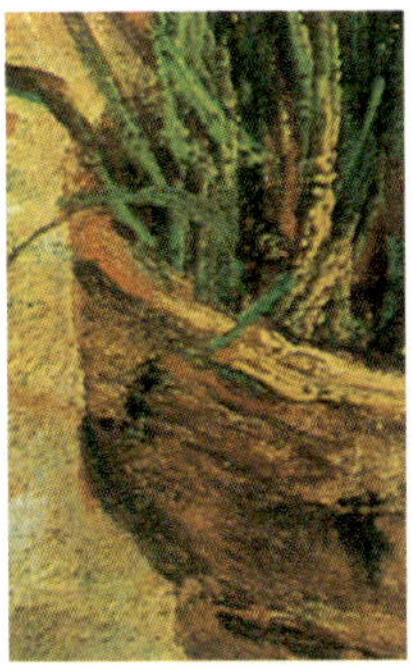

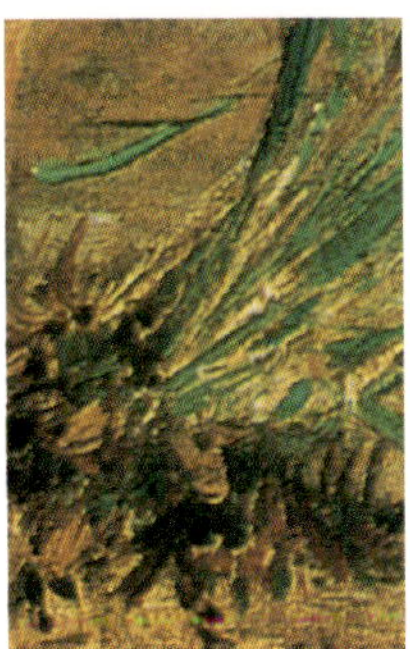

Jean-Baptiste Oudry (1686-1755)

Jean-Baptiste Oudry was born in 1686. King Louis XV often called Jean-Baptiste Oudry to Versailles to paint the royal hounds in the king's presence. He became a member of the "Academy of Painting and Sculpture" in 1719.

Flowerpot with Chives

Vincent van Gogh, 1887
Oil on canvas, 31.5 x 22 cm
Rijksmuseum Vincent van Gogh
Amsterdam, Foundation Vincent van Gogh

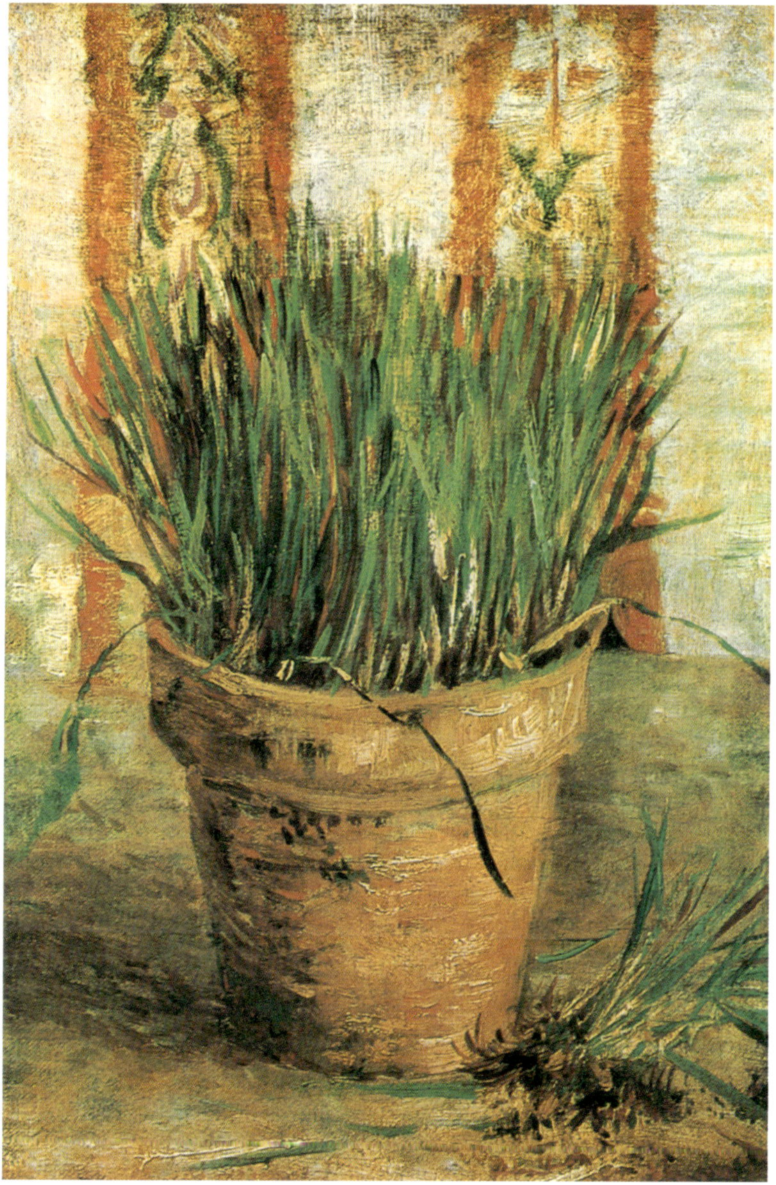

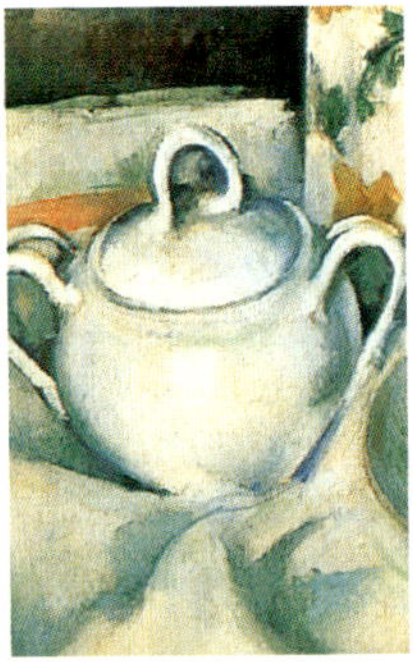

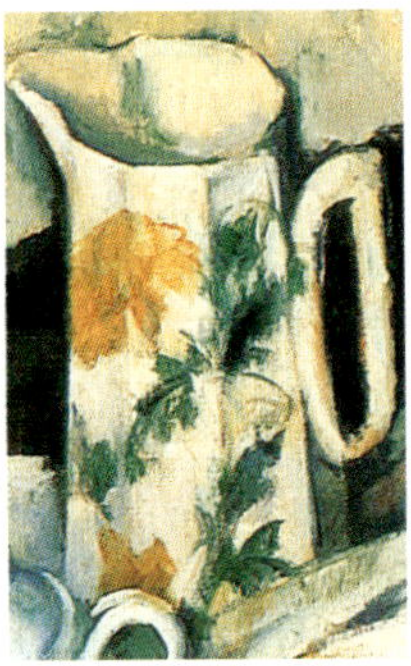

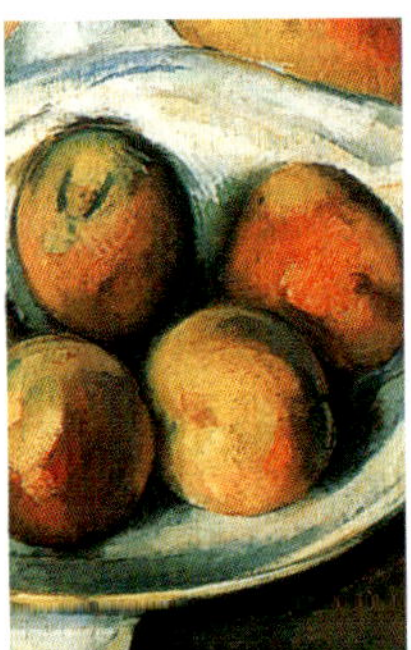

Due to his great success designing tapestries, he was named the 'Director of the Beauvais tapestry manufacturers' and, two years later, director of the Gobelins manufacturers. Oudry died in 1755.

Peaches and Pears

Paul Cézanne, 1888-90
Oil on canvas, 61 x 90 cm
Pushkin Museum of Fine Arts, Moscow

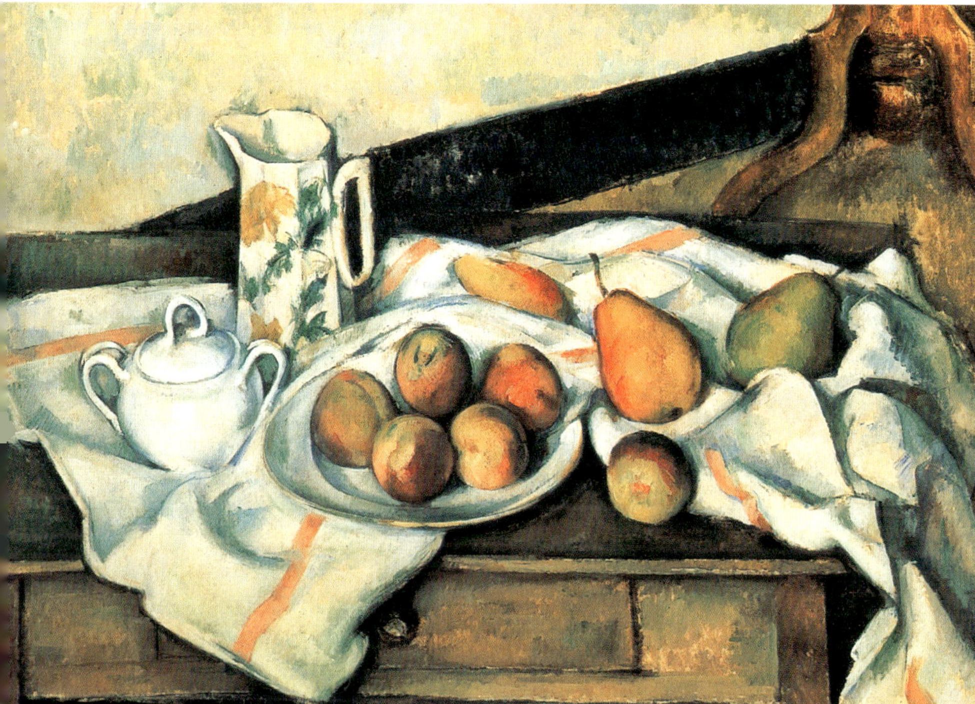

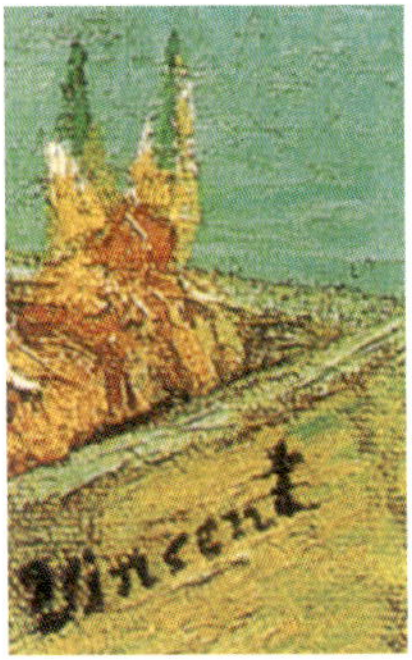

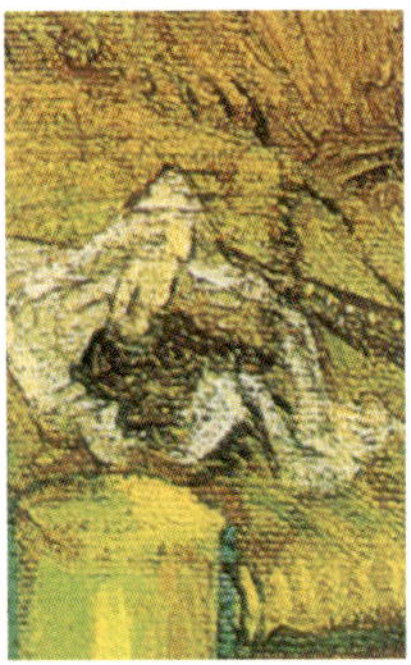

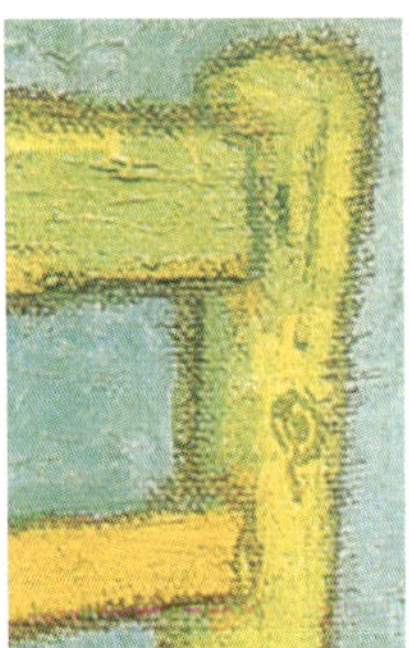

Jean-Baptiste Simeon Chardin

(1699-1779)

Born in 1699 in Paris. "With the use of colour, one can give interest to the dullest things, and makes a master piece with a simple vase and fruits". Chardin helped to elevate still life to a respected category of painting.

Vincent's Chair with His Pipe

Vincent van Gogh, Arles: December 1888
Oil on canvas, 93 x 73.5 cm
National Gallery, London

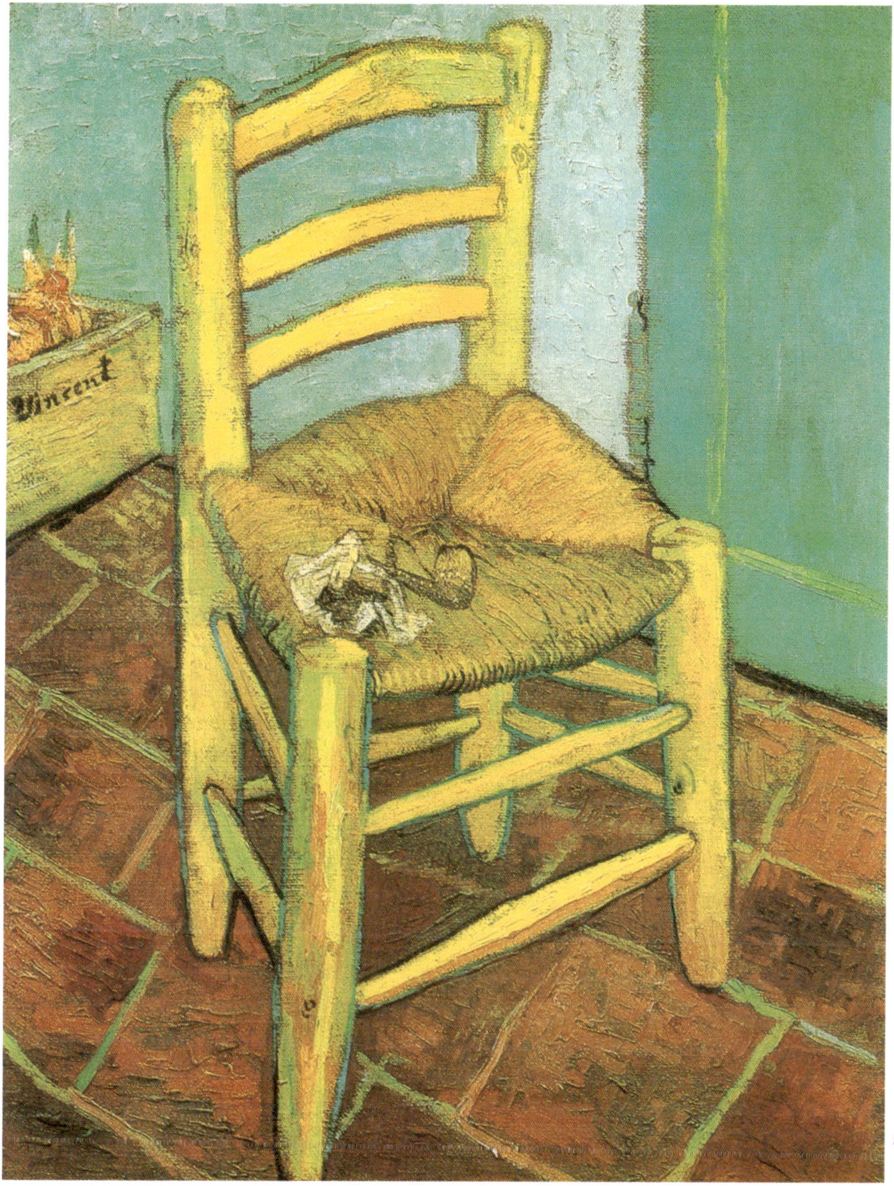
Vincent

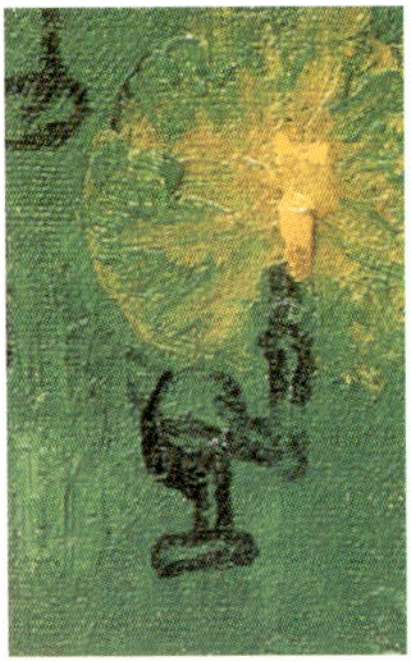

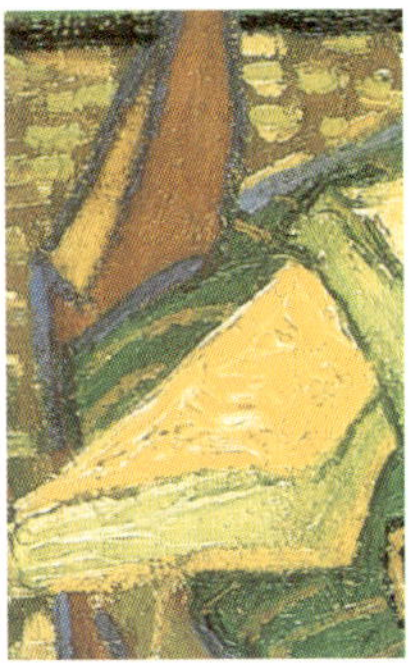

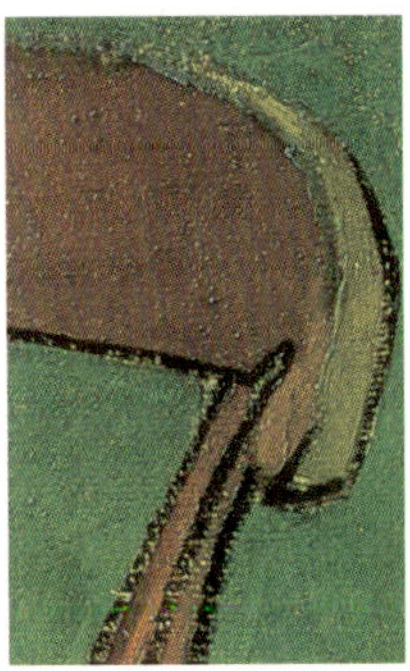

Marcel Proust, a French writer, wrote: "we have learned from Chardin that a pear is as alive as a woman, that an ordinary piece of pottery is as beautiful as a precious stone." Chardin died in 1779 in Paris.

Paul Gauguin's Armchair

Vincent van Gogh, 1888
Oil on canvas, 90.5 x 72.5 cm
Rijksmuseum Vincent van Gogh
Foundation Vincent van Gogh, Amsterdam

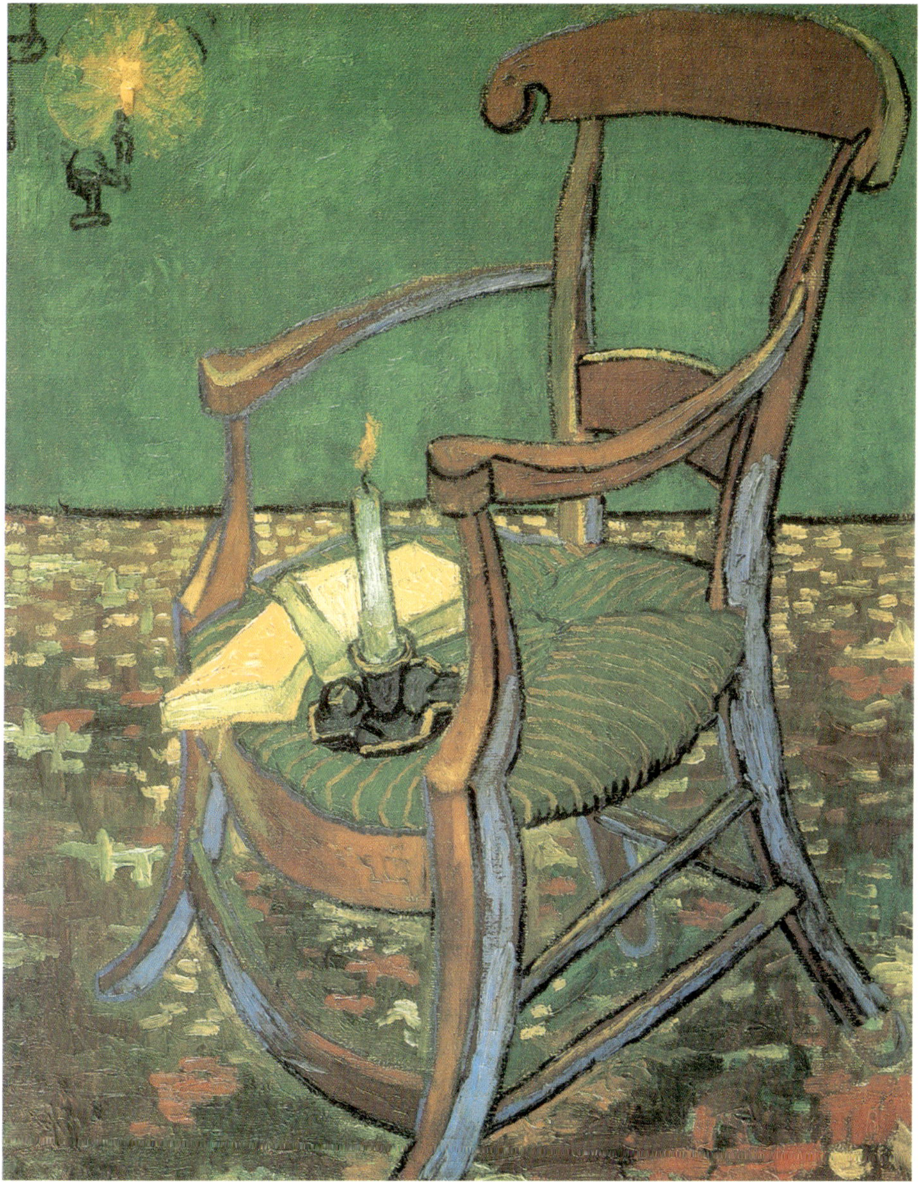

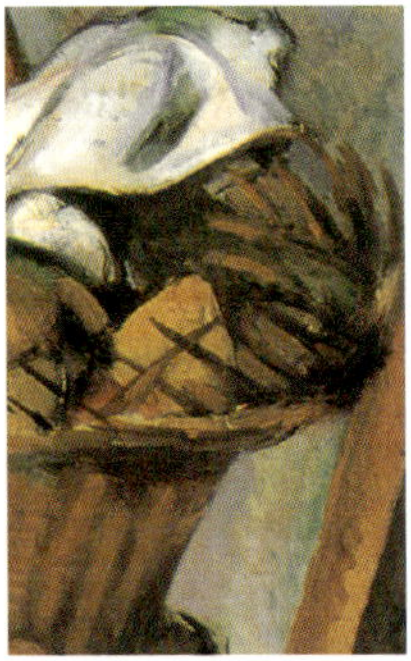

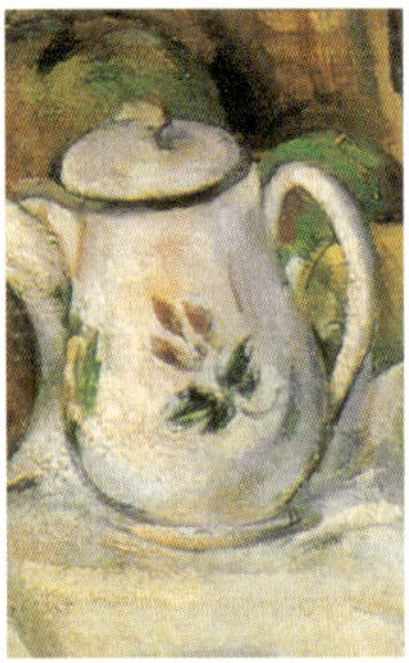

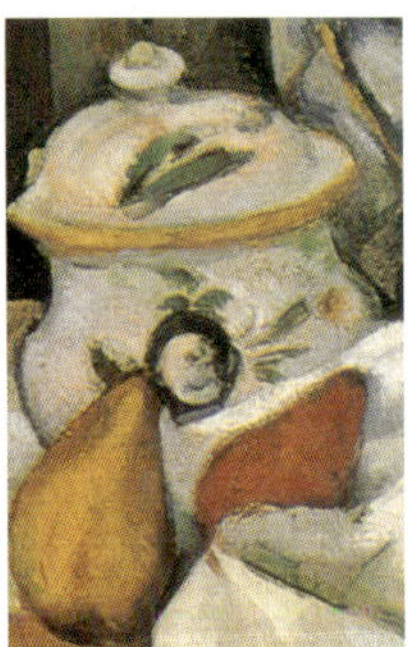

Simon Saint- Jean (1808-1860)

Simon Saint-Jean was born on the 14th of October 1808 in Lyon (France). In his youth he attended the class of Thierriat in the School of Fine Arts in Lyon, where he won a gold medal for a flower painting at the young age of 18.

Still Life with Basket

Paul Cézanne, c. 1888-1890
Oil on canvas
Musée d'Orsay, Paris

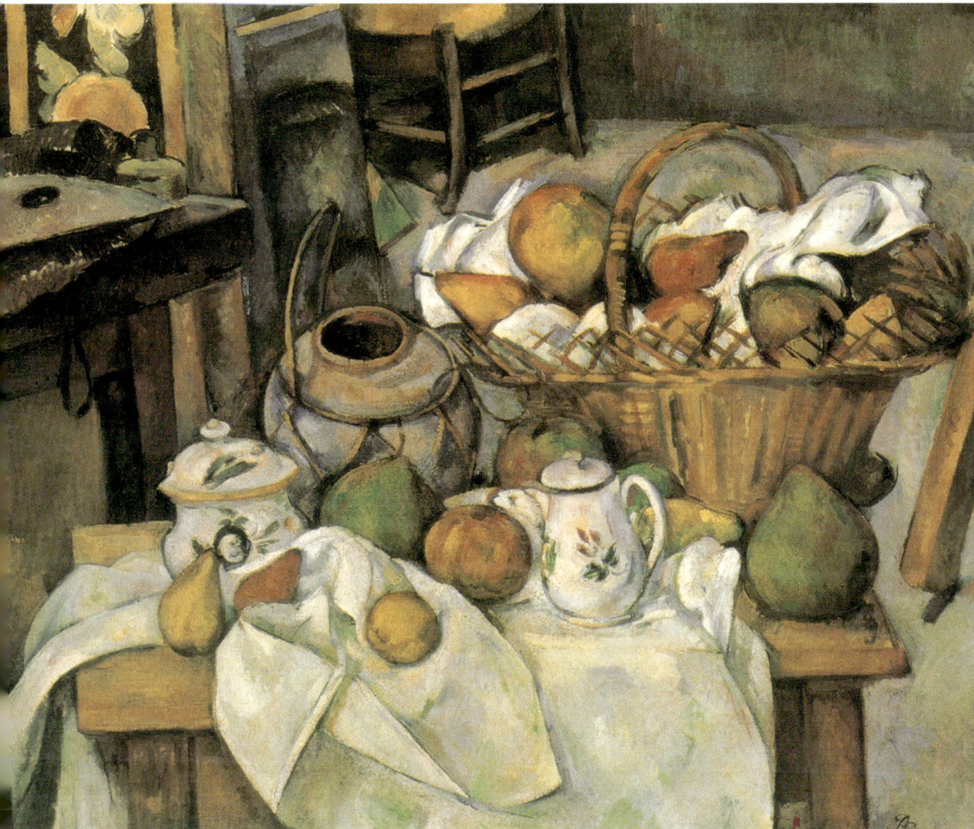

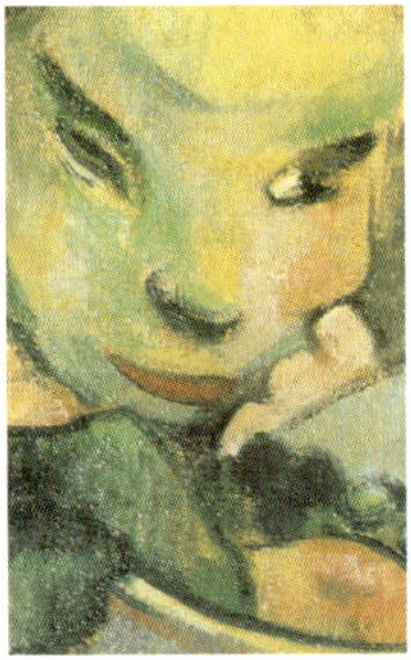

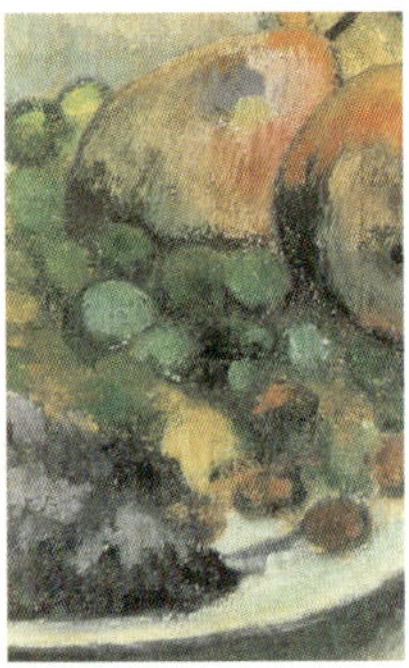

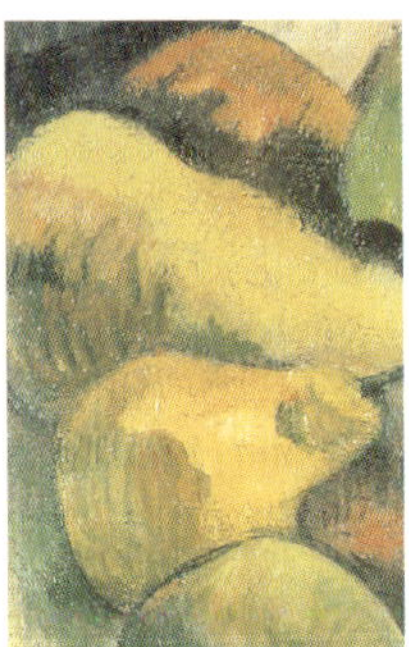

Simon Saint Jean acquired an international reputation with still lifes and flowers that he painted for the Netherlands, Germany, England, Italy and Russia. Six of his still life paintings were exhibited in 1851 at the Great Exhibition in London and in 1855 at the

Still Life with Fruits

Paul Gauguin, 1888
Oil on canvas, 43 x 58 cm
Pushkin Museum of Fine Arts, Moscow

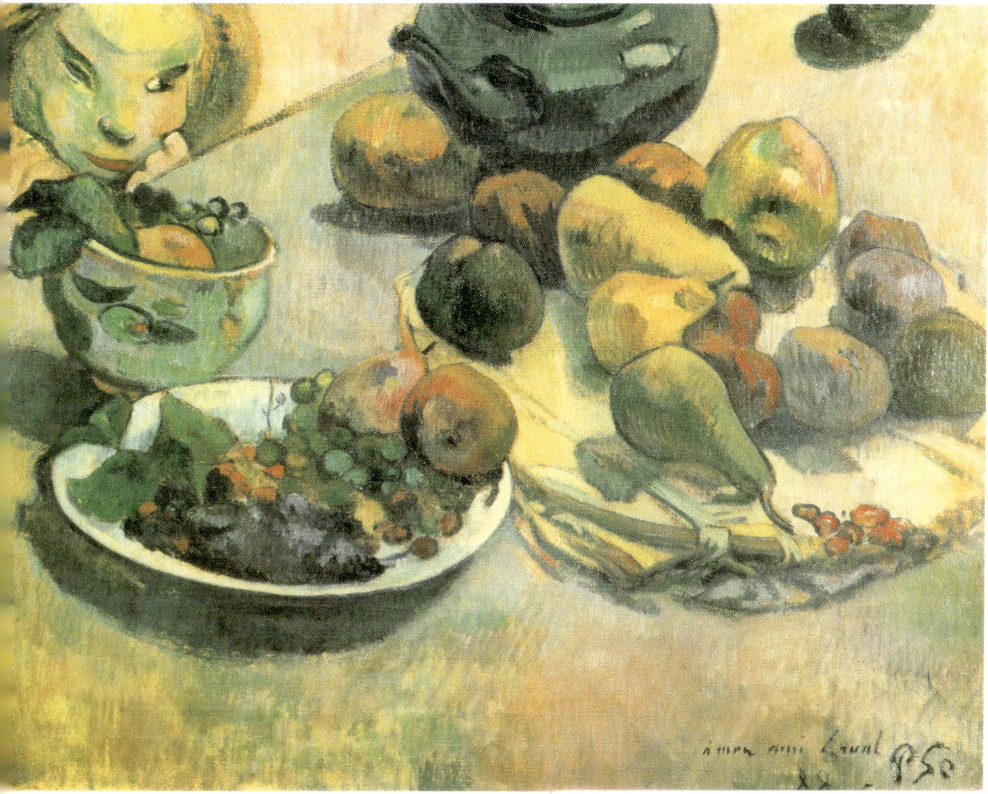

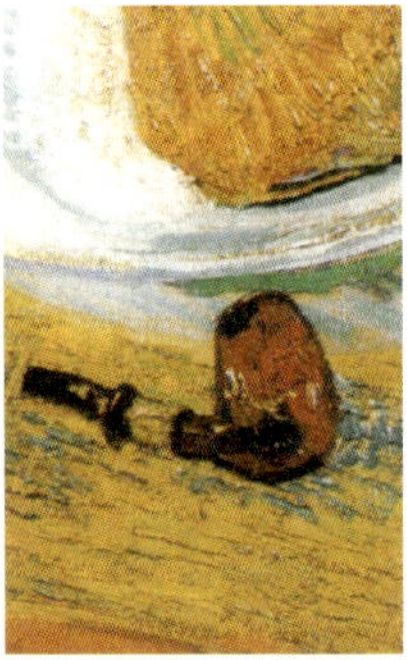

'Exposition Universelle' in Paris, where nine of his paintings were shown. He won the gold medal. Saint-Jean enjoyed, among others, the patronage of Napoleon III, the Empress Eugénie and the 4th Marquess of Hertford. He died on 3rd July 1860.

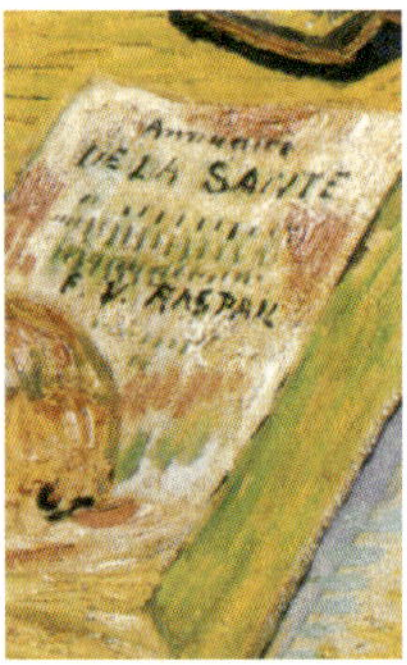

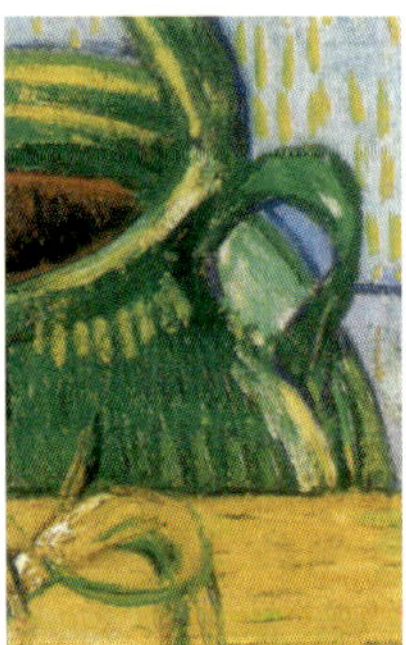

Still Life. Drawing Board with Onions

Vincent van Gogh, 1889
Oil on canvas, 50 x 54 cm
Rijksmuseum Kröller-Müller, Otterlo

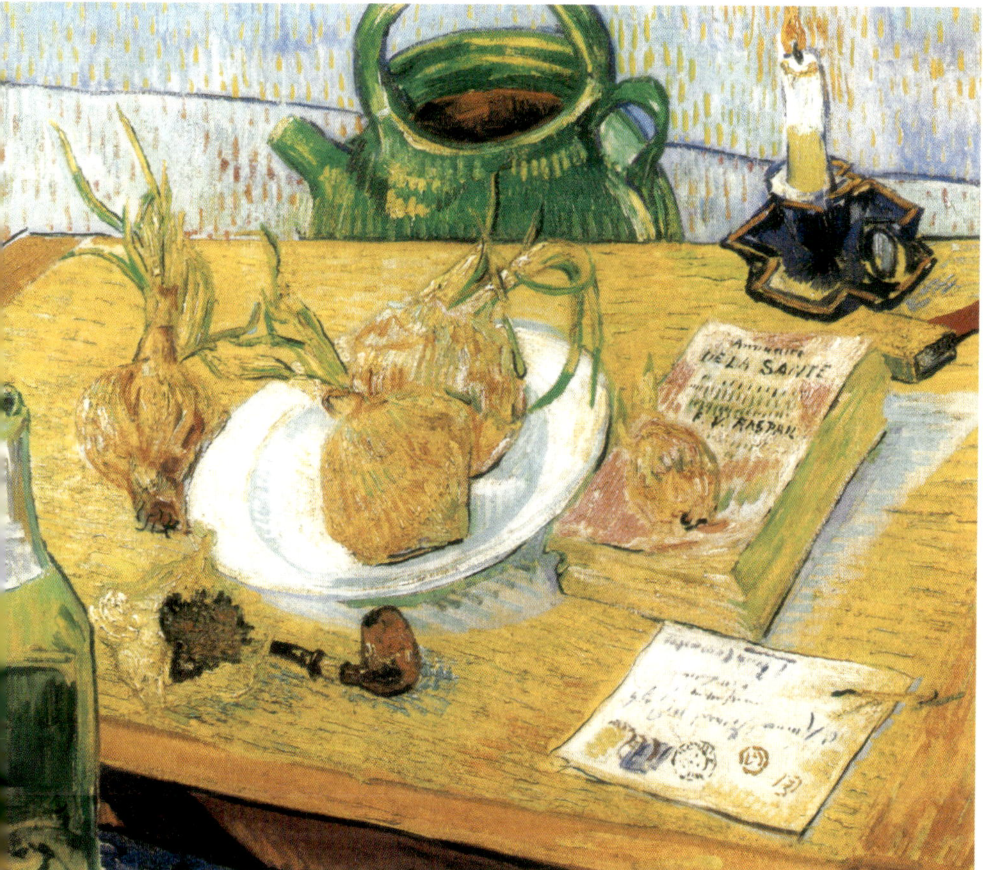
DE LA SANTE
F. V. RASPAIL

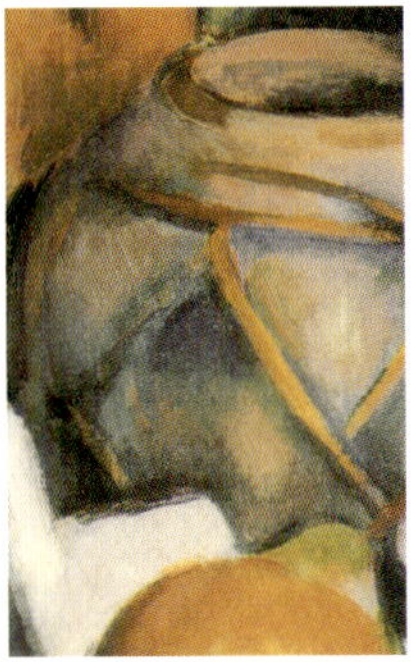

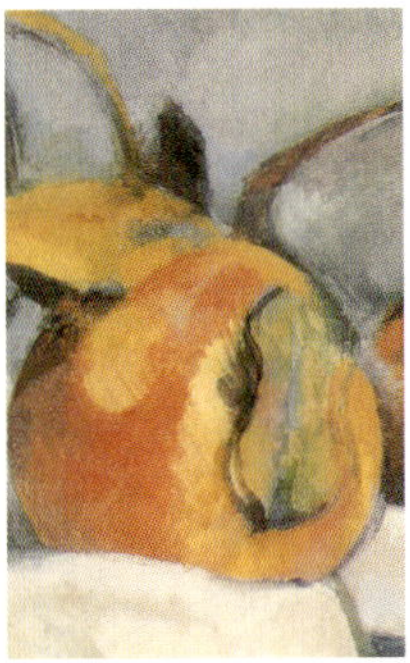

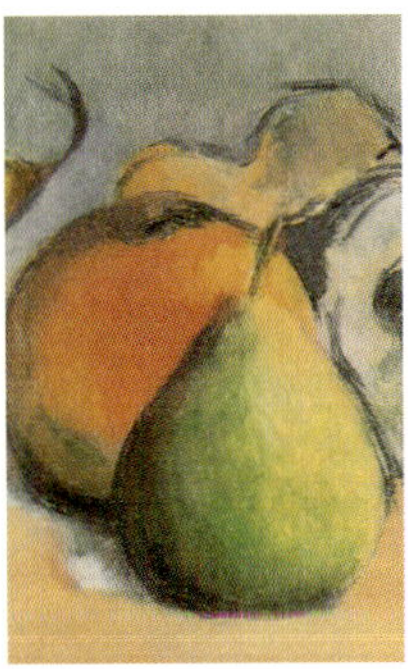

Henri Fantin-Latour (1836-1904)

Henri Fantin-Latour was born in 1836 in Grenoble, France. For Fantin-Latour, still life painting was almost a curse, faced with collectors who wanted nothing else from his immense artistic talent.

Still Life with a Ginger Pot

Paul Cézanne, 1890-1893
Oil on canvas, 46 x 55 cm
Philips Collection, Washington DC

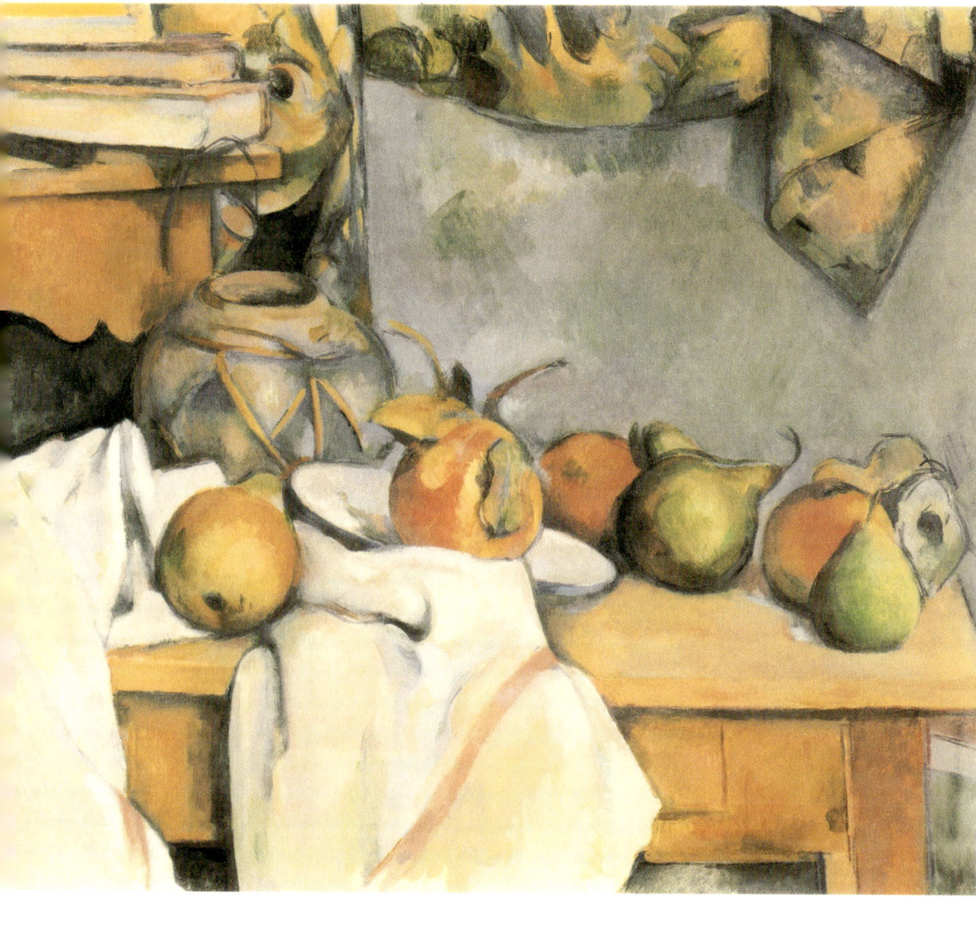

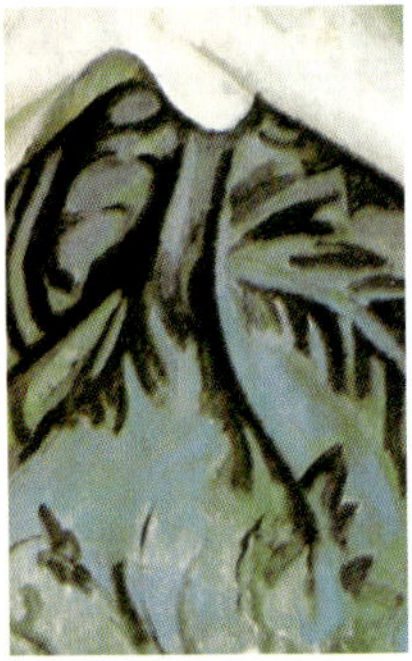

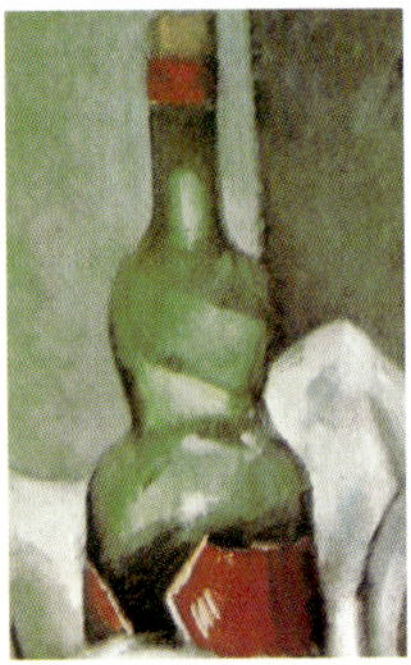

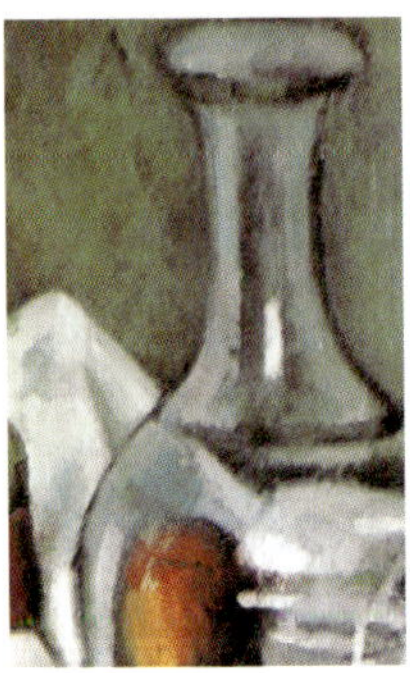

He is known almost exclusively for his delicate still lifes which he excelled in, although his extraordinary figure depictions and portrait groups should have stood the test of time. Many of the best examples of his floral paintings and still lifes can be found in English galleries and museums. Often, when viewed close up, they reveal details and objects which give a realistic impression.

A Bottle of Peppermint

Paul Cézanne, 1893-1895
Oil on canvas, 65.9 x 82.1 cm
National Gallery of Art, Washington DC

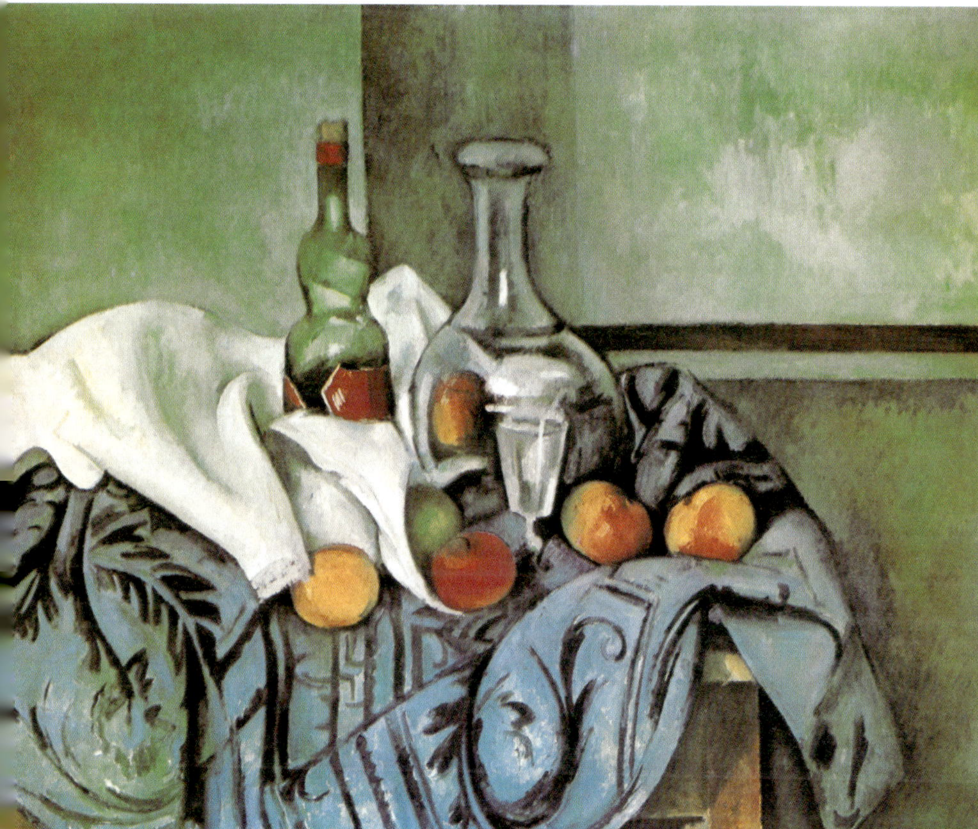

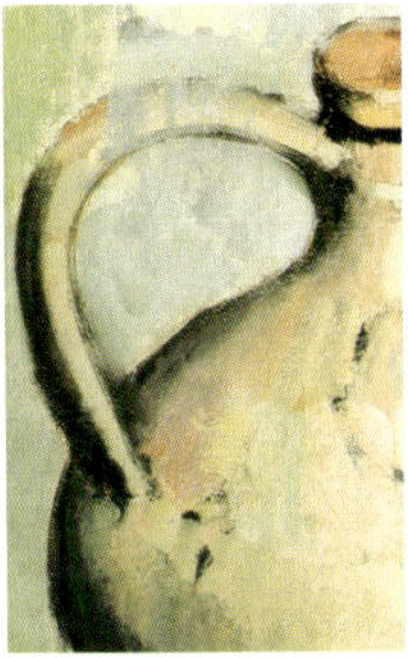

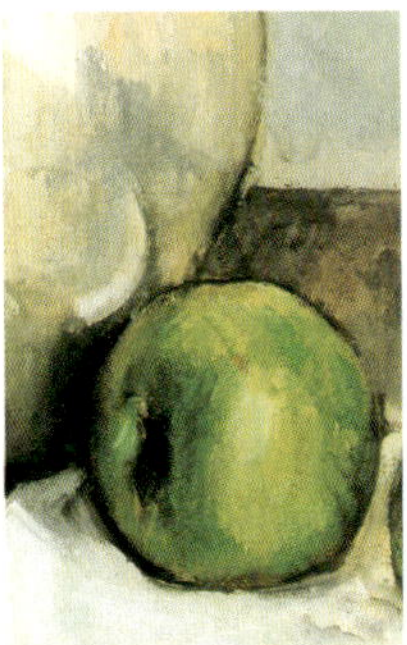

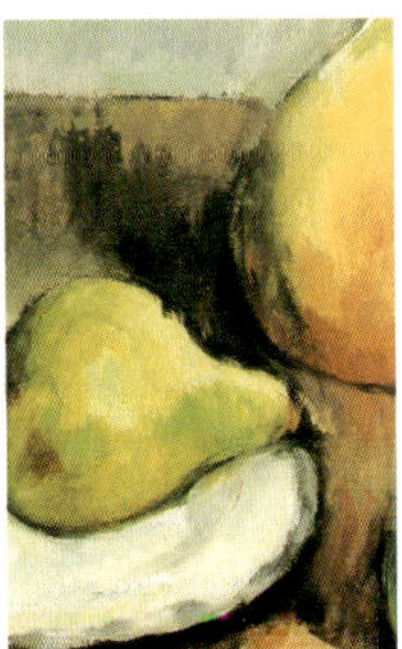

They combine meticulous drawing with intricate brushwork and lovely harmonies of colours. In this way his still lifes, like his portraits, have a realistic quality and great pictorial depth. Fantin-Latour sold many flower paintings on the Anglo-Saxon art market. He died in 1904 in Normandy.

Still Life with Pitcher and Fruits

Paul Cézanne, 1893-1894
Oil on canvas, 43.2 x 62.8 cm
Berggruen Collection, Paris

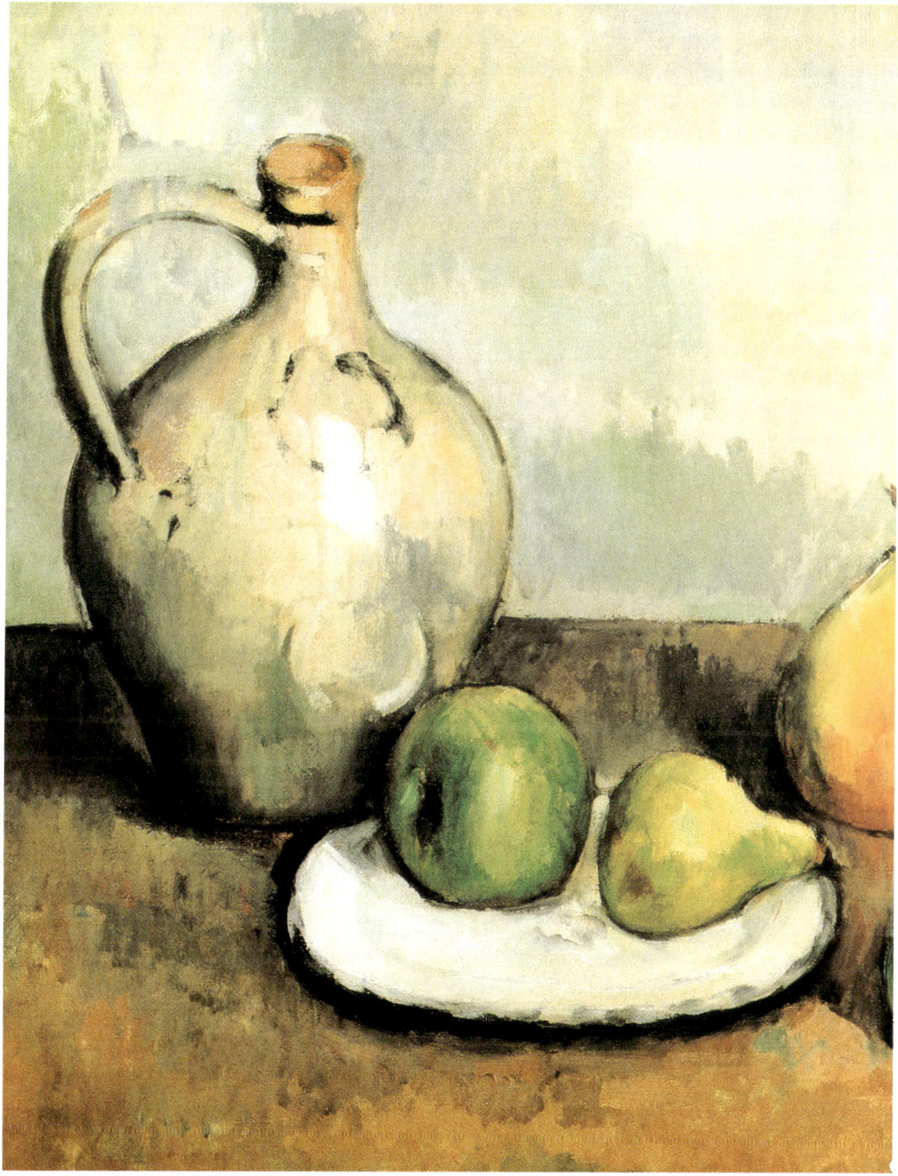

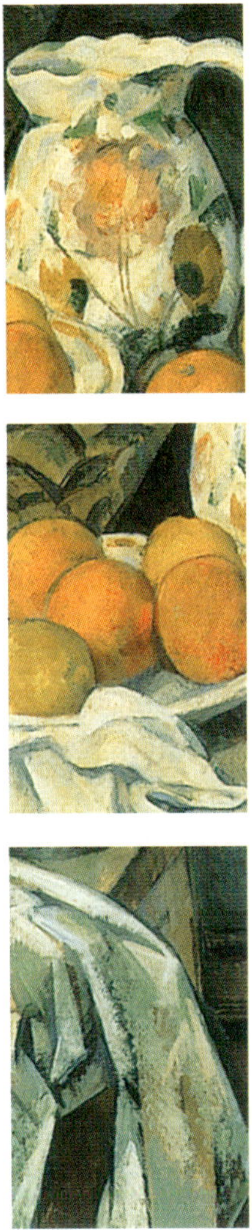

Nicolae Grigorescu (1838-1907)

The painter Nicolae Grigorescu holds a foremost place in Romanian art and in Romanian culture. He was born in Pitaru-Dambovitza, a village near Bucharest, in 1838. Thanks to a study subsidy from the Moldavian authorities, Grigorescu was able to go to Paris.

Still Life with Drapery

Paul Cézanne, c.1895
Oil on canvas, 53 x 72 cm
The Hermitage, Saint Petersburg

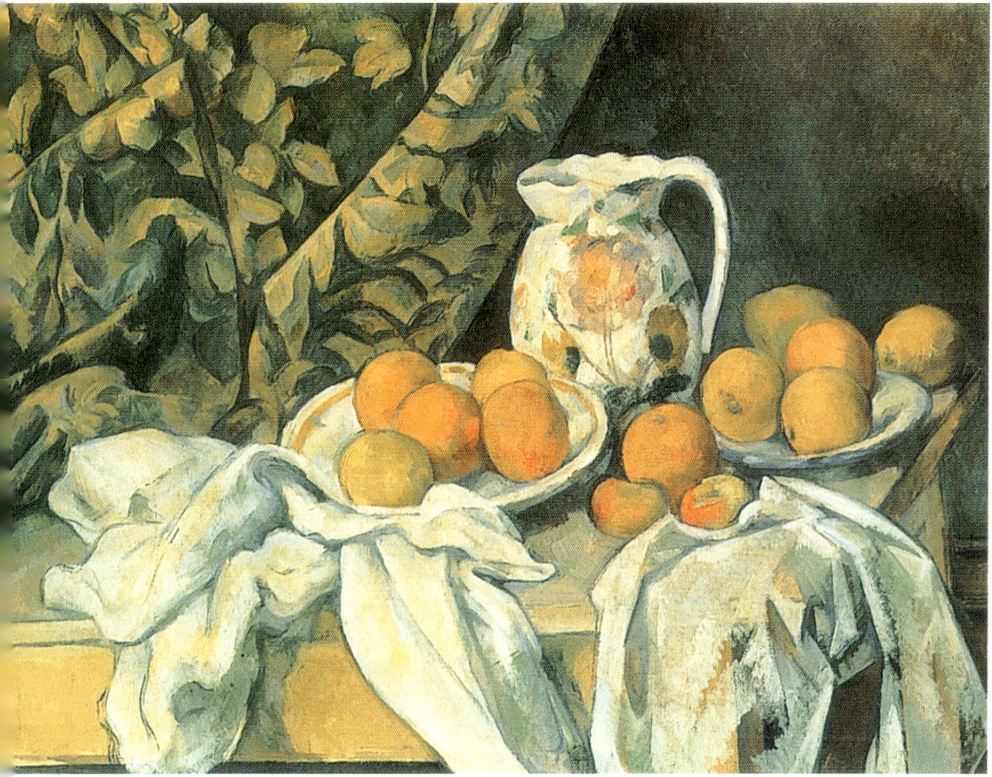

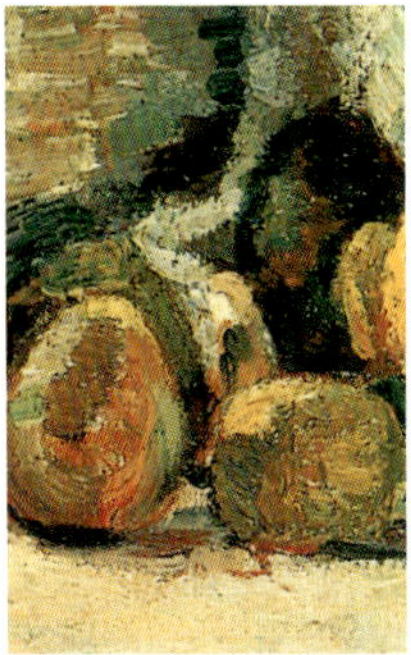

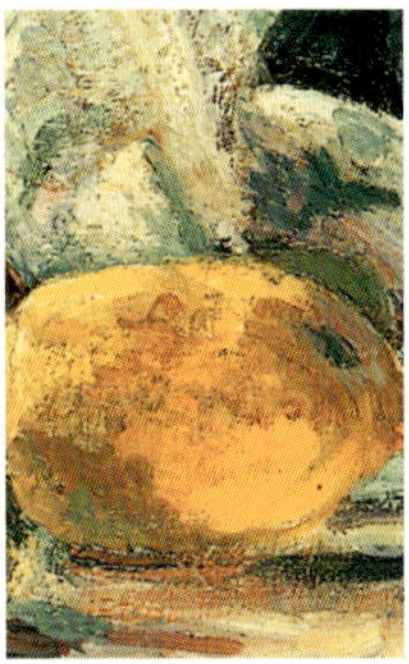

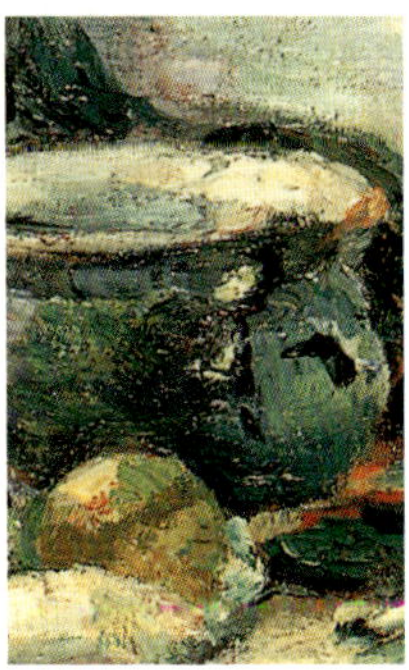

From that moment on, the artist's life and career flourished. The outcome was a massive oeuvre of over 3,000 works, comprehensive, original and unitary, including a great number of flower and still life paintings. He worked on them with a sincere passion, far from the conventionality of his contemporaries.

Blue Pot and Lemon

Henri Matisse, 1897
Oil on canvas, 39 x 46.5 cm
The Hermitage, Saint Petersburg

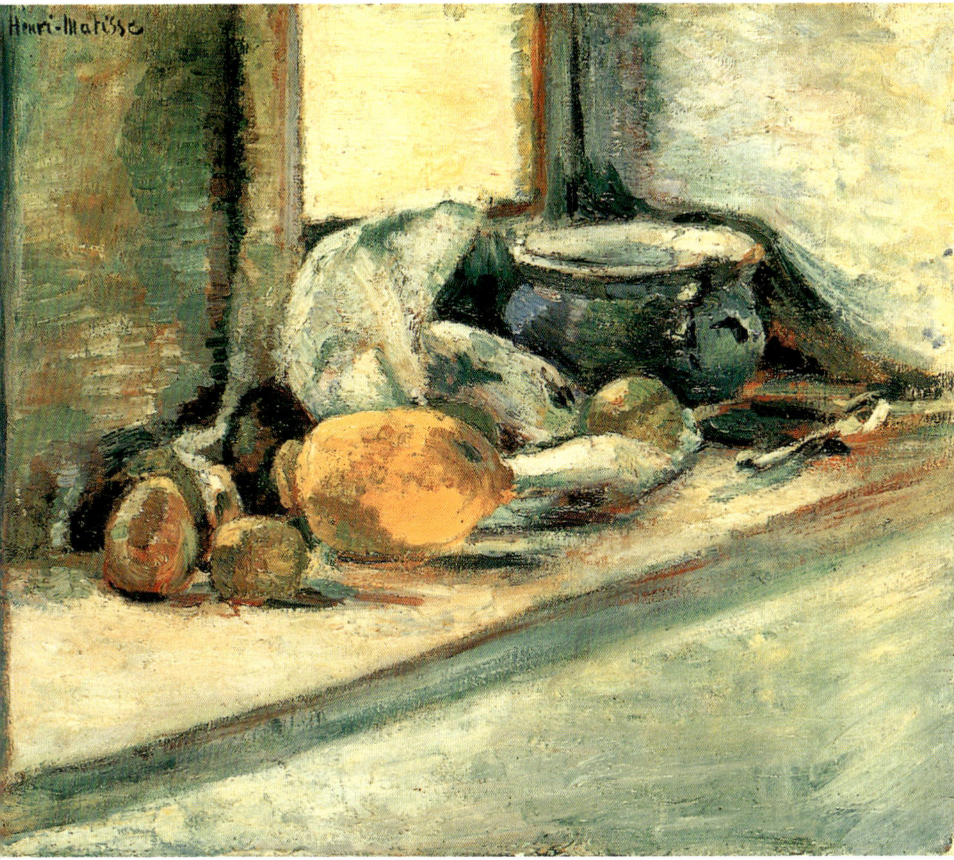
Henri-Matisse

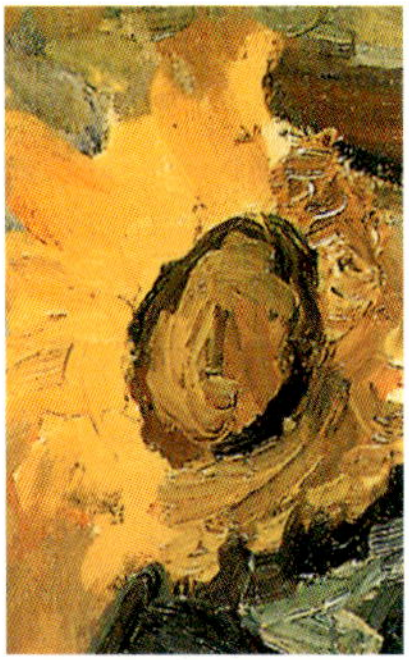

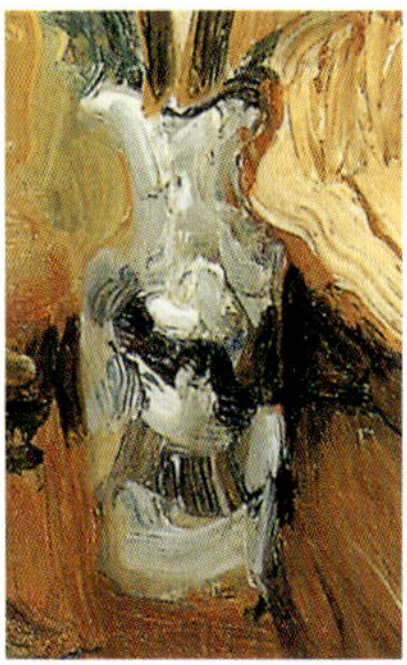

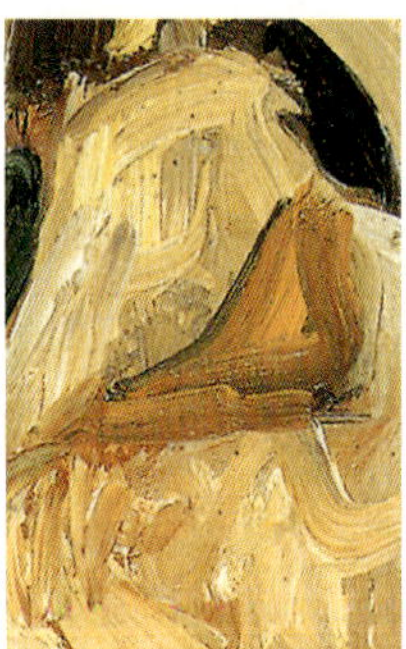

Grigorescu is also famous because, like a real war correspondent, he immortalised scenes from the principal events of the Russian-Romanian-Turkish war. After a long stay in France, he returned to his native land of Romania. He built a house in Campina, where he died in 1907. Today it is the "Nicolae Grigorescu" Museum.

Vase of Sunflowers

Henri Matisse, c.1898
Oil on canvas, 46 x 38 cm
The Hermitage, Saint Petersburg

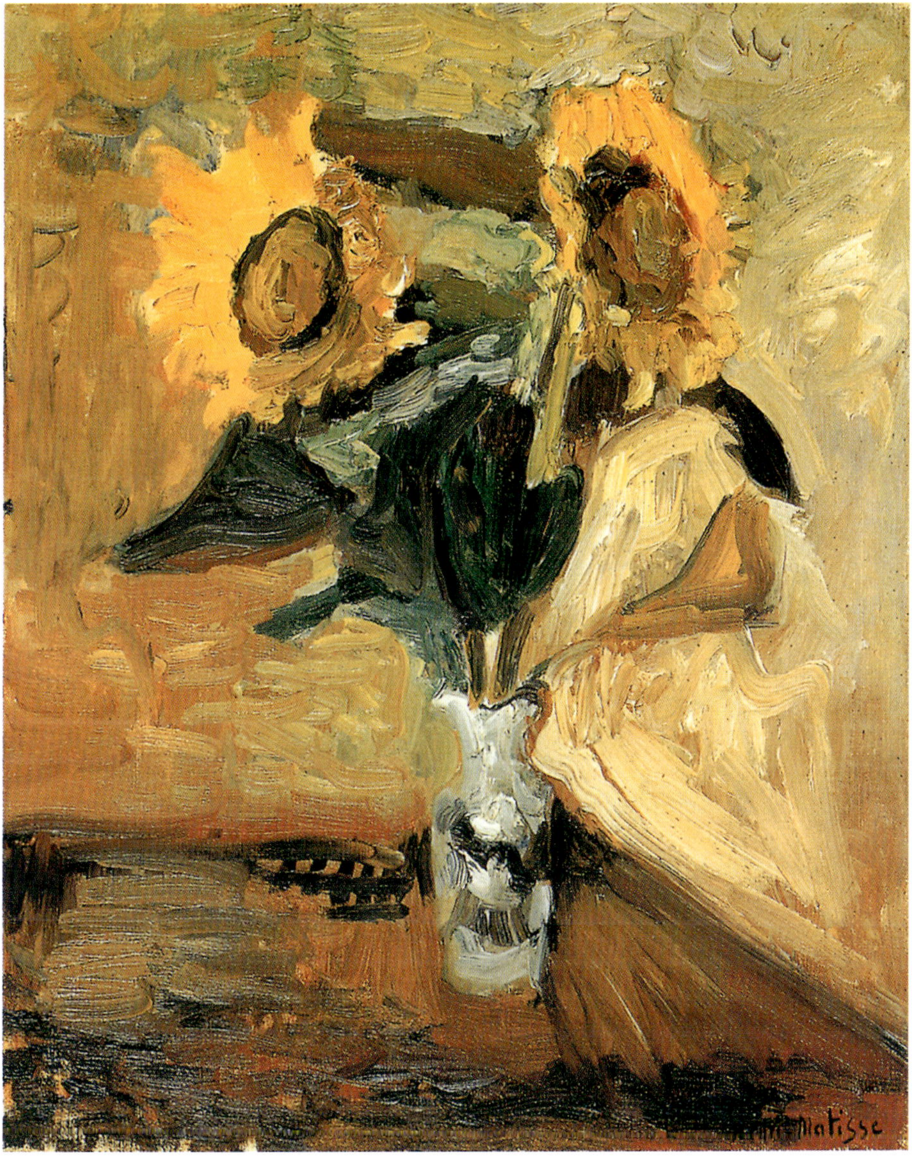
Matisse

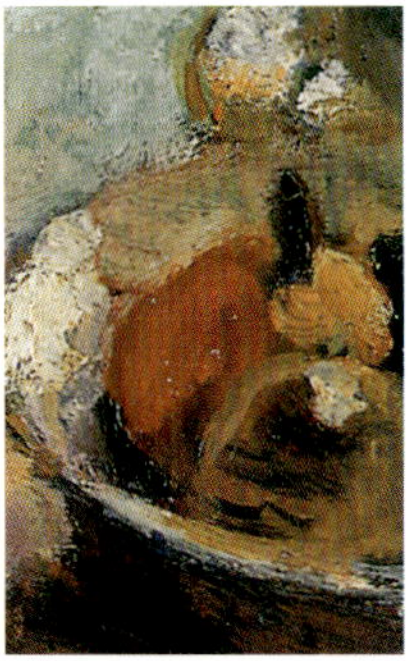

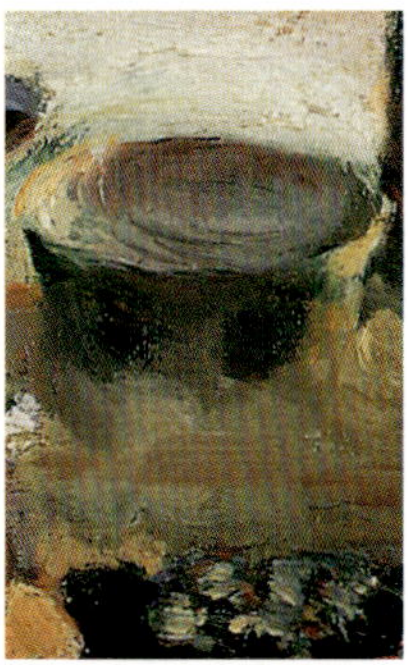

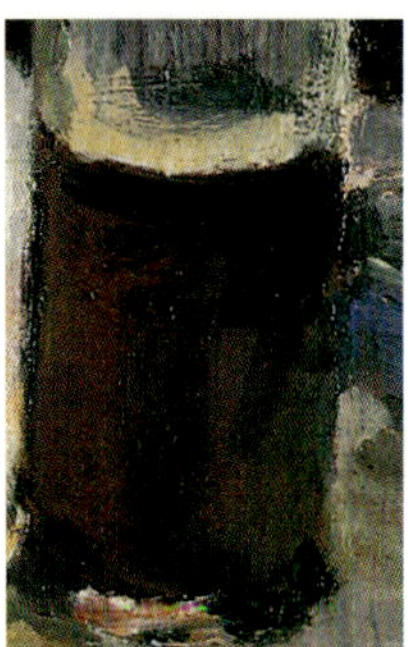

Paul Cézanne (1839-1906)

Paul Cézanne, born in 1839 in Aix-en-Provence, France, was probably the greatest of modern still-life painters. He painted more than 170 still life paintings in his lifetime.

Fruits and Teapot

Henri Matisse, c. 1898
Oil on canvas, 38.5 x 46.5 cm
The Hermitage, Saint Petersburg

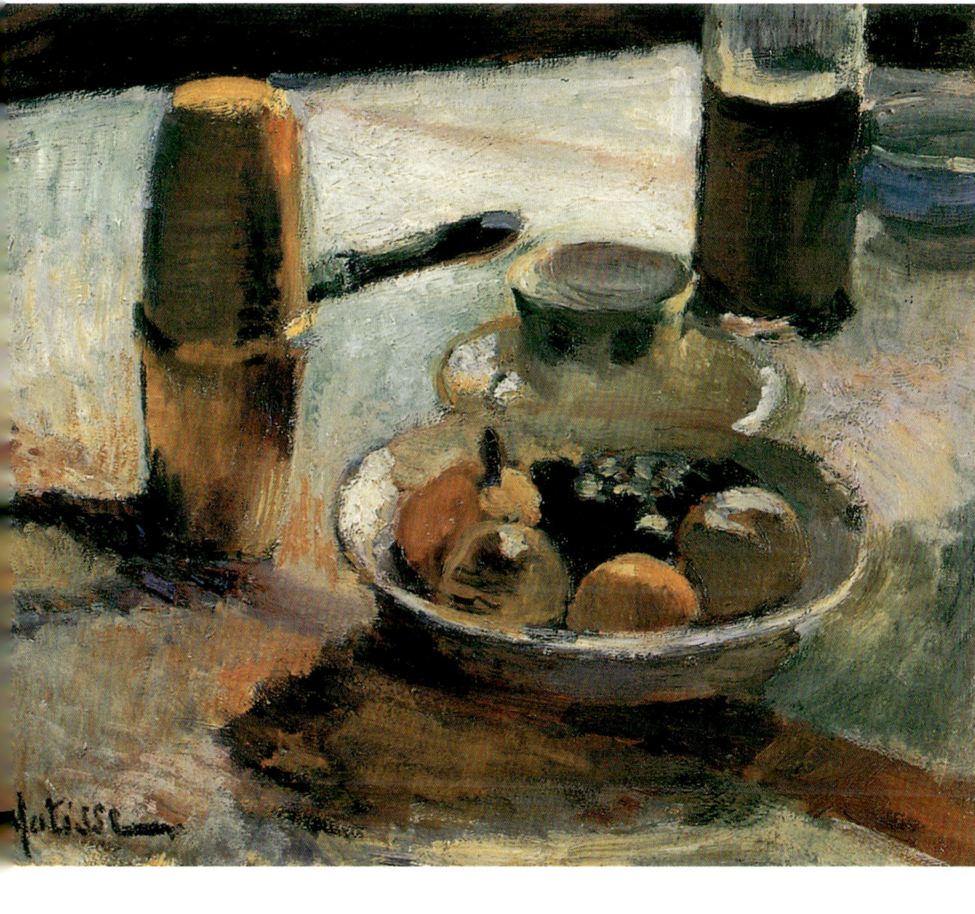
Matisse

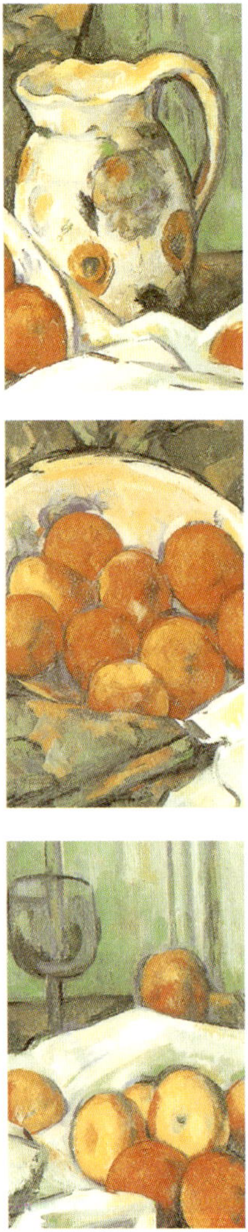

It is likely that Paul Cezanne found still life to be the perfect vehicle for his revolutionary perception of space and depth of perspective. He changed the course of history of painting and we can consider that his experiments led directly to the development of Cubist still life painting in the 20th century.

Dish with Fruits and Drapery

Paul Cézanne, 1898-1899
Oil on canvas, 53 x 72 cm
The Hermitage, Saint Petersburg

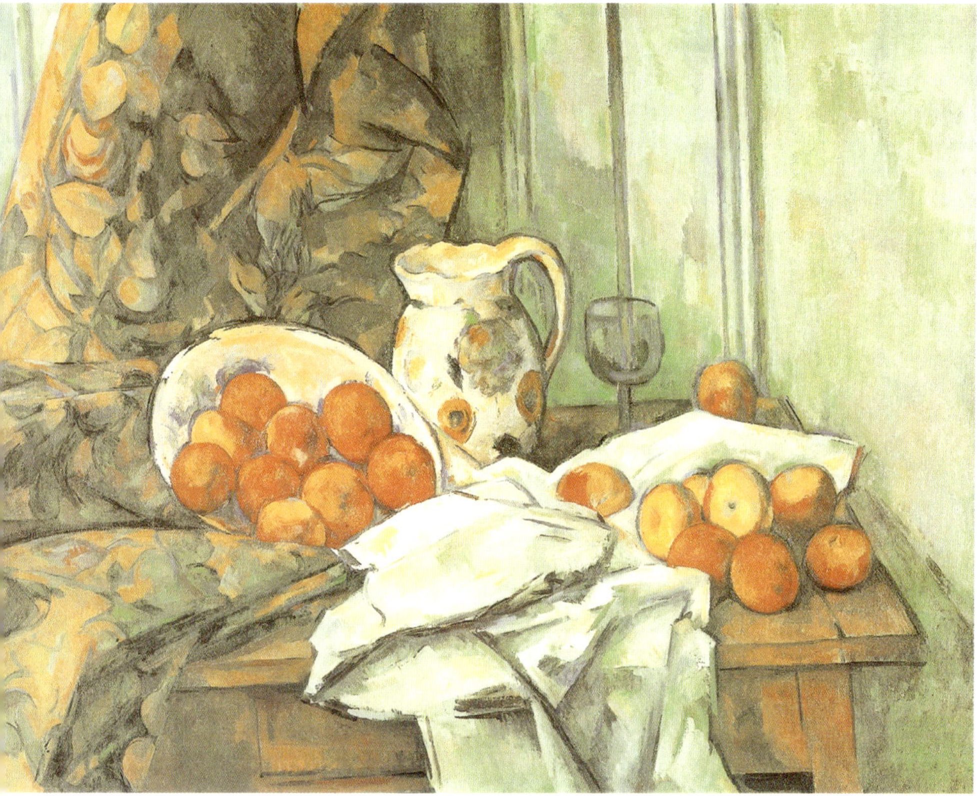

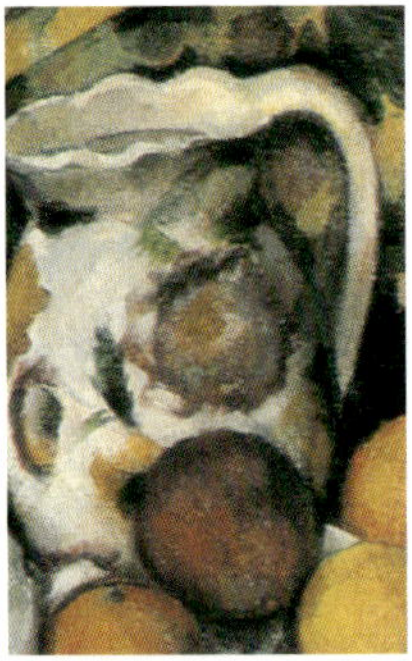

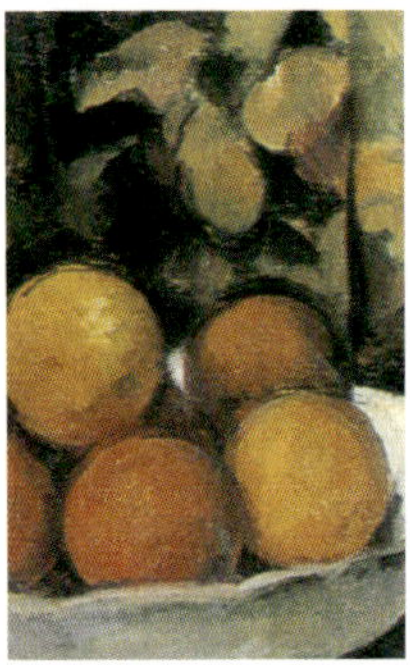

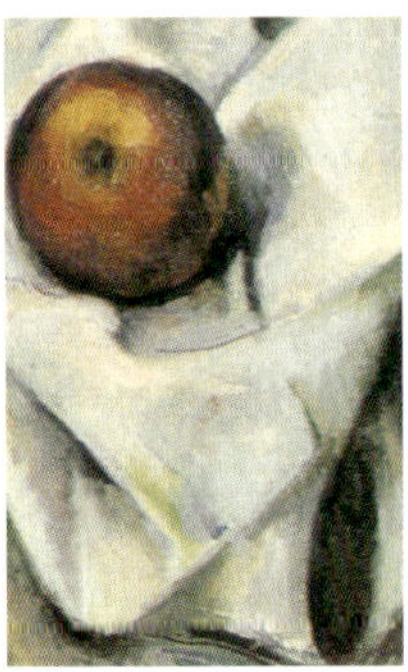

Paul Cezanne often used contrasting colours to describe the play of light and, as he explained in his own words: "I try to show internal construction of forms." Apples were Cezanne's favourite subject. He painted them with simplicity and delicate tonal harmony. They are readily identifiable, but they are not true to nature.

Apples and Oranges

Paul Cézanne, 1898-1899
Oil on canvas, 74 x 93 cm
Musée d'Orsay, Paris

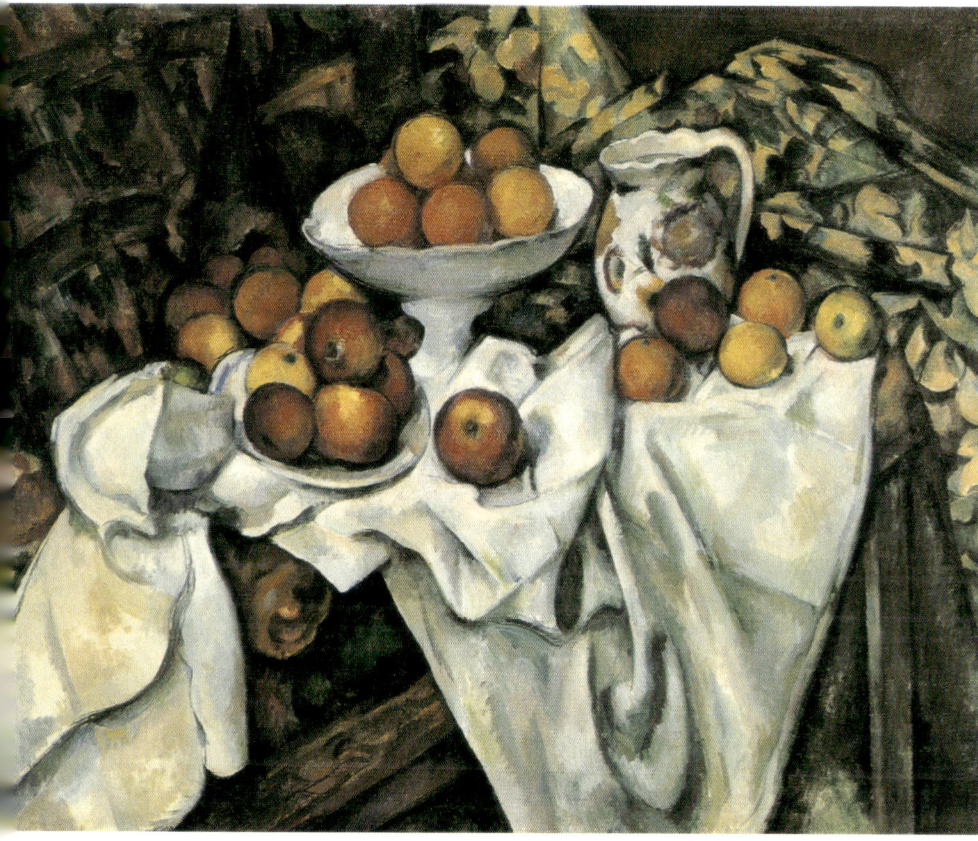

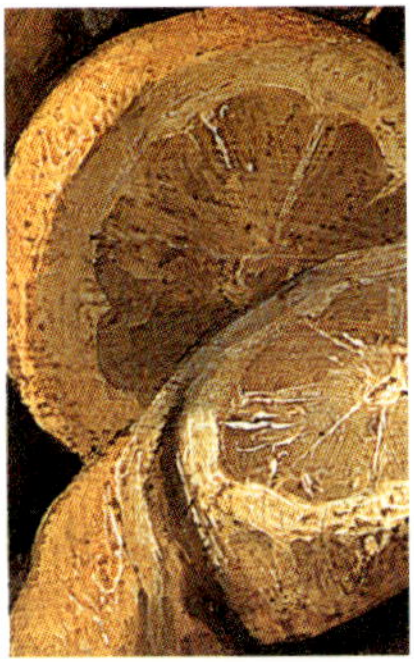

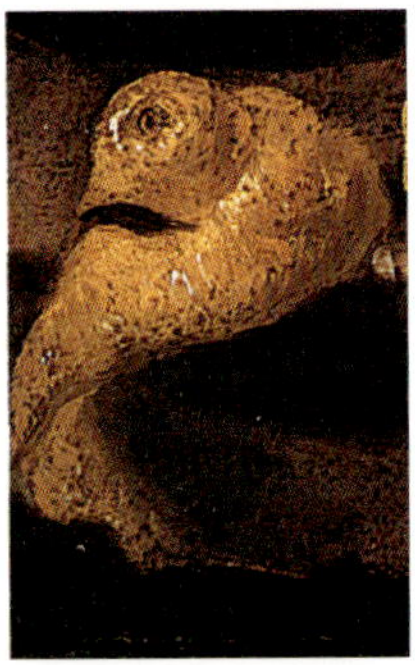

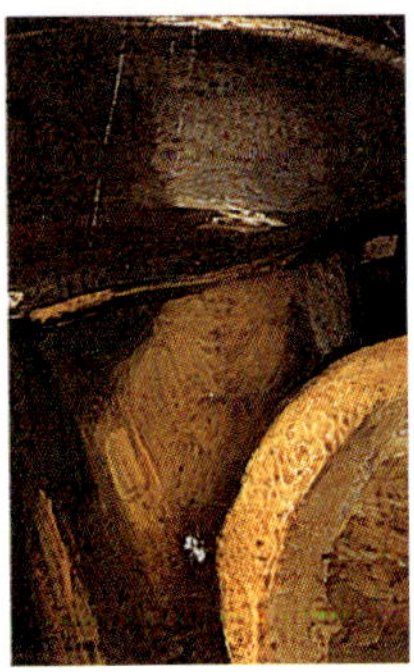

Cezanne loved to make ordinary objects, such as a cloth, some apples, a vase or a bowl and, later in his career, plaster sculptures look unfamiliar. That makes Cezanne's still lifes at the same time so traditional and avant-garde. He died in 1906.

Still Life with Lemons

Nicolae Grigorescu
oil on cardboard, 22 x 28.5 cm
Art Museum, Constanta

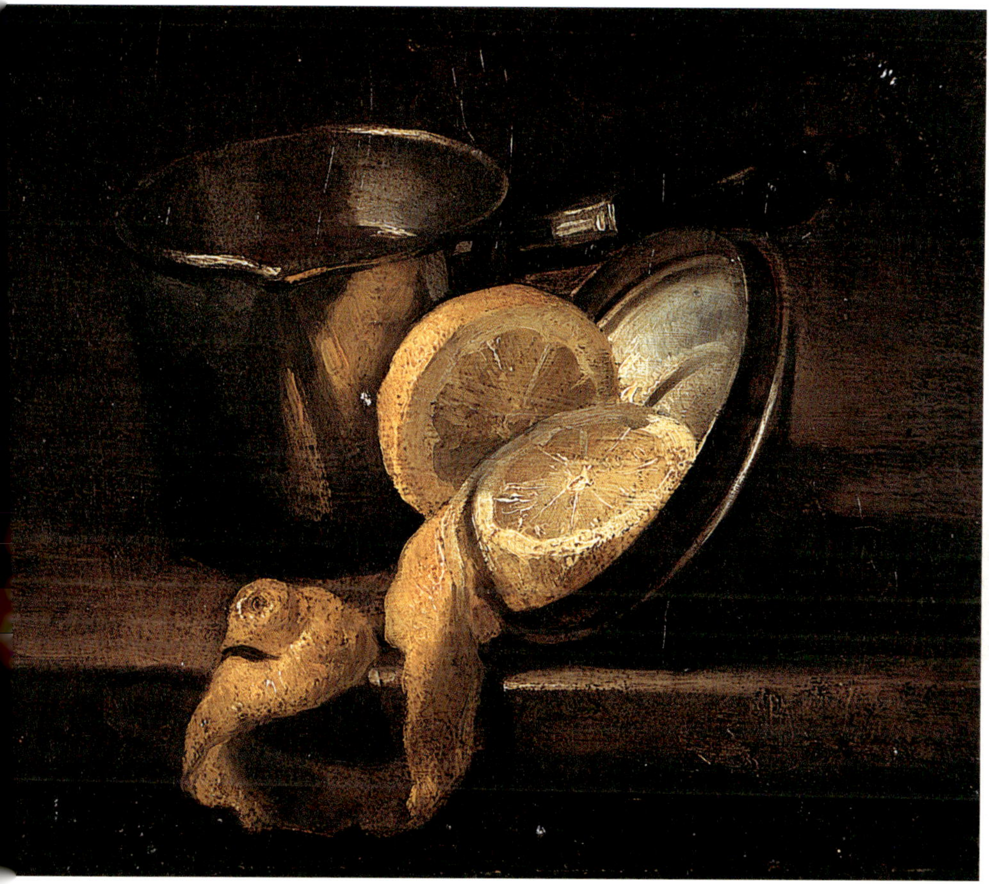

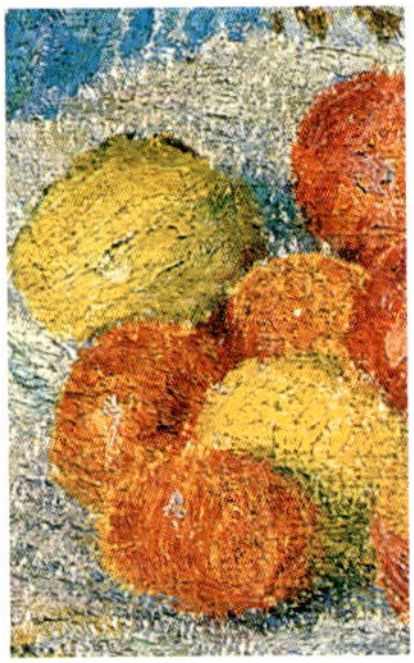

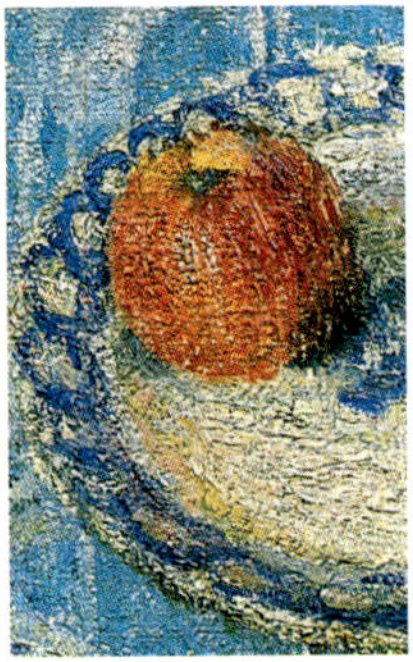

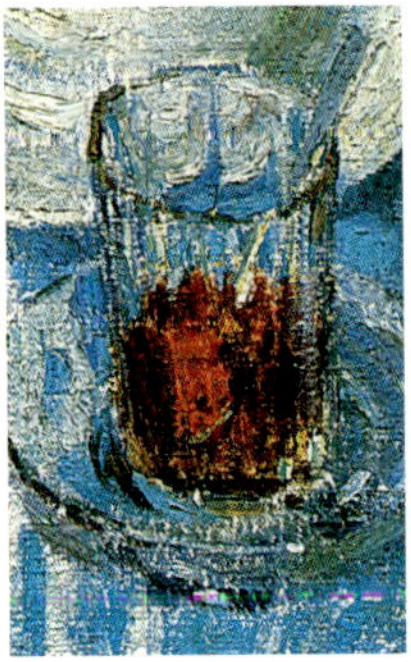

Claude Monet (1840-1926)

Born in Paris in 1840, Claude Monet was an unequalled genius of composition and colour. During his lifetime he produced about 65 still life paintings. More than half of them represent floral paintings.

The Blue Tablecloth

Igor Grabar, 1916
Oil on canvas, 115 x 97 cm
Russian Museum, Saint Petersburg

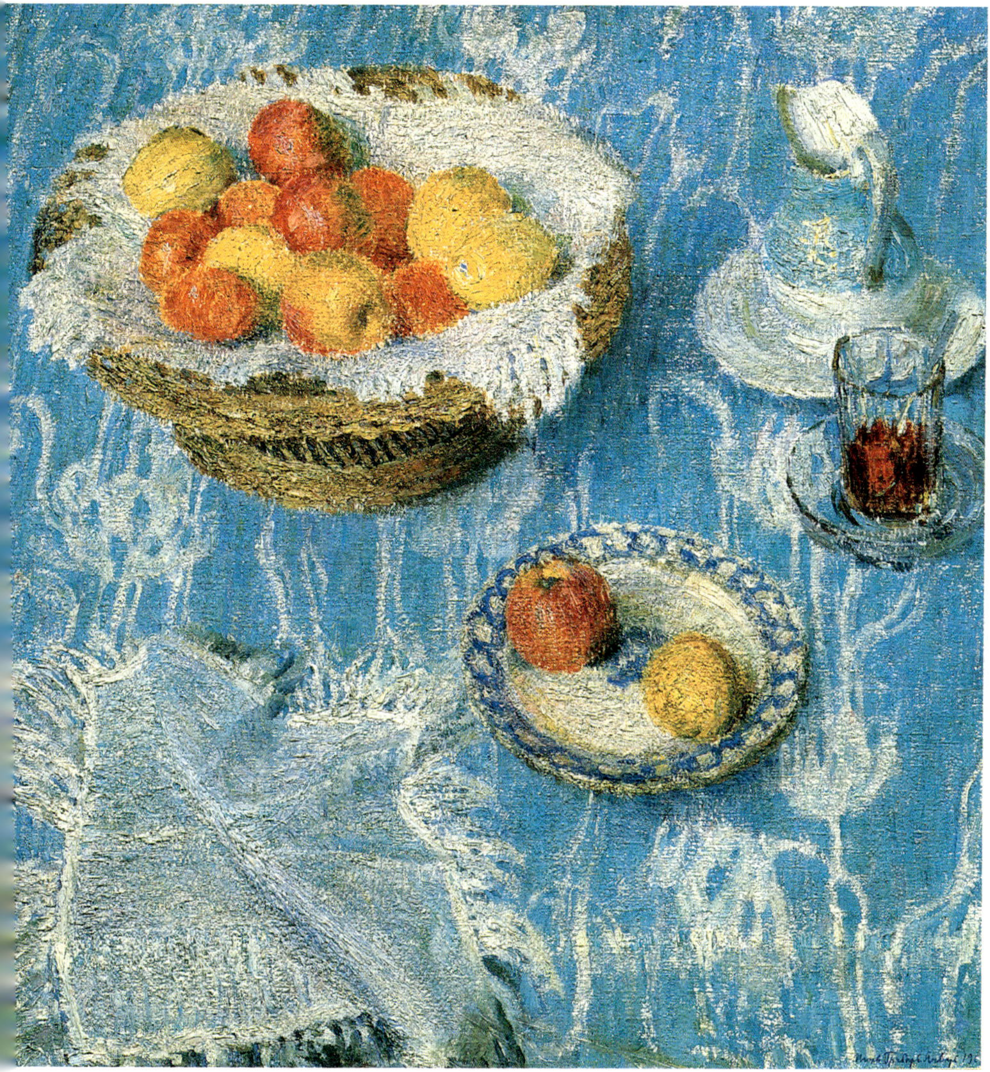

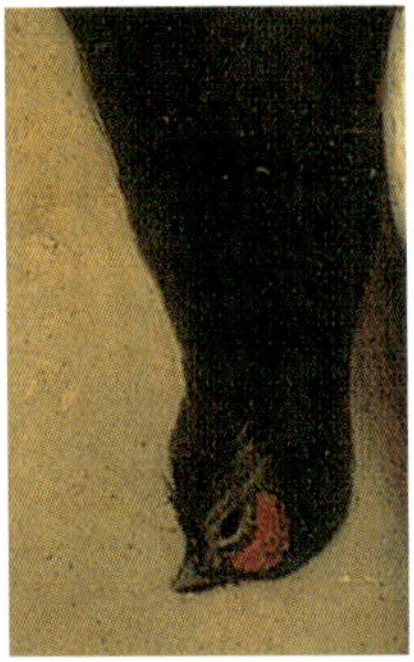

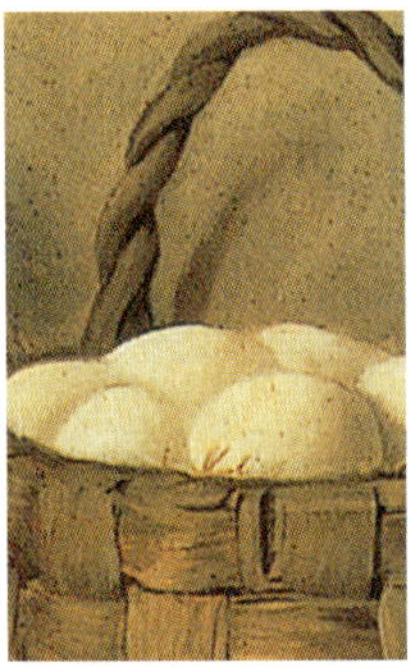

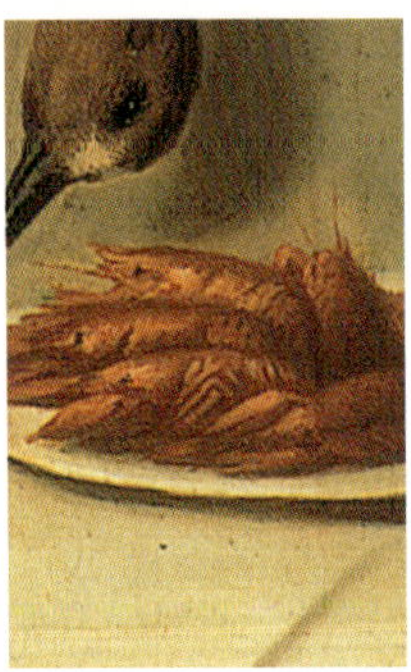

Monet produced his first flower painting in 1864, which he sent to Rouen for an exhibition. He once explained to a friend: "What I need most of all are flowers, always, always." Still life paintings do not account for an important part of Monet's entire oeuvre.

Still Life with Dead Game

Hippolyte Robillard
early 19th century, after 1875
The Hermitage, Saint Petersburg

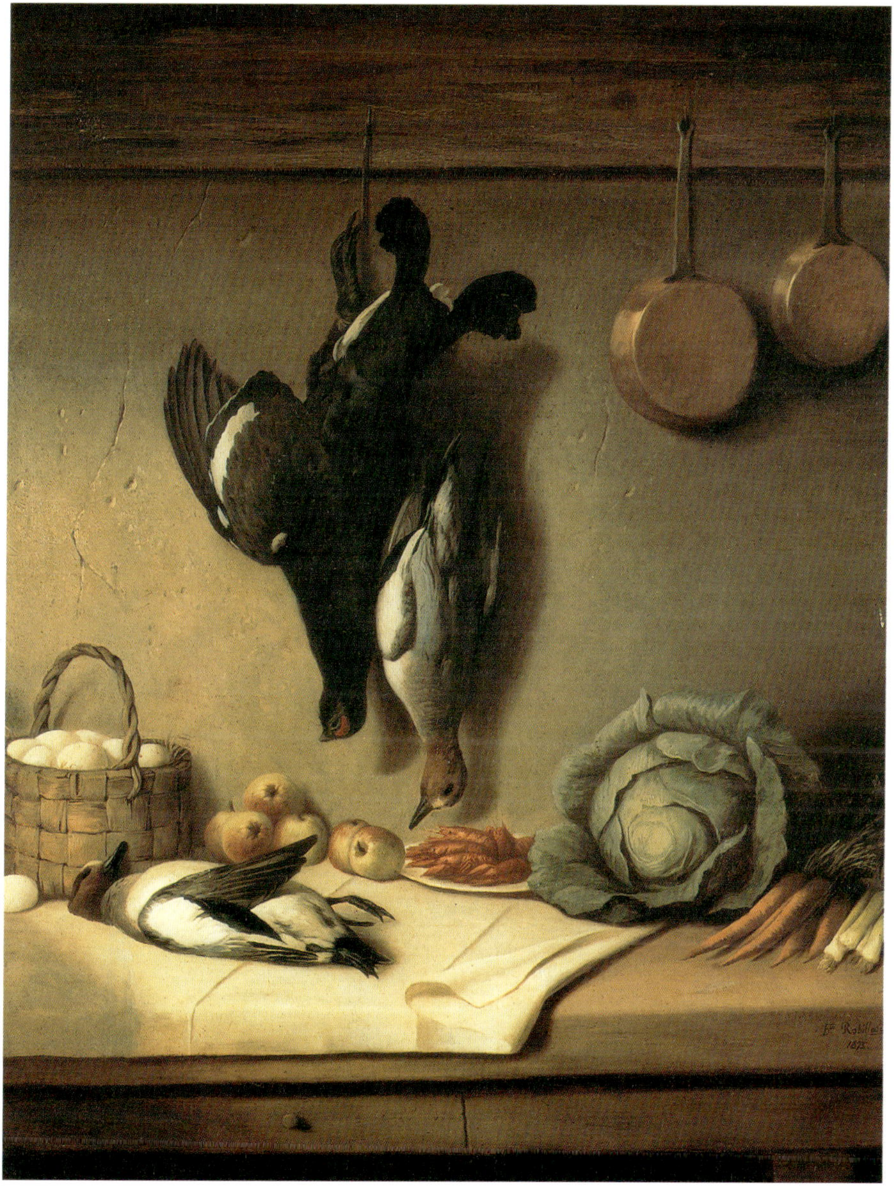

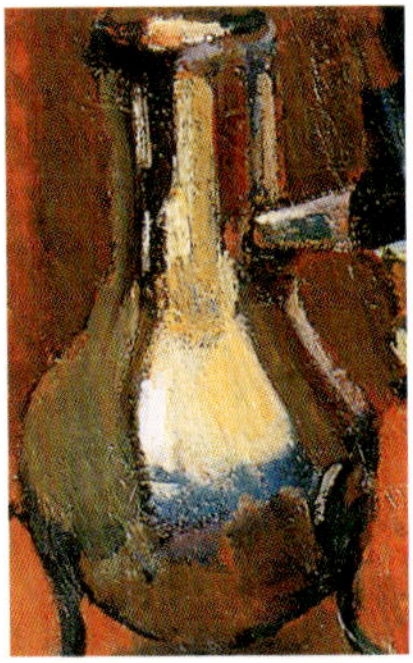

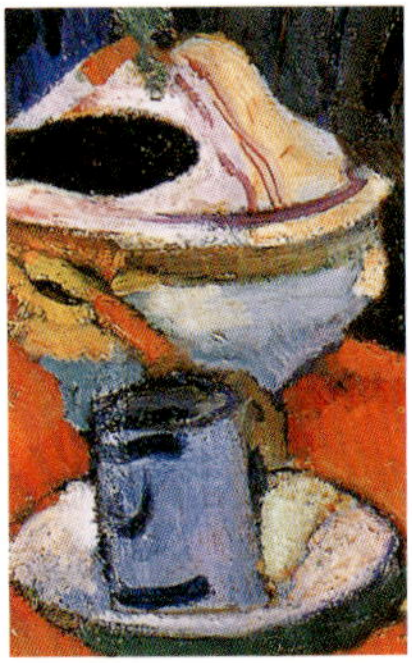

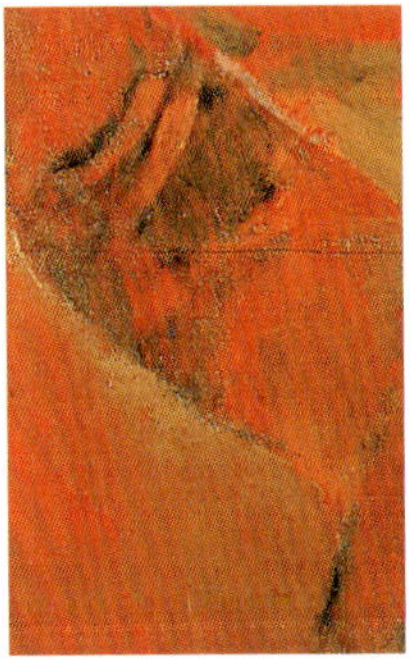

However, he painted 36 decorative panels of fruit and flowers for the dining-room doors of the Parisian art dealer Durand-Ruel. Despite the boldness of his colours and the extreme simplicity of his compositions, Monet was recognised as a master of meticulous observation, an artist who sacrificed neither the true

Crockery on the Table

Henri Matisse, 1900
Oil on canvas, 97 x 82 cm
The Hermitage, Saint Petersburg

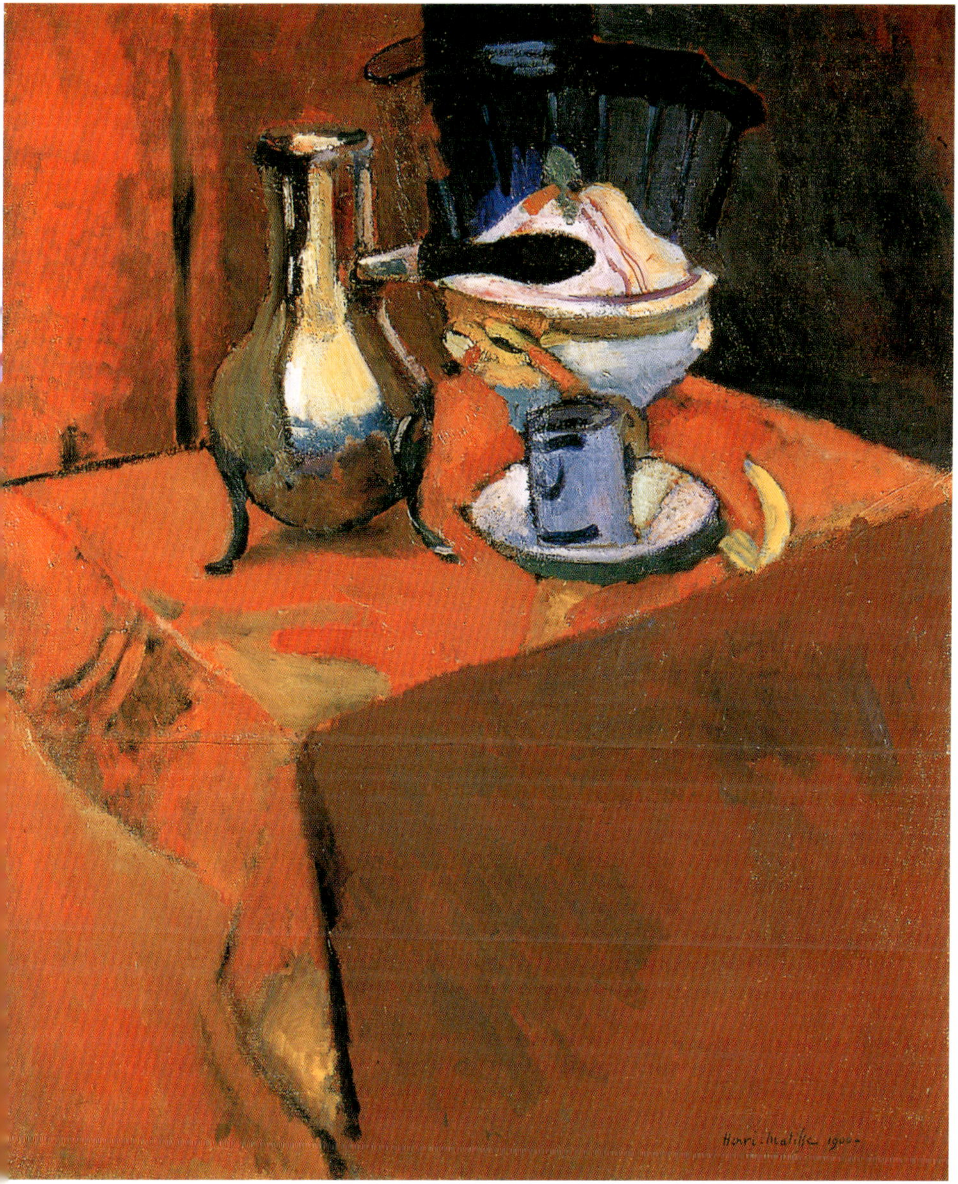

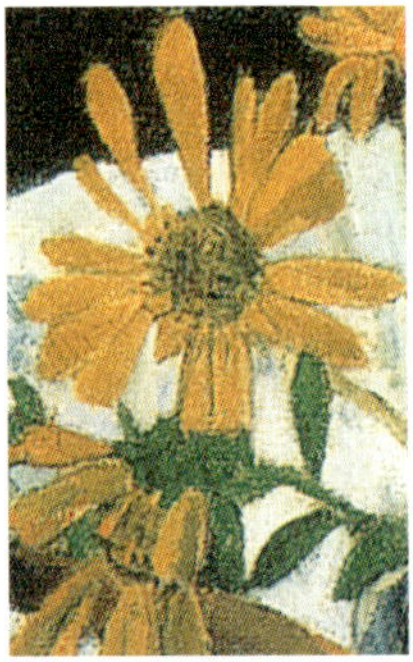

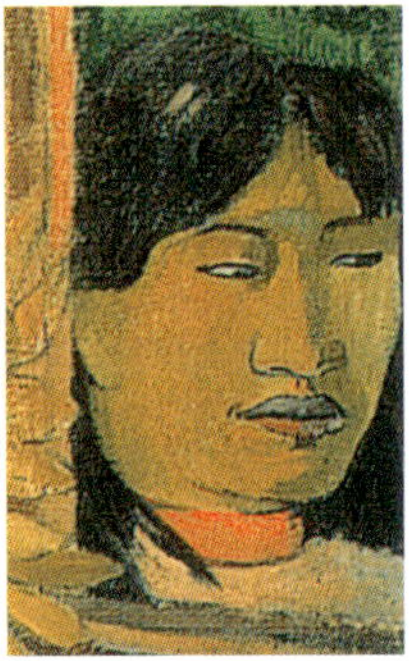

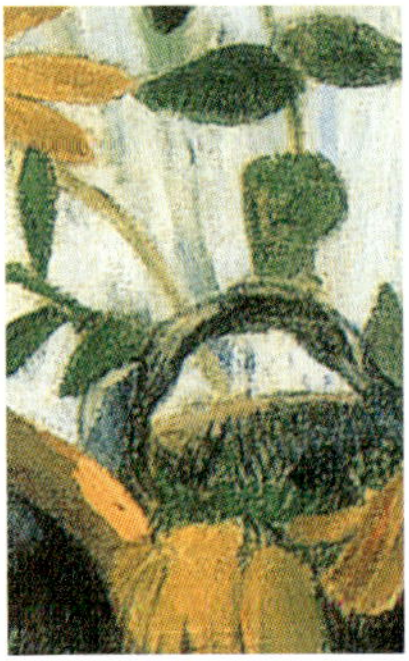

complexities of nature nor the intensity of his own feelings. Monet died in Giverny of lung cancer on the 5th of December 1926, after he had finished his last series of paintings depicting his flower-filled garden and the pond covered with his famous water lilies, *Les Nymphéas.*

Sunflowers

Paul Gauguin, 1901
Oil on canvas, 72 x 91 cm
The Hermitage, Saint Petersburg

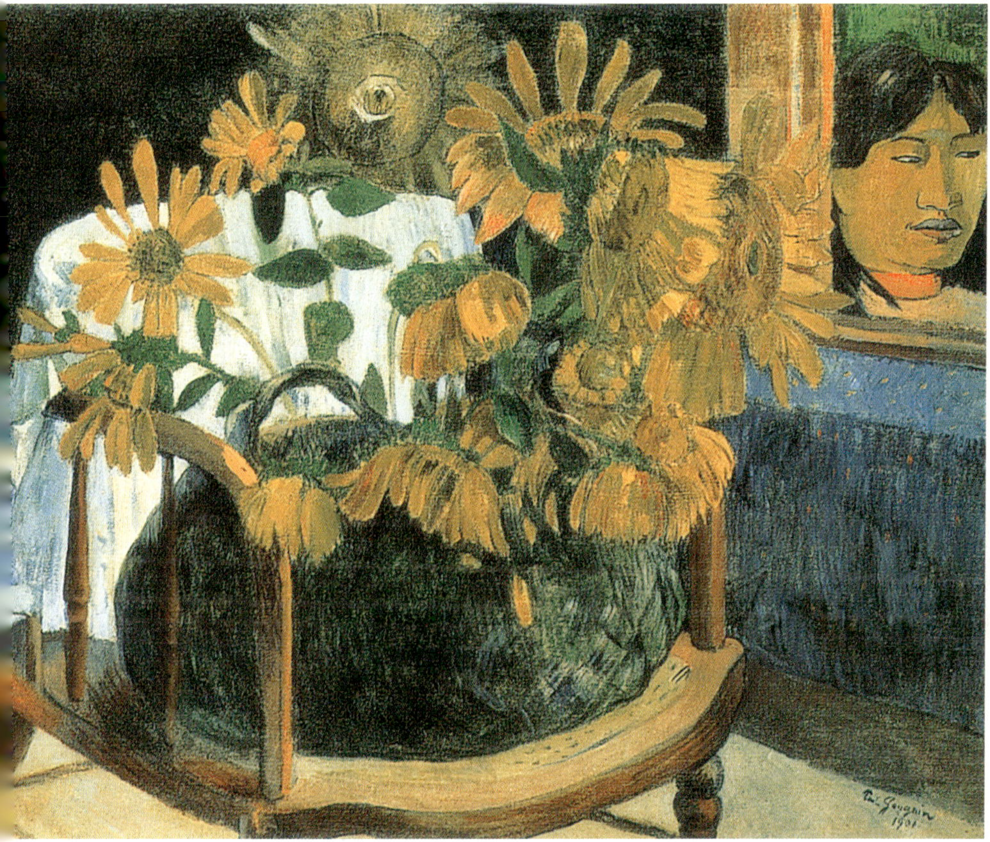

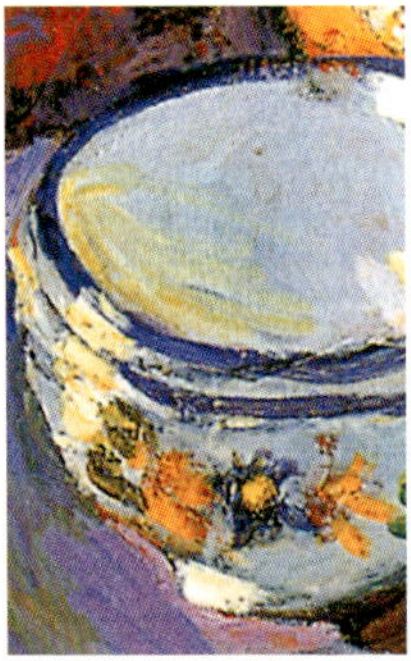

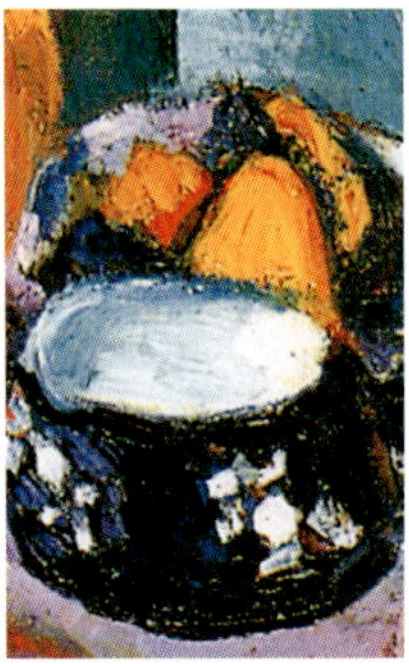

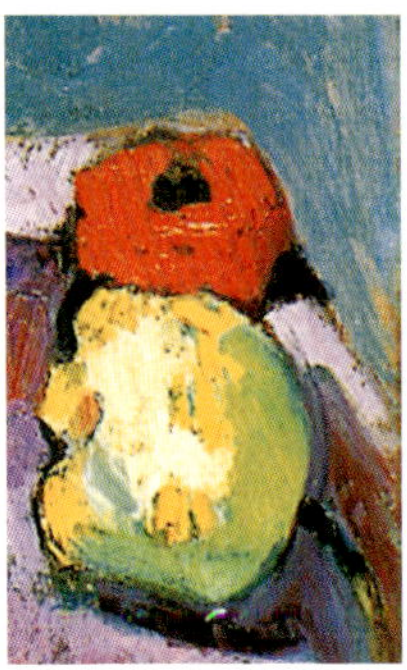

Auguste Renoir (1841-1919)

Renoir once explained to his son Jean; "Believe me, anything can be painted. Of course, it is better to paint a pretty girl or a pleasant landscape – but you can paint anything."

Crockery and Fruits

Henri Matisse, c. 1901
Oil on canvas, 51 x 61.5 cm
The Hermitage, Saint Petersburg

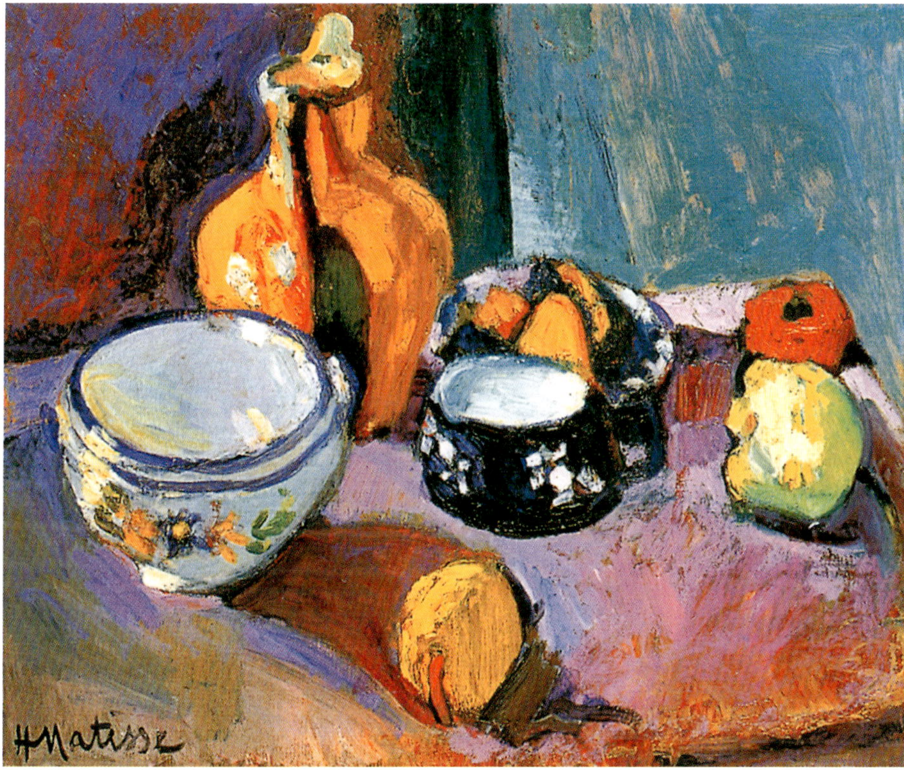
H Matisse

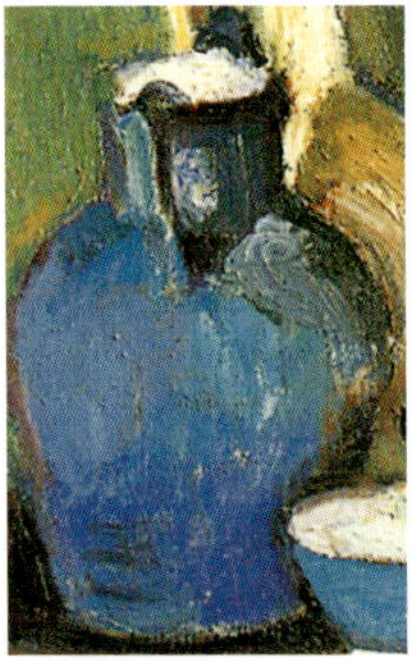

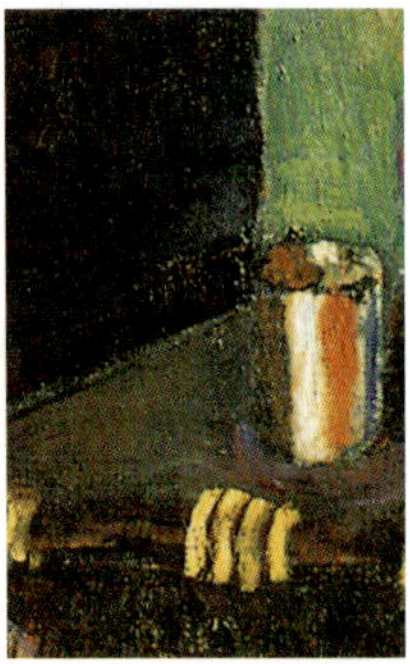

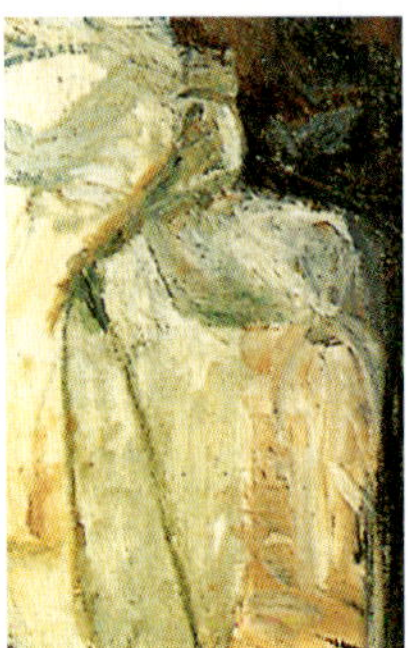

Renoir's still life paintings served as a refreshing respite from bigger assignments. Nevertheless, the brilliant colours of Renoir's still life paintings and the harmony of his lines have never been equalled.

Blue Jug

Henri Matisse, before 1901
Oil on canvas, 66 x 74 cm
Pushkin Museum of Fine Arts, Moscow

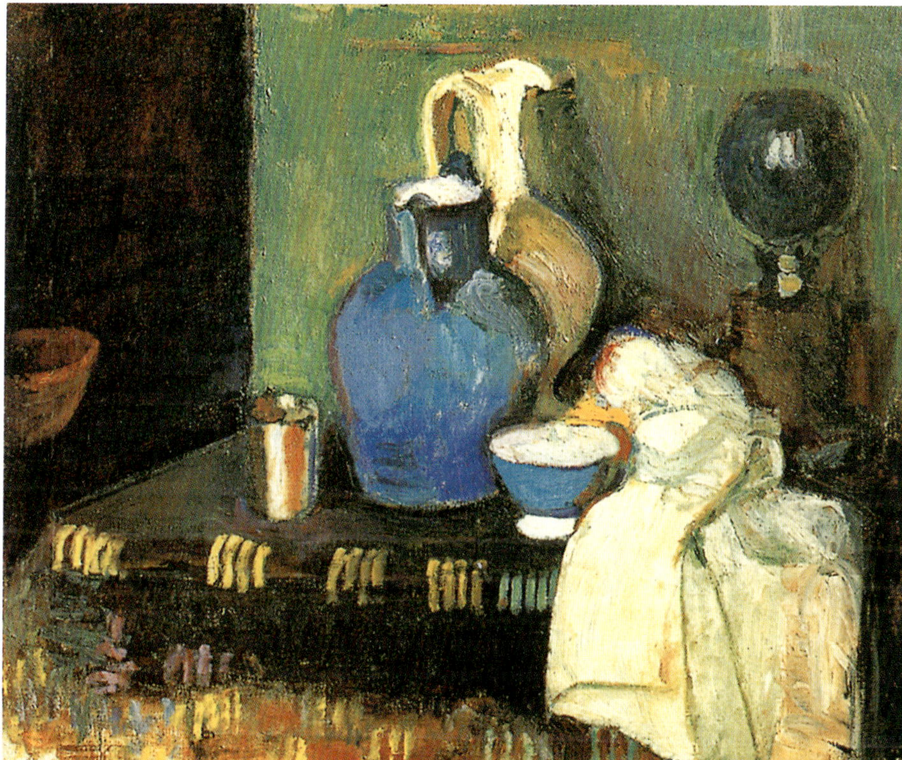

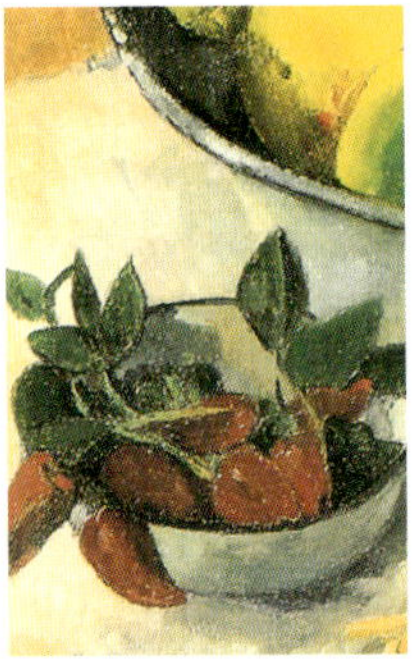

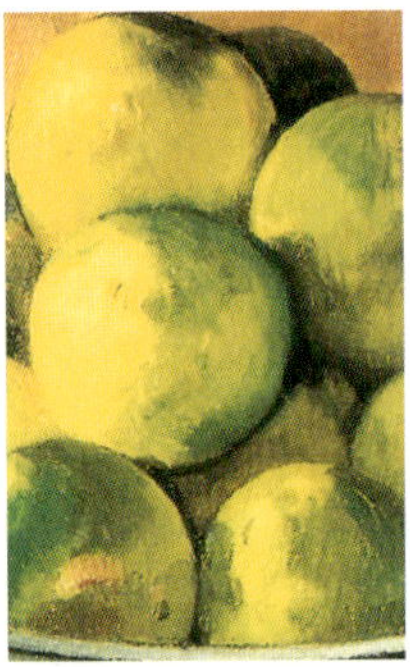

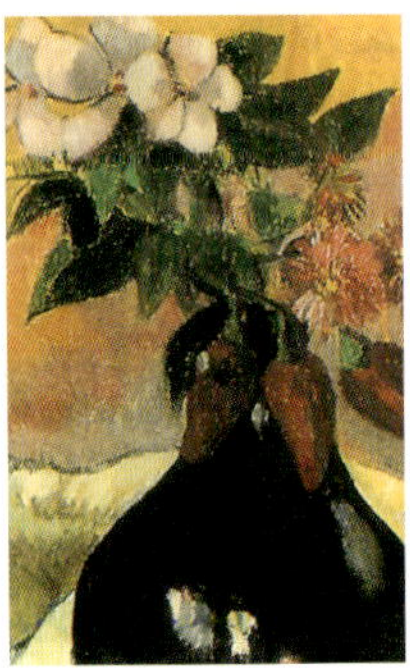

This applies in particular to the fragile charm of his floral still lifes which he mainly painted in the middle and at the end of his career. Vollard, a Parisian art dealer and friend, once explained: "Madame Renoir knew what she was doing when she brought him from the garden in Essoyes, her home village,

Still Life with Grapefruit

Paul Gauguin, c. 1901
Oil on canvas, 66 x 76 cm
private collection

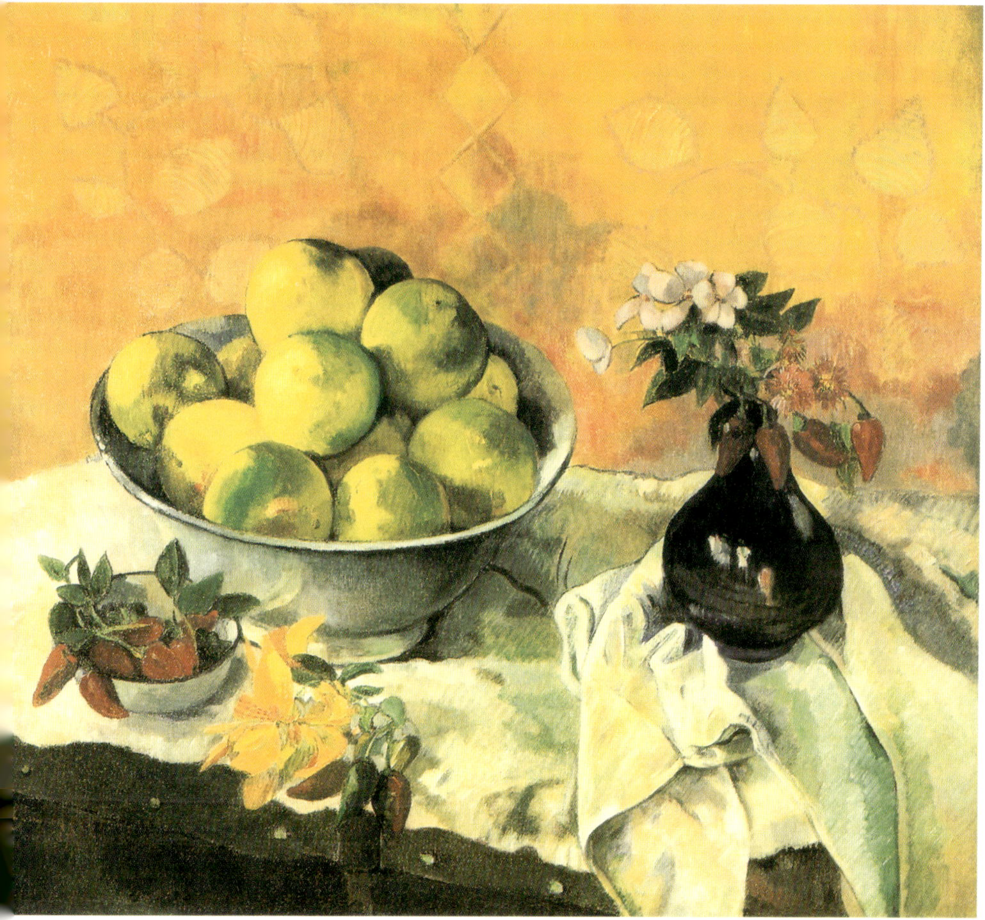

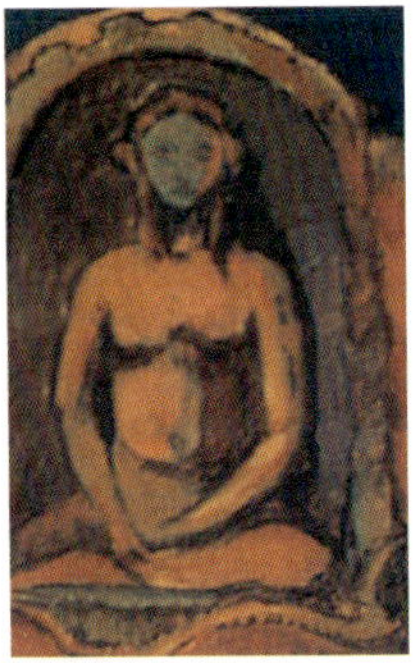

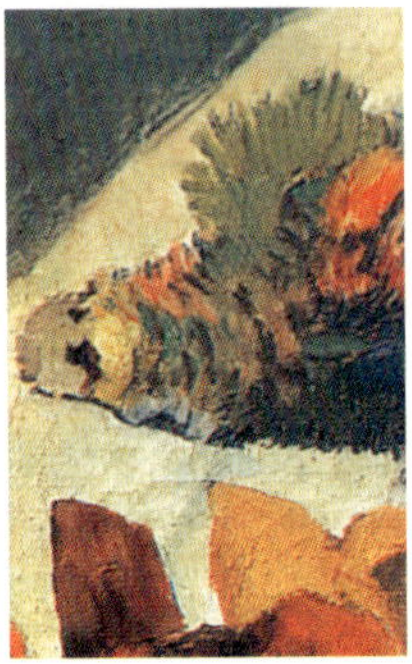

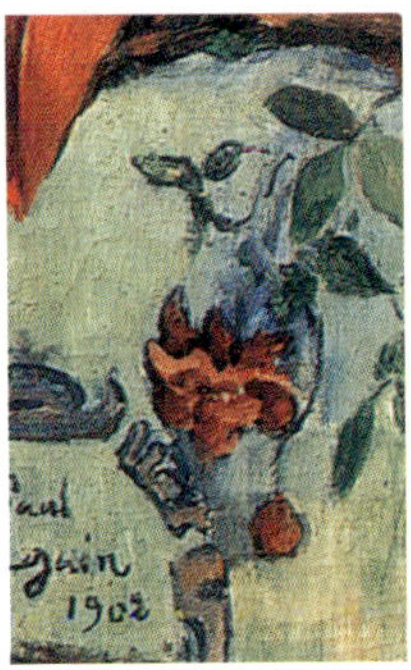

the flowers of the season and placed them in his studio". Renoir would simply say: "When my wife composes a bouquet, I need only sit down and paint it." He was always fond of flowers and he painted fruit whenever they caught his eye. Renoir's repertoire as a painter embraced everything, including the still life paintings.

Still Life with Exotic Birds

Paul Gauguin, 1902
Oil on canvas, 62 x 76 cm
Pushkin Museum of Fine Arts, Moscow

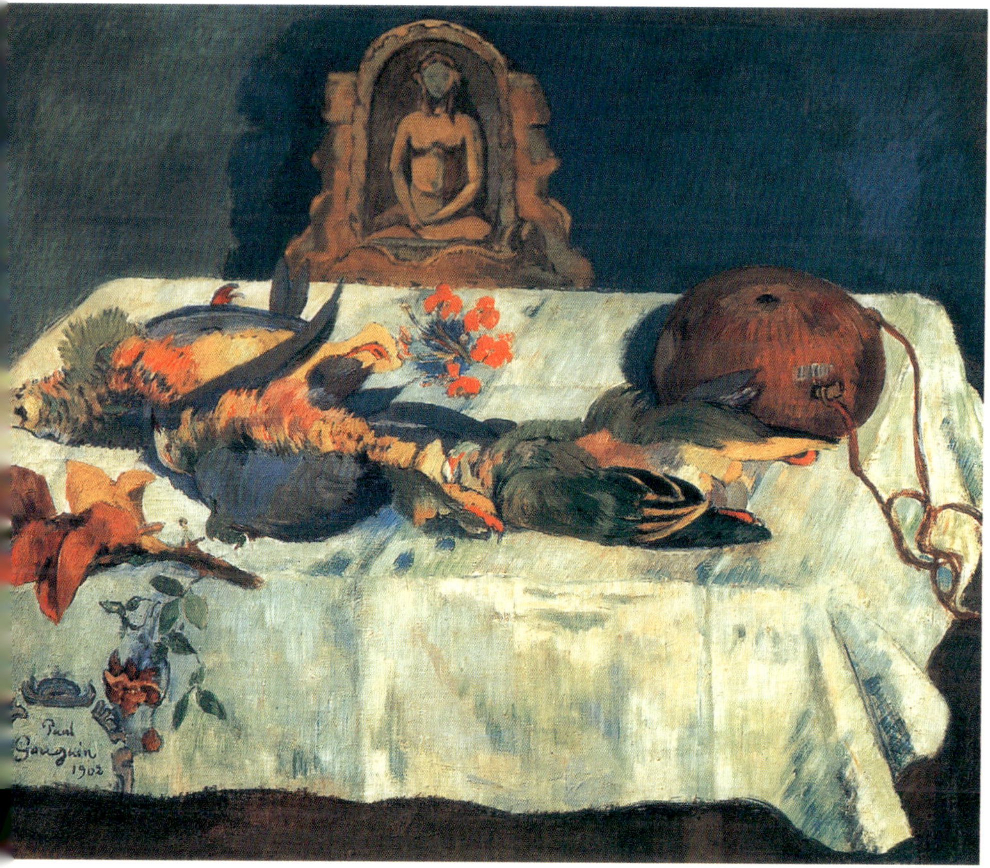
Paul
Gauguin
1902

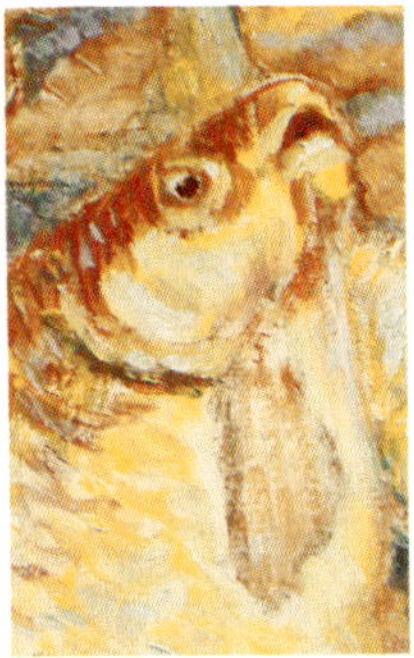

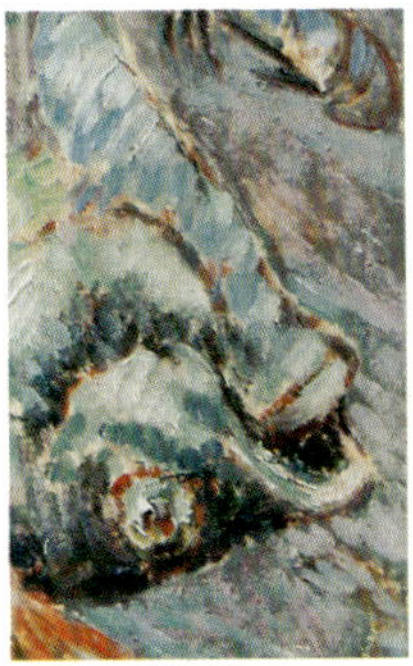

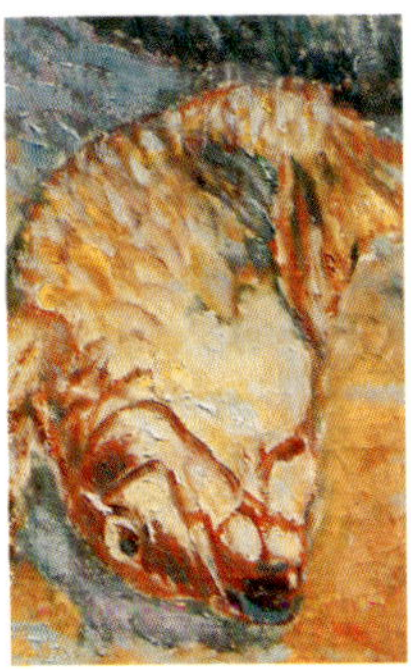

But his ventures into that genre were rather haphazard and it remained somewhere in the background as far as his work as a whole was concerned. However, Renoir's still life paintings have a unique texture and light that places his work among that of the world's finest artists.

Fish in the Setting Sun
(Fish at Dusk)

Mikhail Larionov, 1904
Oil on canvas, 100 x 95.5 cm
Russian Museum, Saint Petersberg

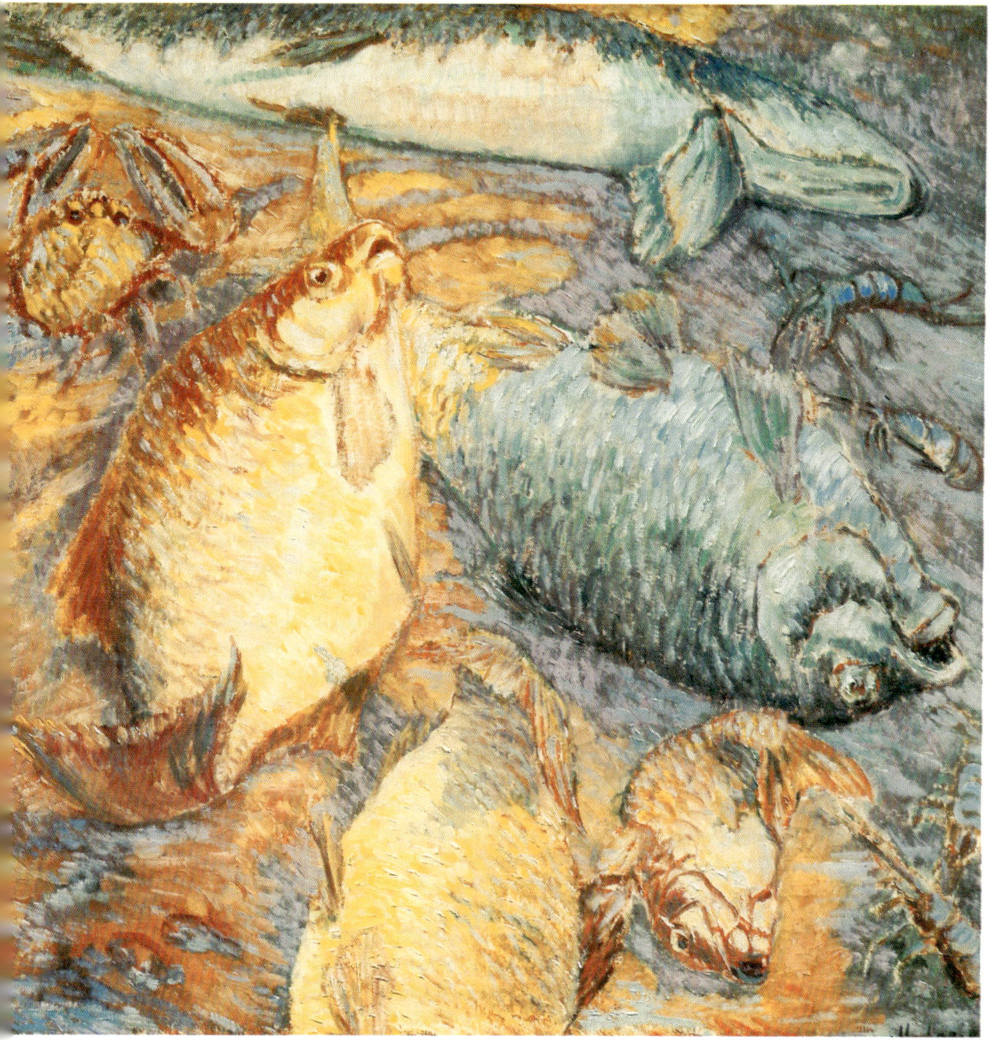

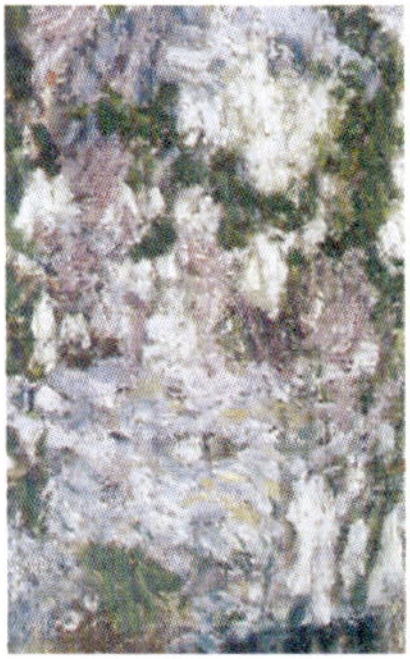

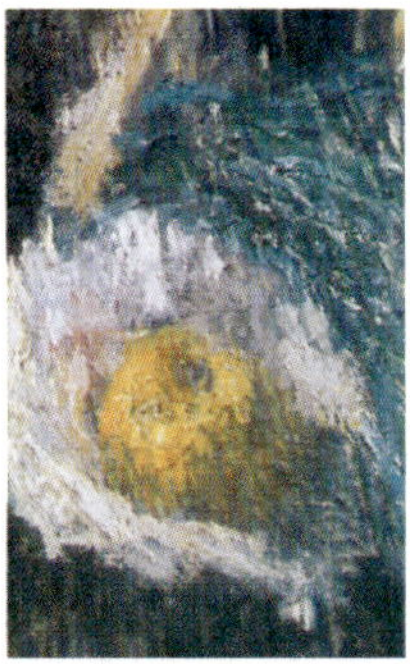

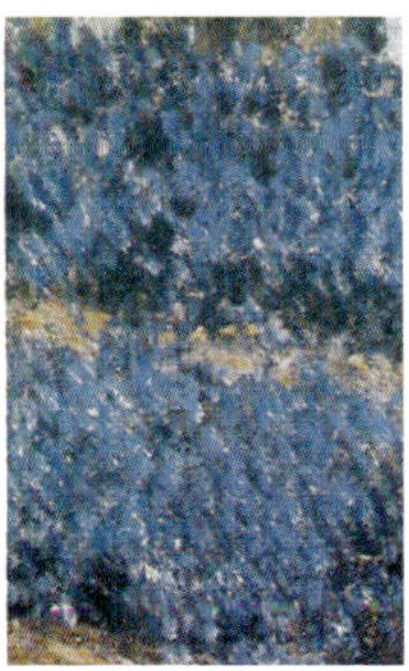

Ilya Repin (1844-1930)

Ilya Repin was the most gifted of the group known in Russia as "The Itinerants". Most of Repin's powerful work deals with the social dilemmas of Russian life in the 19th century.

Flowers and Fruit on the Piano

Igor Grabar, 1904
Oil on canvas, 79 x 101 cm
Russian Museum, Saint Petersburg

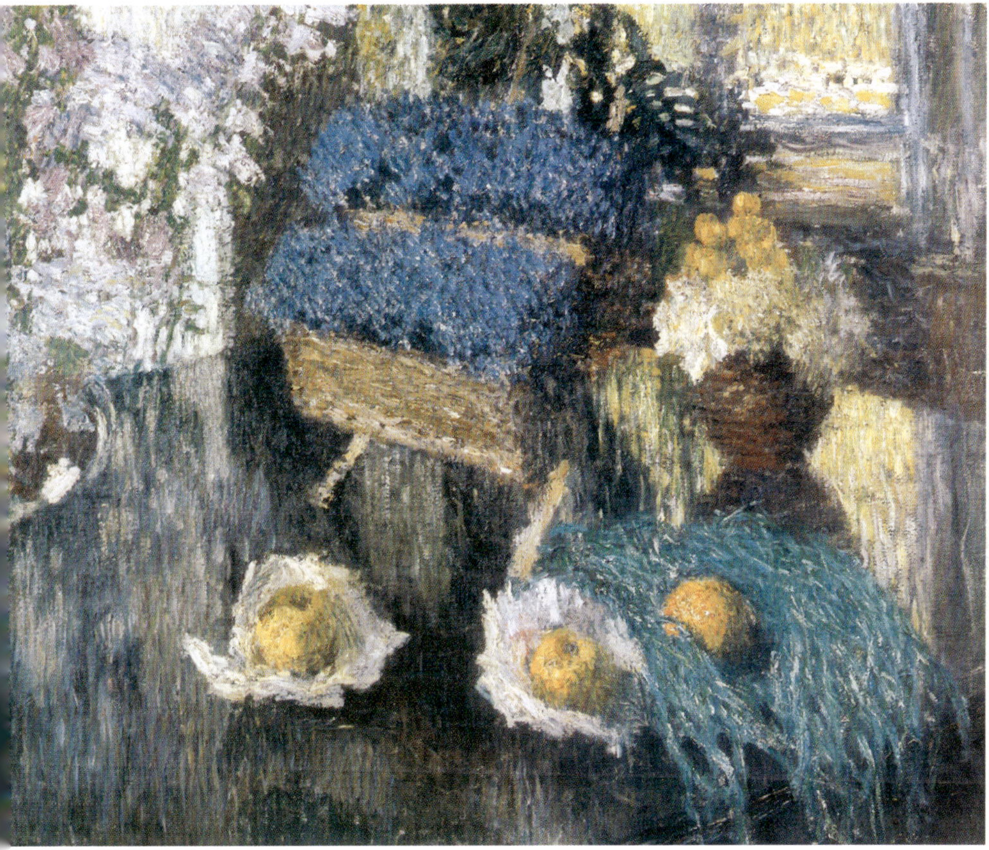

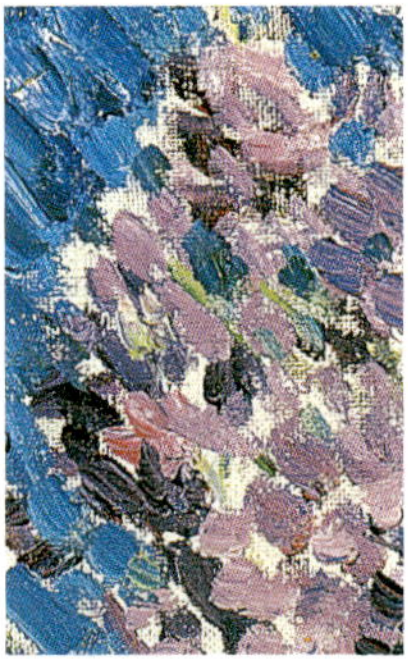

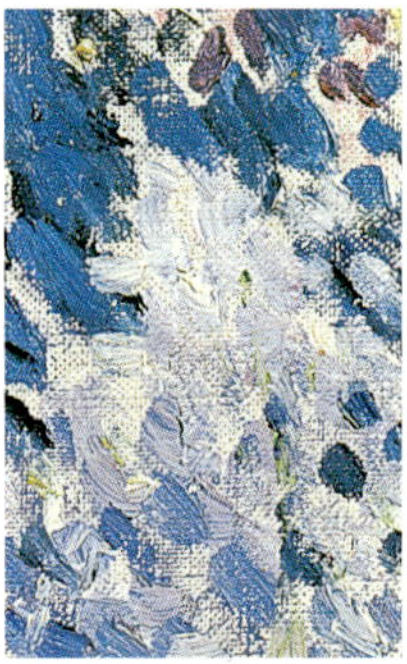

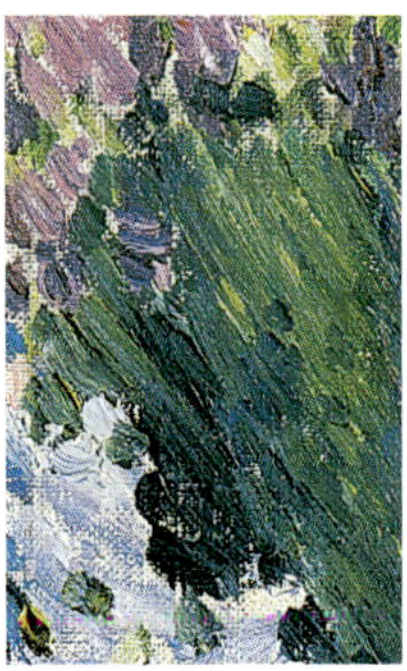

He established his reputation in 1873 with the celebrated picture *Barge Haulers of the Volga,* symbol of the oppressed Russian people pulling their chains. This struggle against the autocracy inspired many works including *Confession* and *The Arrest of the Propagandist* or *They did not expect him.*

Flowers (Two Bouquets)

Mikhail Larionov, 1904
Oil on canvas, 49 x 47 cm
From the former collection of A.K
Tomilina-Larionova, Paris

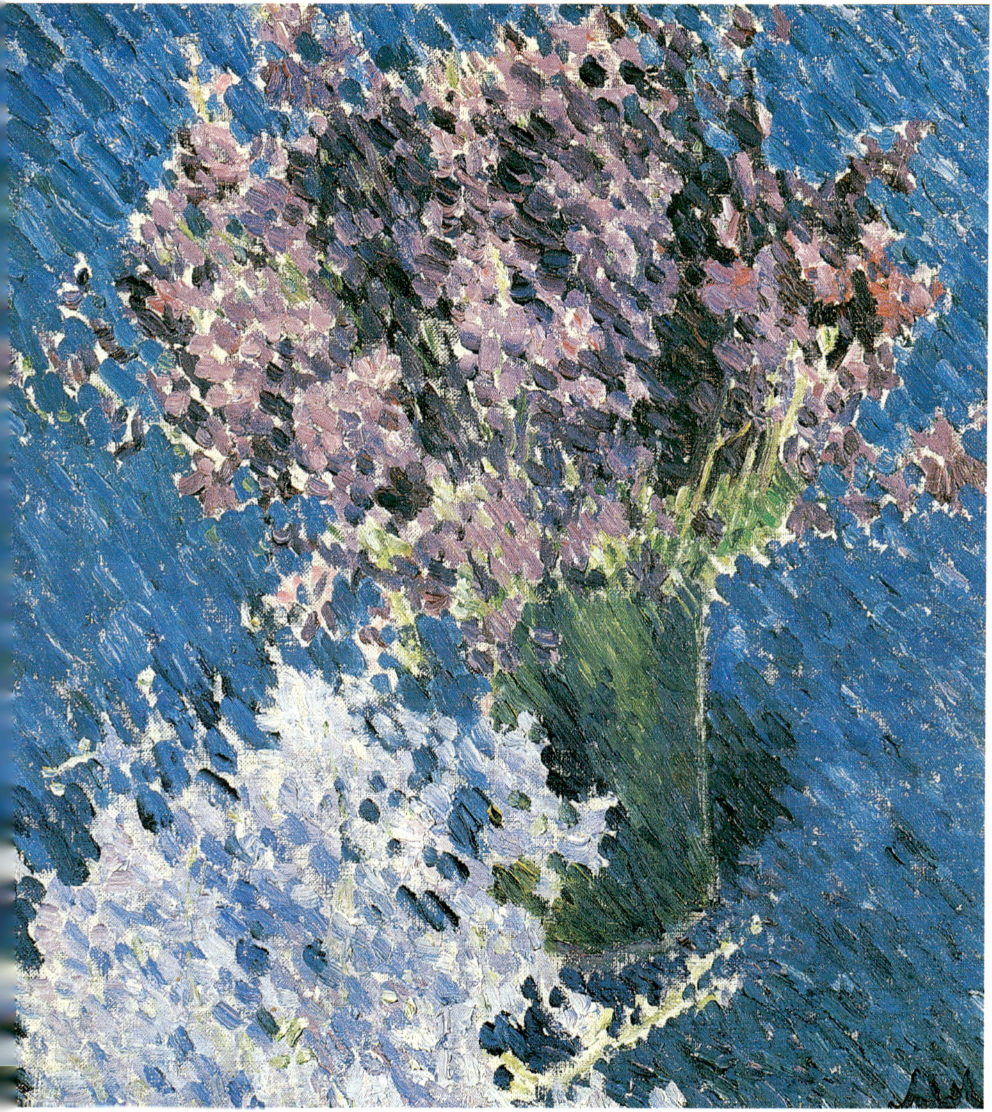

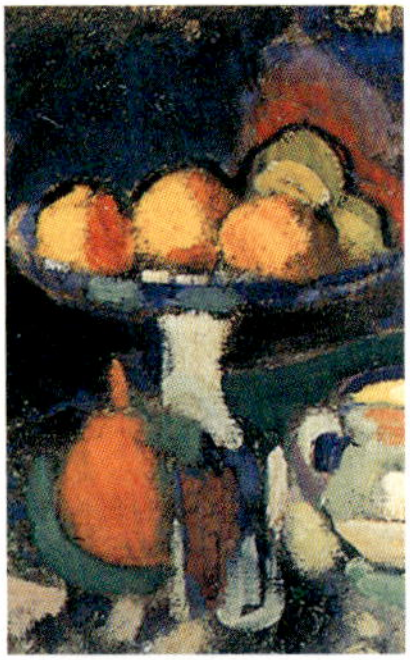

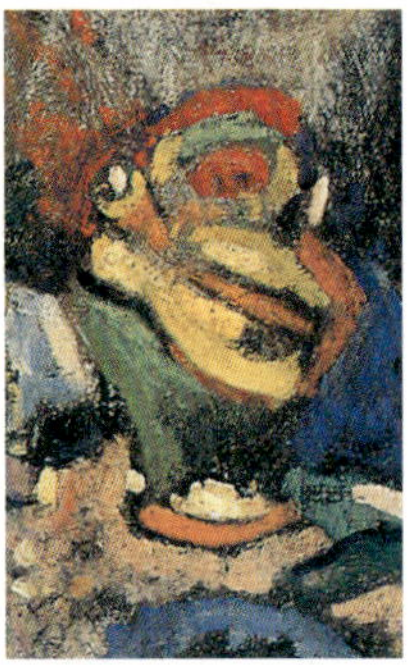

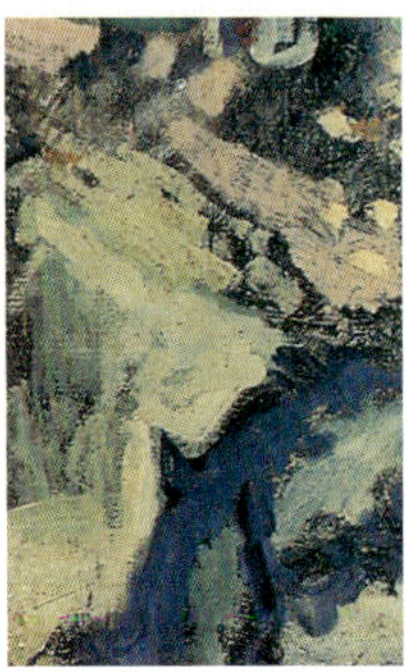

He also painted Russia's official history in such works as *Ivan the Terrible and his Son* and executed many portraits, among which those of Mussorgsky, Borodin and Tolstoy stand out. Repin also enjoyed a career as a still life painter.

Vase, Bottle and Fruits

Henri Matisse, 1905-1906
Oil on canvas, 73 x 92 cm
The Hermitage, Saint Petersburg

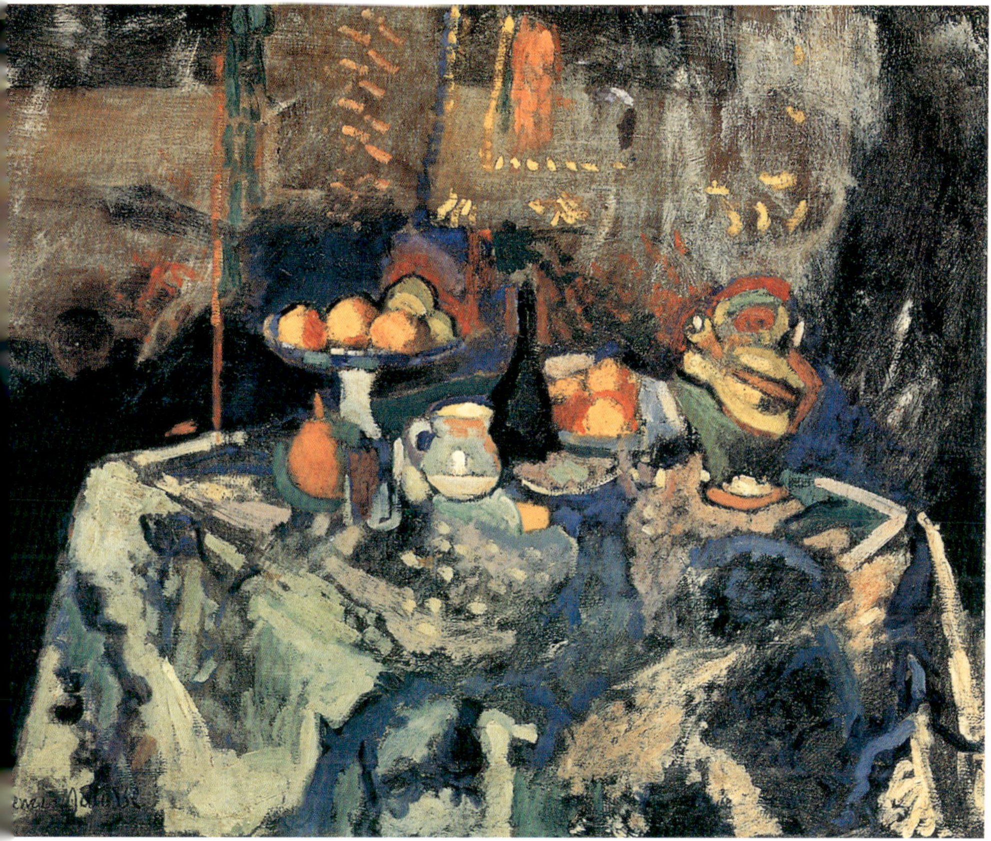

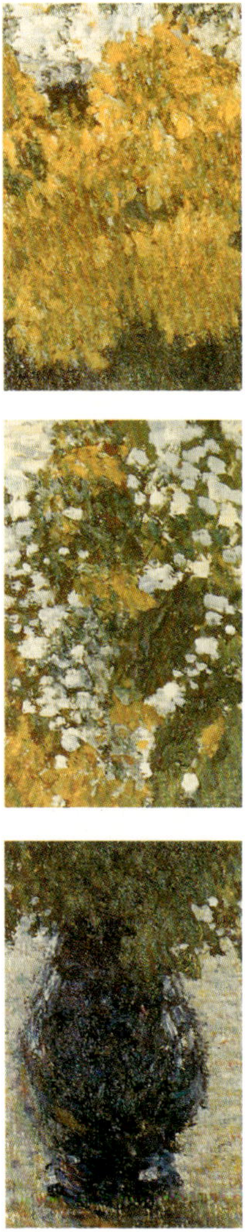

His works, which depart from the academic constraints of their predecessors, are both delicate and possess powerful plasticity. Even there, he reached a superior masterly skill, finds new accents to transcribe the coloured and brilliant vibration of the sensitive appearances.

Chrysanthemums

Igor Grabar, 1905
Oil on canvas, 98 x 98 cm
Tretyakov Gallery, Moscow

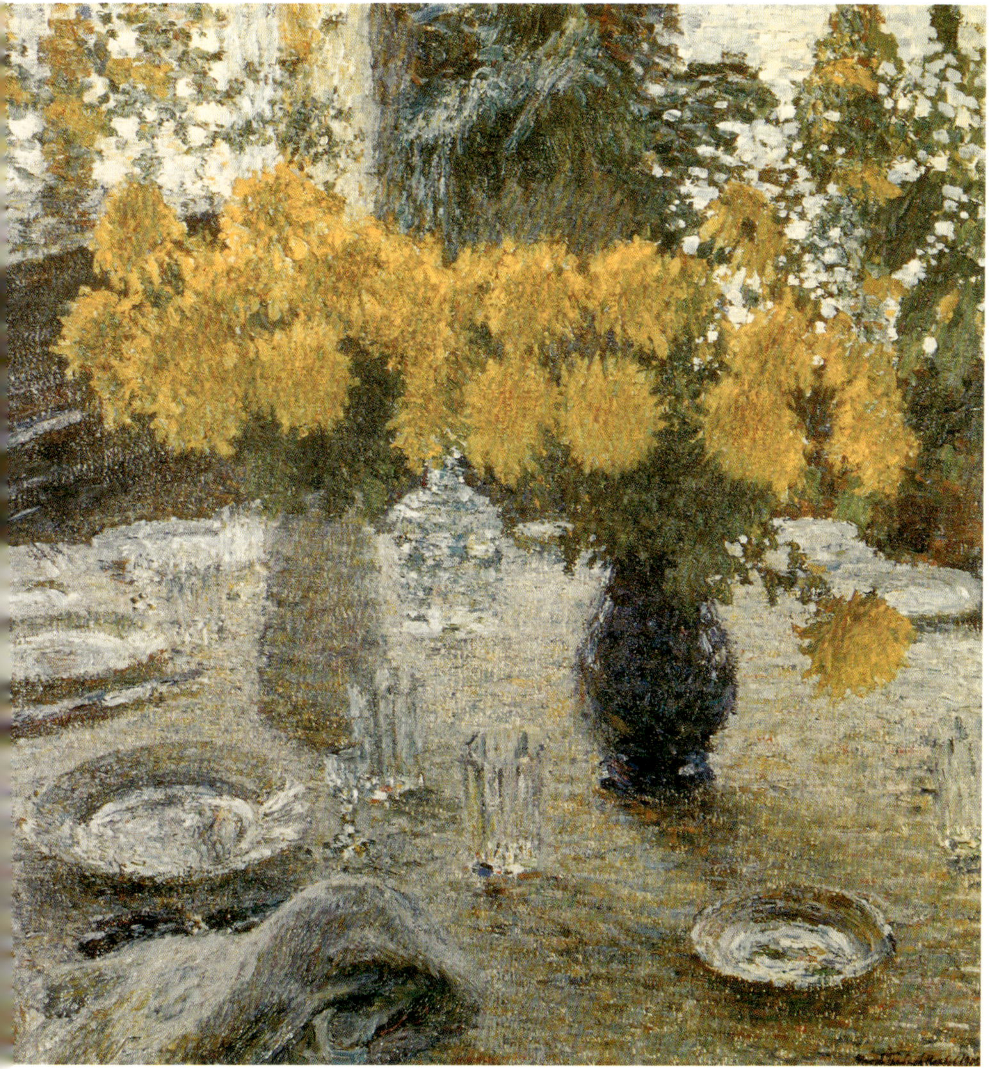

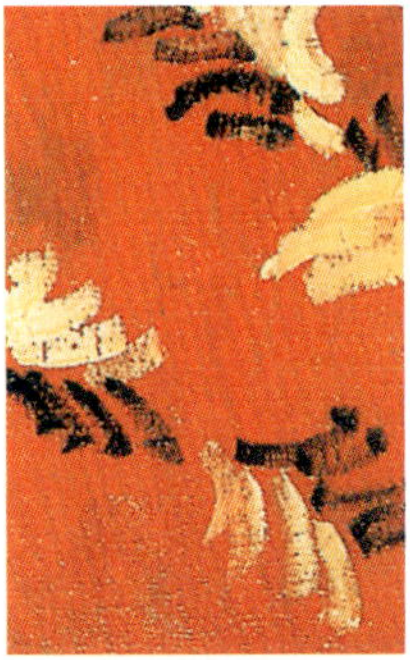
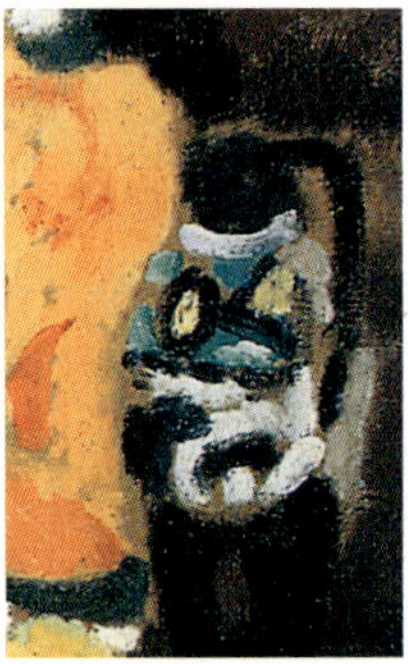
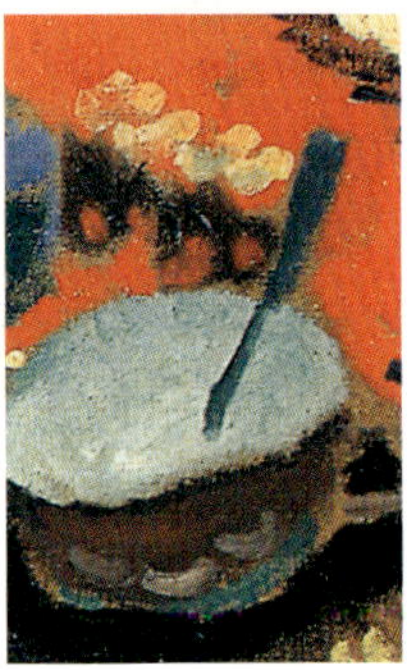

Paul Gauguin (1848-1903)

Paul Gauguin was first a sailor, then a successful stockbroker in Paris. In 1874 he began to paint at the weekends as a Sunday painter. Nine years later, after a stock-market crash, he felt confident of his ability to earn a living for his family by painting and he resigned.

Crockery and Fruits on Black and Red Table-cloth

Henri Matisse, 1906
Oil on canvas, 61 x 73 cm
The Hermitage, Saint Petersburg

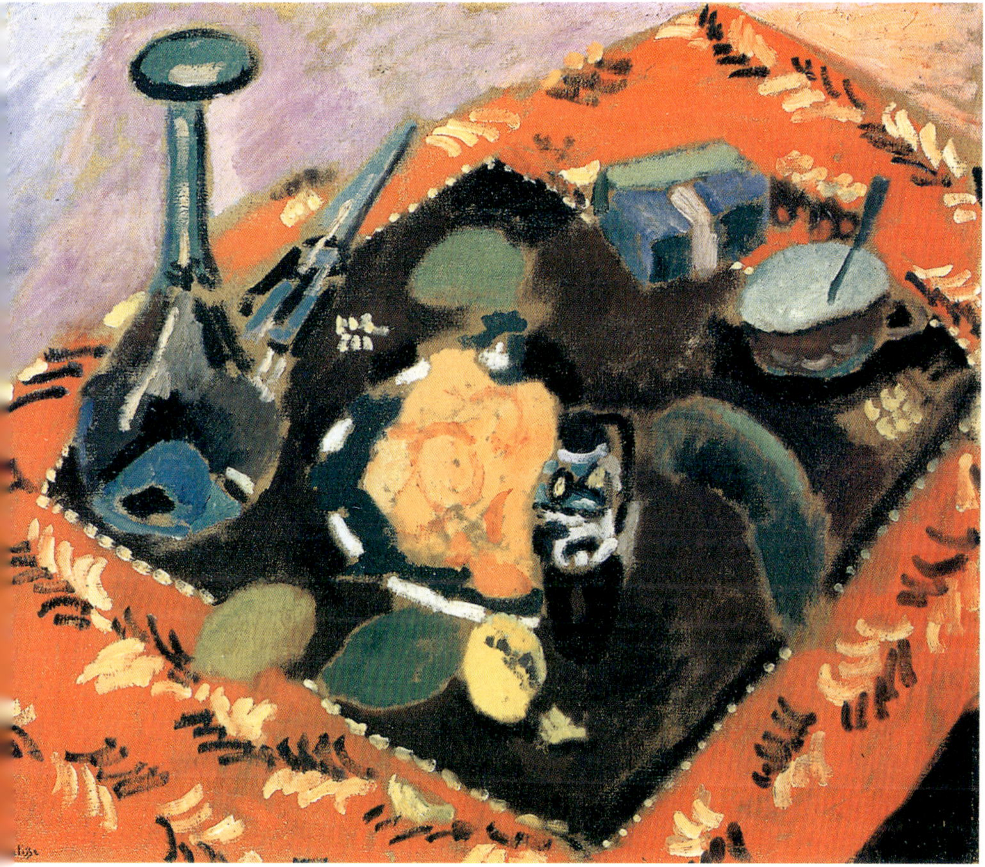

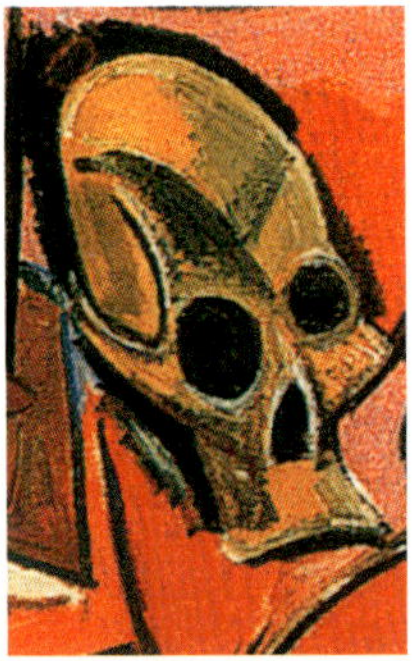

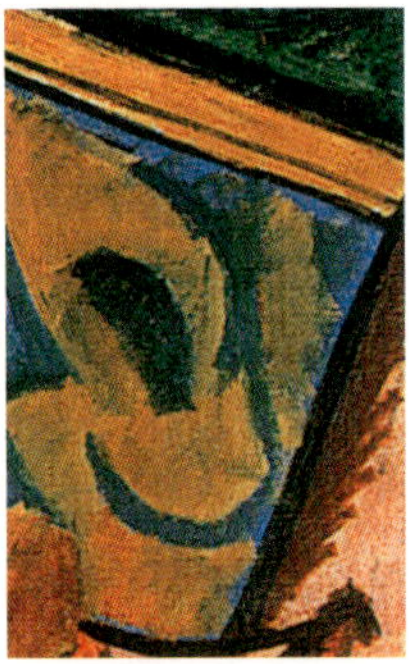

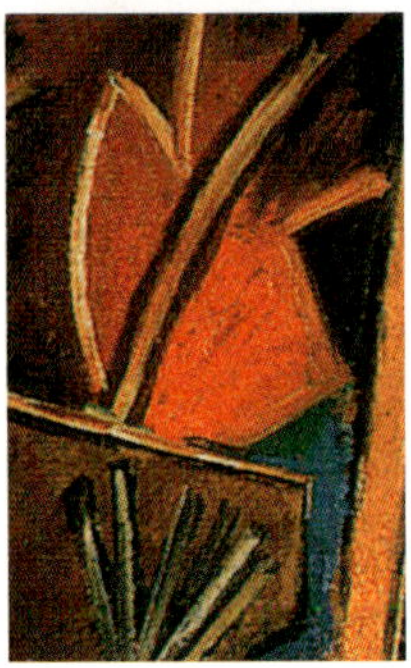

Following the lead of Cezanne, Gauguin painted still lifes from the very beginning of his artistic career. He even owned a still life by Cezanne, which is shown in his painting "Portrait of Marie Lagadu" behind her. This work obviously influenced him in painting his own still lifes.

Composition with a Skull

Pablo Picasso, 1907
Oil on canvas, 116.3 x 89 cm
The Hermitage, St Petersburg

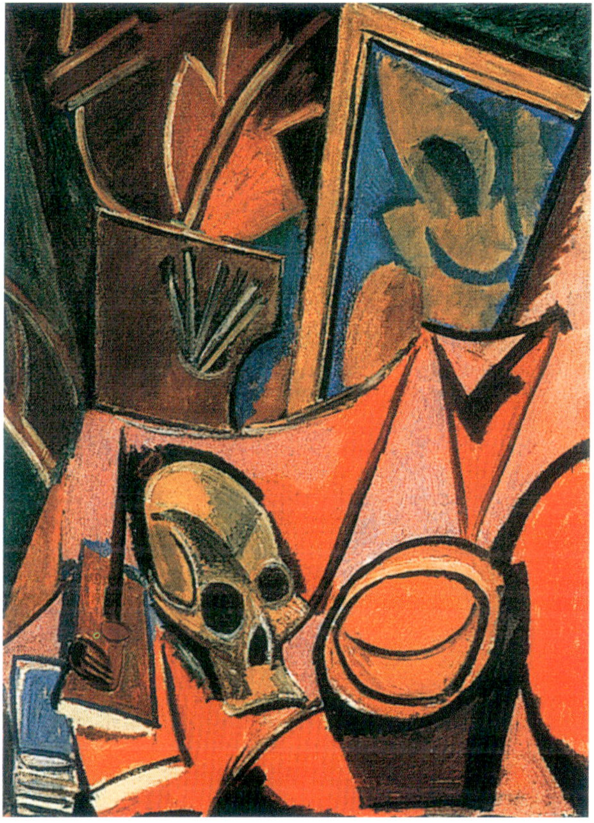

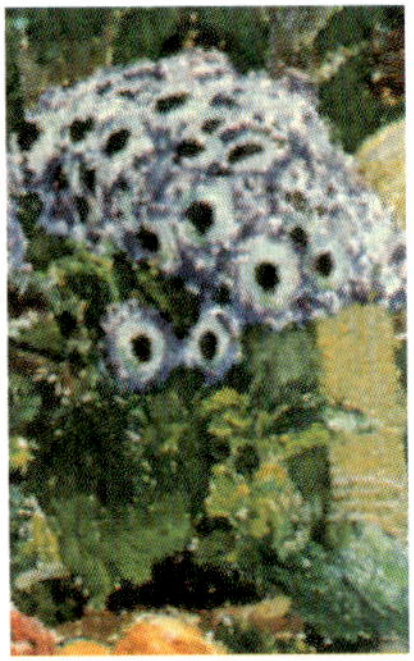

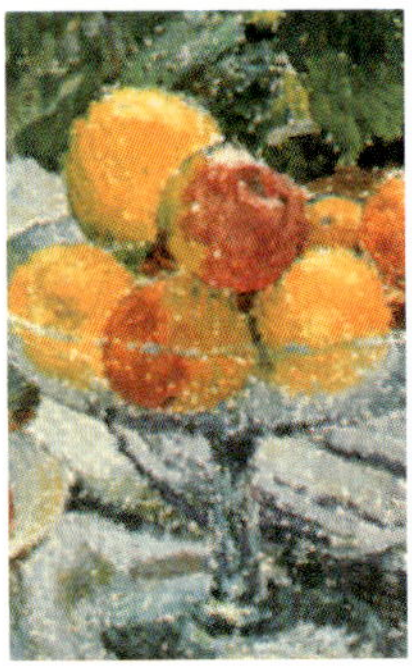

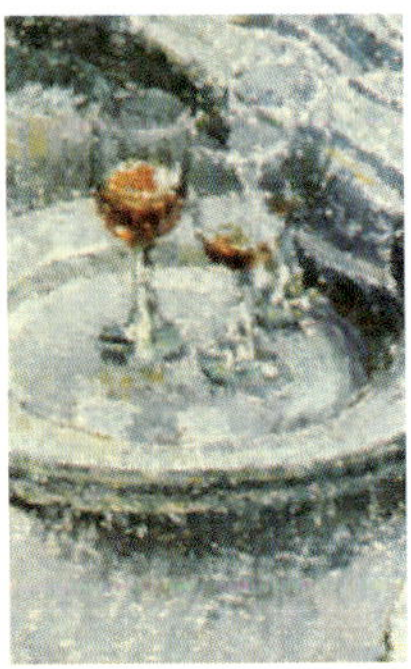

His transverse oval still lifes can be regarded as preliminary versions of "Still Life with Sunflowers", painted in 1901. They were inspired by self-grown sunflowers in Tahiti, where he remained until his death in 1903. In Tahiti, Gauguin discovered primitive art, with its flat forms and violent colours, belonging to an untamed nature.

The Uncleared Table

Igor Grabar, 1907
Oil on canvas, 100 x 96 cm
Tretyakov Gallery, Moscow

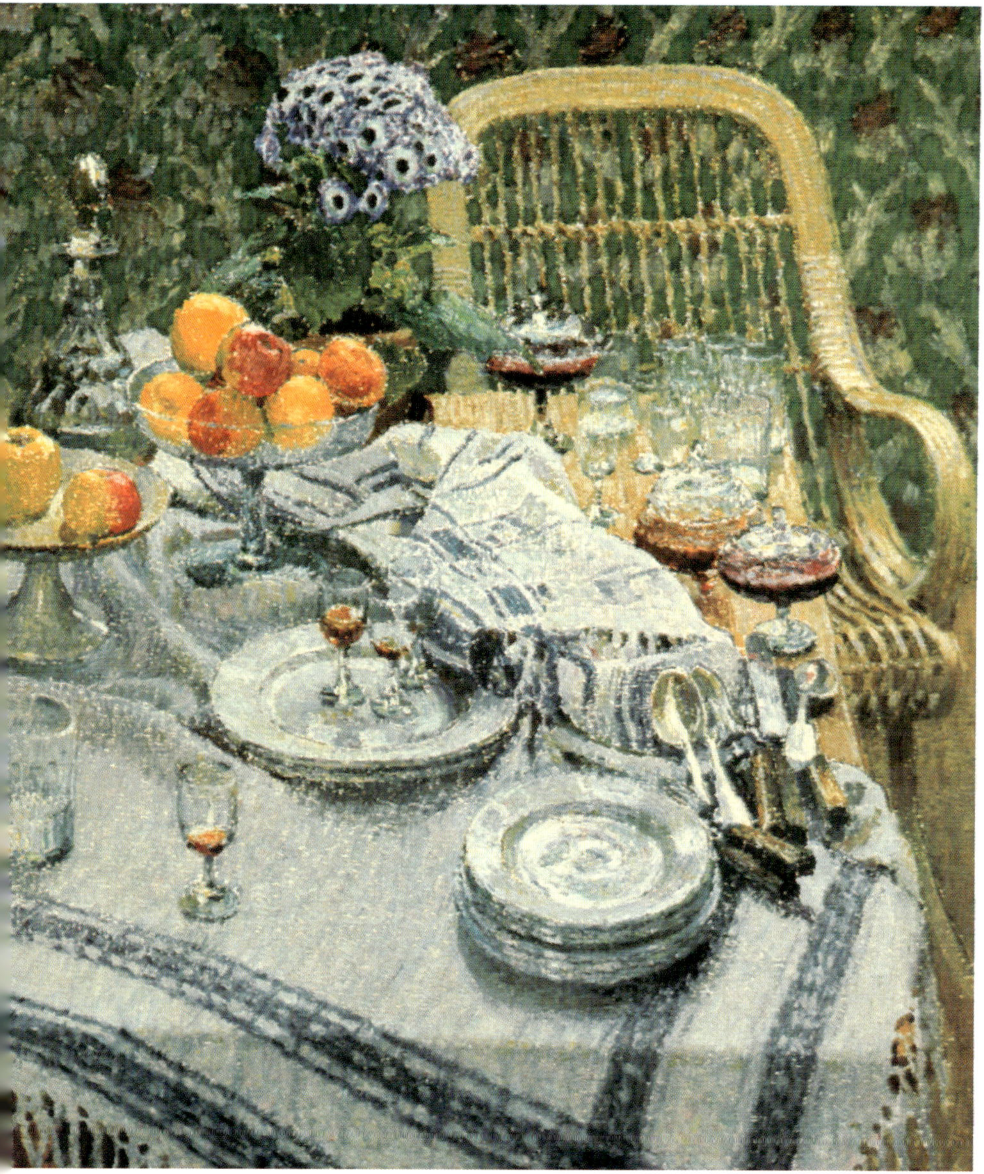

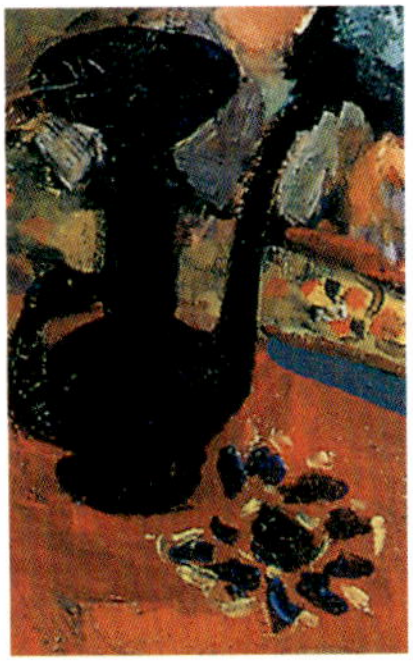

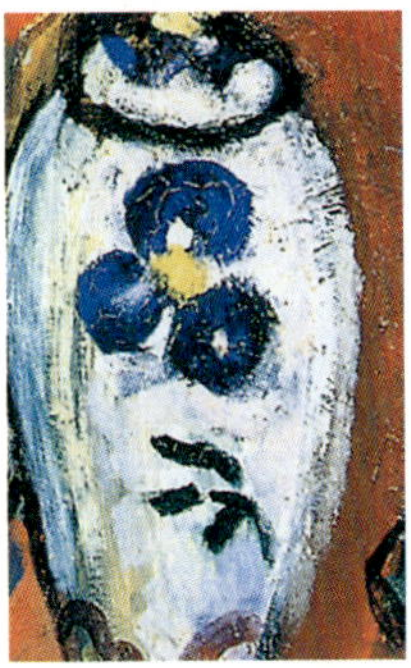

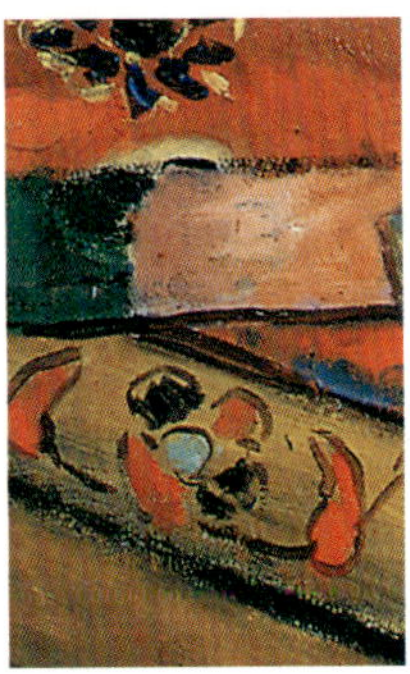

With absolute sincerity, he transferred them onto his canvas. All his still life paintings mirror his style: radical simplifications of drawing, brilliant, pure, bright colours, an ornamental type composition and deliberate flatness of planes – the style, which he called himself "synthetic symbolism".

Statuette and Vase on Oriental Carpet

Henri Matisse, 1908
Oil on canvas, 89 x 105 cm
Pushkin Museum of Fine Arts, Moscow

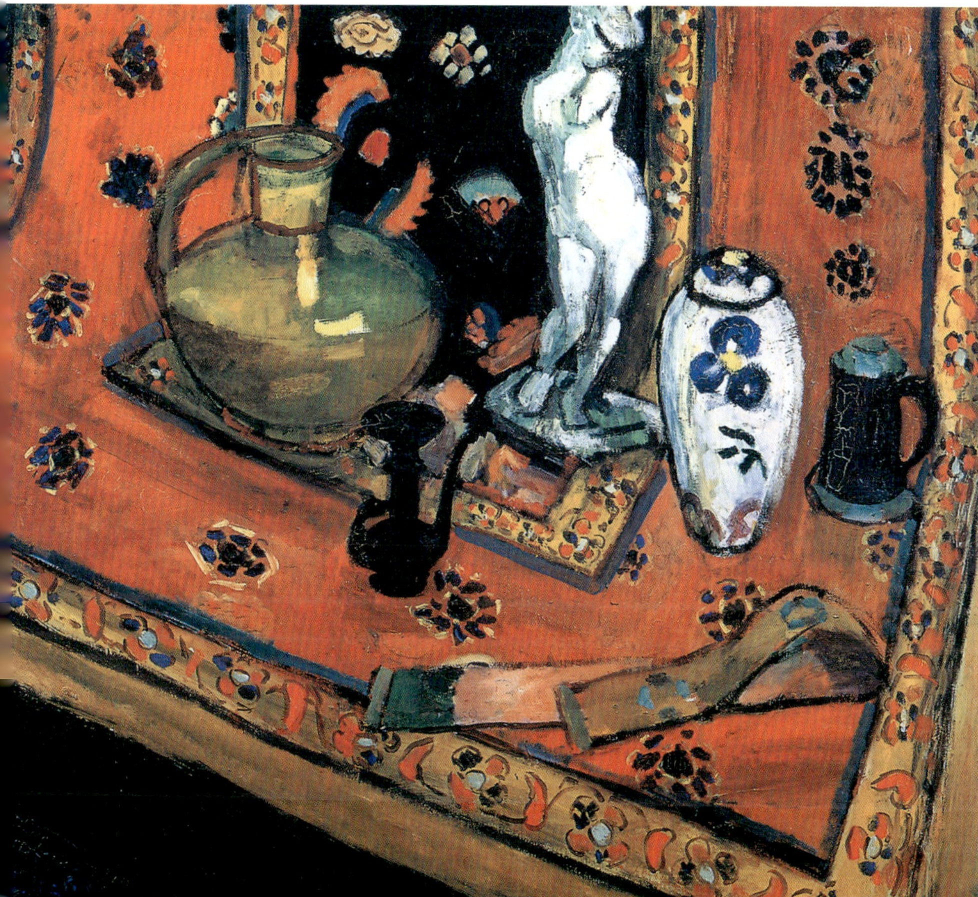

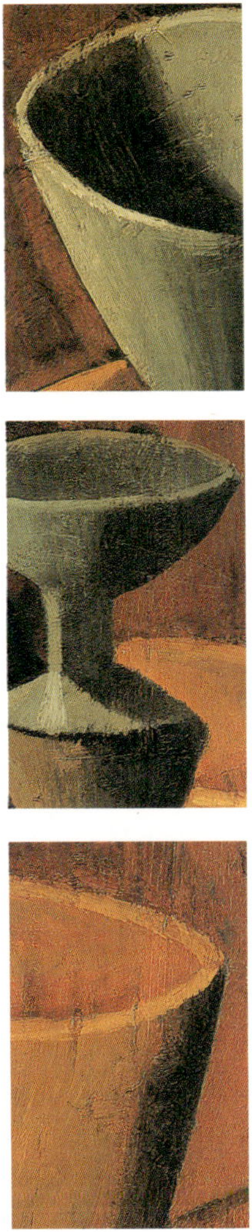

Vincent van Gogh (1853-1890)

Van Gogh was born in 1853 in Groot-Zundert and suffered numerous professional and personal crises. In 1881, following a period of poverty and moral distress (which would affect him all his life), Van Gogh began to paint with a sombre realism.

Decanter and Tureens

Pablo Picasso, 1908
oil on cardboard, 66 x 50.5 cm
The Hermitage St. Petersburg

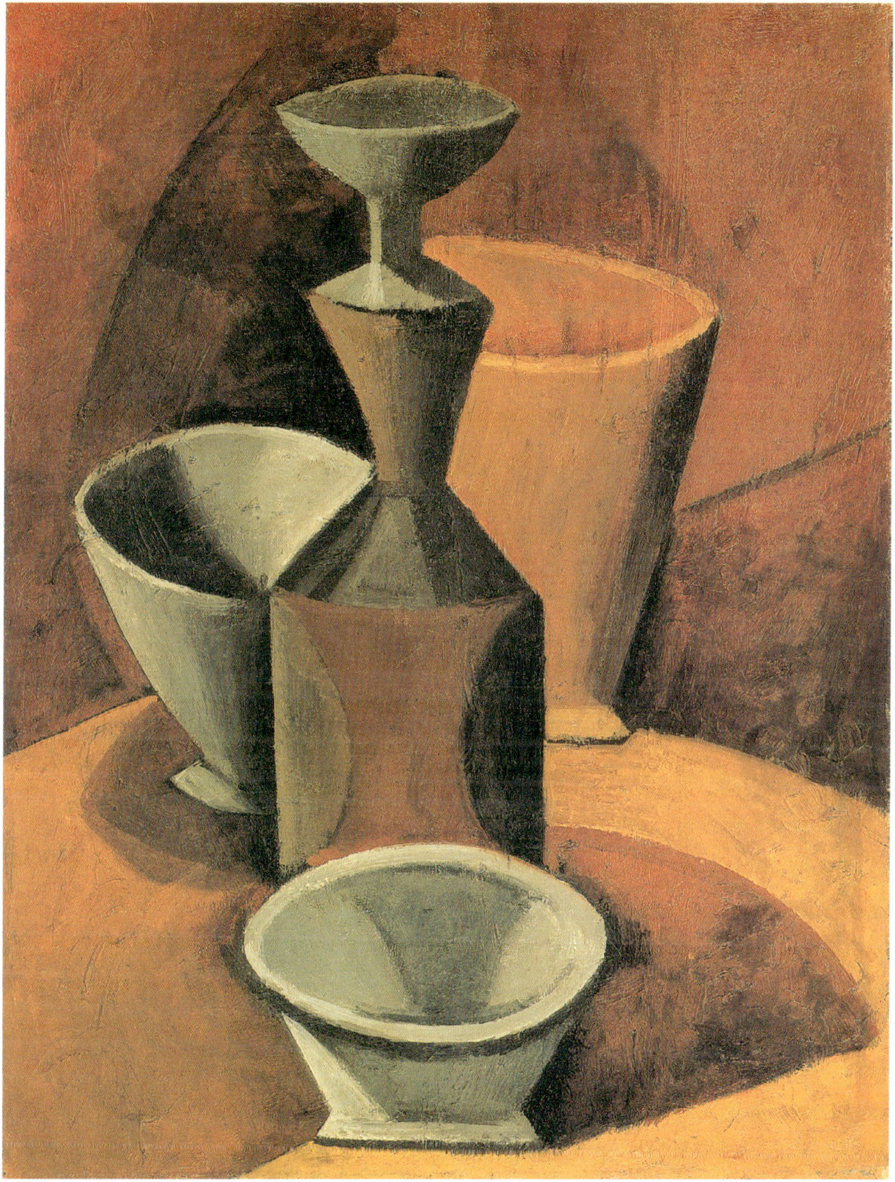

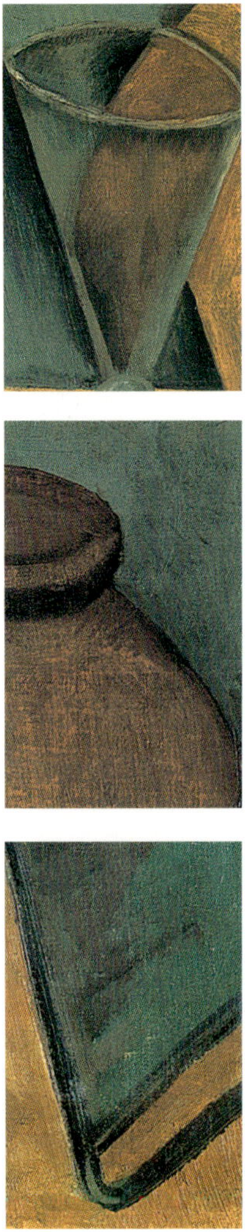

But as from 1885 (notably after having seen the works of art of Rubens) van Gogh discovered the bright colours which would be an integral part of the rest of his work. Then, in Paris, he met several Impressionist painters (such as Pissarro, Degas and Gauguin,

Pot, Wineglass and Book

Pablo Picasso, 1908
Oil on canvas, 55 x 46 cm
The Hermitage, Saint Petersburg

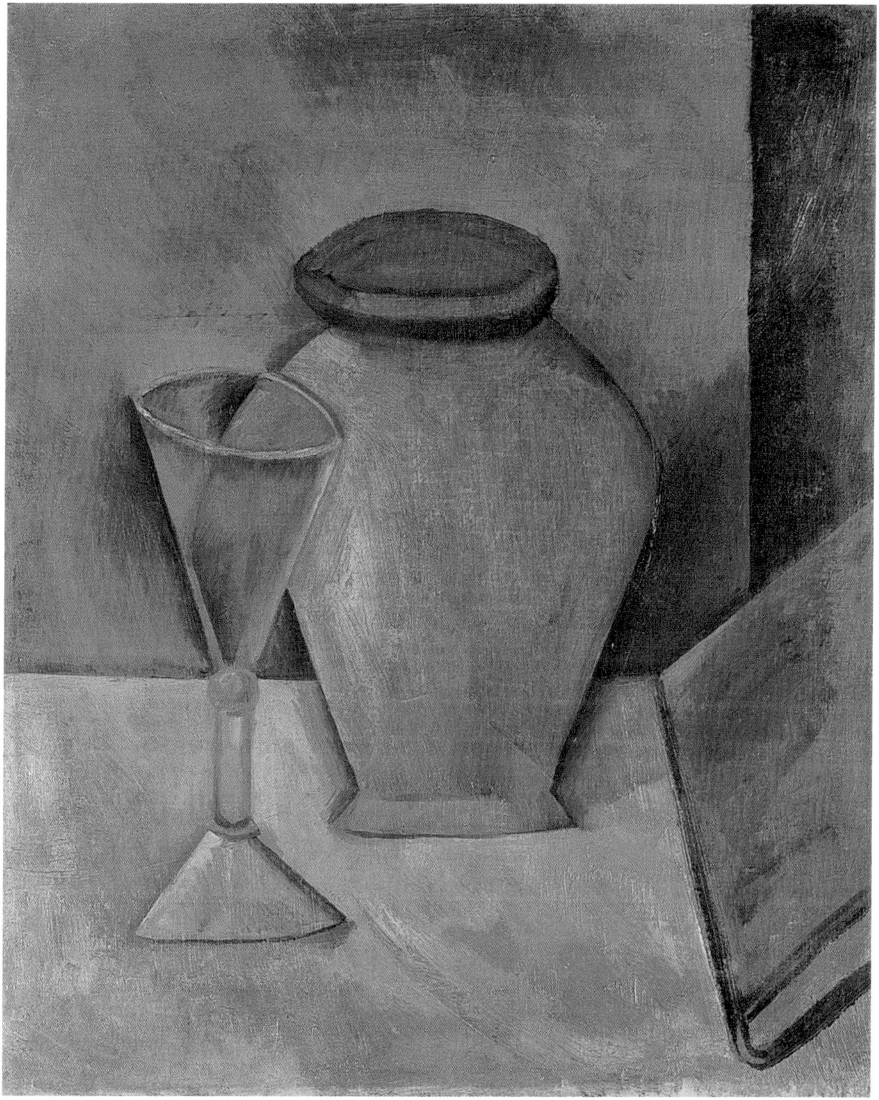

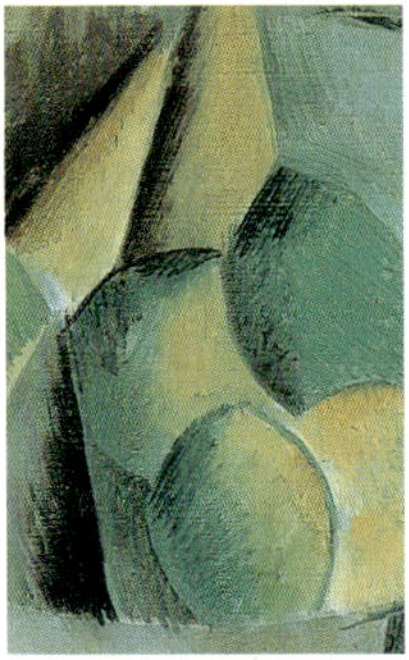

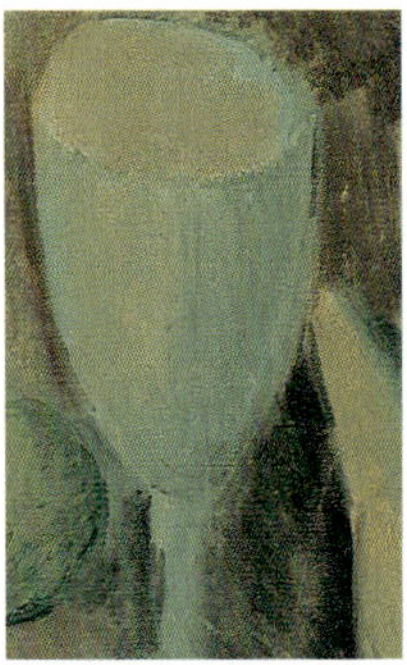

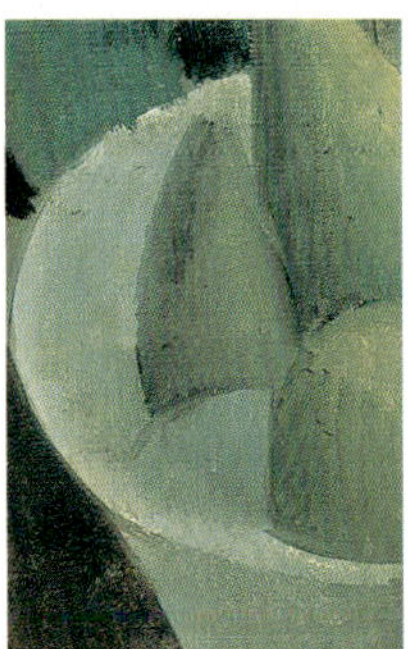

who would become his friends) from whom he would appropriate a light pallet and technique. He settled in Provence, France, in 1888 and abandoned Impressionism for more vigorous brushstrokes and dazzling colours.

Compotier, Fruit and Wineglass

Pablo Picasso, 1909
Oil on canvas, 92 x 72.5 cm
The Hermitage, St. Petersburg

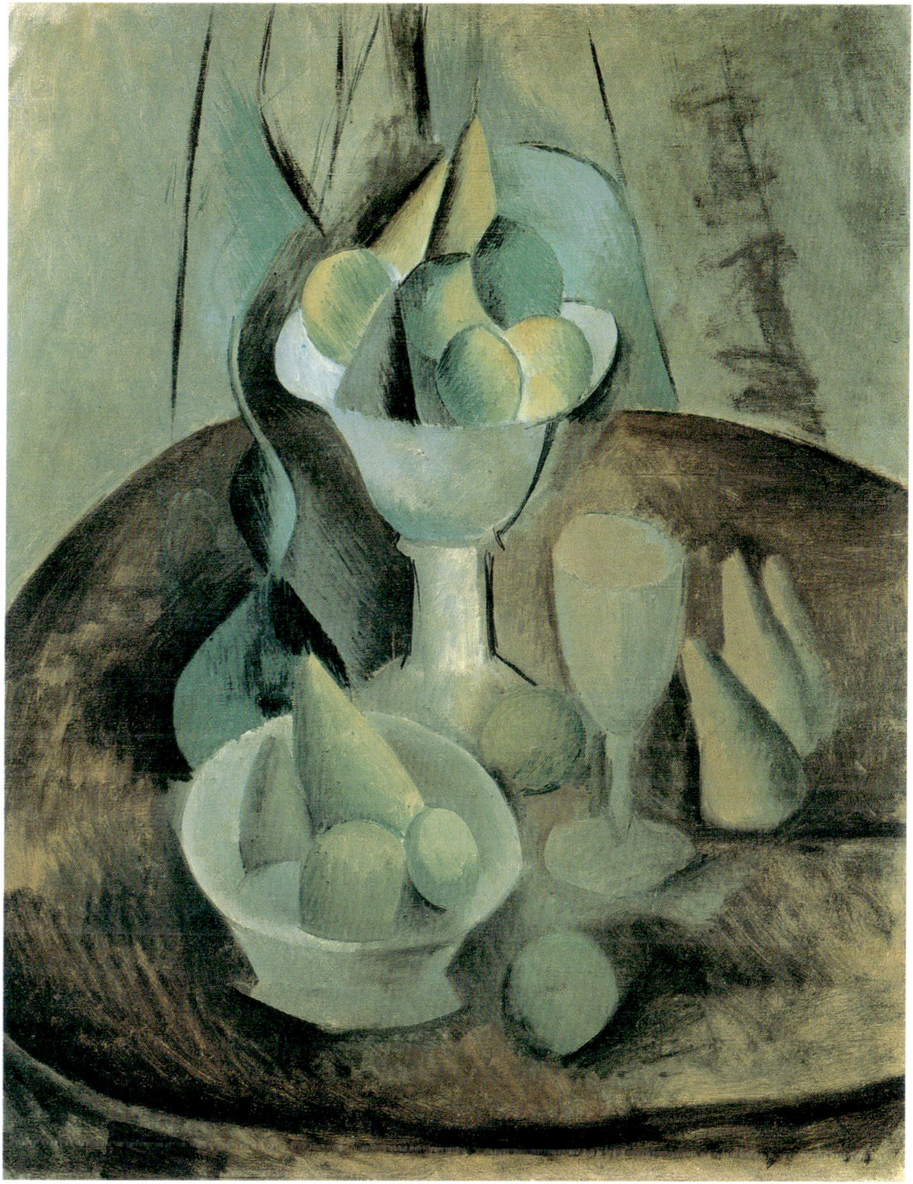

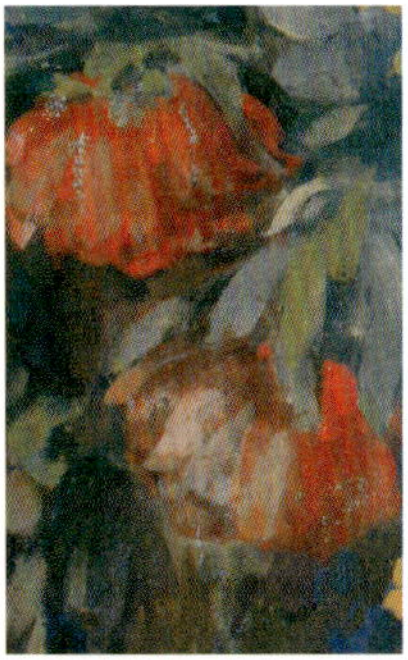
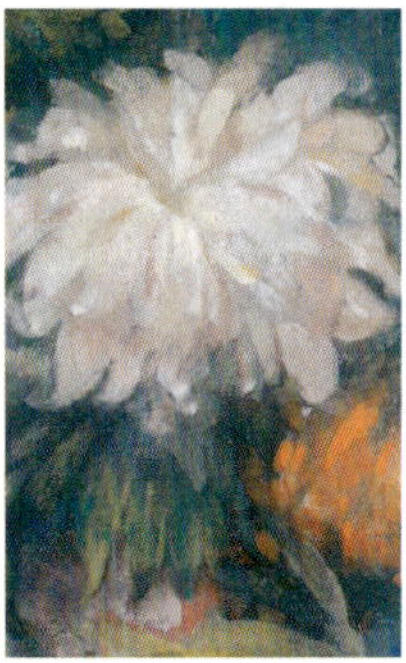
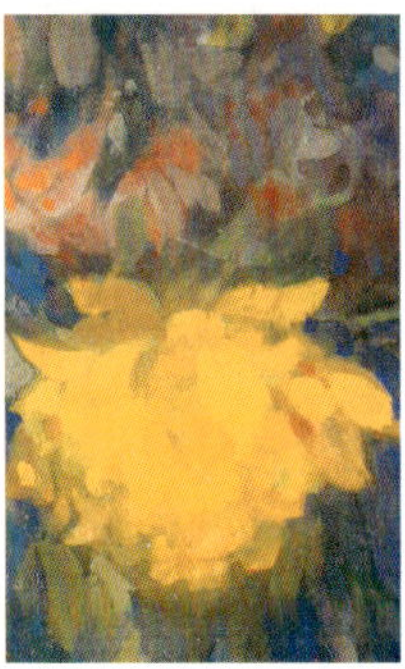

In the middle of August, he started the cycle of the sunflowers for the guest room: "I am hard at it, painting with the same enthusiasm as a Marseillais eating bouillabaisse, which won't surprise you when you know that what I love is the painting of some big sunflowers.

Peonies

Nikolai Sapunov, 1908
Tempera on canvas, 107 x 98 cm
Tretyakov Gallery, Moscow

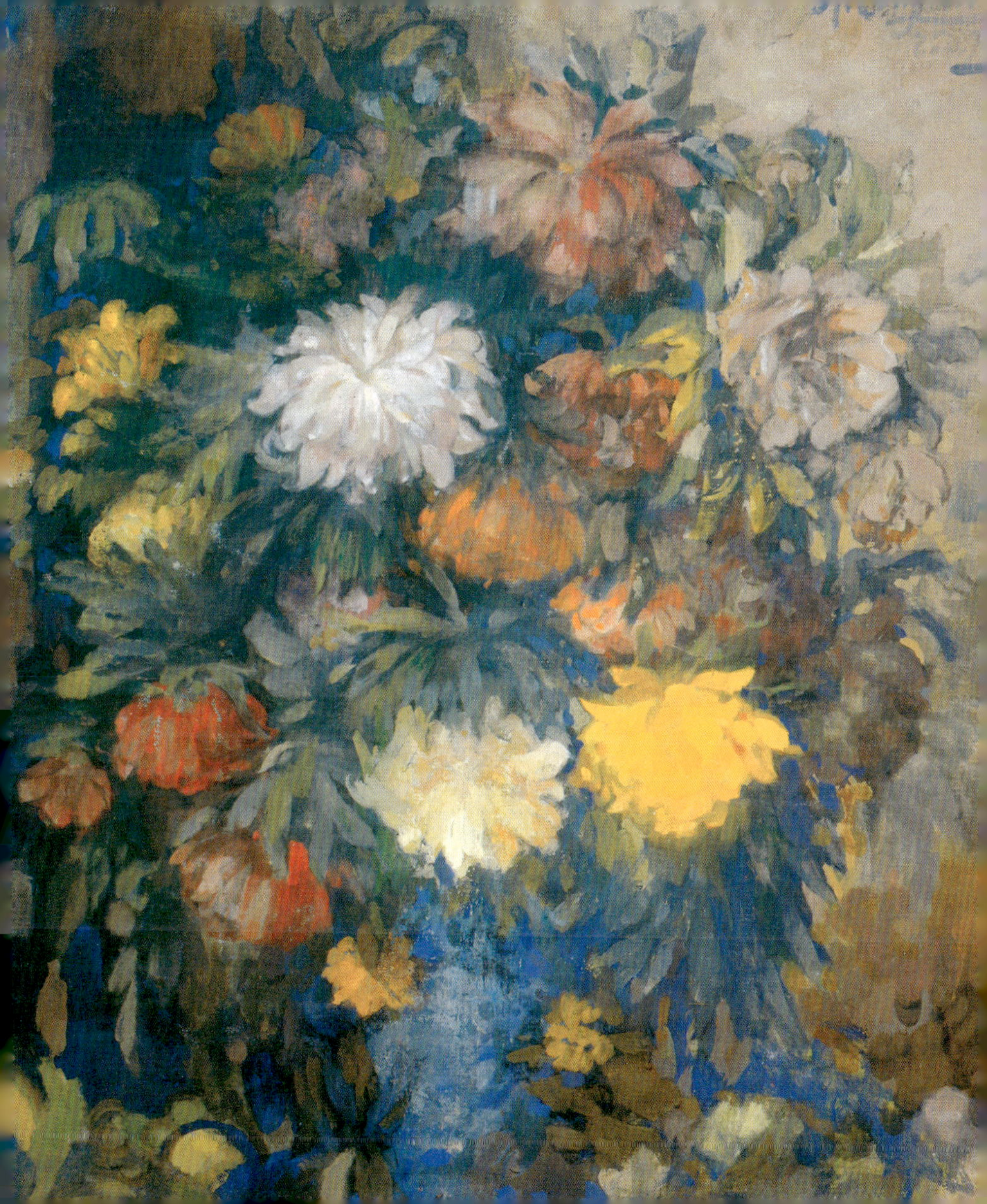

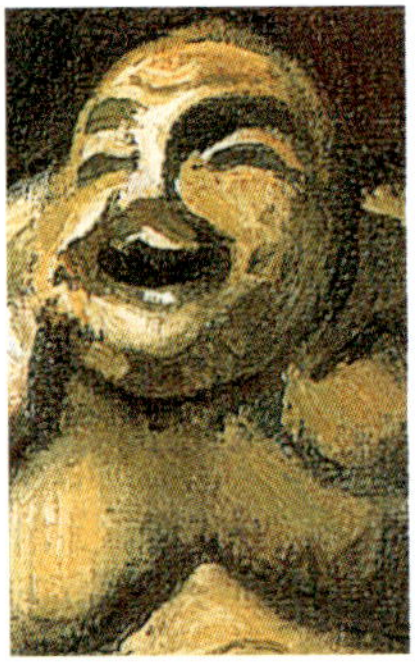

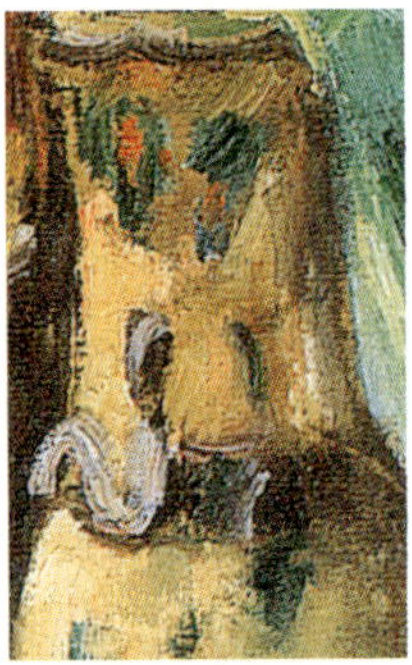

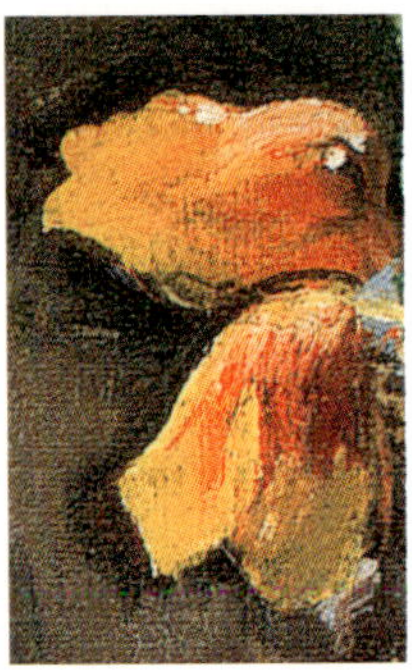

I have three canvases going – First, three huge flowers in a green vase, with a light background [...]; Then, three flowers, one gone to seed, having lost its petals, and one a bud against a royal-blue background [...]; Finally, twelve flowers and buds in a yellow vase [...]

Still Life with a Statuette of Buddha

Othon Friesz, 1909
Oil on canvas, 51 x 42 cm
The Hermitage, Saint Petersburg

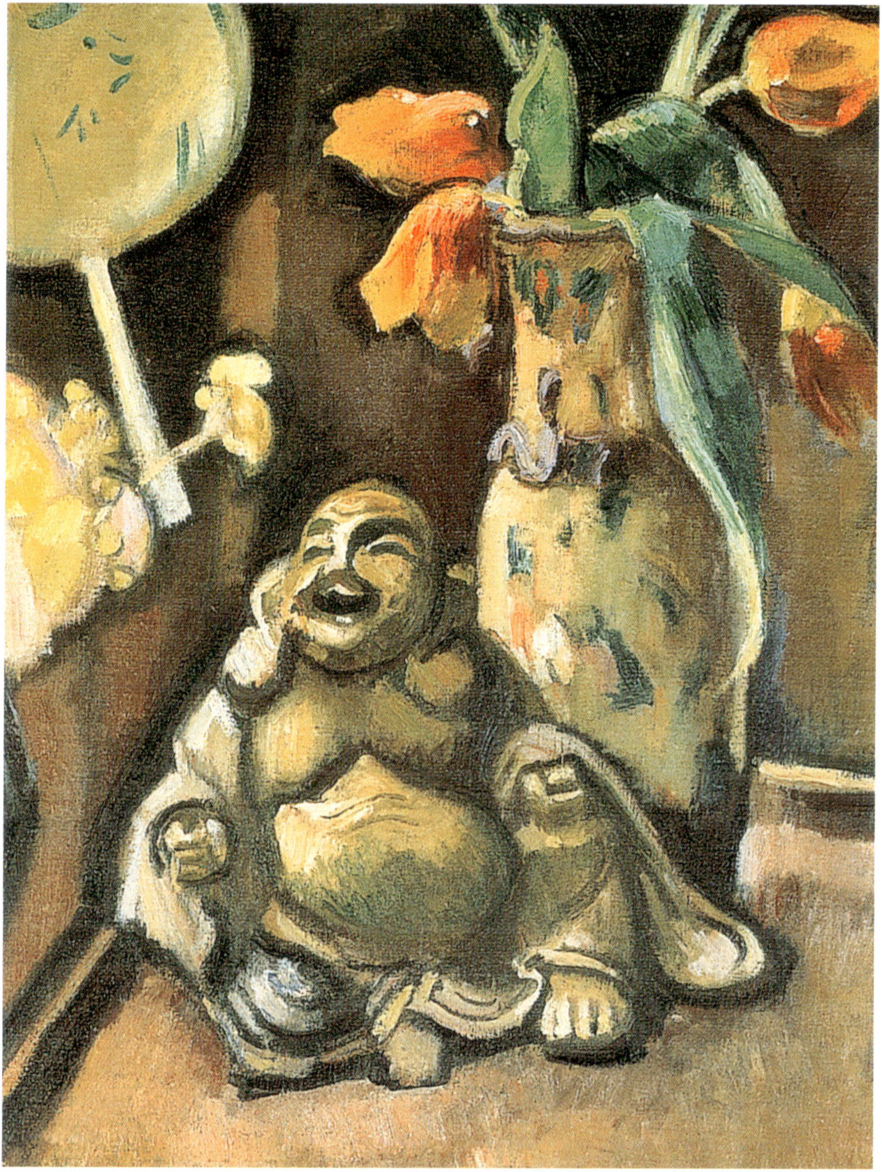

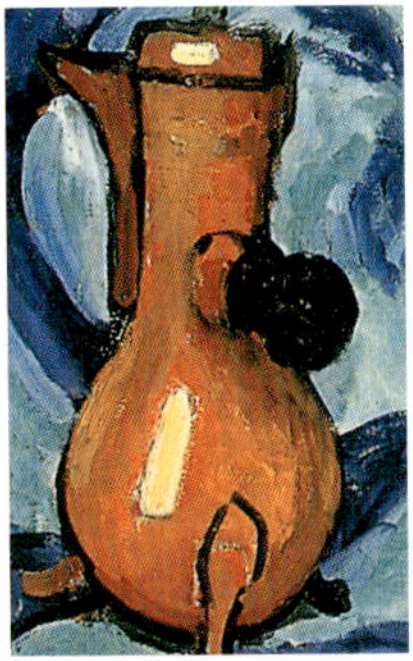

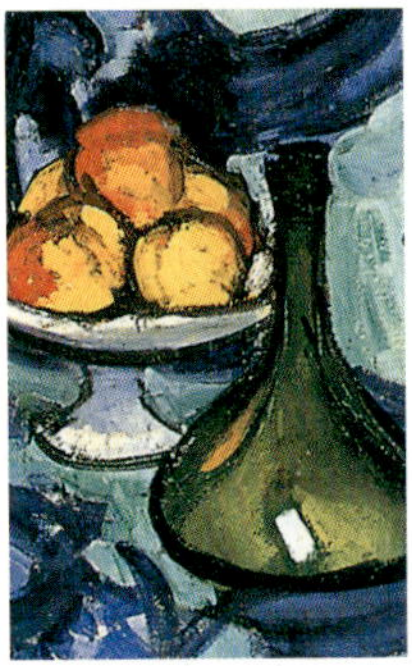

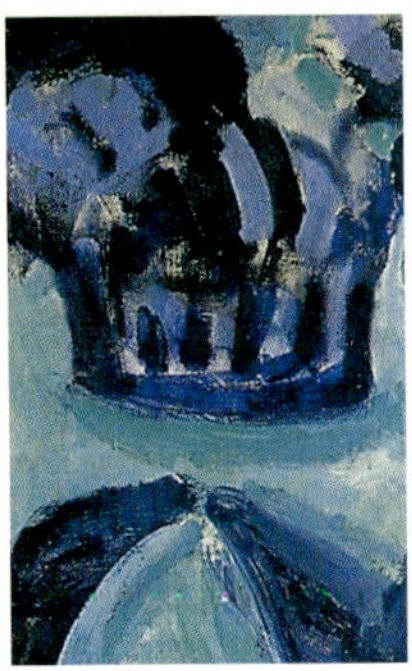

The last one is therefore light on light, and I hope it will be the best [...] If I carry out this idea there will be a dozen panels. So the whole piece will be a symphony in blue and yellow." Of the projected twelve sunflower pictures,

The Blue Table-Cloth

Henri Matisse, 1909
Oil on canvas, 88.5 x 116 cm
The Hermitage, Saint Petersburg

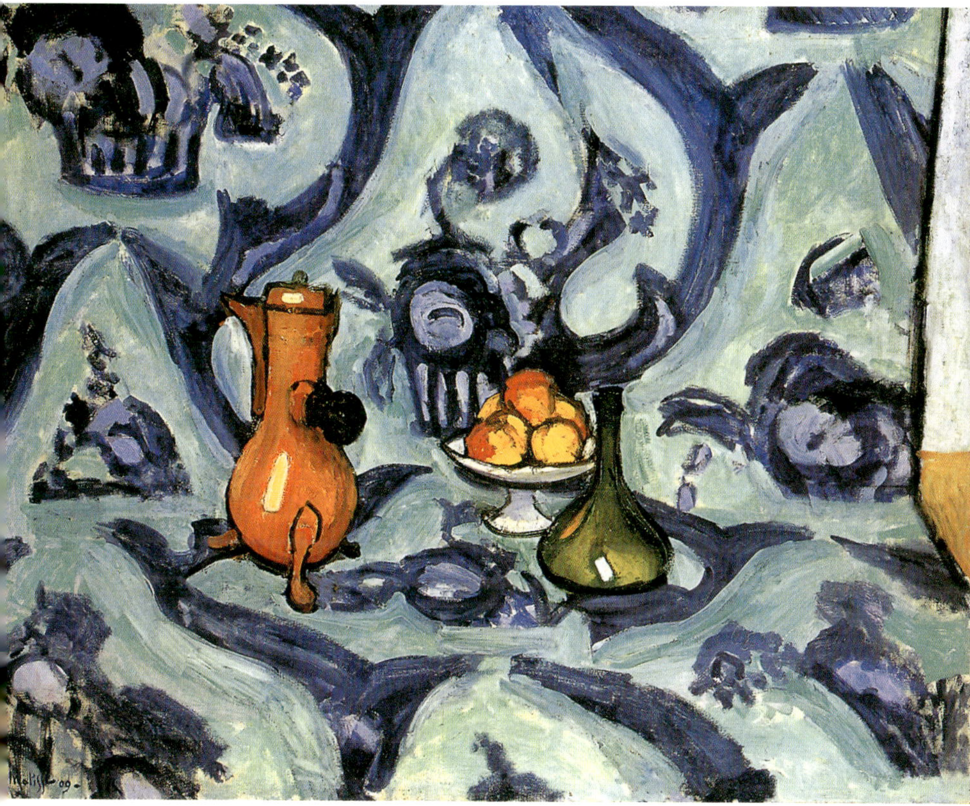

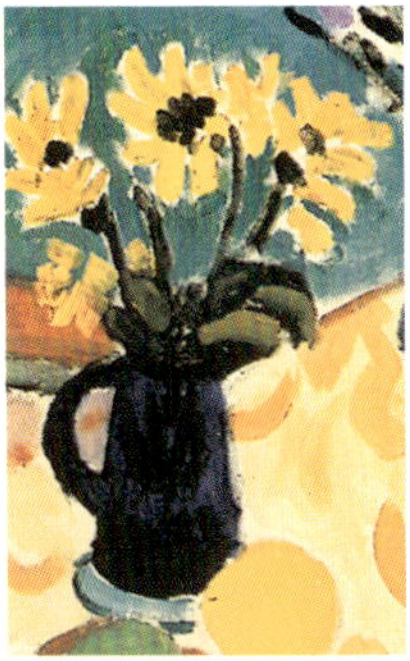

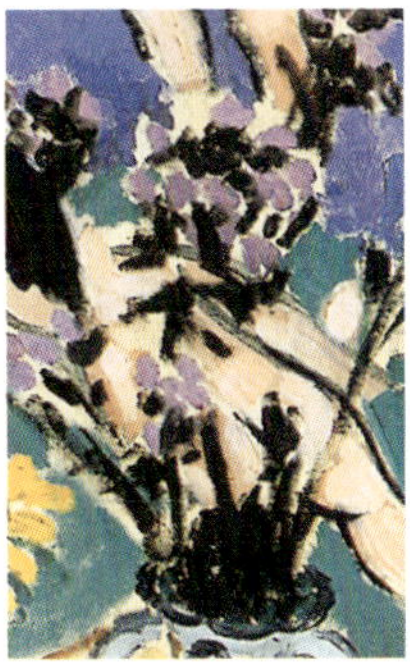

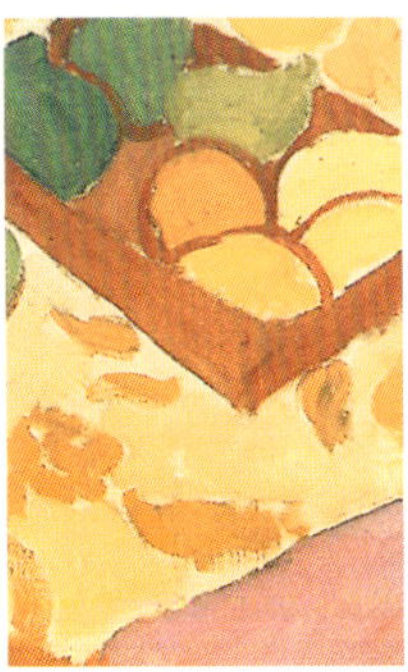

he completed only two, because the 'models' disappeared too quickly. Vincent produced many remarkable "Vanitas" still lifes, including his "Still Life with Bible". At first glance, this canvas seems to recall 17th-century still lifes,

Fruits, Flowers and the Wall Painting "The Dance"

Henri Matisse, 1909
Oil on canvas, 89.5 x 117.5 cm
The Hermitage, Saint Petersburg

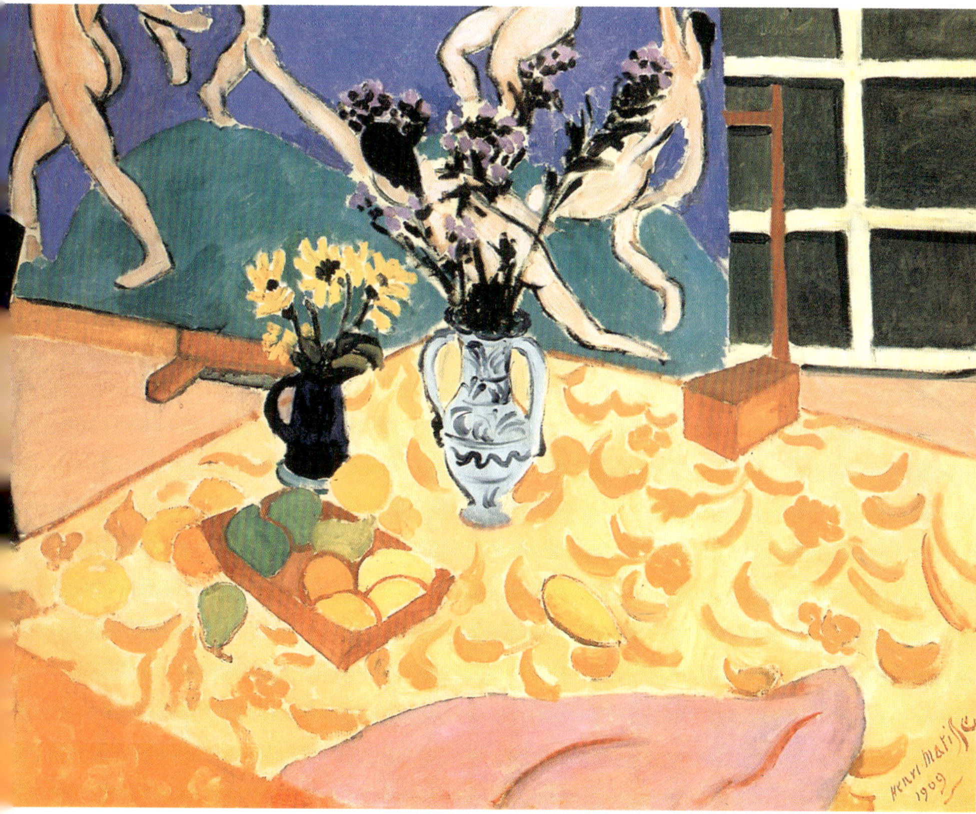
Henri Matisse
1909

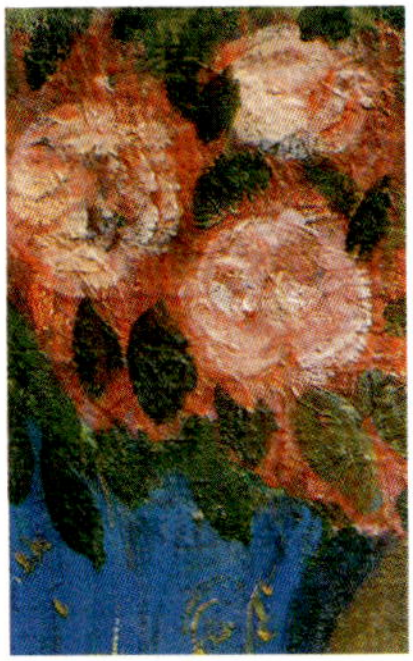

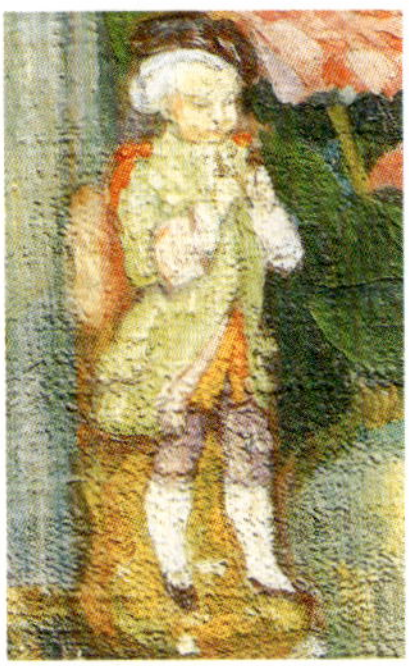

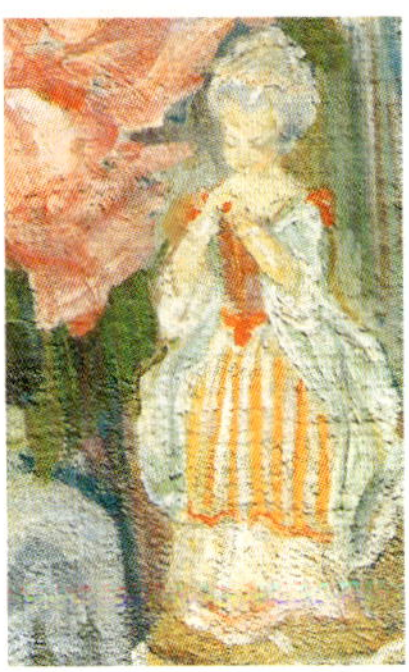

because at that time, the Bible was considered a symbol of mortality and the transience of knowledge. This Bible had belonged to him, and was a symbol of his rather conventional faith and strict way of life. Next to the Bible is a copy of *La joie de vivre* by the French author Emile Zola.

Still Life with Porcelain Figurines and Roses

Sergei Sudeikin, 1909
Oil on canvas mounted on cardboard
44 x 43.5 cm
Russian Museum, Saint Petersburg

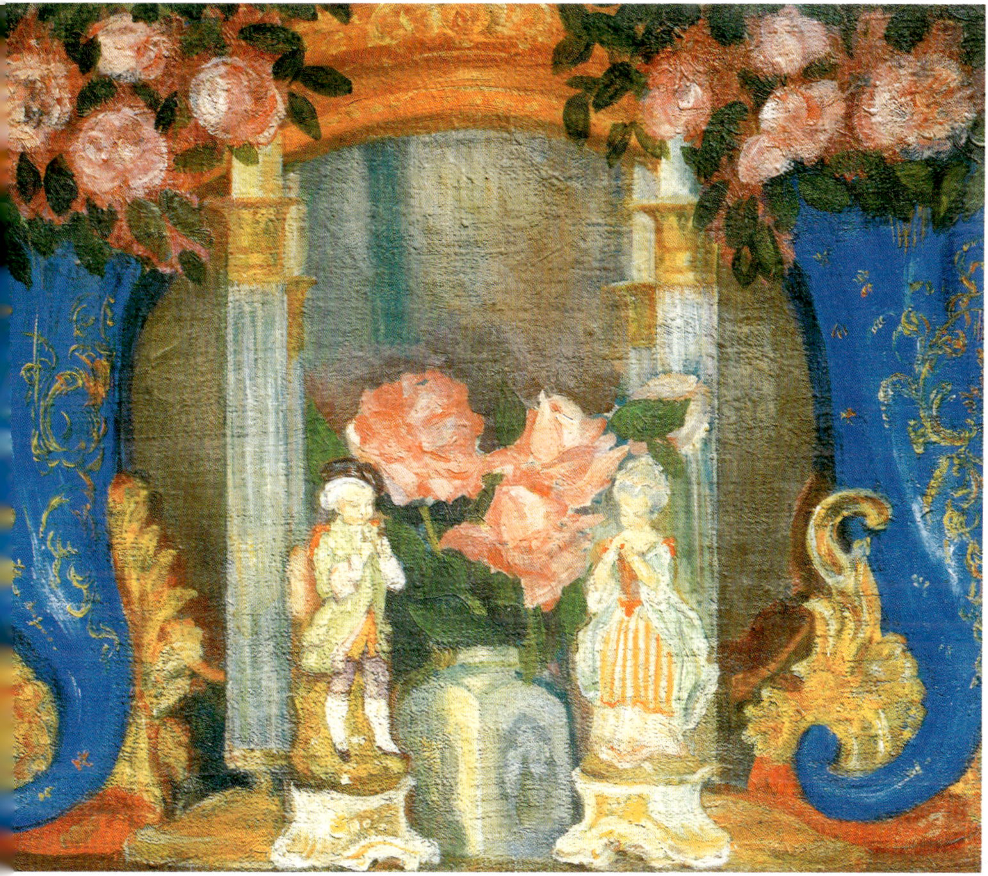

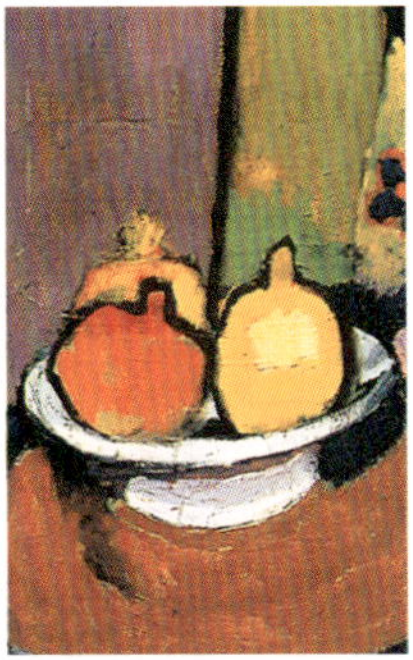
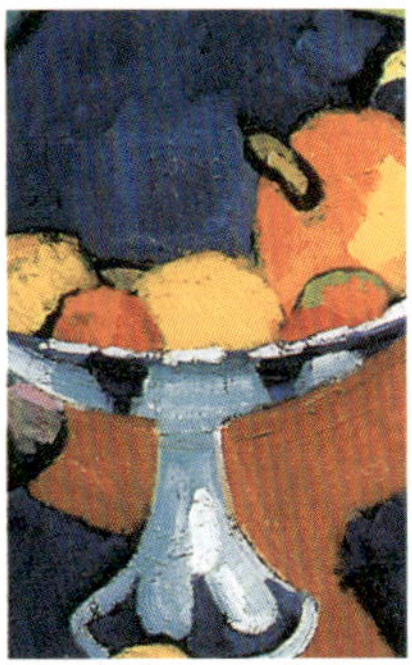
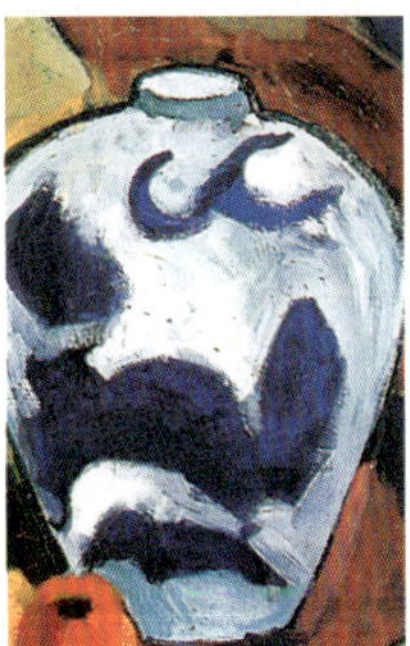

At this time, Van Gogh was fascinated by the works of Zola, seeing in them a kind of bible for modern life. By contrasting these two books, Vincent might have wanted to show his critical stance towards his father.

Fruits and Bronze

Henri Matisse, 1910
Oil on canvas, 90 x 118 cm
Pushkin Museum of Fine Arts, Moscow

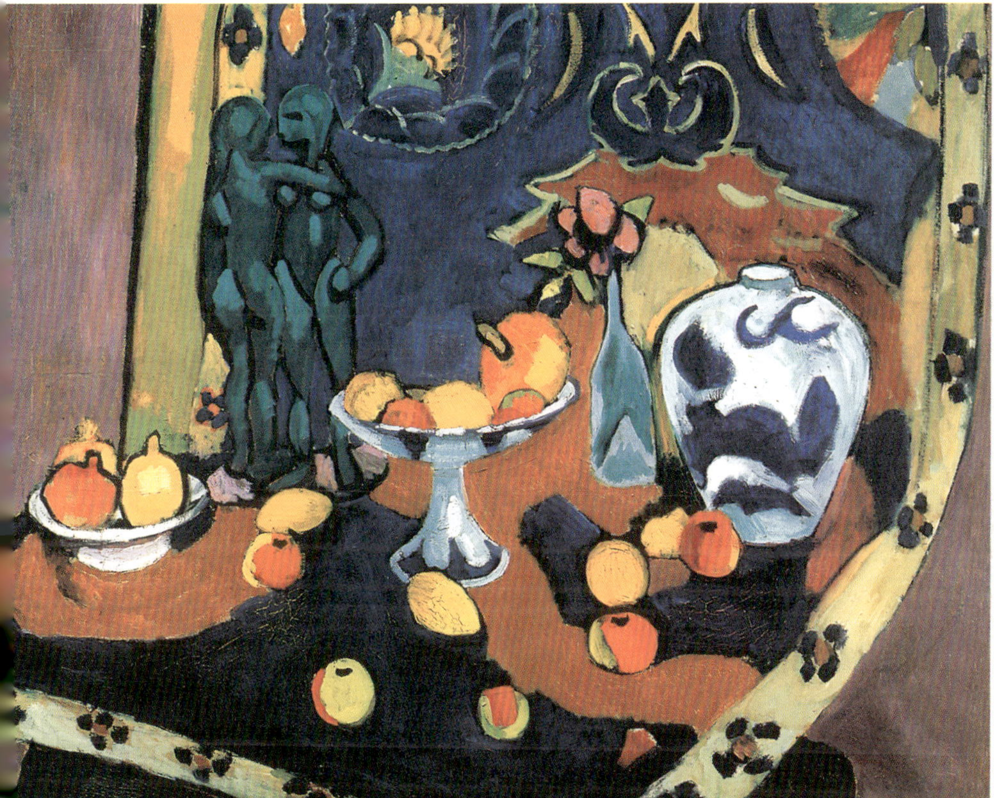

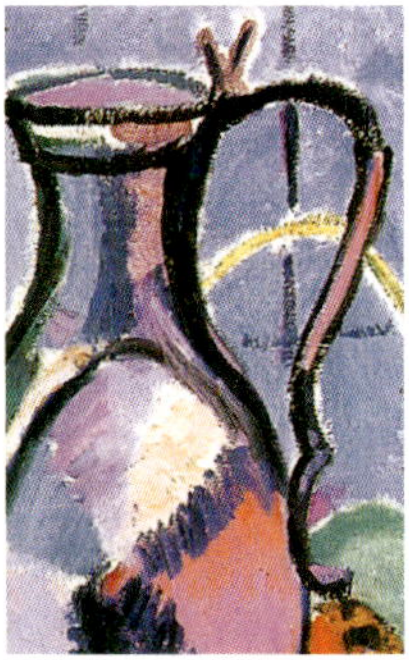
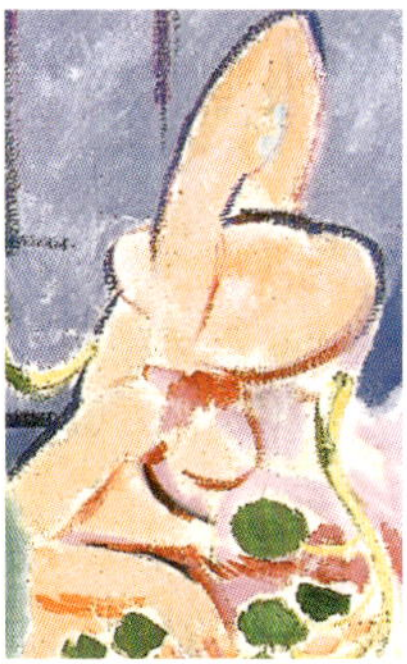
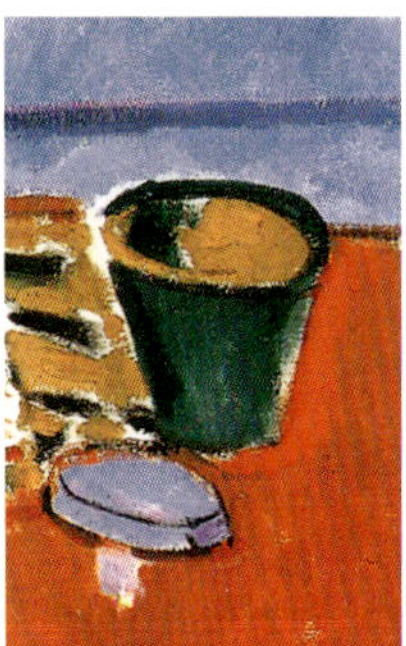

In 1889, Van Gogh was voluntarily admitted to an asylum in Saint-Rémy-de-Provence where he painted several more flower canvases based on the harmony of yellow, green, blue and purple while vast panels of saturated colour make up the background. Van Gogh committed suicide in July 1890.

Pink Statuette and Jug on Red Chest of Drawers

Henri Matisse, 1910
Oil on canvas, 90 x 117 cm
The Hermitage, Saint Petersburg

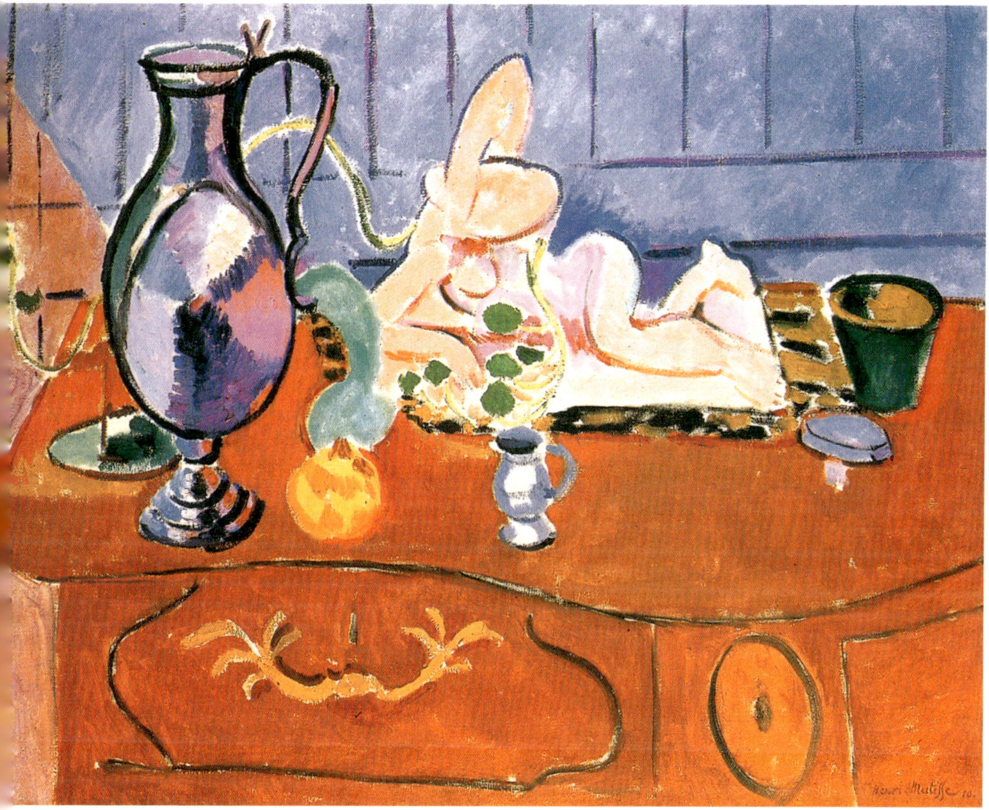

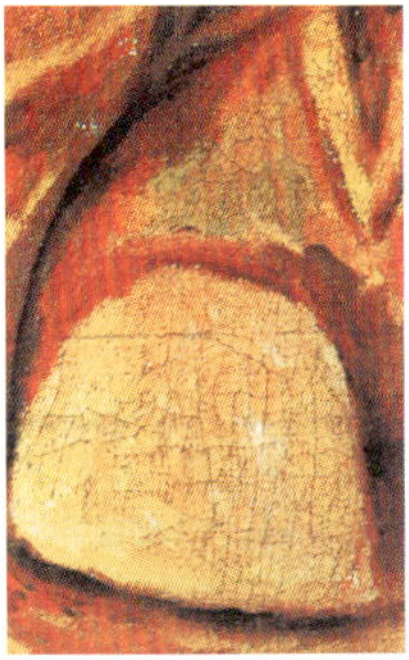

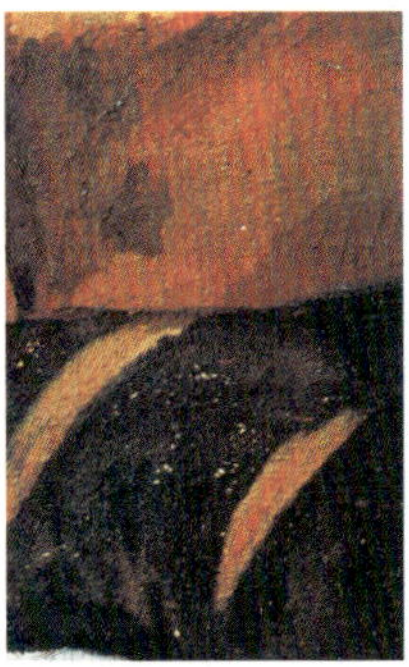

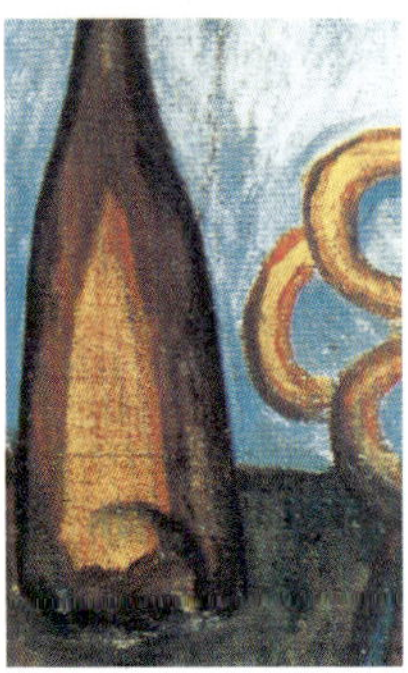

Henri Matisse (1869-1954)

The work of Matisse communicates his quest for chromatic depth and for balance (combining passion and reason, joy of life and torments of the spirit).

Bread

Mikhail Larionov, c. 1910
Oil on canvas, 102 x 84 cm
private collection, Paris

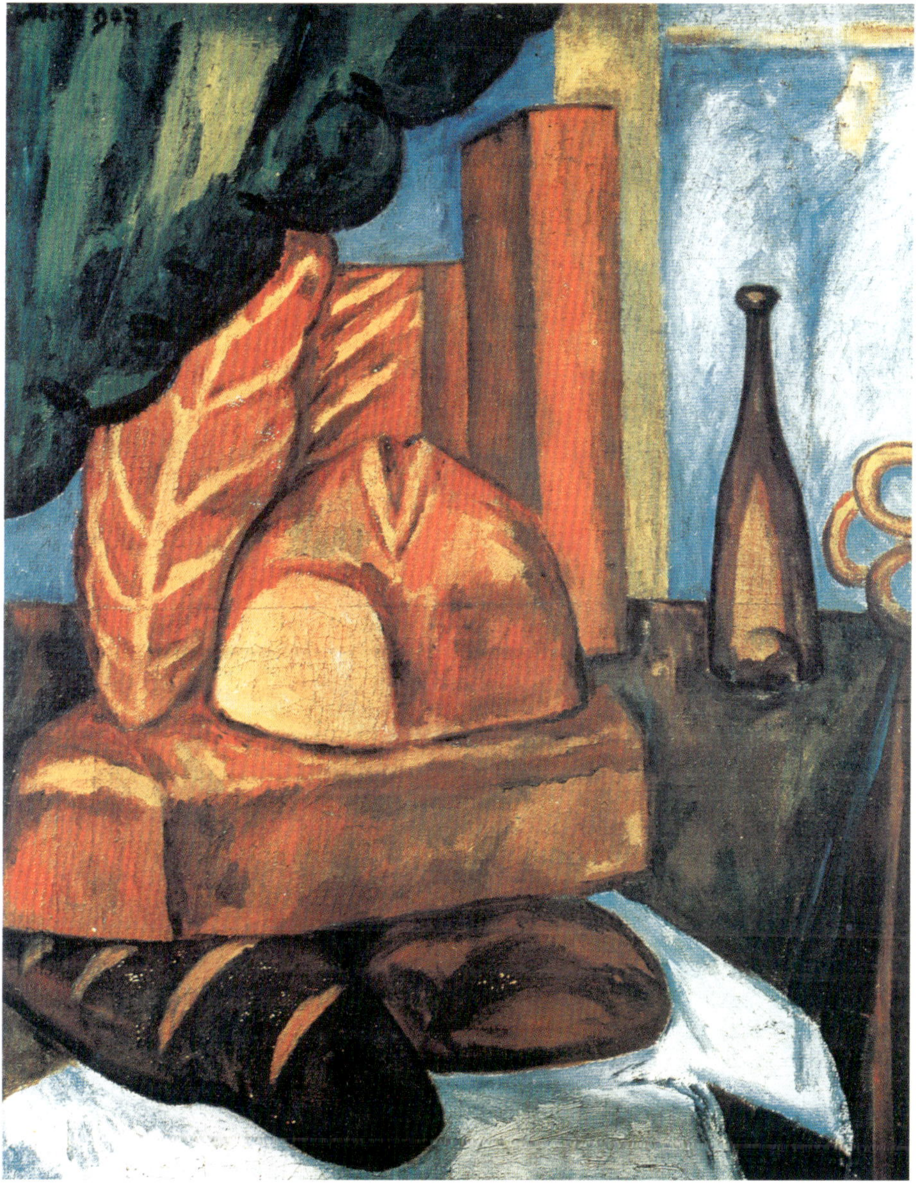

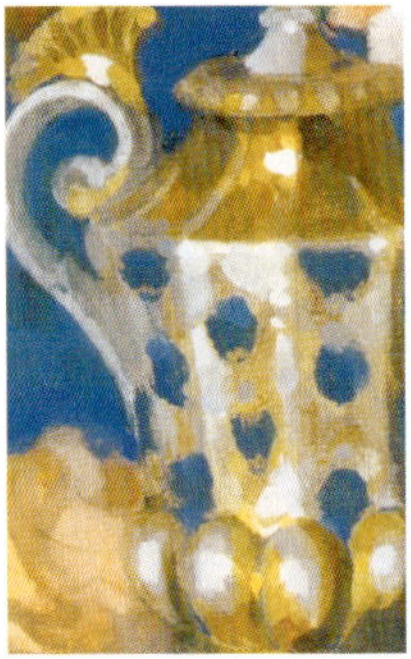

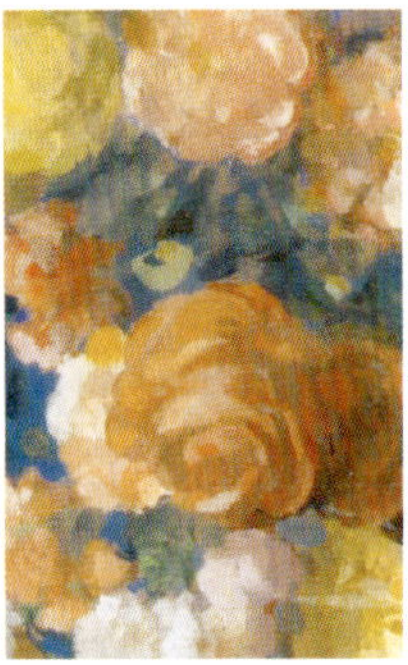

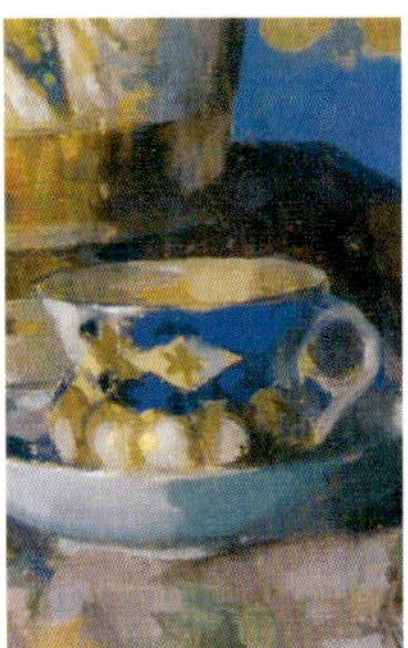

He assimilated and combined lessons from the Impressionists and from Cézanne and the neo-Impressionists to achieve a particular form of brushstroke and the plastic quality of paint layering, as seen in *Tournesols dans un vase (Sunflowers in a vase).*

Still Life with Vase and Flowers

Nikolai Sapunov, 1910
tempera on canvas, 118 x 114 cm
Tretyakov Gallery, Moscow

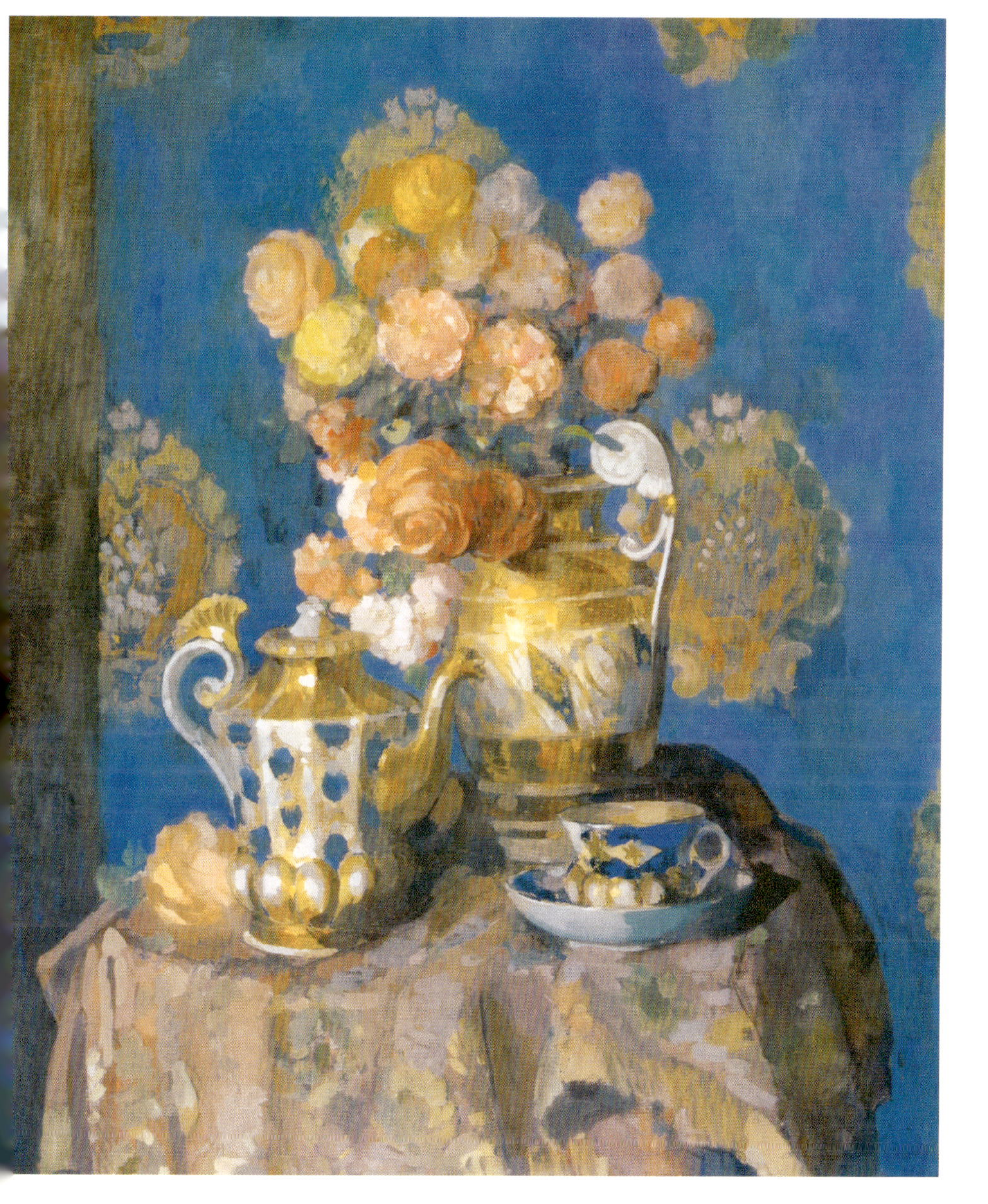

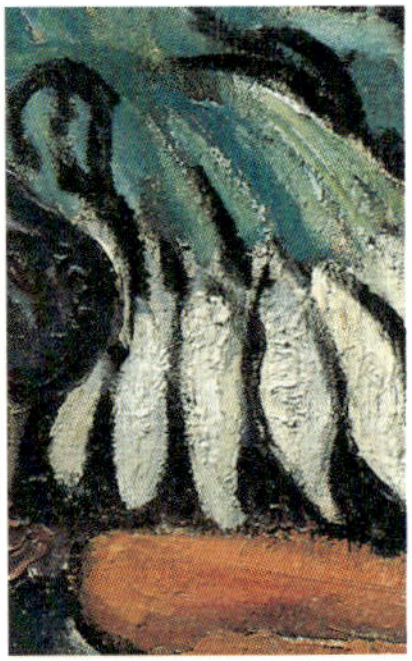

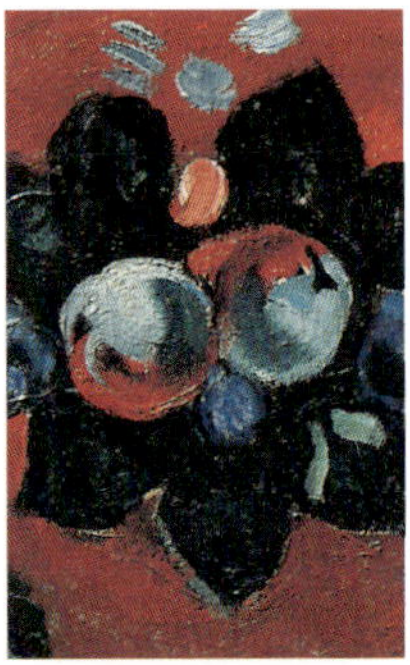

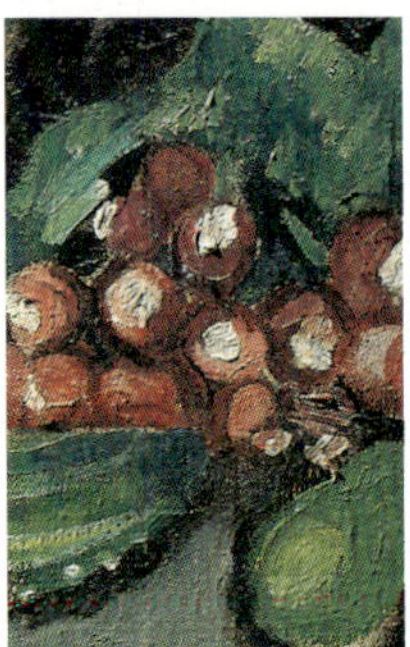

Like his other paintings, his flowers are drawn by colour which gives them their strength, and this is reinforced by the violence of contrasts. His great freedom of expression is organised around colour. In his own words:

Tray and Vegetables

Pyotr Konchalovsky, 1910
Oil on canvas, 73 x 92 cm
Russian Museum, Saint Petersburg

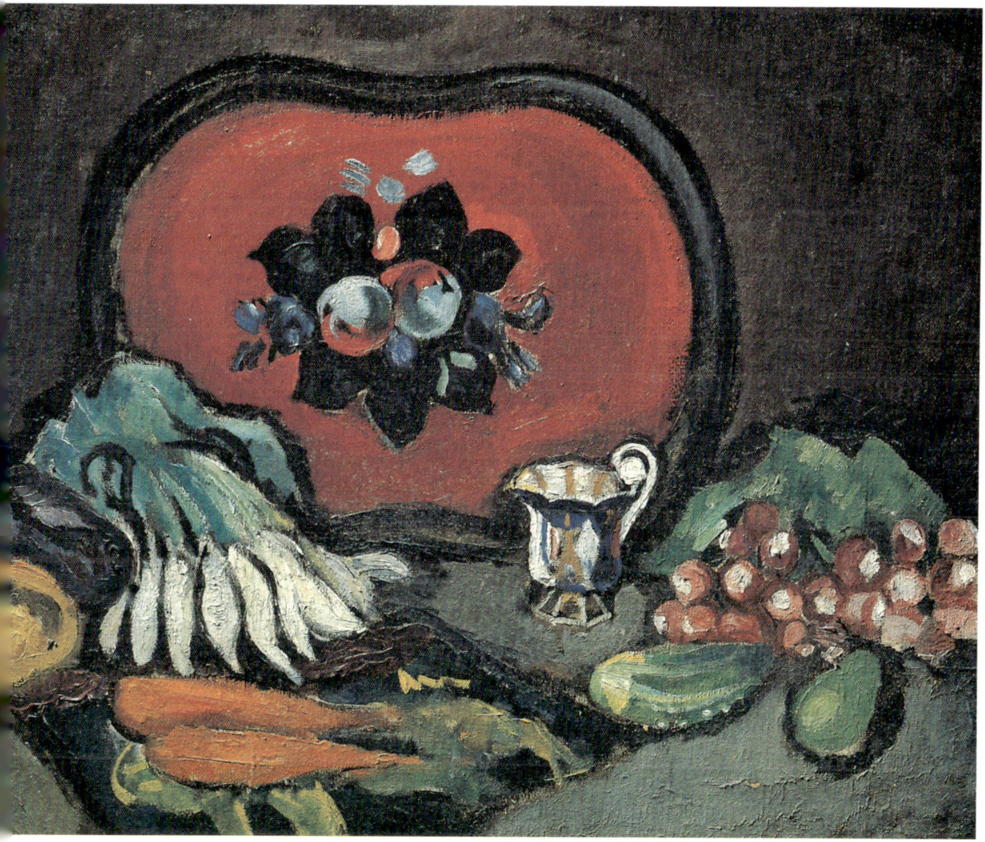

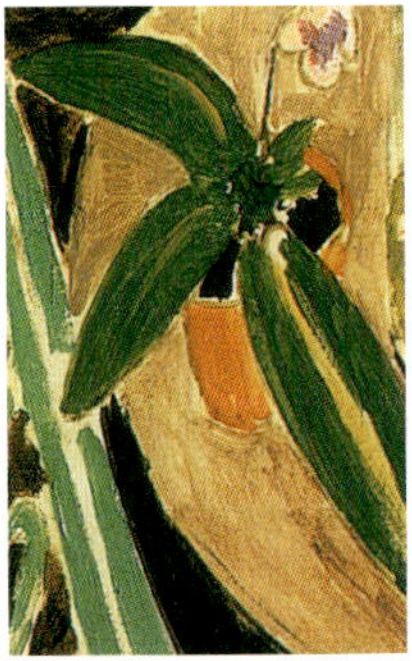

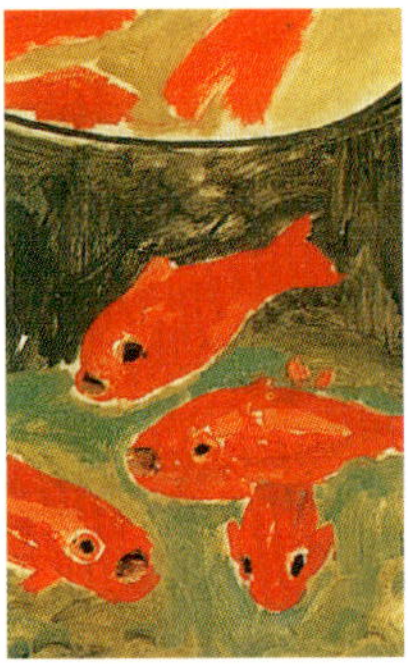

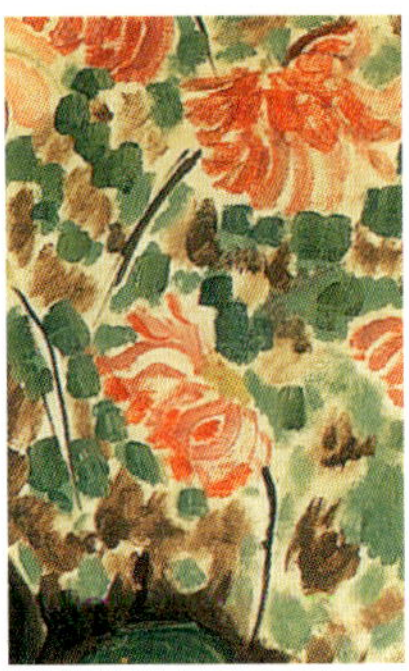

"An avalanche of colour remains without strength. Colour only reaches its full expression when it is organised and when it corresponds to the intensity of the artist's emotion". Matisse, the artist of colour and decoration, delighted in painting serene and joyful pictures, based on

Goldfish

Henri Matisse, 1911
Oil on canvas, 147 x 98 cm
Pushkin Museum of Fine Arts, Moscow

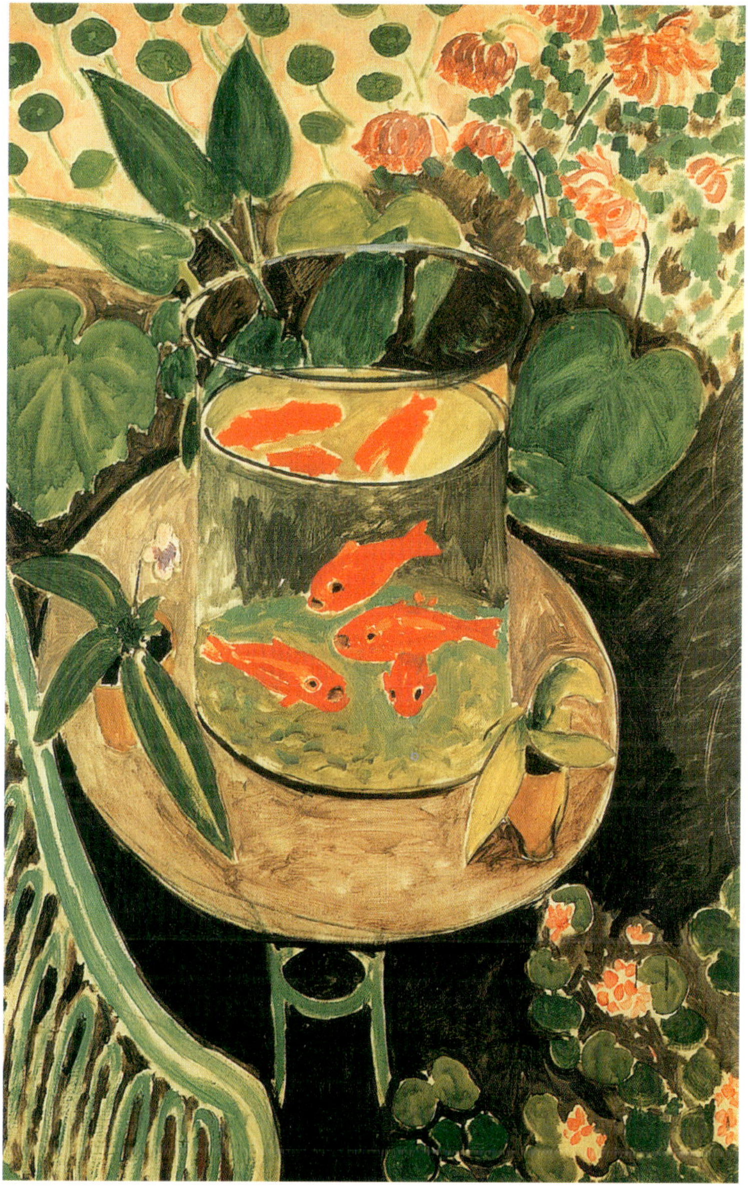

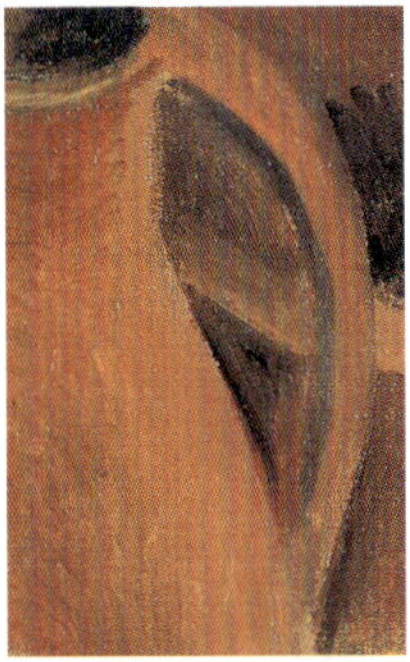
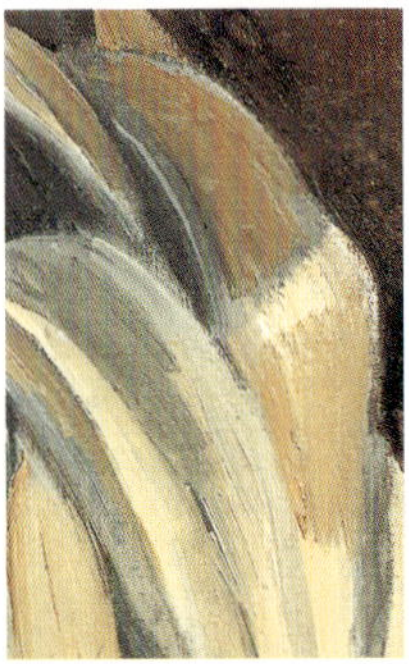
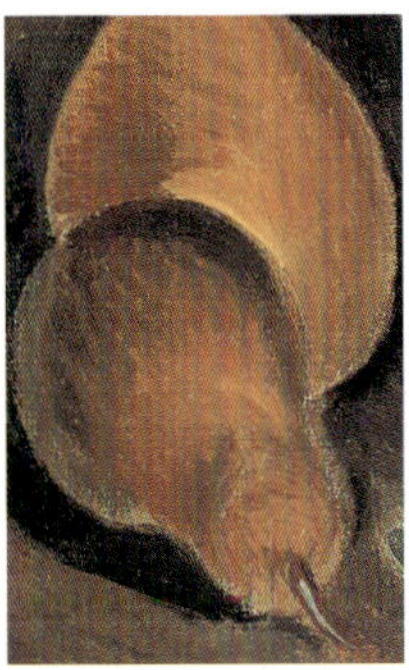

the use of bright and wonderful colours. He was a member of the group that was dubbed "Les Fauves" (literally, "the wild beasts") because of the extremes of emotionalism in which they indulged their use of vivid colours, and their distortion of shapes.

Still Life. Earthen Jug, White Napkin

André Derain, c. 1911
Oil on canvas, 60 x 49 cm
The Hermitage, Saint Petersburg

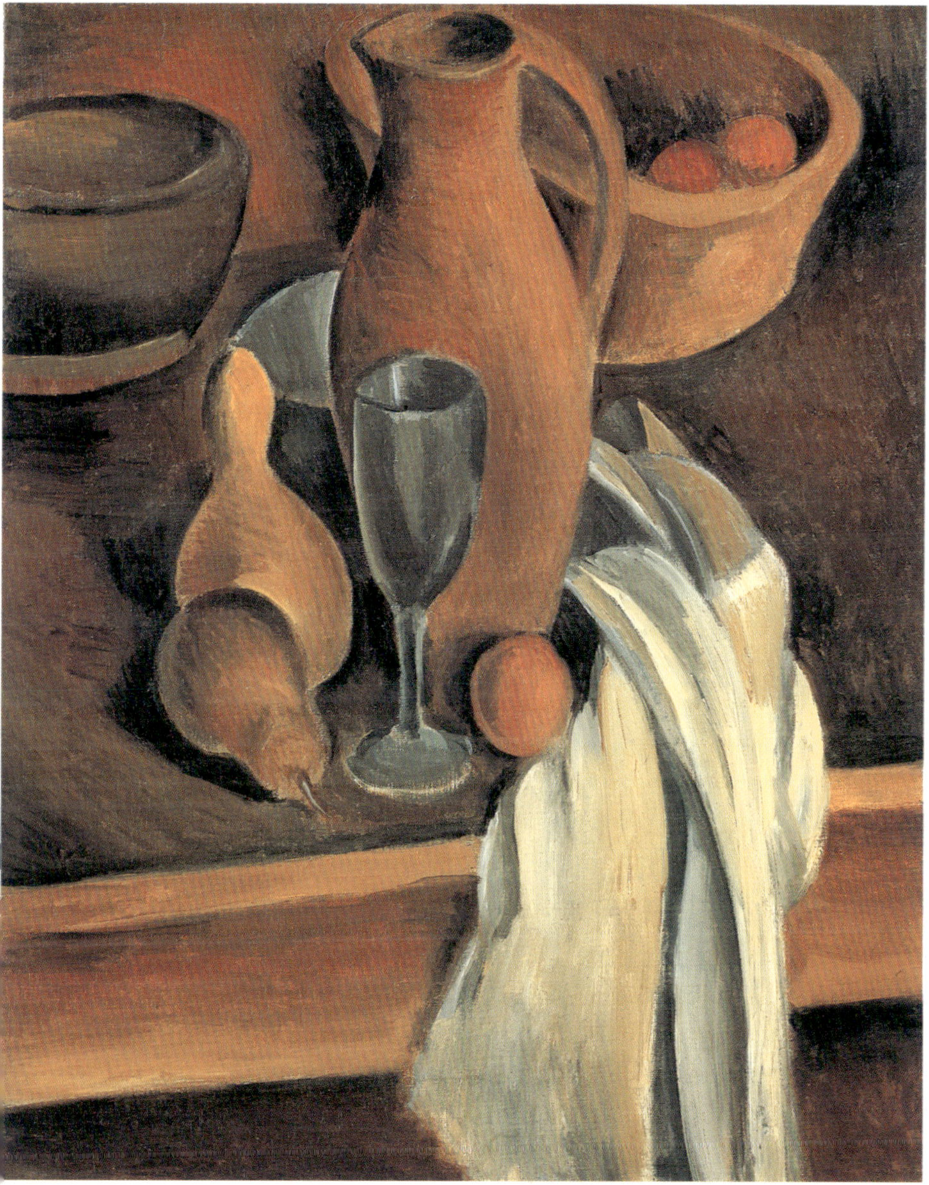

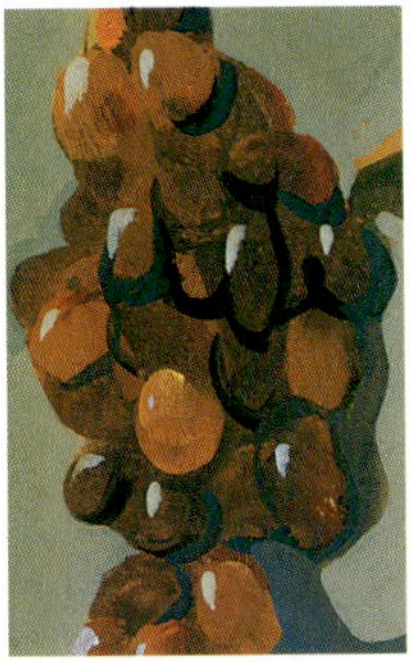

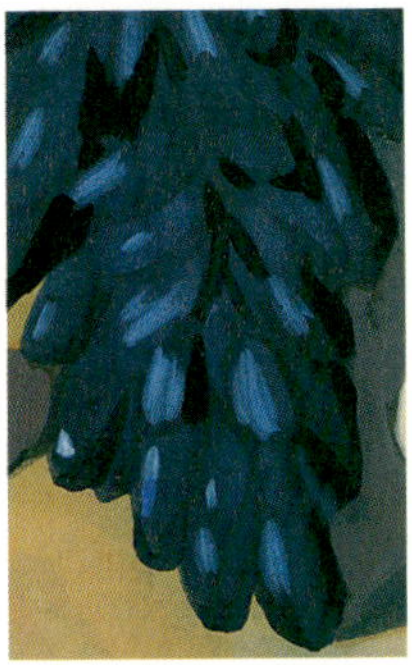

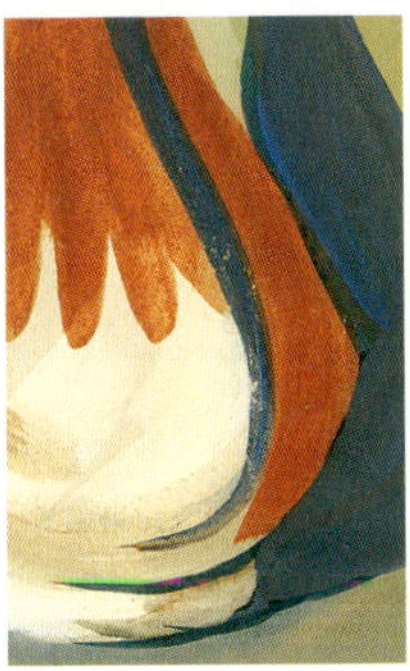

Still, while Matisse may not have considered himself a Fauvist, he always acknowledged the movement's importance. In the 19th century, the genre of still life was considered inferior to the elaborate historical paintings.

Still Life. Grapes

Martiros Saryan, 1911
tempera on board, 43.5 x 64 cm
Tretyakov Gallery, Moscow

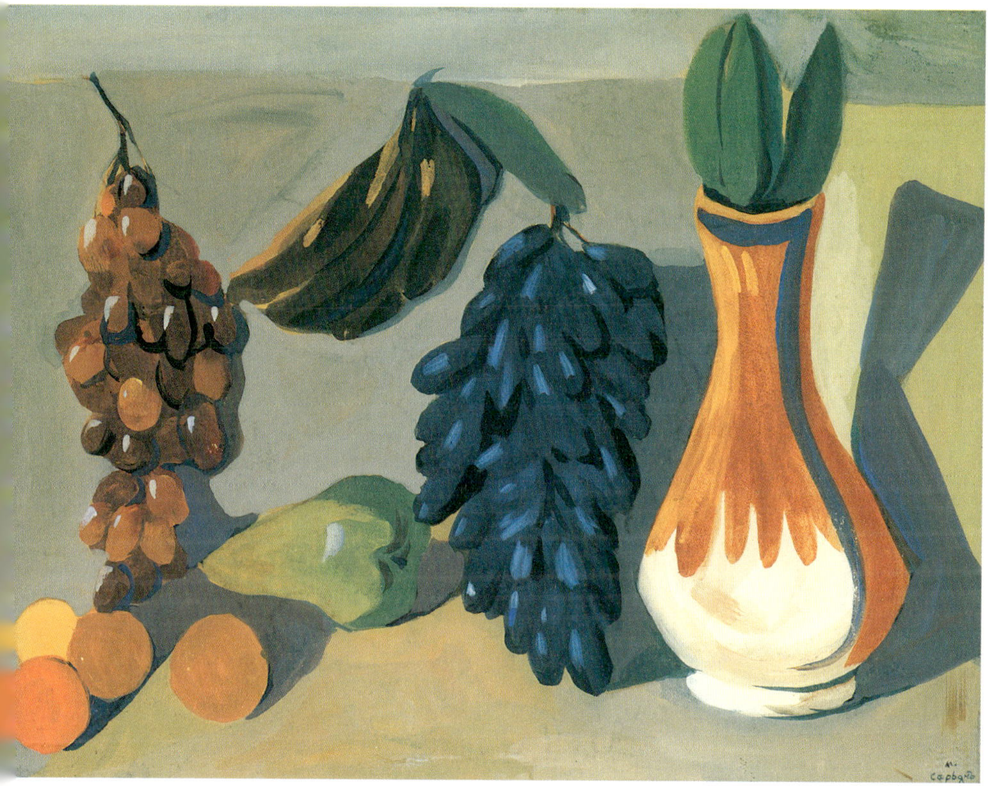

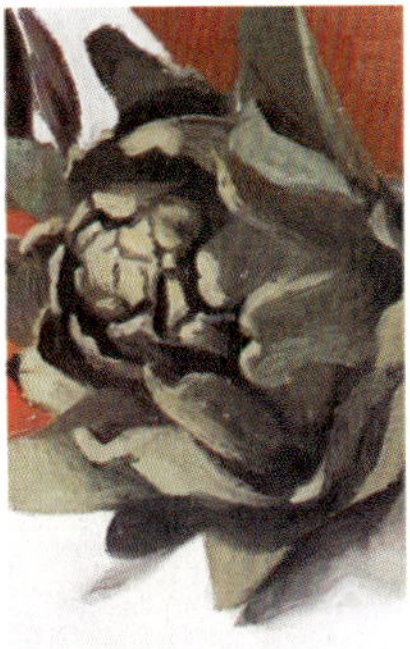

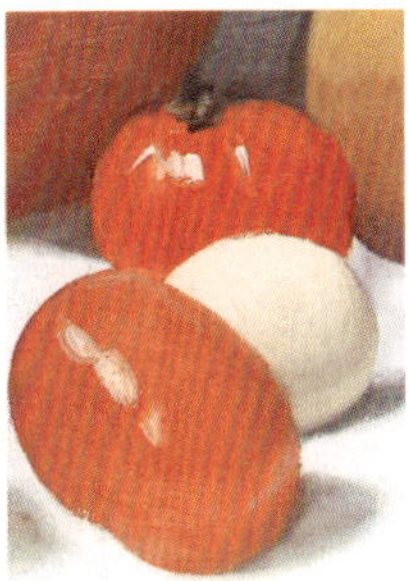

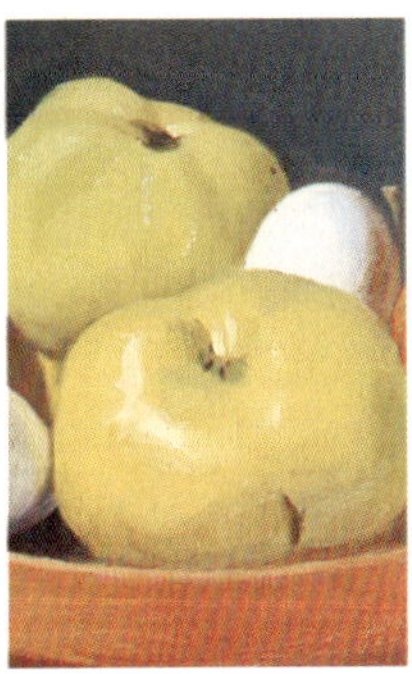

The Impressionists changed all this, allowing Matisse to paint still lifes boldly and freely. He once said: "Exactitude is not truth". His goal was total pictorial harmony and absolute essence. His "Goldfish in a bowl", for example, is the absolute essence of a fish.

Still Life with Tomatoes

Félix Vallotton, 1911
Oil on canvas, 66 x 81 cm
M.C.B.A. Lausanne

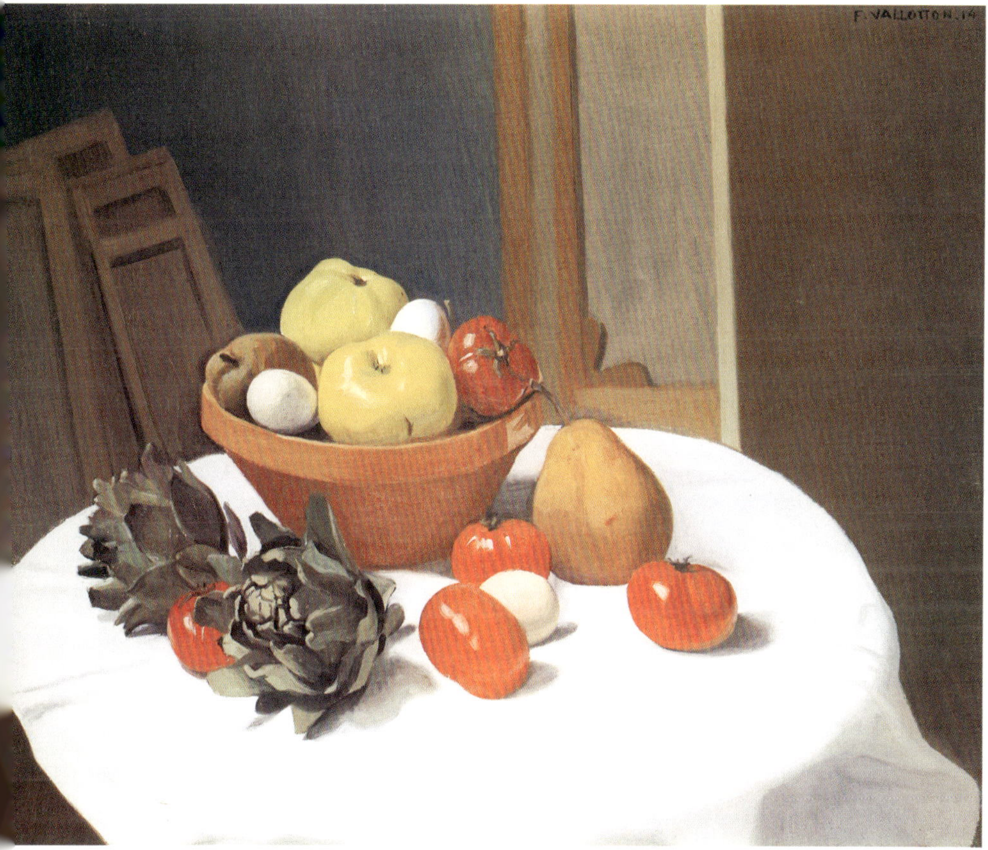
F. VALLOTTON.14

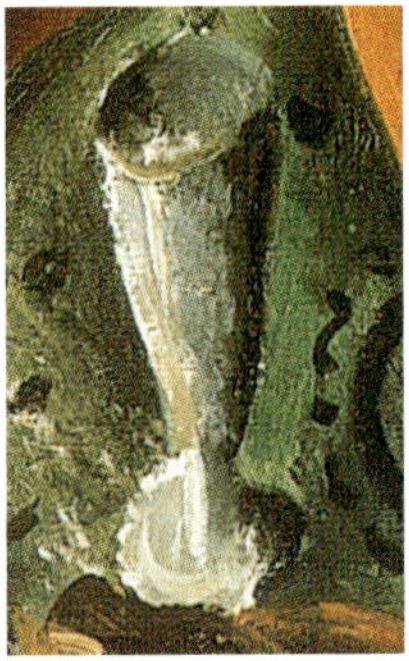

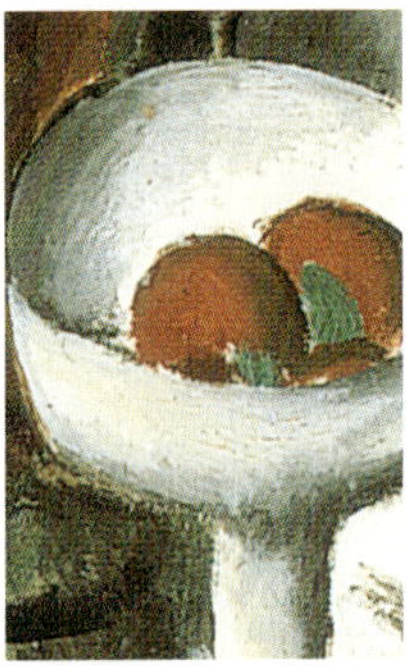

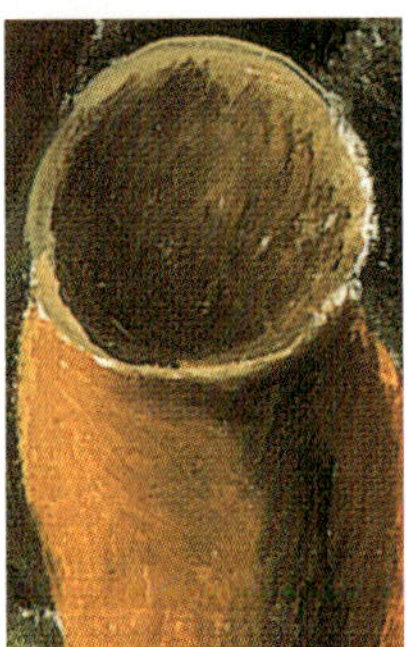

Matisse's work is neat and careful. His goldfish are goldfish and his lemons are lemons. He paints the joy of flowers and fruits but above all he paints colour. Matisse's "Still Life with a Magnolia" is a luscious reaffirmation and celebration of life.

Table and Chairs

André Derain, c.1912
Oil on canvas, 87 x 85.5 cm
The Hermitage, Saint Petersburg

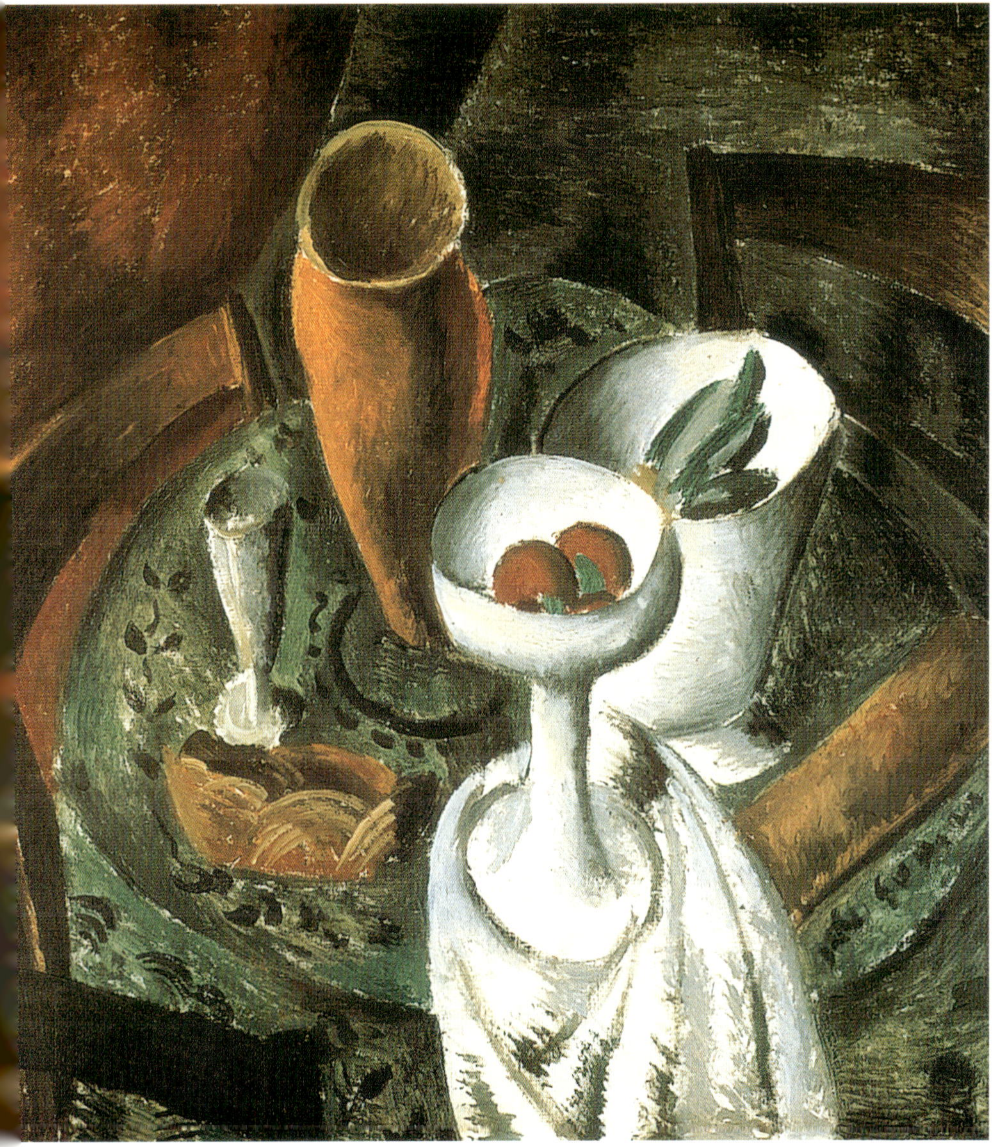

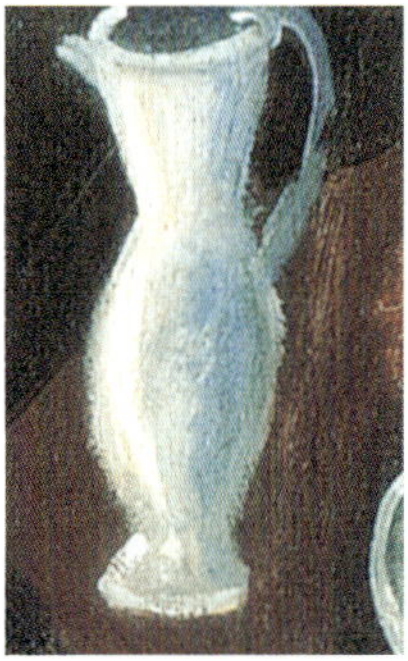

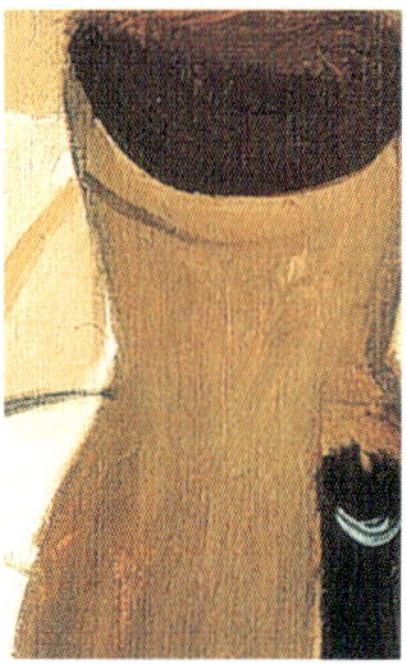

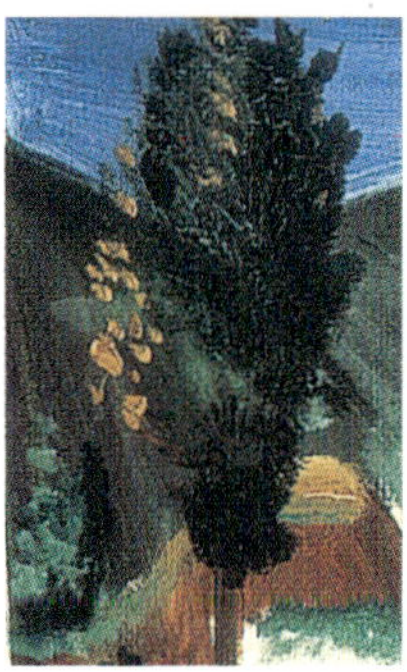

Henri Matisse embodies a style and a personality that has become almost synonymous with words like bright and radiant but his supreme achievement, which may be seen in all his work, was to liberate colour from its traditional realistic function and to make it the foundation of a decorative art of the highest order.

Still Life in Front of the Window

André Derain, 1912-13
Oil on canvas, 128 x 79 cm
Pushkin Museum of Fine Arts, Moscow

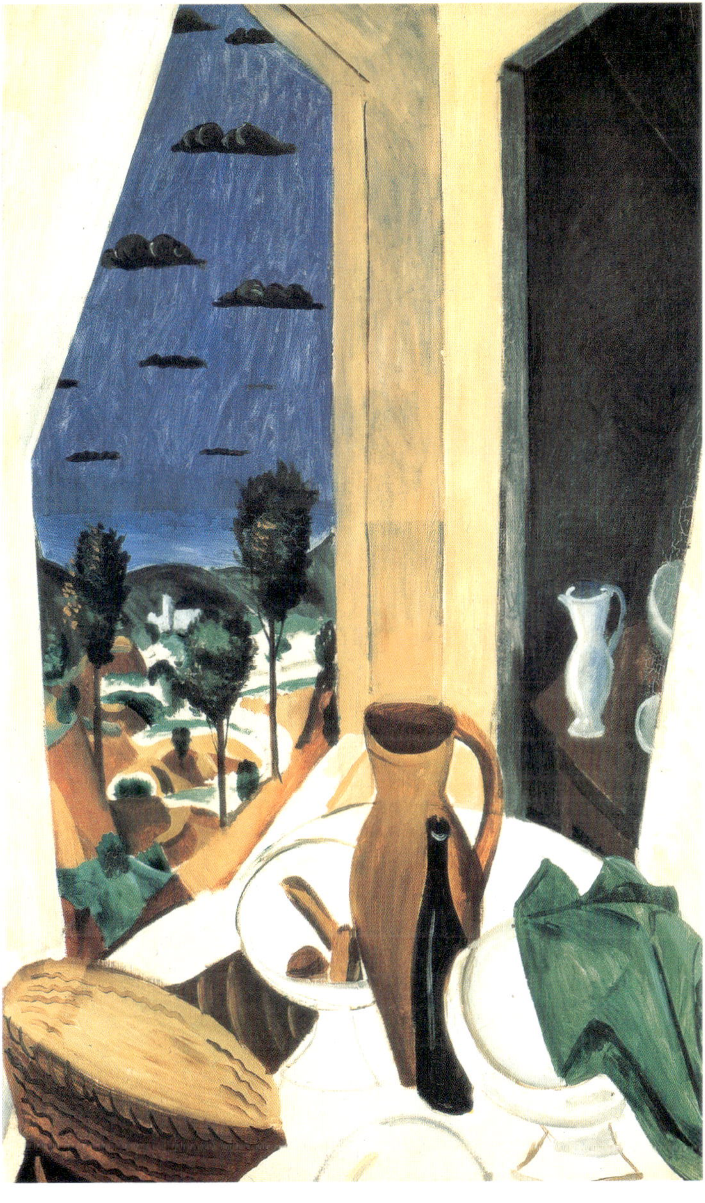

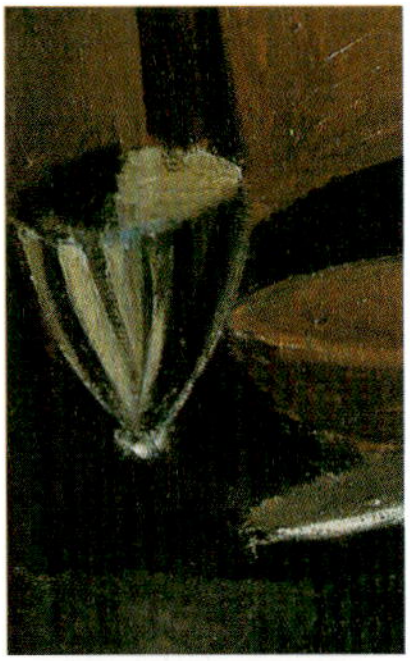

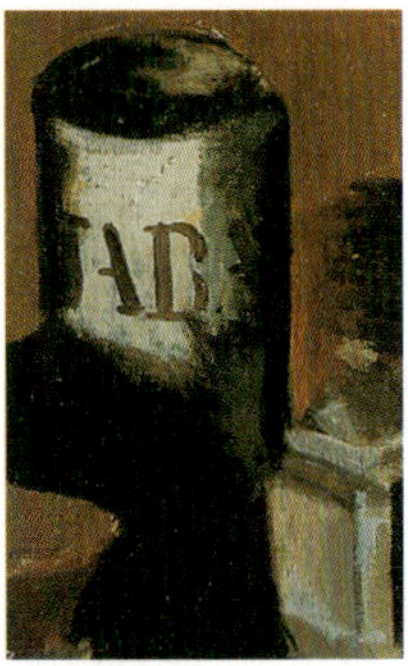

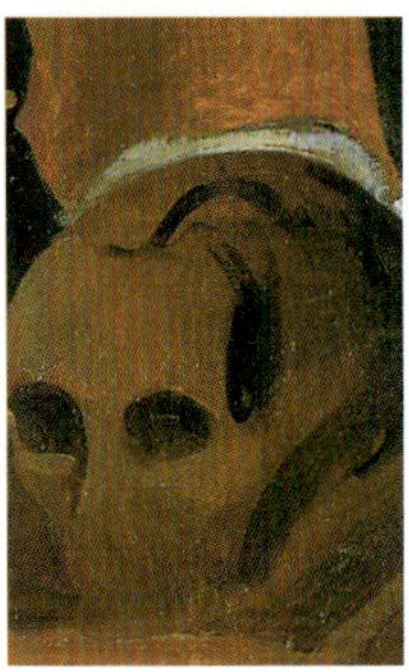

Igor Grabar (1871-1960)

Born in Budapest in 1871. Both Igor Grabar and Konstantin Korovin produced delightful still lifes in the Impressionist idiom, such as *The Uncleared Table* and *The Blue Tablecloth*. Grabar died in Moscow in 1960.

Still Life with Skull

André Derain, c. 1912
Oil on canvas, 72 x 119 cm
The Hermitage, Saint Petersburg

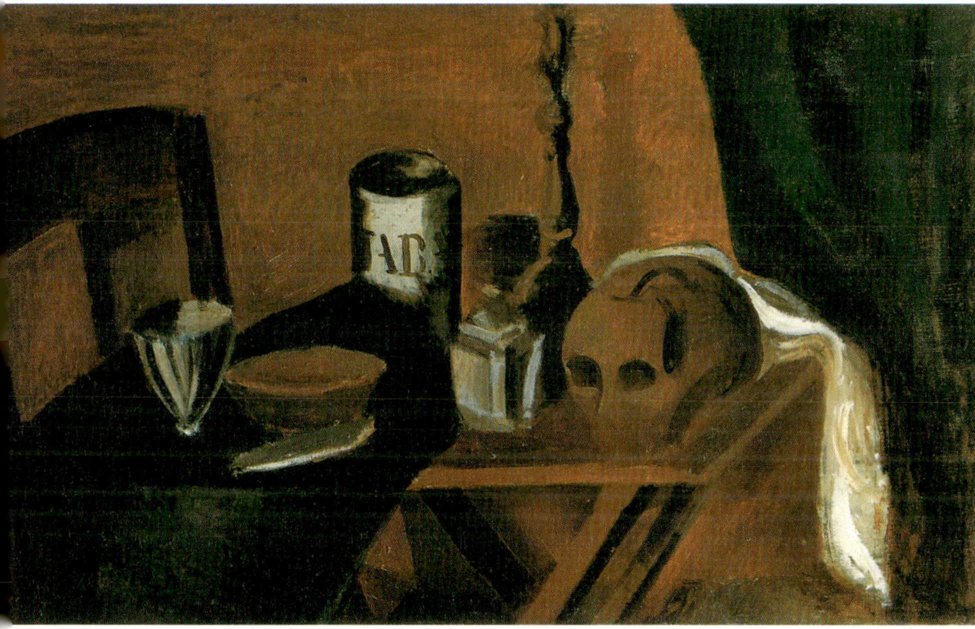
AB

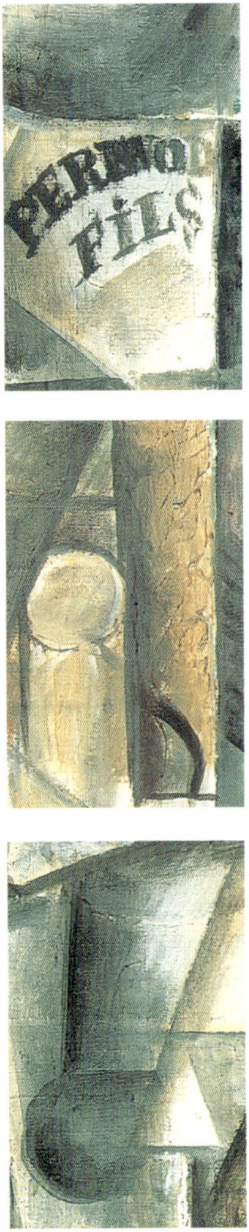

Kuzma Petrov-Vodkin (1878-1939)

Quite different from any of these were the still lifes of Kuzma Petrov-Vodkin, who became an influential theorist and teacher. At the time of the formation of the Blue Rose group he was working in North Africa (which had an impact on his treatment of light and the human figure), but he was able to participate in the *Golden Fleece* exhibitions.

A Table in a Café
(A Bottle of Pernod)

Pablo Picasso, 1912
Oil on canvas, 45.5 x 32.5 cm
The Hermitage, St. Petersburg

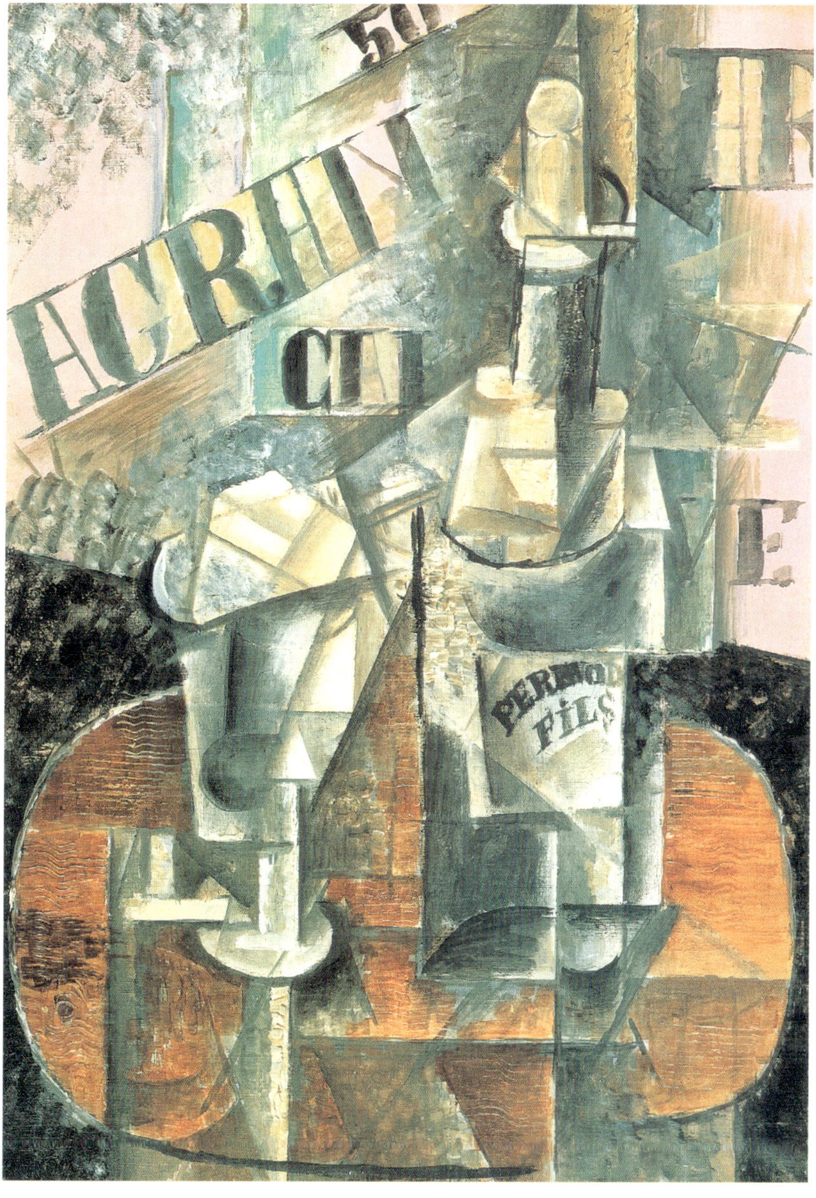

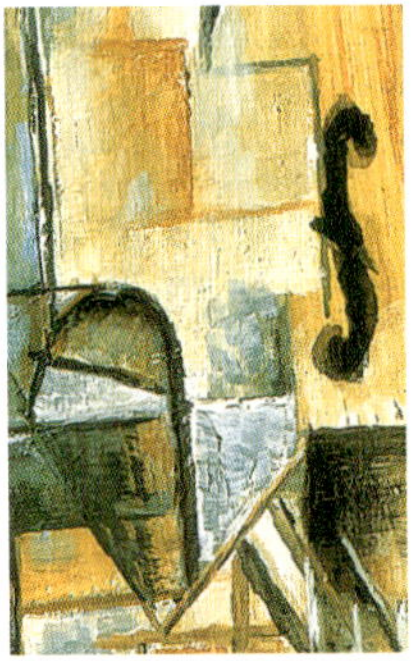

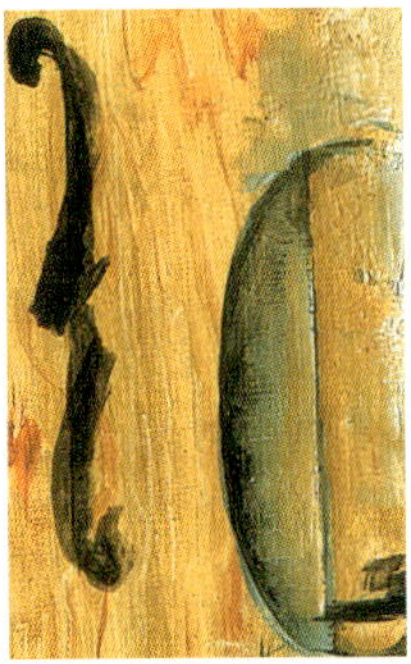

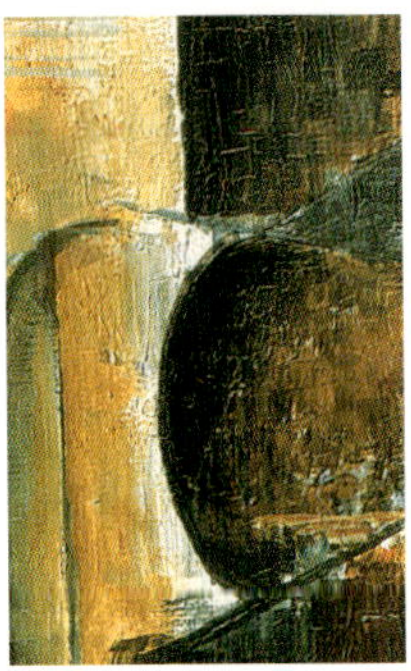

According to Petrov-Vodkin, "the new way of looking at things is markedly an absence of vertical and horizontal lines". Many of his later paintings are notable for their "spherical perspective", but in *Morning Still Life* the intriguing tension of the composition derives from his use of "tilted space".

Violin

Pablo Picasso, 1912
Oil on canvas, 55 x 46 cm
The Pushkin Museum of Fine Arts, Moscow

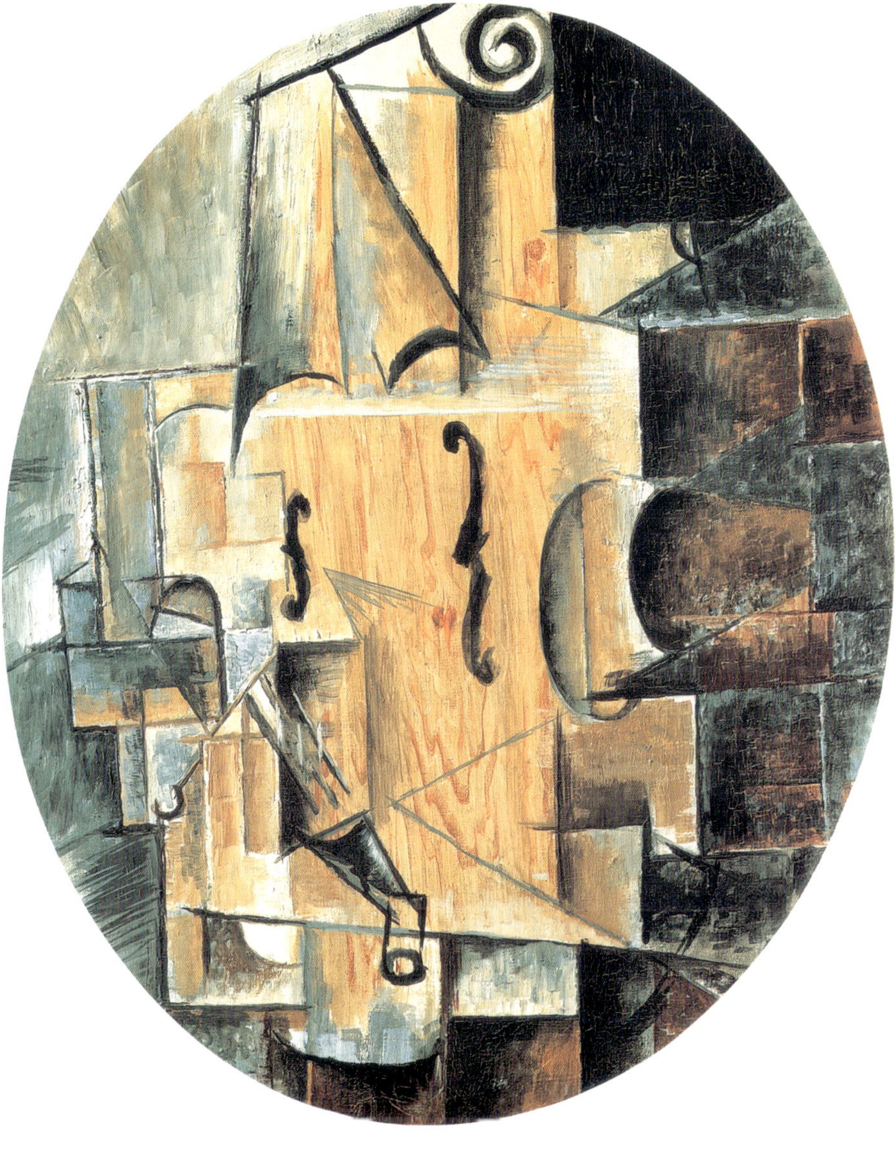

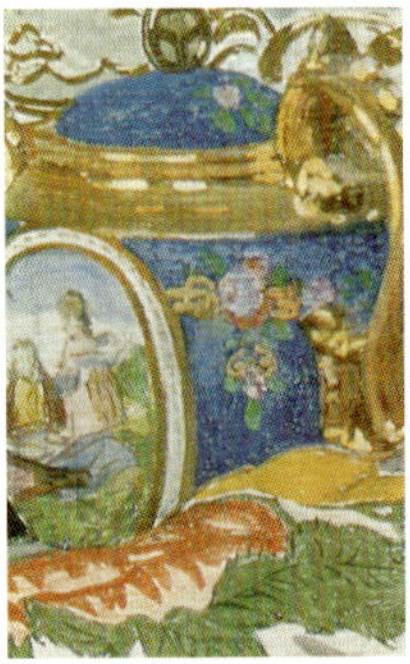

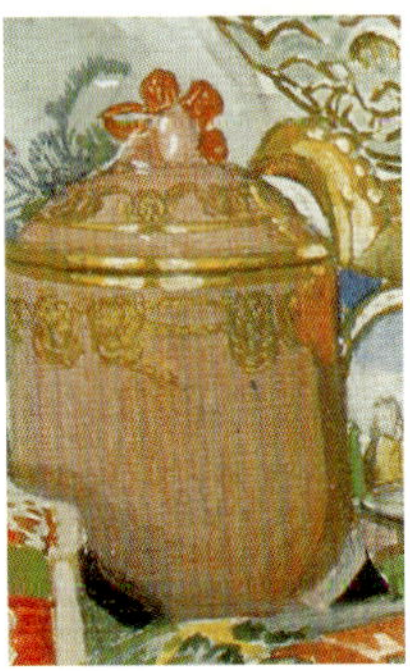

Othon Friesz (1879-1949)

Othon Friesz was born in 1879. He followed courses at the Havre School of Fine Arts where he became friendly with Raoul Dufy. Friesz produced, though not exclusively, a great number of floral portraits.

Still Life with Flowers and China

Alexander Golovin, 1912
tempera on plywood, 88.5 x 70.5 cm
Brodsky Memorial Museum, Saint Petersburg

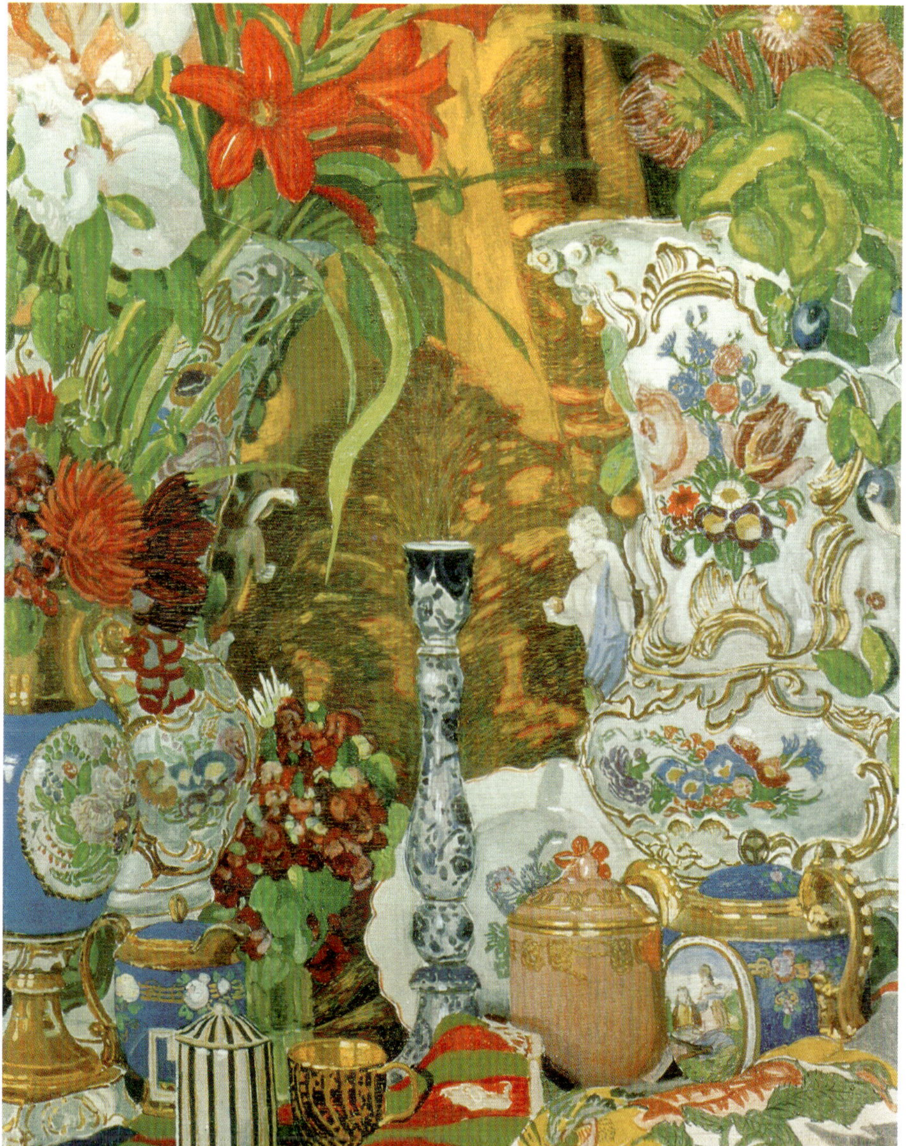

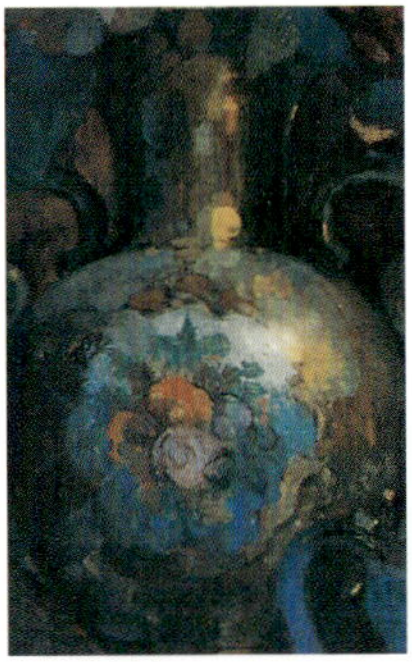

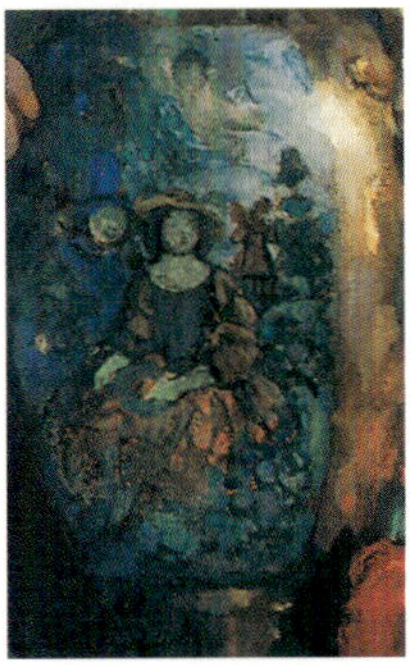

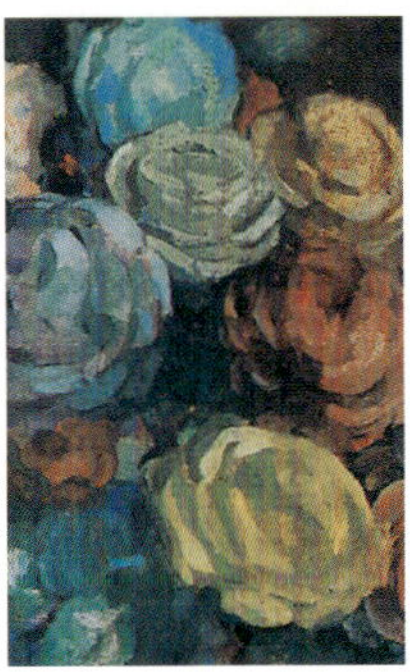

At the beginning of his career Friesz was closely involved in the Fauve movement in which the orchestration of pure colour plays the most important role, and then he evolved towards something more structured, a move probably inspired by Cézanne.

Still Life with Vase, Flowers and Fruit

Nikolai Sapunov, 1912
tempera on canvas, 147.2 x 115.8 cm
Tretyakov Gallery, Moscow

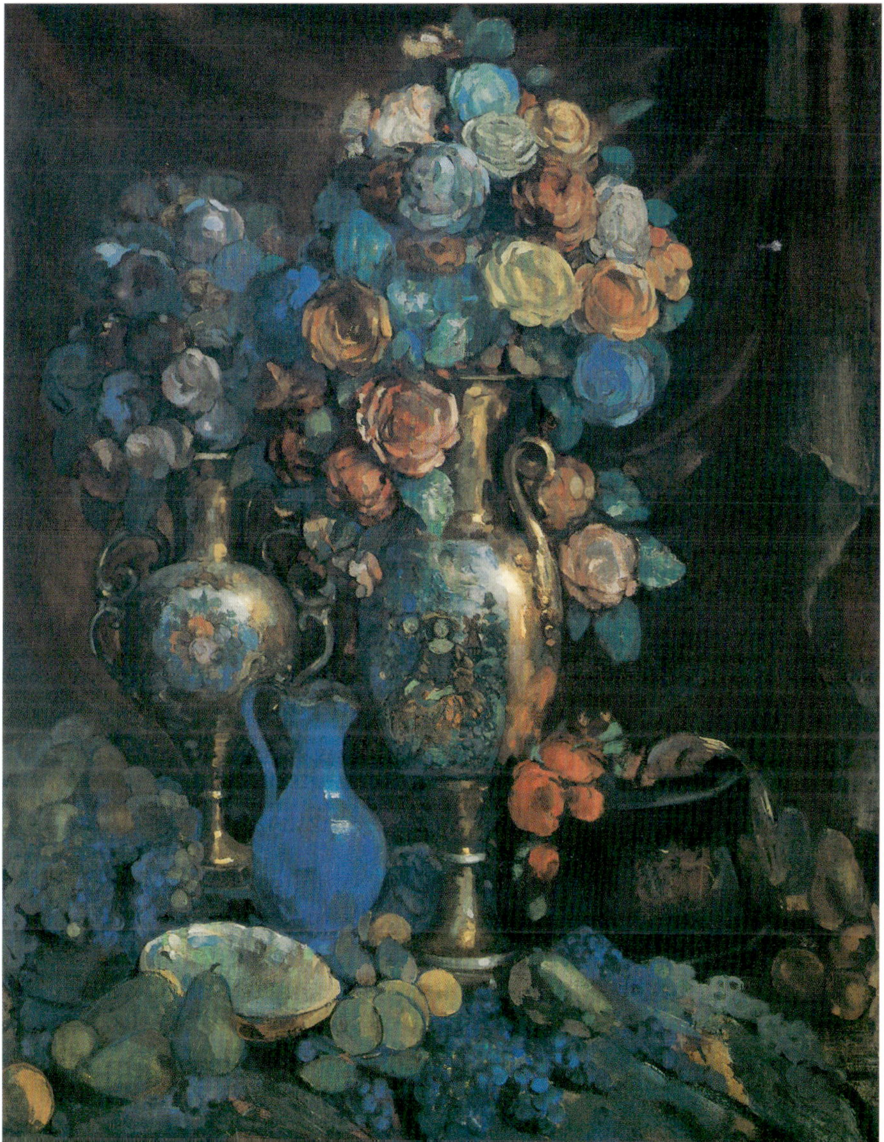

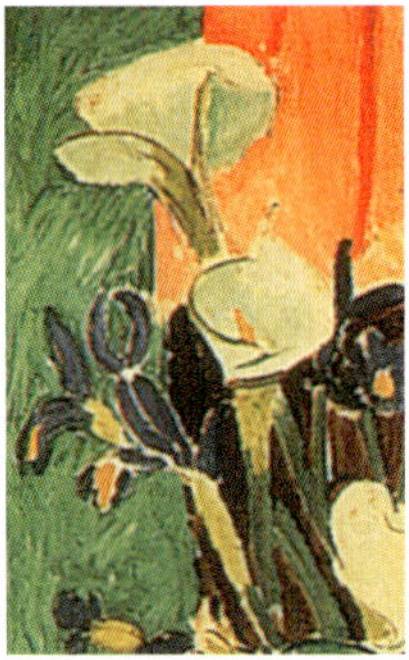

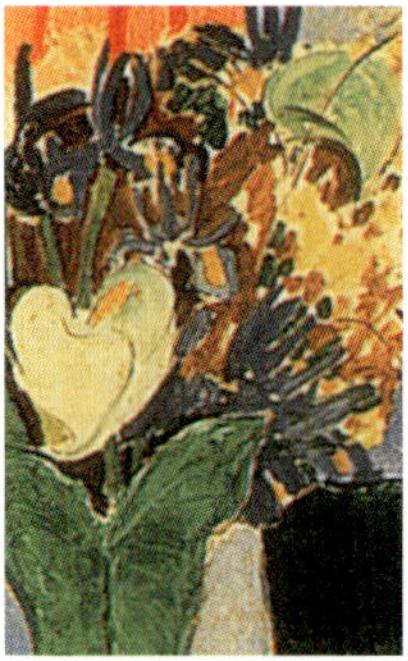

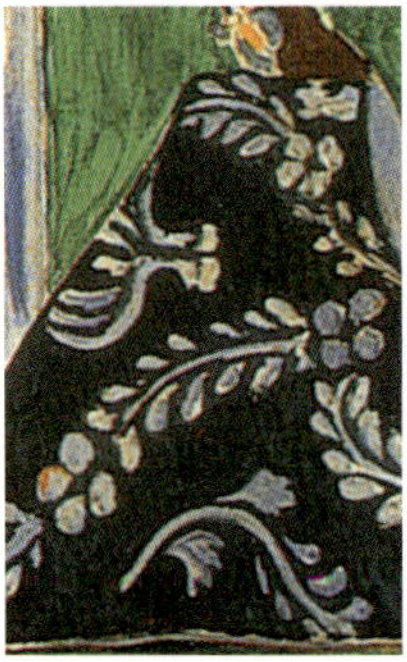

His pallet became more muted (he used mainly ochres, browns, greens and blues), the lines are rigid and the shapes were outlined thickly. His paintings are based on the direct observation of what is real to which he adds the necessary modifications for expressing personal feelings. Othon Friesz died in Paris in 1949.

Still Life. Arum Lilies, Iris, and Mimosa

Henri Matisse, 1913
Oil on canvas, 147 x 98 cm
Pushkin Museum of Fine Arts, Moscow

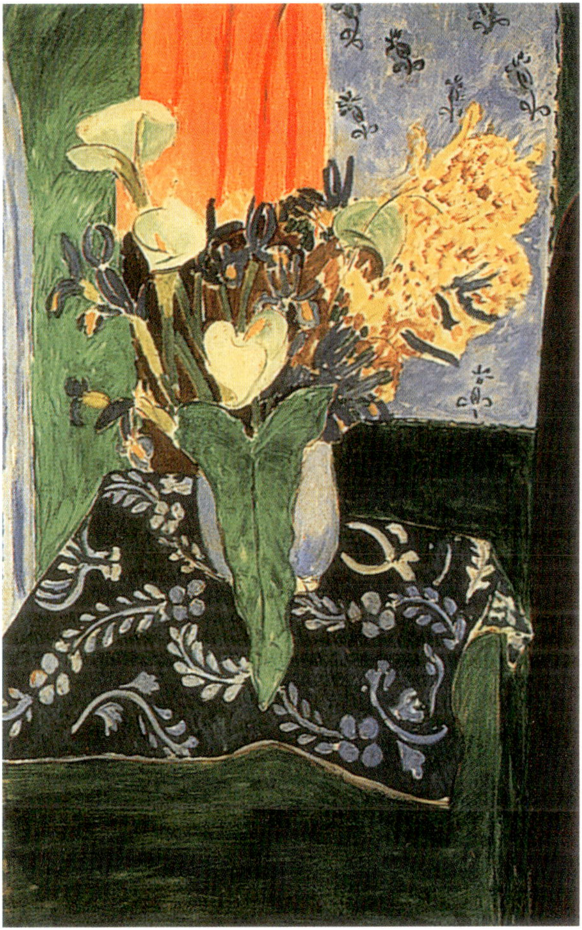

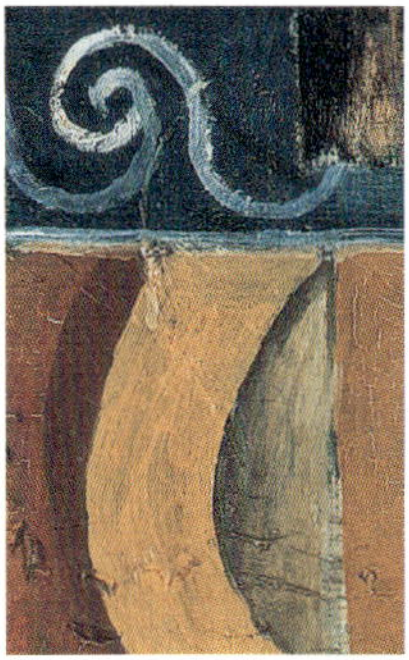

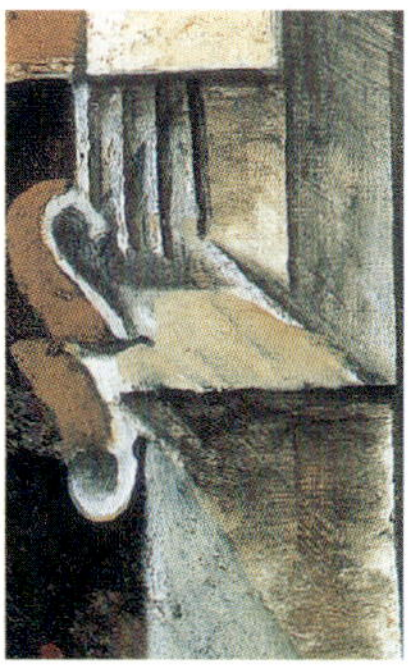

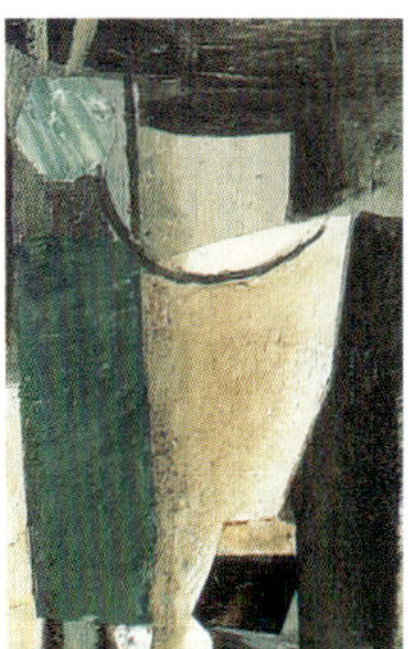

Alexander Kuprin (1880-1960)

He was a painter and graphic artist, and he studied at the Voronezh School of Painting and Drawing (1896), the school of Painting and Drawing of Lew Dmitriyev-Kavkazsky in St. Petersburg (1902-04), the school of Konstantin Yuon in Moscow (1904-05), and the Moscow

Violin and Guitar

Pablo Picasso, 1913
Oil on canvas, 65 x 54 cm
The Hermitage, Saint Petersburg

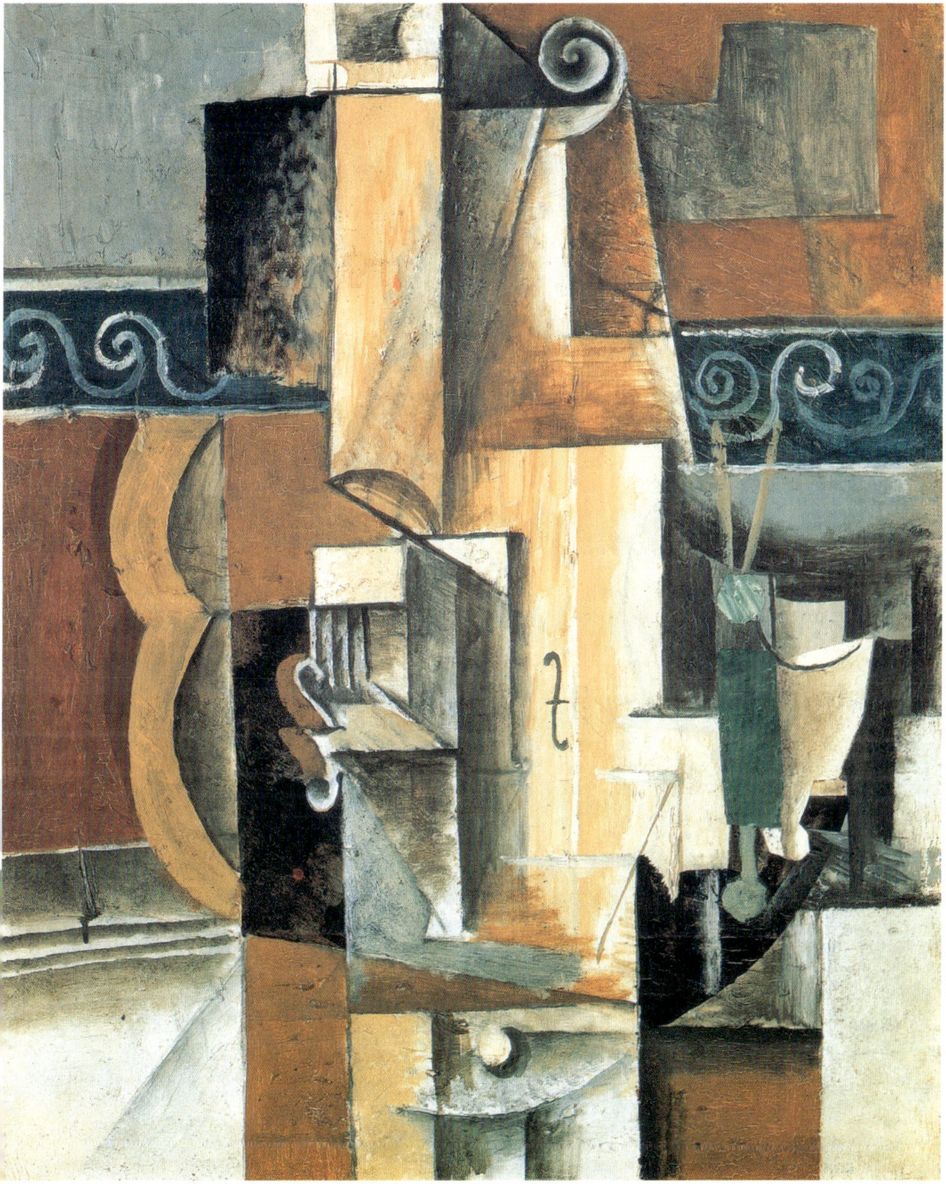

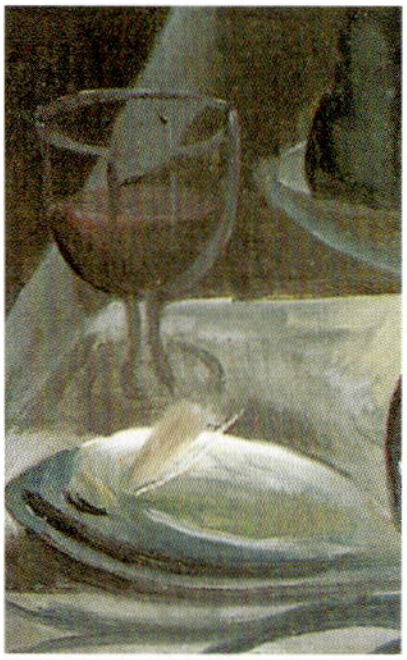

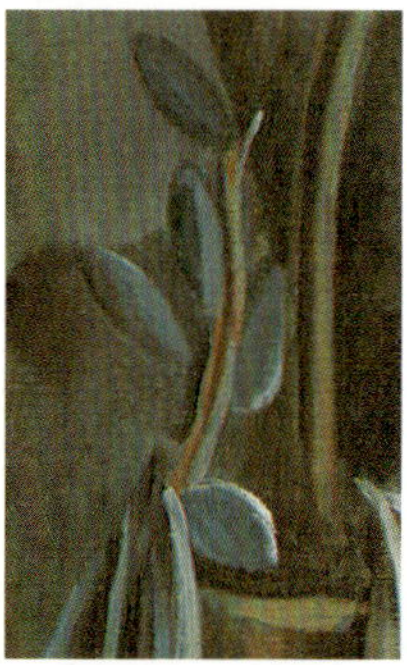

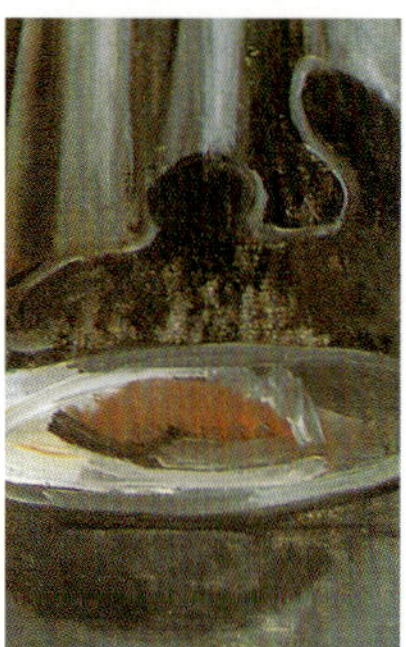

Institute of Painting, Sculpture and Architecture (1906-10) under Konstantin Korovin, Nicolai Kasatkin, Leonid Pasternak, and Abram Arkhipov. Kuprin participates in exhibitions from 1906.

Still Life

André Derain, c. 1913
Oil on canvas, 100.5 x 118 cm
The Hermitage, Saint Petersburg

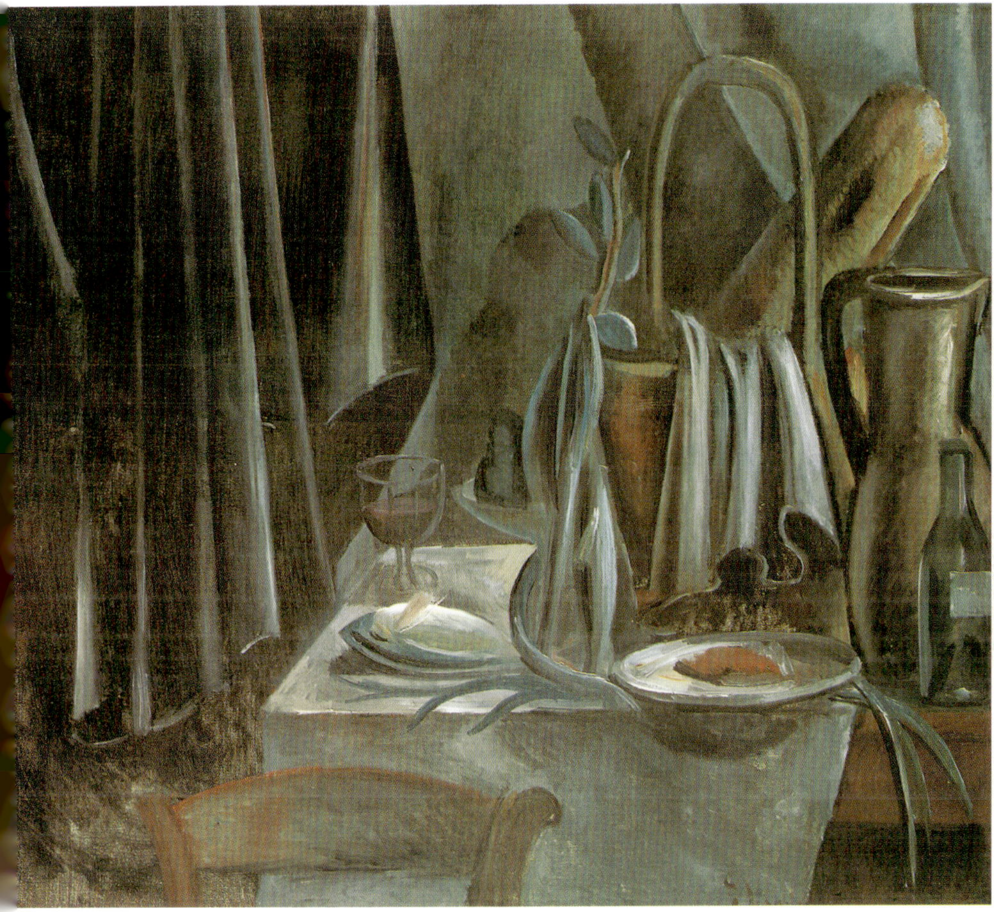

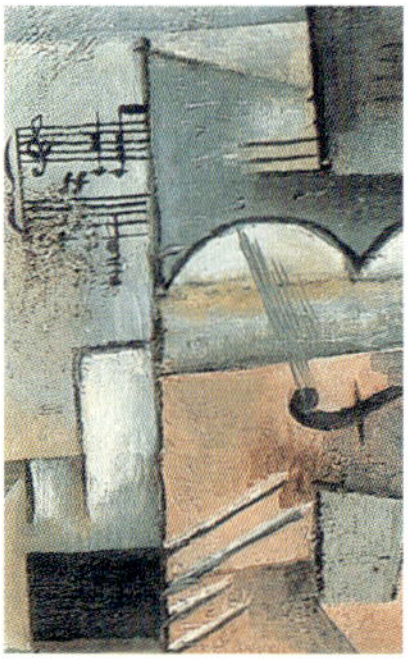

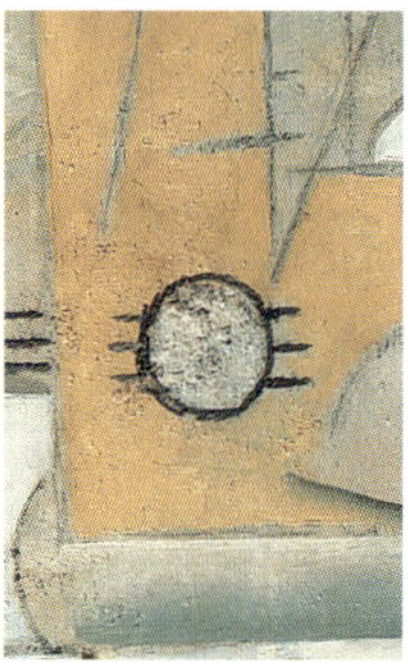

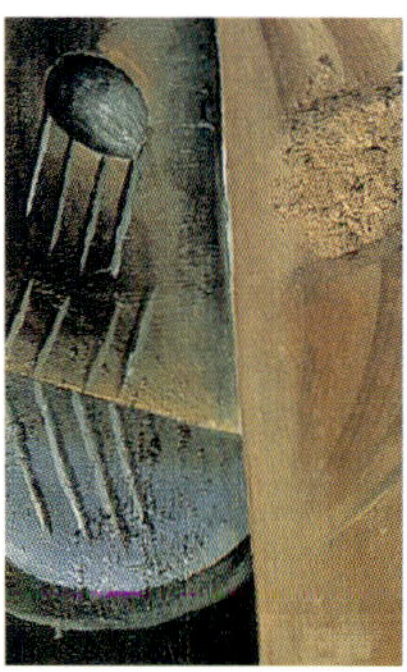

At the Knave of Diamonds exhibitions bolder experimental styles were in evidence – discernible influences ranging from Matisse and Cézanne to Primitivism, Expressionism and various types of Cubism.

Musical Instruments

Pablo Picasso, 1913
oilcloth, ripoline, oil, plaster
wood shavings, 98 x 80 cm
The Hermitage, Saint Petersburg

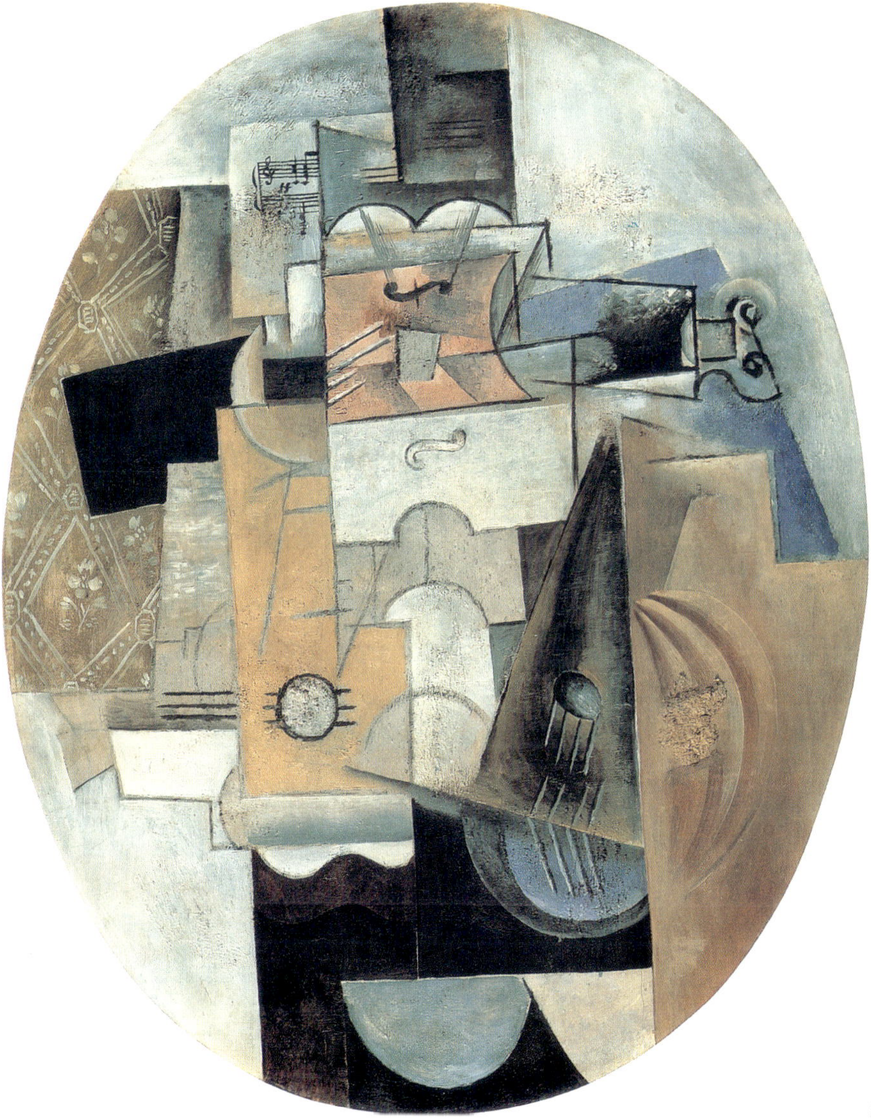

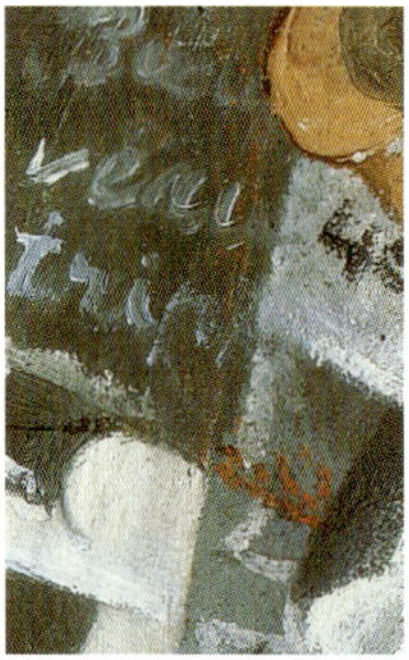

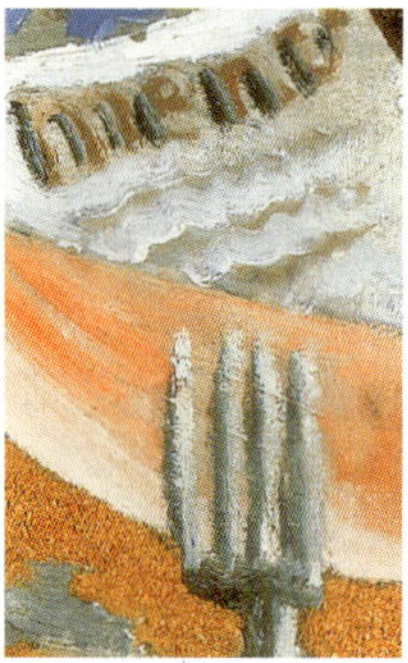

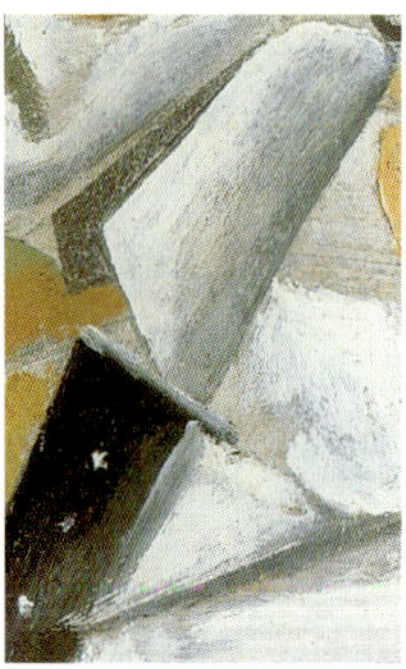

Four of the most active founder members of the group were Alexander Kuprin, Pyotr Konchalovsky (1876-1956), Ilya Mahkov (1881-1944) and Robert Falk (1886-1958). All four produced still lifes that played with colour and form.

Tavern (The Ham)

Pablo Picasso, c.1914
oil and sawdust on cardboard
29.5 x 38 cm (oval)
The Hermitage, St Petersburg

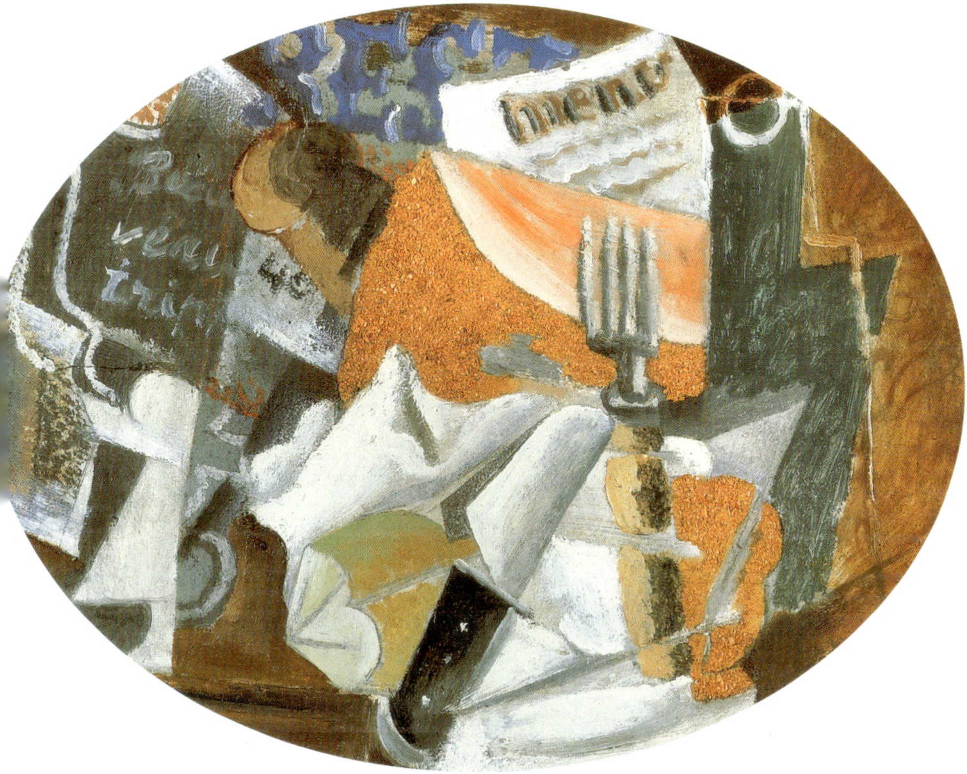

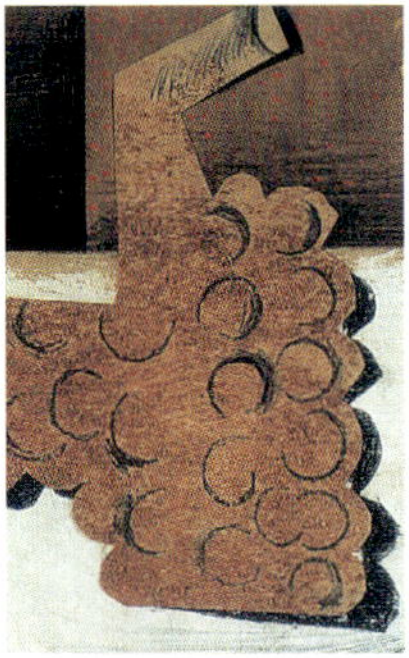

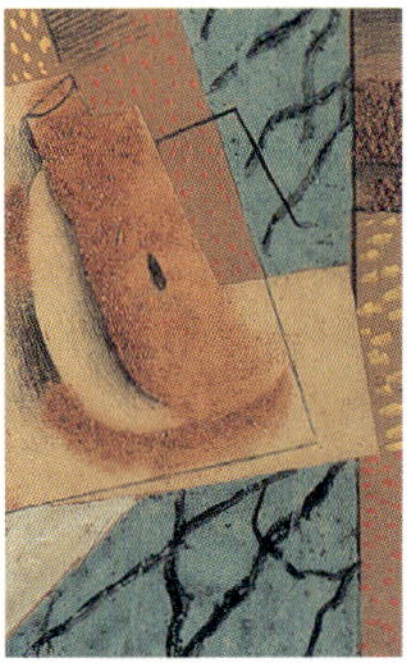

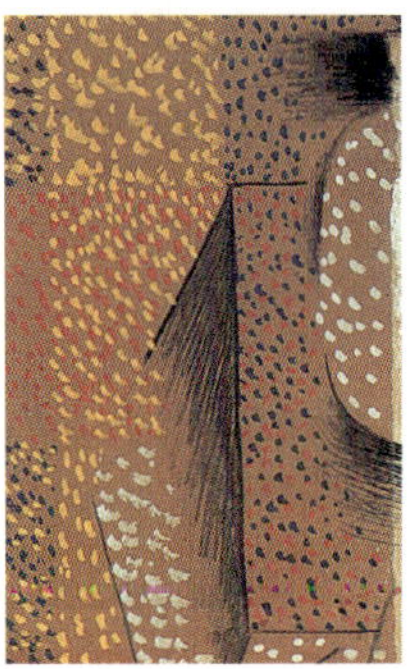

This creative playfulness resulted in pictures like the ones by Kuprin and Konchalovsky. Many of Mashkov's still lifes feature fruit or loaves – sometimes stylized and sometimes so realistic that they are almost palpable.

Fruit Vase and Bunch of Grapes

Pablo Picasso, 1914
paper, gouache, tempera
sawdust and pencil on cardboard
67.7 x 57.2 cm
The Hermitage, Saint Petersburg

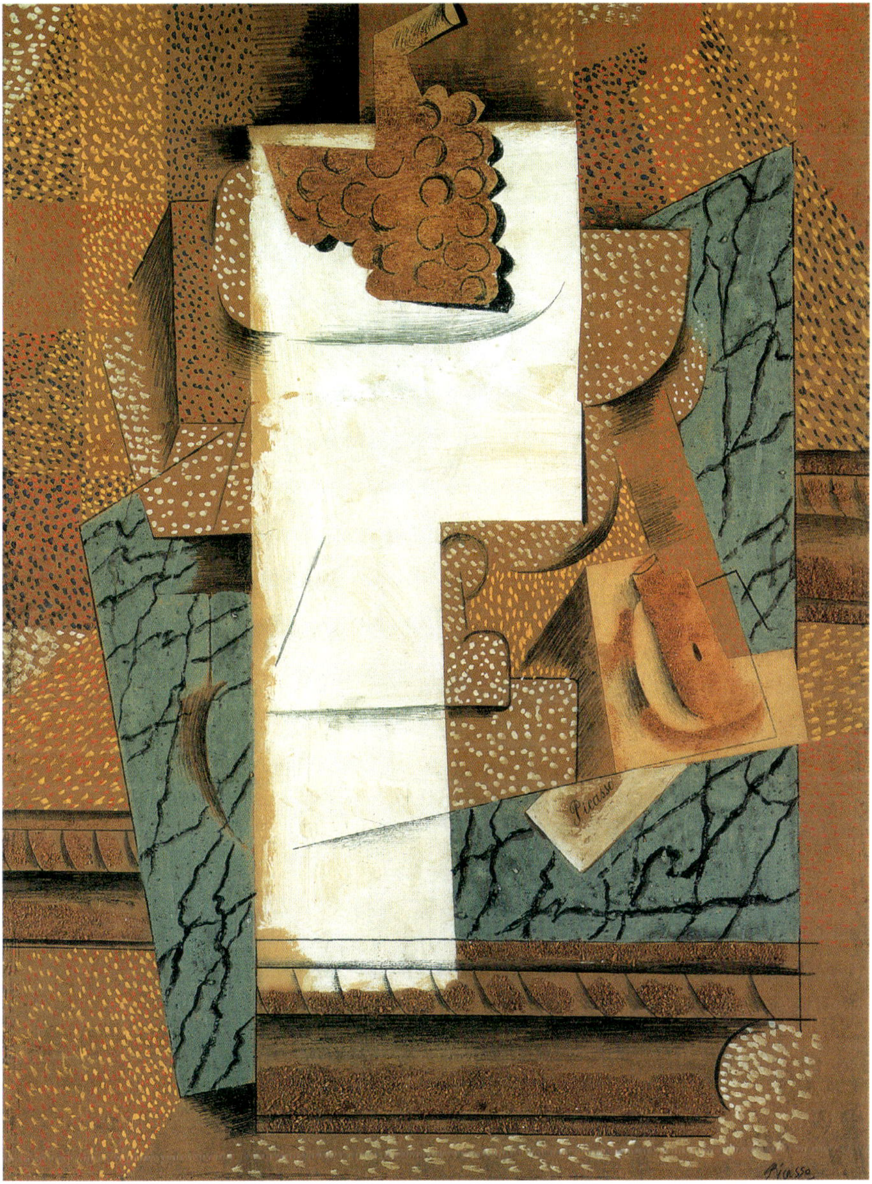
Picasso
Picasso

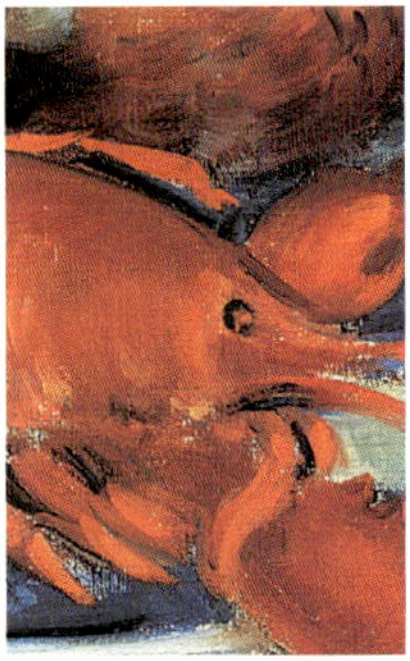

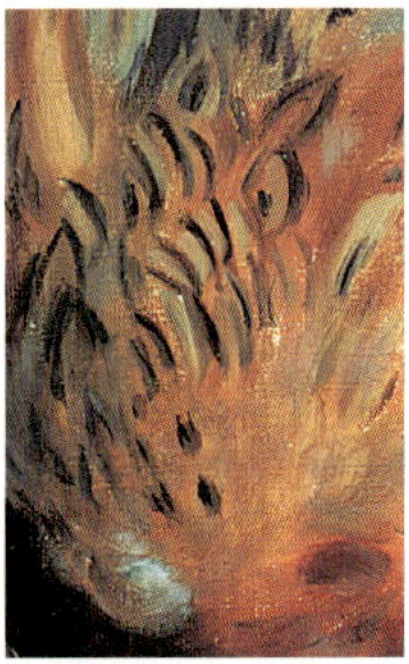

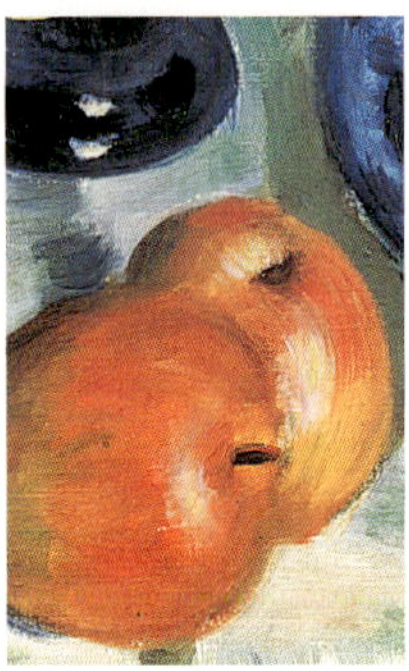

He was engaged in pedagogical work as an assistant to Korovin at the Free Art Studios in Moscow, and taught at the art studios in Nizhni Novgorod and Sormovo (1920-22), at the Moscow Textile Institute (1928-32), and Stroganov School (1946-52). He lived and worked in Moscow from 1904 until his died in 1916.

Still Life with Pheasants

Boris Kustodiev, 1914
Oil on canvas, 41 x 40 cm
Kustodiev Picture Gallery, Astrakhan

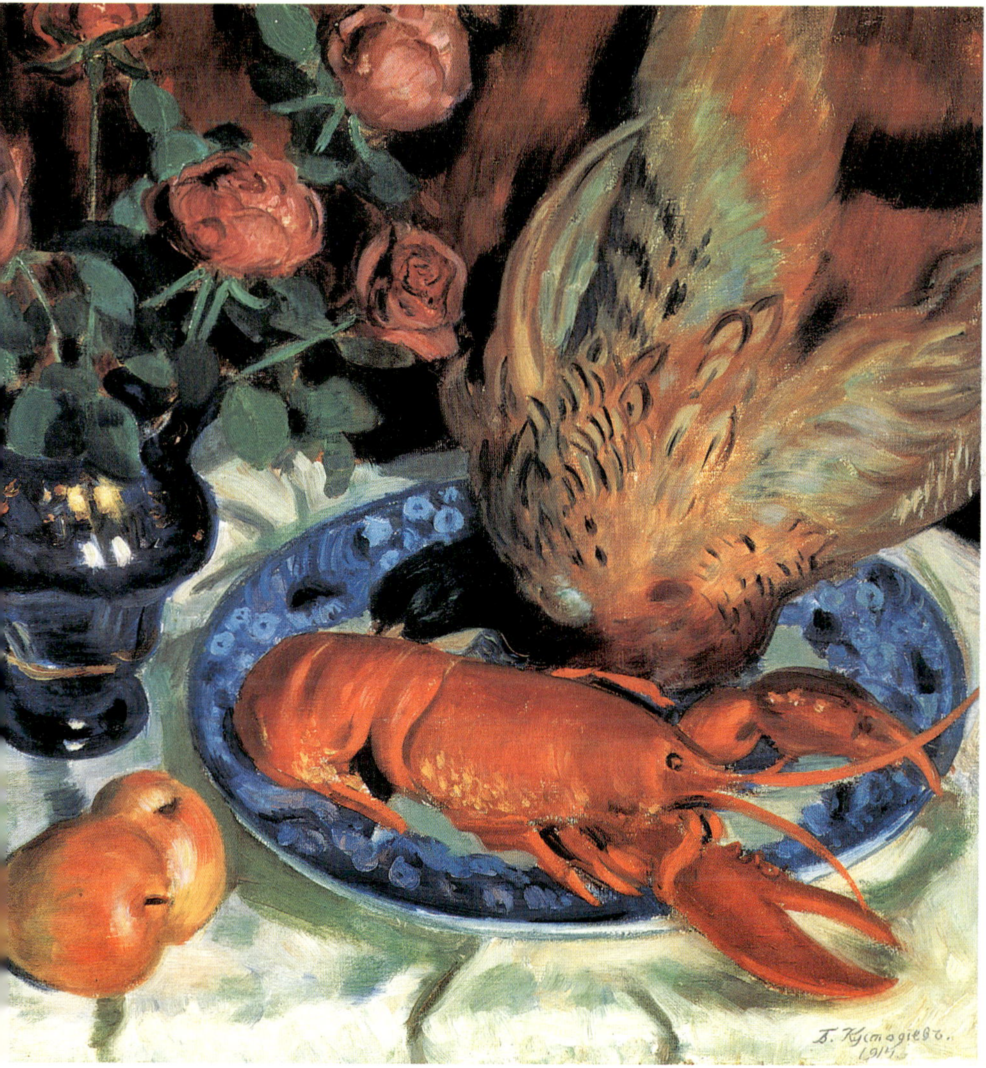
Б. Кустодiевъ.
1914

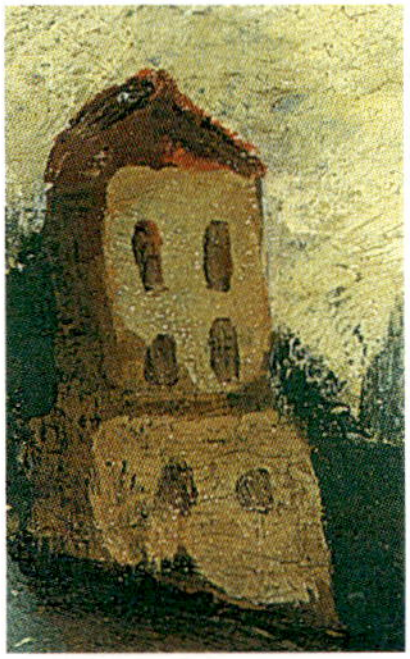

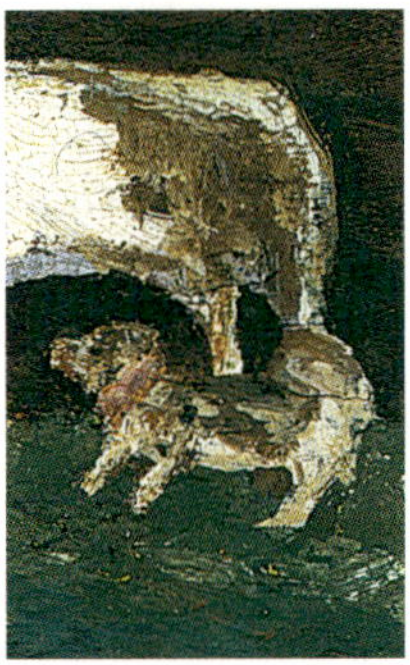

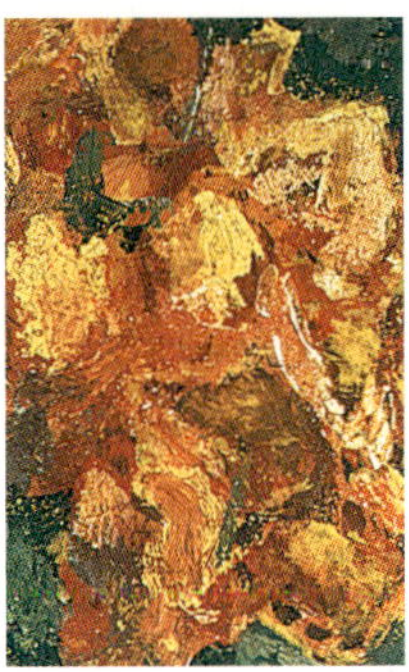

Martiros Saryan (1880-1972)

Like Larionov, the Armenian painter Martiros Saryan studied under Korovin and Serov at the Moscow College of Painting and Sculpture, where he became friendly with Sudeikin, Kuznetsov and Petrov-Vodkin – all brilliant colourists.

Still Life with a Tray

Sergei Sudeikin, 1914
Oil on canvas, 51 x 62.5 cm
private collection, Saint Petersburg

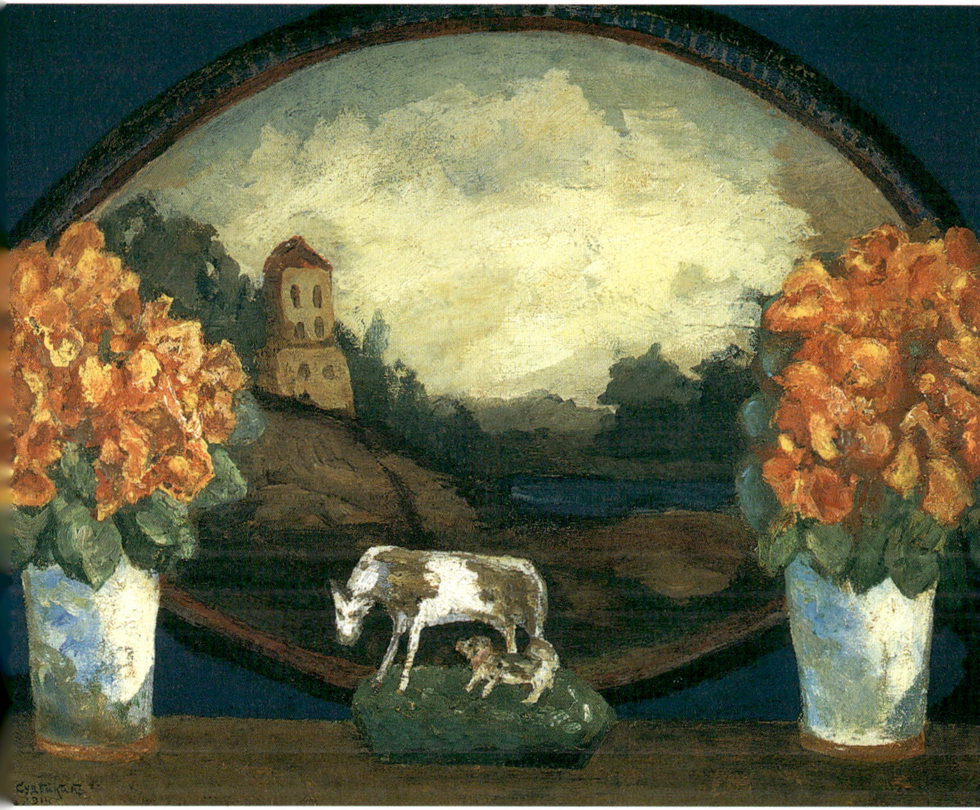

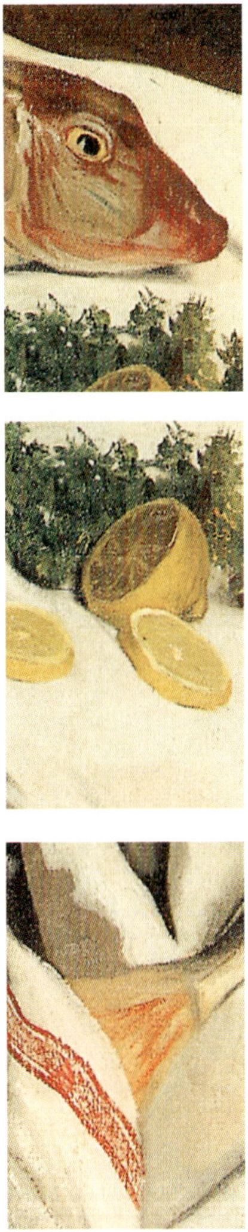

His still lifes, like his portraits and landscapes, have a remarkable zest. Many of them feature fruit, vegetables or flowers painted in vibrant, sun-drenched colours. A few include Eastern elements, as in *Buddhist Still Life*.

Still Life with Gurnet

Félix Vallotton, 1914
Oil on canvas, 44 x 55 cm
Private collection

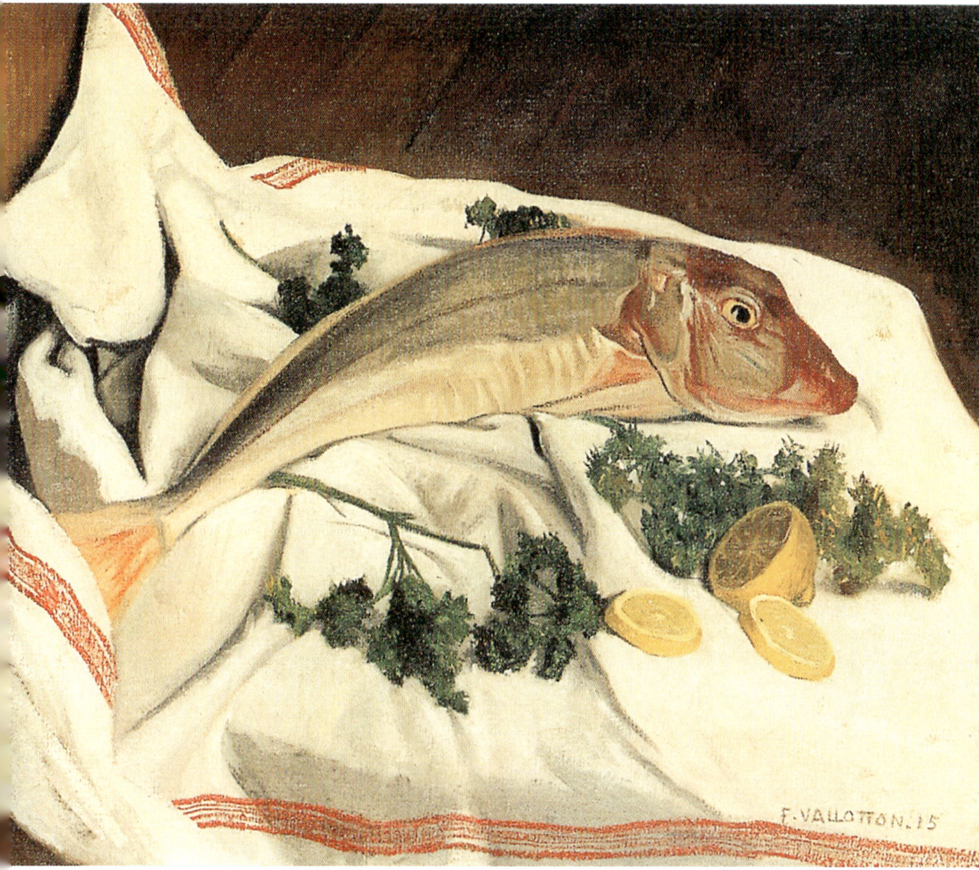
F. VALLOTTON. 15

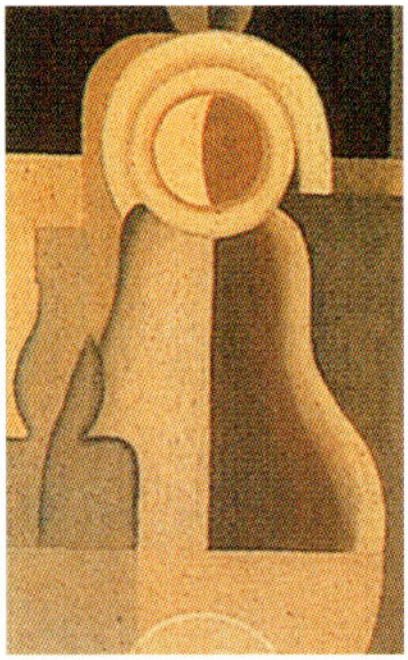

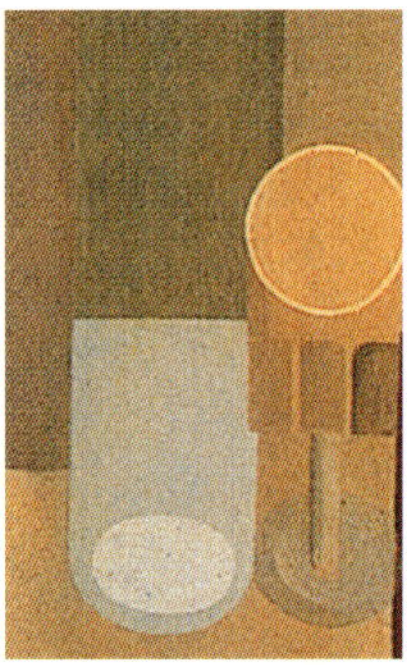

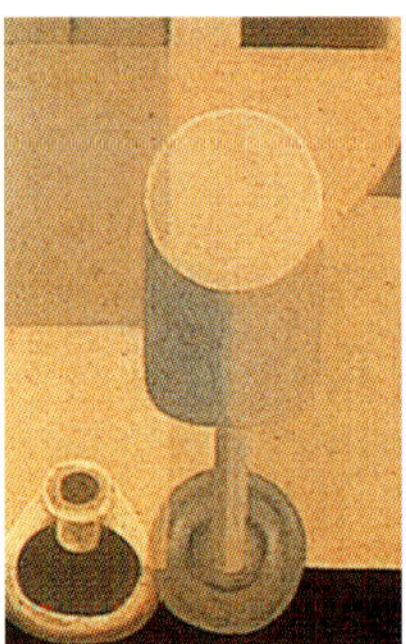

He participated in exhibitions from 1907, including those of the Blue Rose (1907) and World of Art (1913-15). He was also a member of the Union of Russian Artists (1910-1911) and The Four Arts Society (1925-1929). He lived and worked in Yerevan from 1921 until he died in 1972.

Still Life with Vessels

Amédée Ozenfant, 1886-1966
Oil on canvas, 72 x 60 cm
The Hermitage, Saint Petersburg

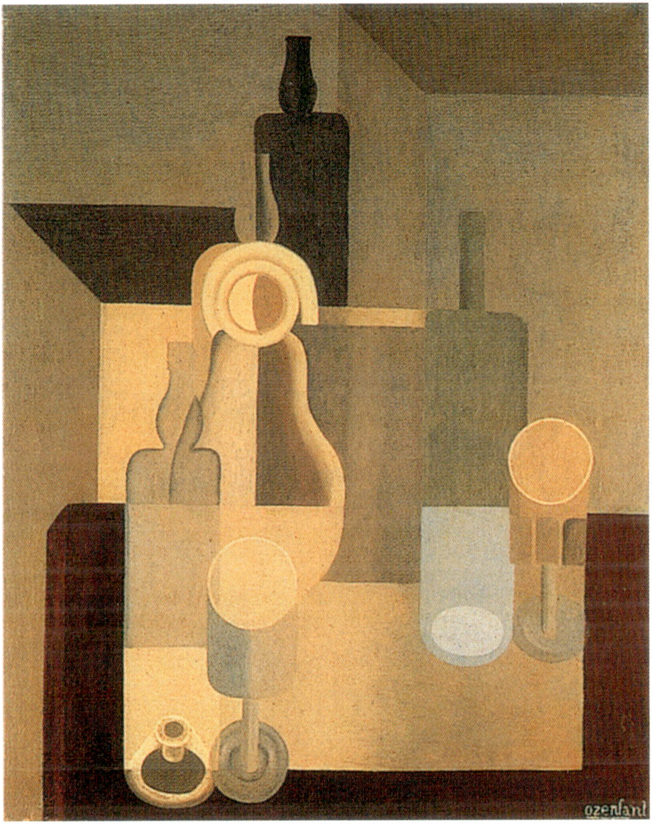
ozenfant

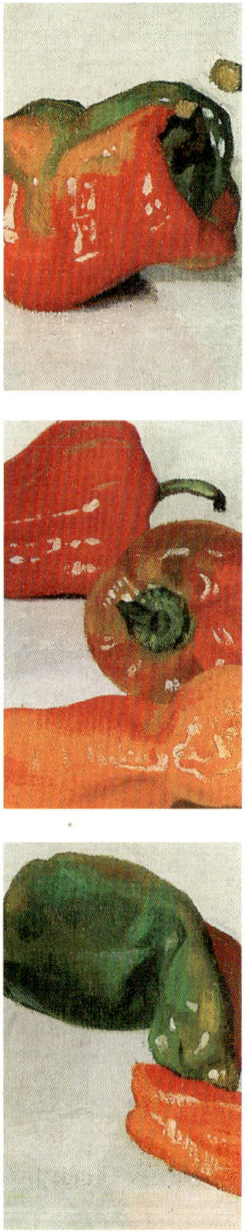

Nikolai Sapunov (1880-1912)

Among the artists of the Blue Rose group, Nikolai Sapunov and Serguei Sudeikin (1882-1946) were noted for their colourful theatre designs. Both were enthusiastic admirers of Russian crafts and decorative traditions – hence "Primitivist" (folk-inspired) colours of their paintings – and often included nostalgic ephemera, such as antique figurines,

Still Life
Red Pimentoes on a White Lacquered Table

Félix Vallotton, 1915
Oil on canvas, 46 x 55 cm
Museum of Fine Arts, Soleure
Dübi-Müller Foundation

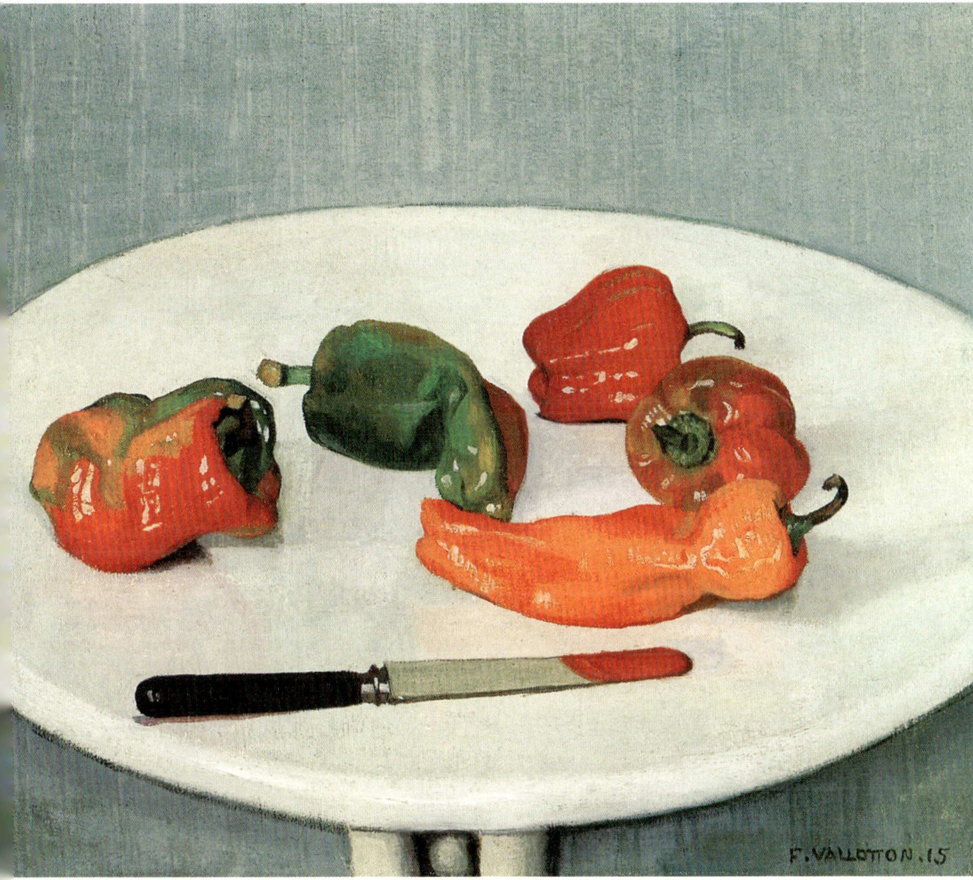
F. VALLOTTON. 15

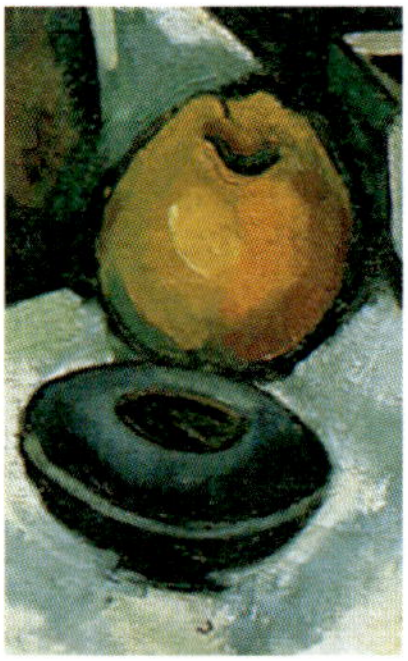

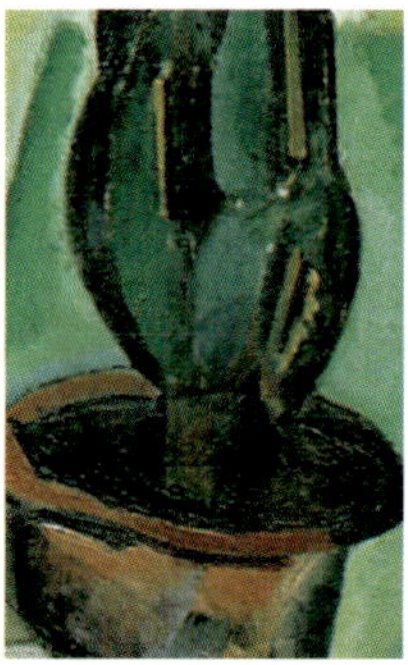

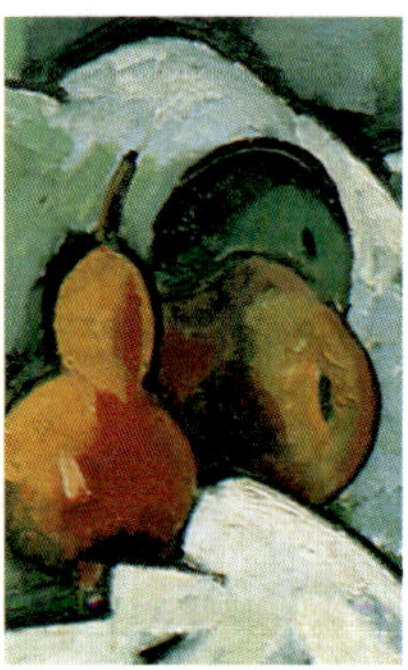

hand-painted trays and old toys, in their still lifes. Like Grabar, Sapunov produced still life paintings remarkable for their handling of colour, though in terms of tonal range the two artists could scarcely have been less similar.

Still Life. Cactus and Fruits

Alexander Kuprin, 1918
Oil on canvas, 96.5 x 113 cm
Location unknown

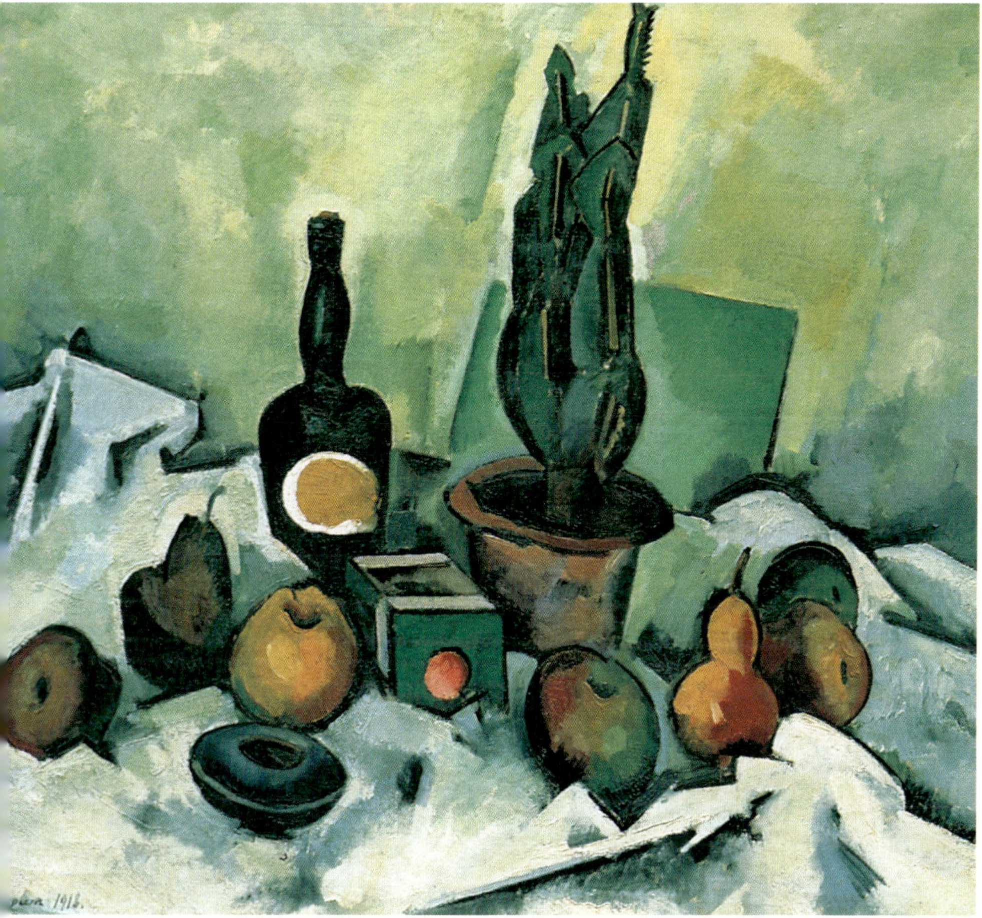

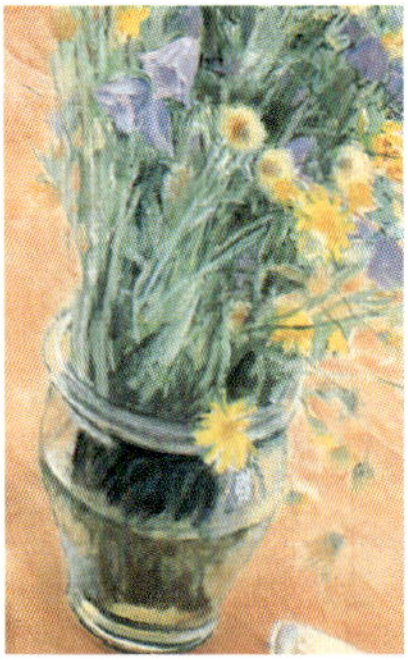

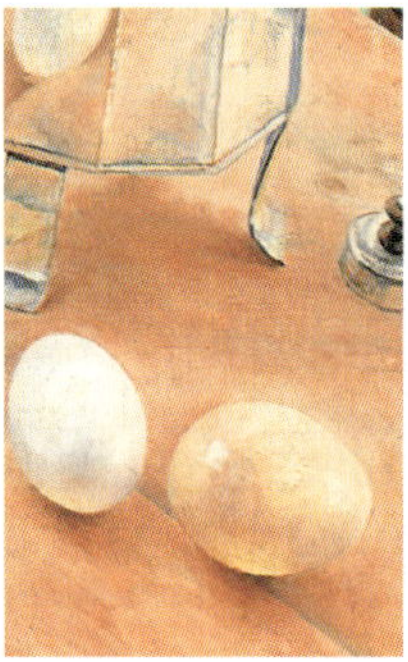

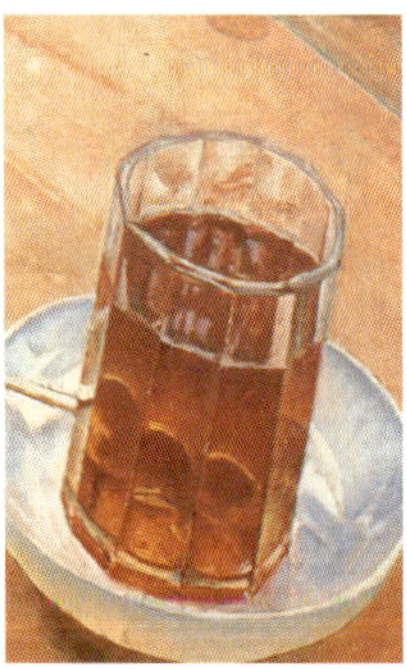

Mikhail Larionov (1881-1964)

Mikhail Larionov was born in 1881 in Tiraspol, Russia. From childhood he painted the nature he saw in his large garden. From the beginning of the 20th century Larionov developed in his flower painting an original and "poetic" type of impressionism characterised by a more synthetic effect and research into the large plastic forms.

Morning Still Life

Kuzma Petrov-Vodkin, 1918
Oil on canvas, 66 x 88 cm
Location unknown

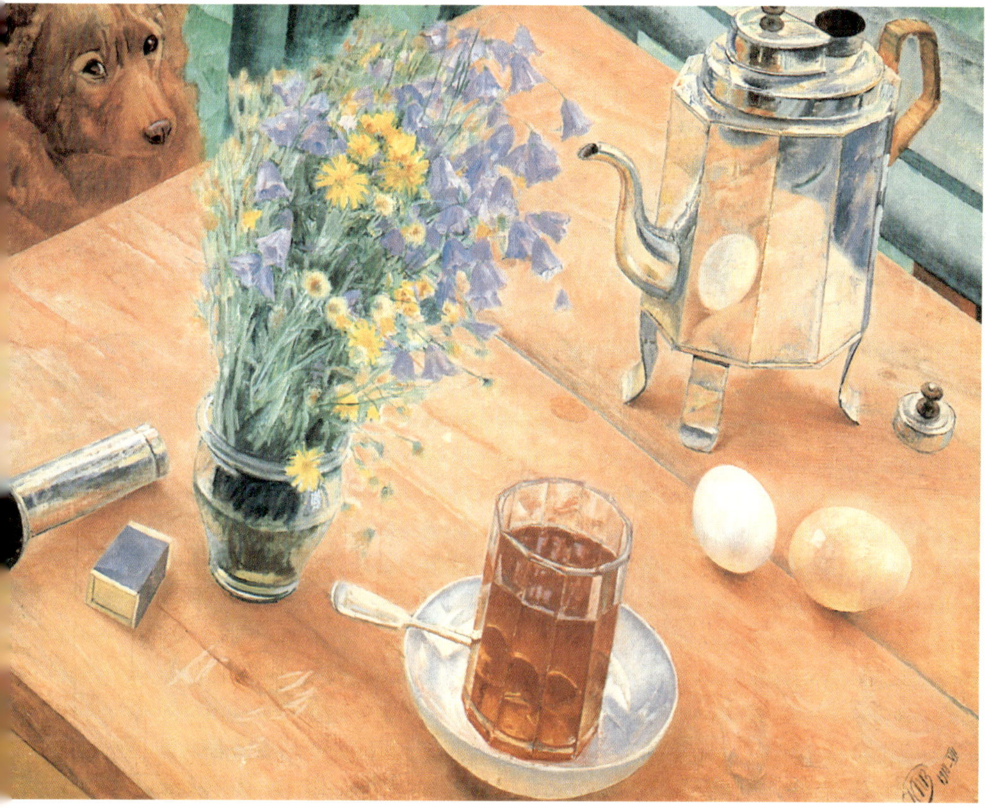

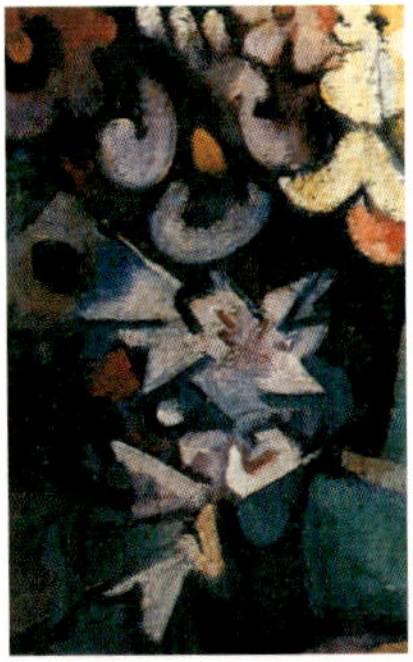

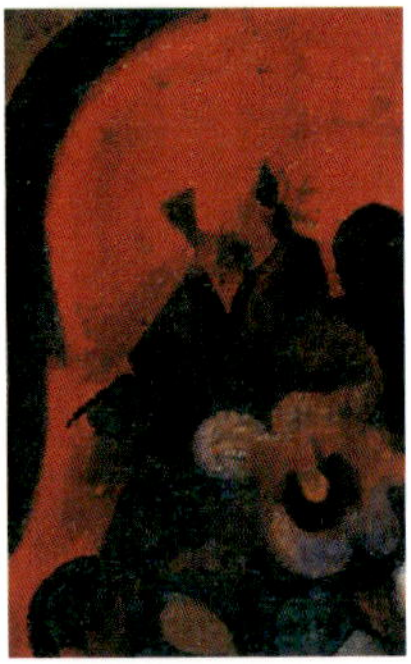

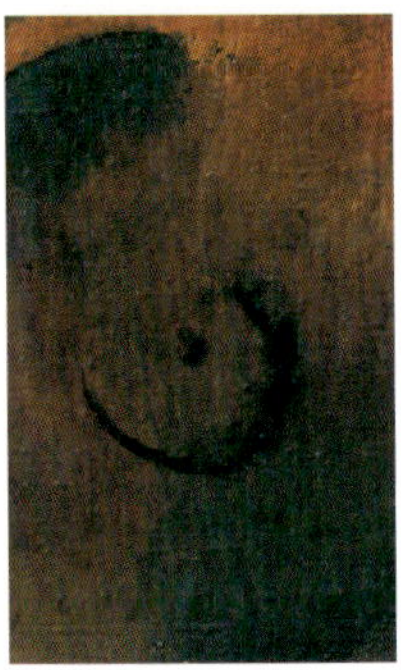

Larionov's very particular method can be seen in his depictions of floral still lifes. His innate sense of colour reveals harmonious combinations which are lively, intense, contrasting and complementary. His quick, nervous brushstrokes depict the subject in a light and authentic way.

Large Still Life with Artificial Flowers
a Red Tray and a Wooden Plate

Alexander Kuprin, 1919
Oil on canvas, 140 x 168 cm
Russian Museum, Saint Petersburg

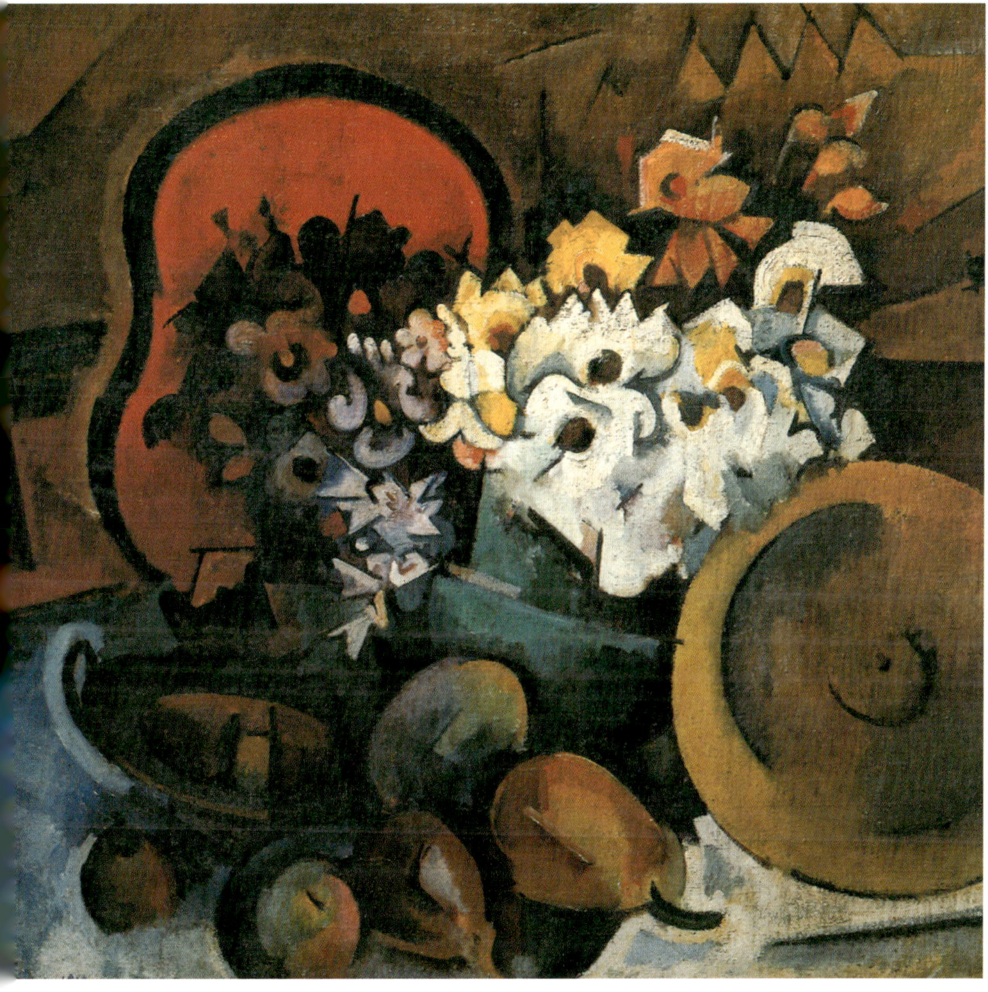

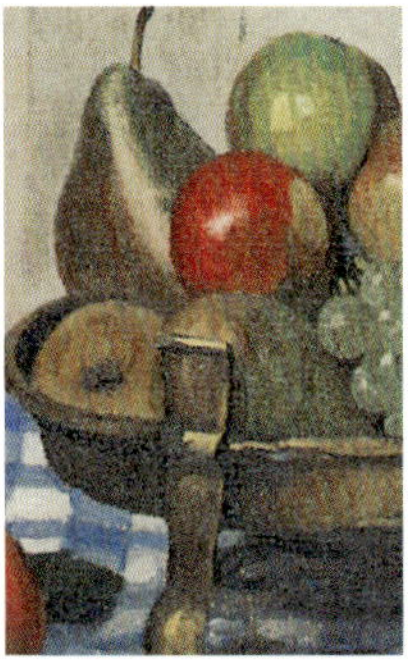
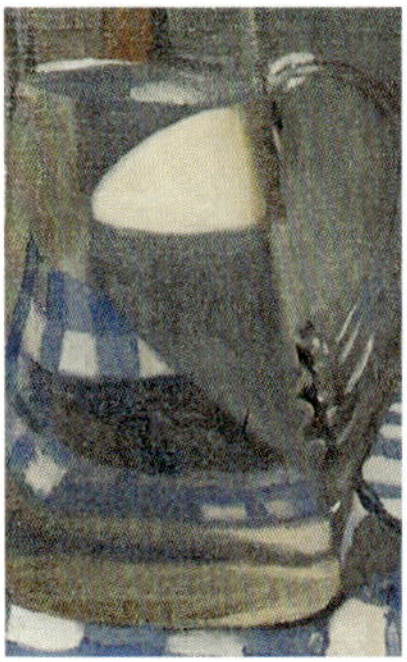
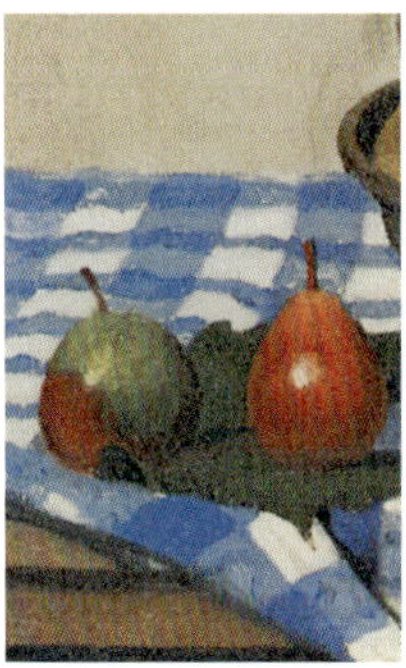

For this artist the chromatic scale would progressively become a whole separate means of expression. In his depictions of flowers Larionov wished to capture the ephemeral mix of colour and reproduce in its variations the vagaries of nature.

Still Life with Blue Check Cloth

Félix Vallotton, 1919
Oil on canvas, 54 x 73 cm
Private collection

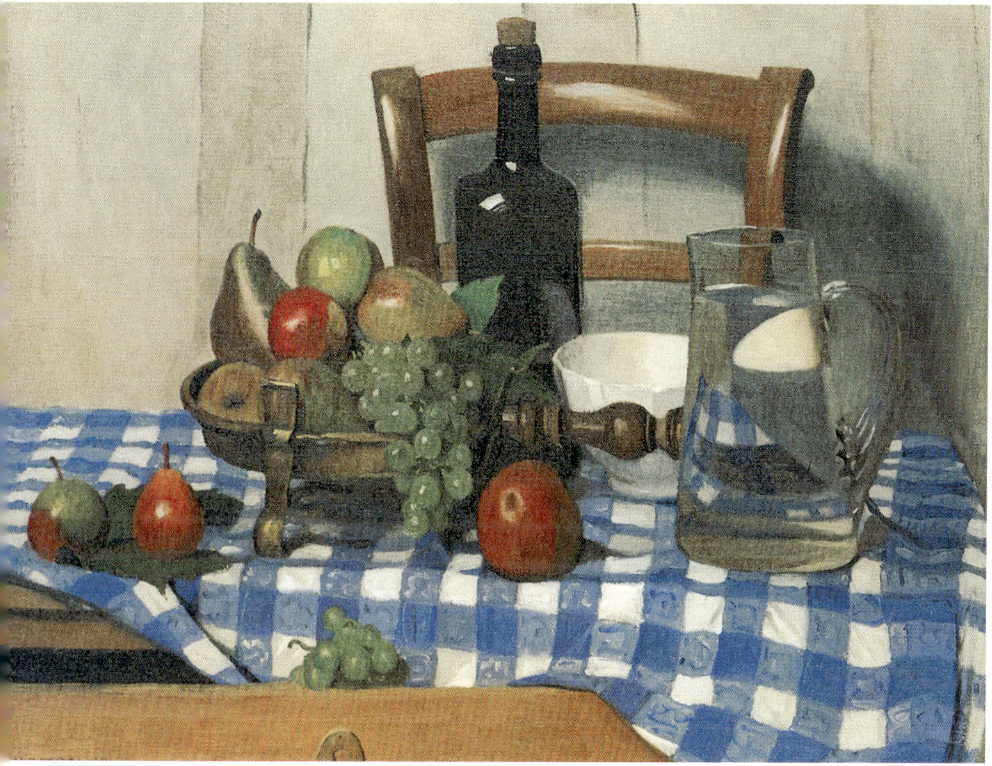

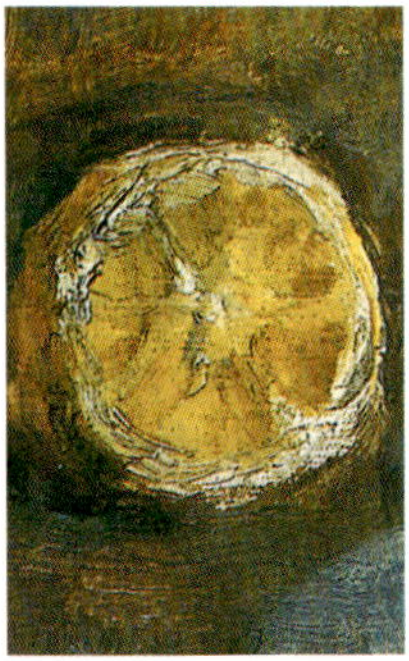

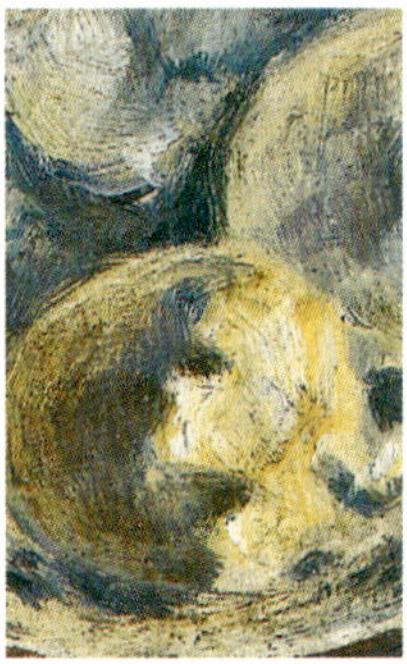

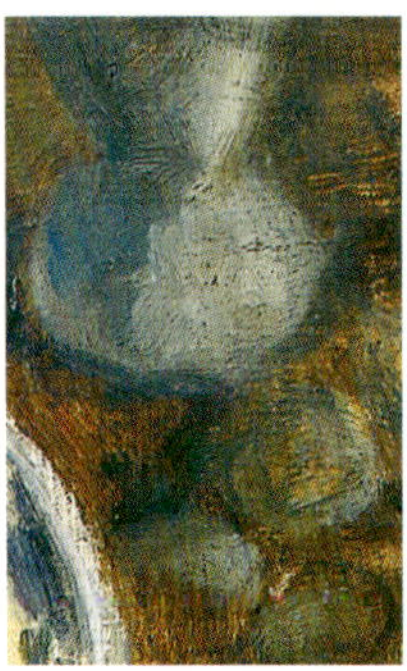

The typical luminous quality of his canvases, like in *Le rosier (The Rose Bush)* for example, is not due to colour effects but to the colours themselves and to the pictoral organisation of the painting. After 1904, his painting adhered more to the "fauve" movement,

Still Life with a Lemon and an Egg

Mikhail Larionov, 1920s
Oil on canvas, 23.5 x 37.5 cm
Russian Museum, Saint Petersburg

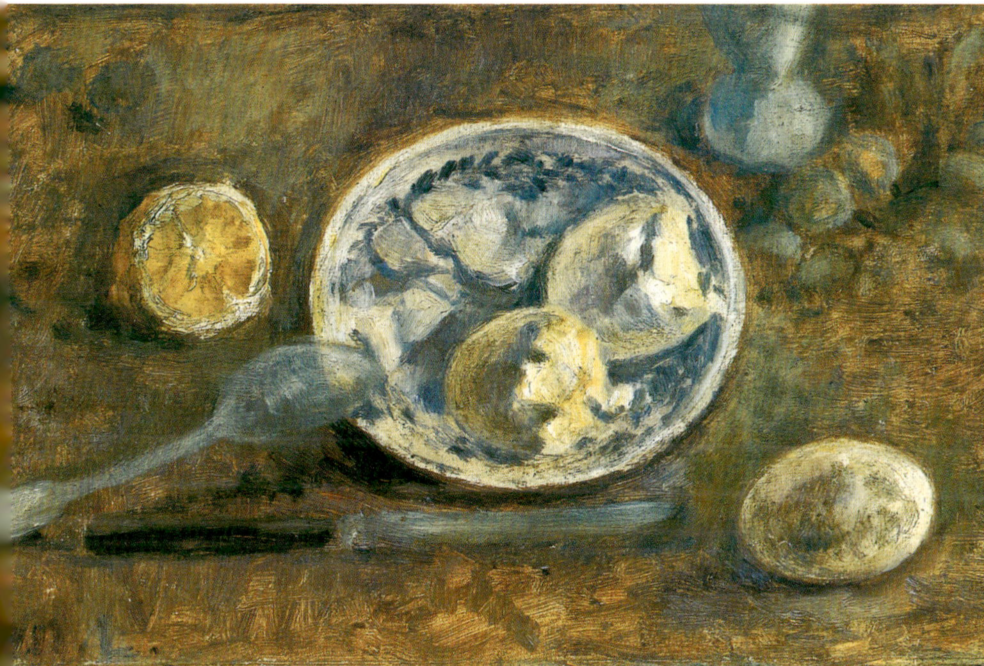

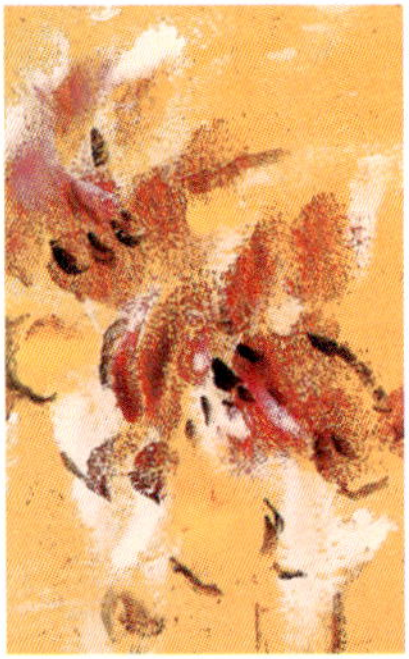

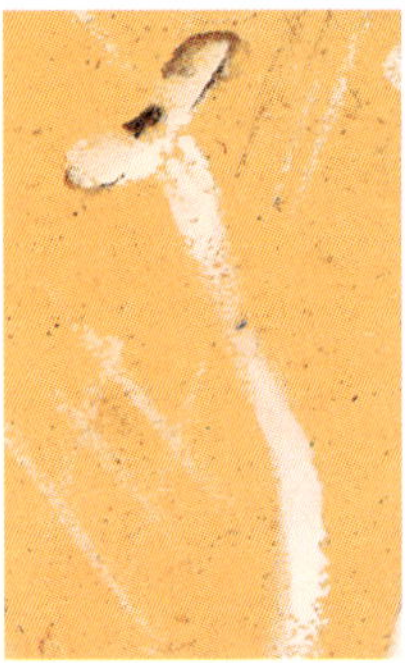

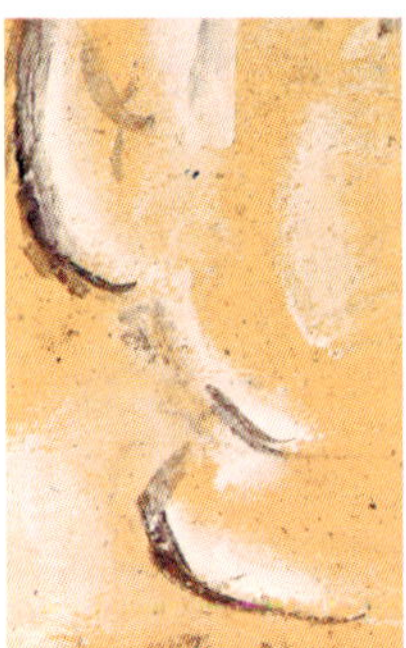

it was less spontaneous and the colour was purer and more lively. After a brilliant career, Mikhail Larionov died in Fontenay-aux-Roses, France, in 1964. The style of Larionov's still lifes went through several phases.

Still Life with a Portrait

Mikhail Larionov, 1920s
gouache on paper, 34.3 x 22.4 cm
Russian Museum, Saint Petersburg

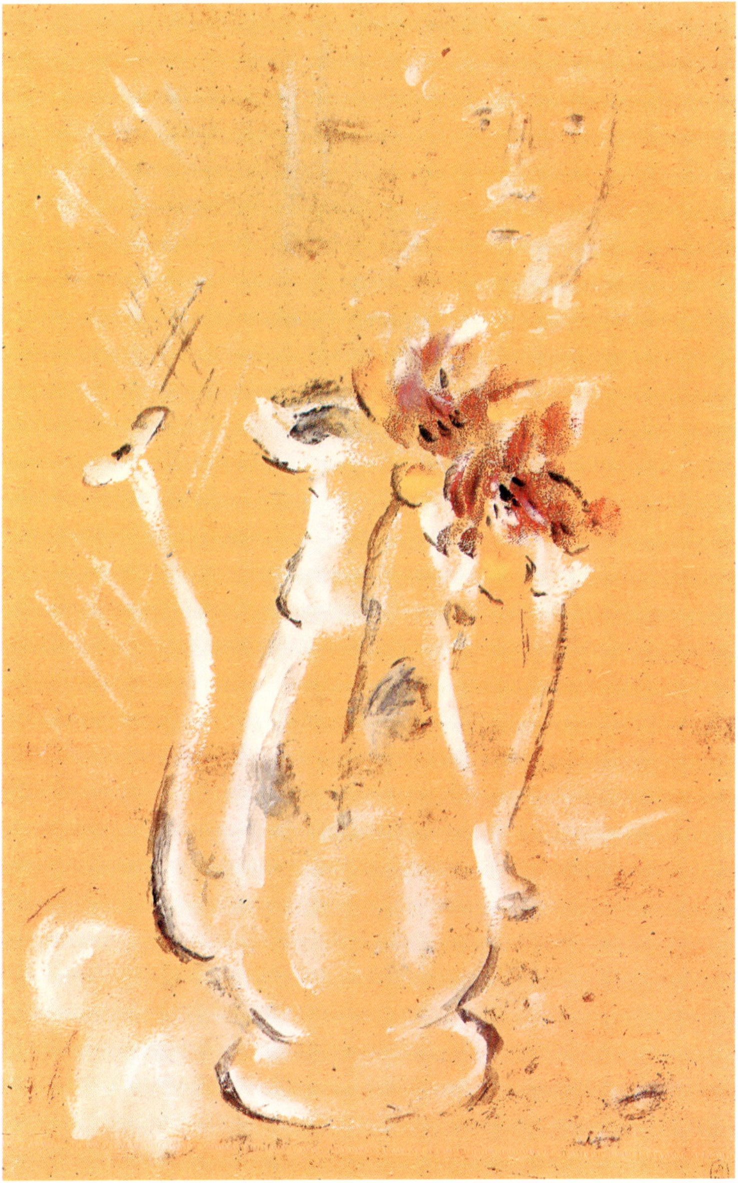

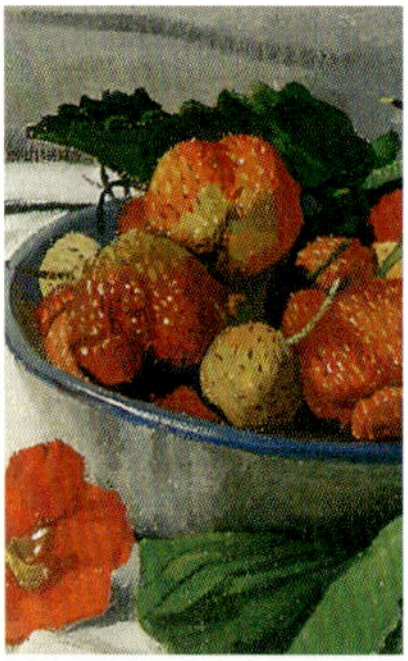

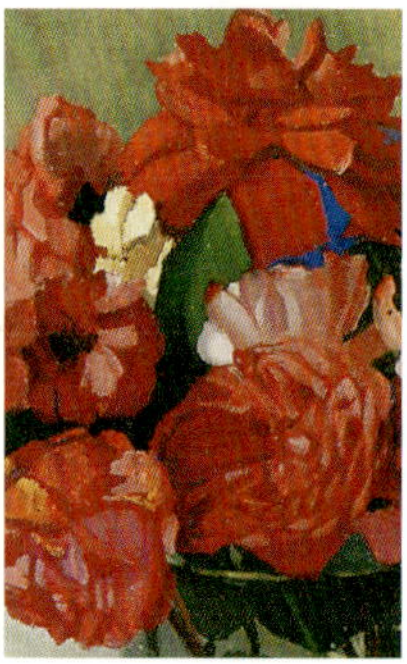

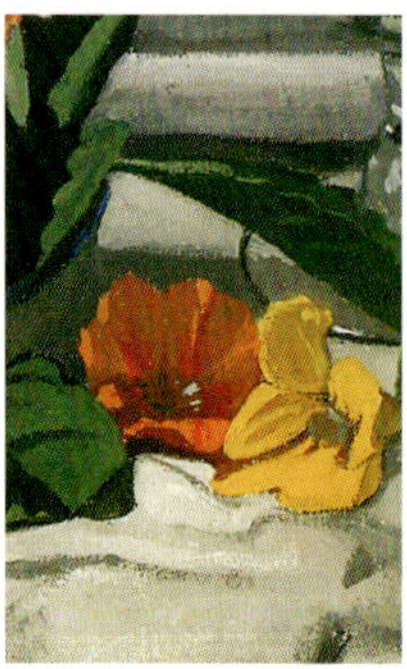

Works such as *Fish in the Setting Sun* and *Flowers (Two bouquets)*, which date from 1904, have an Impressionist quality, but around that time he began to experiment with more intense colours, resulting in the Fauve-like idiom of *Pears*.

Flowers and Strawberries

Félix Vallotton, 1920
Oil on canvas, 61 x 73 cm
Private collection

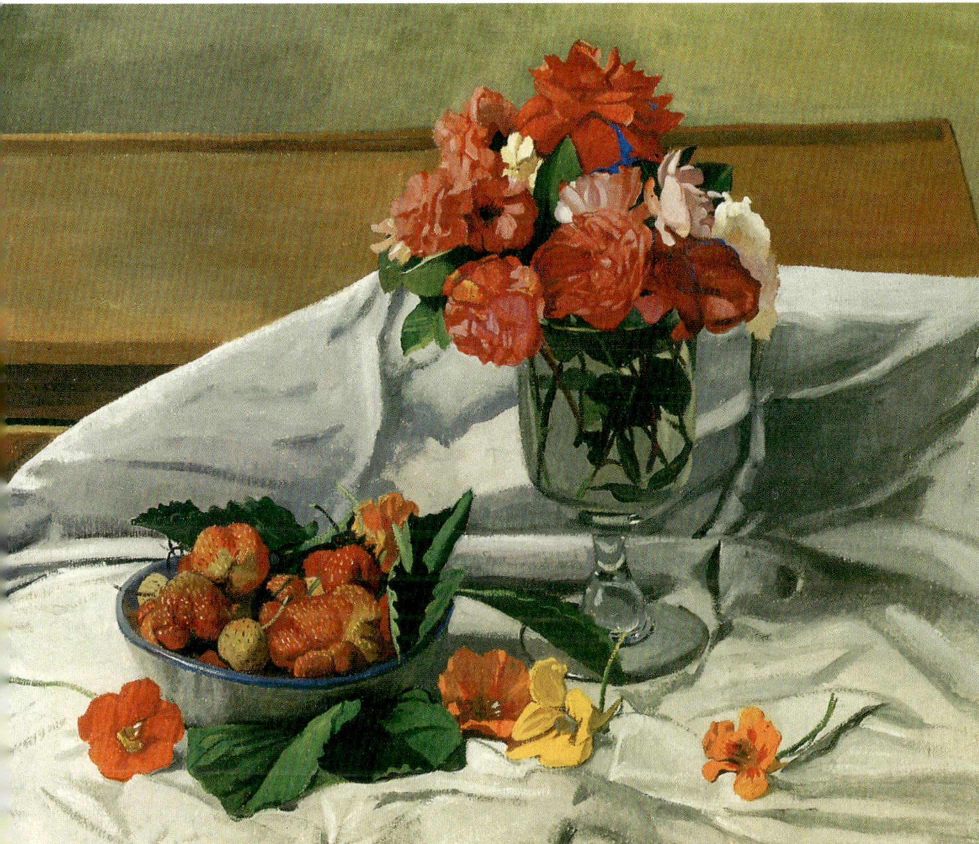
F. VALLOTTON. 20

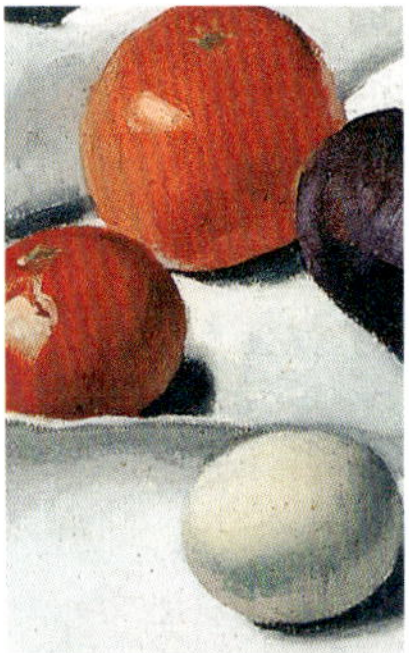

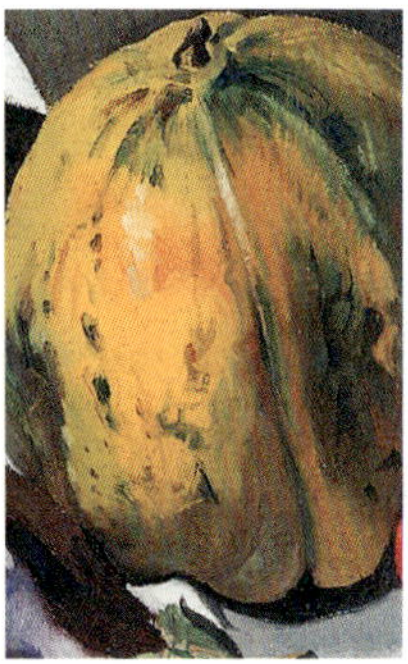

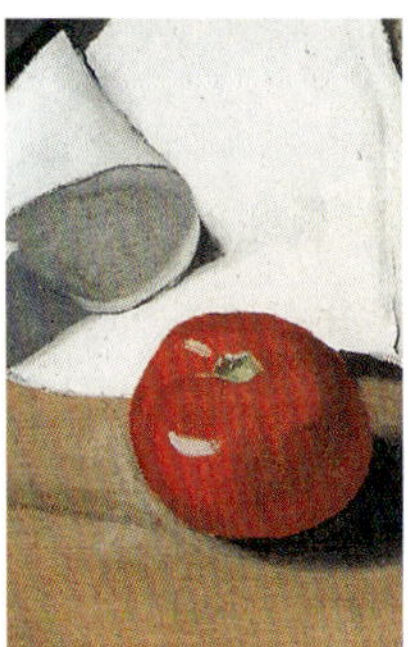

Between 1907 and 1913, Larionov and Goncharova poured out a stream of Primitivist pictures, using elements and styles culled from folk art – especially tradesmen's signboards and *lubki* (the Russian wood-cuts, similar to English chapbooks, that had become immensely popular in the seventeenth century).

Still Life with Large Earthenware Jar

Félix Vallotton, 1923
Oil on canvas, 81 x 65.3 cm
Galerie Vallotton, Lausanne

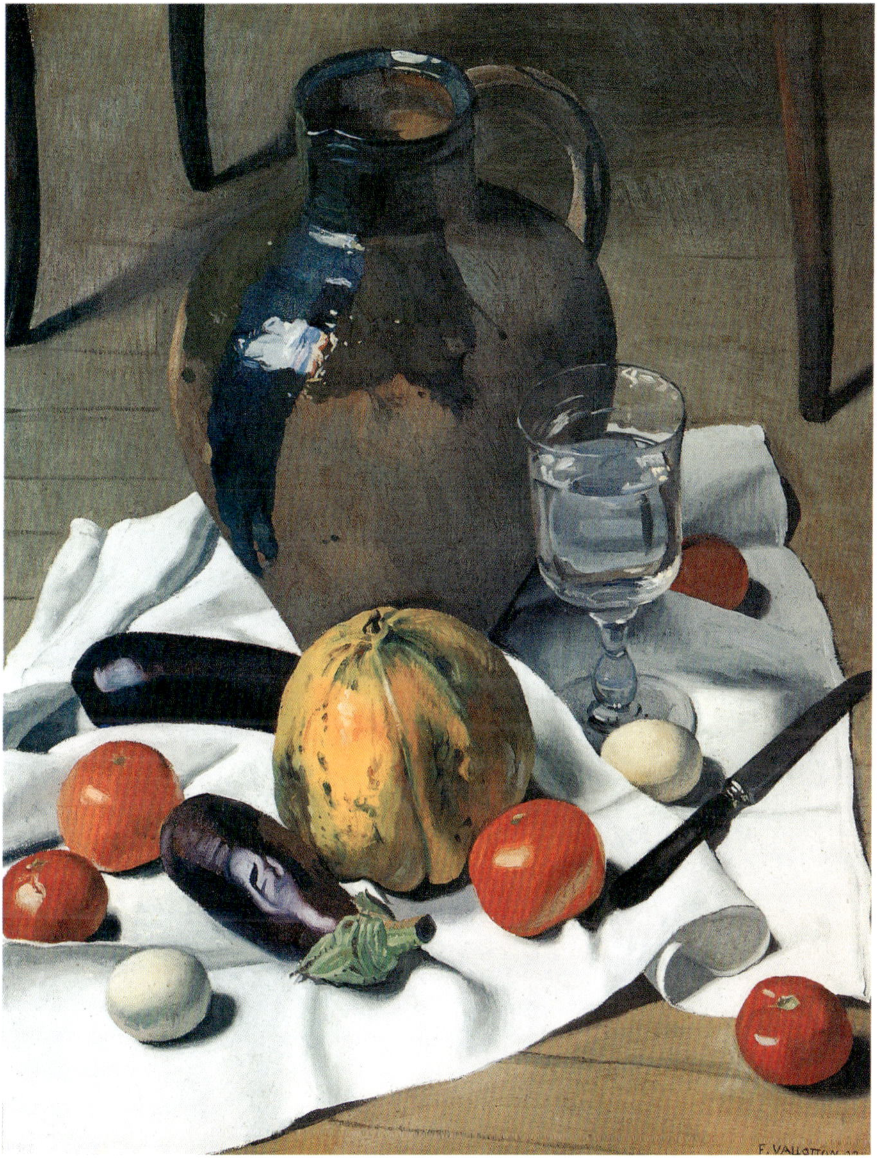
F. VALLOTTON

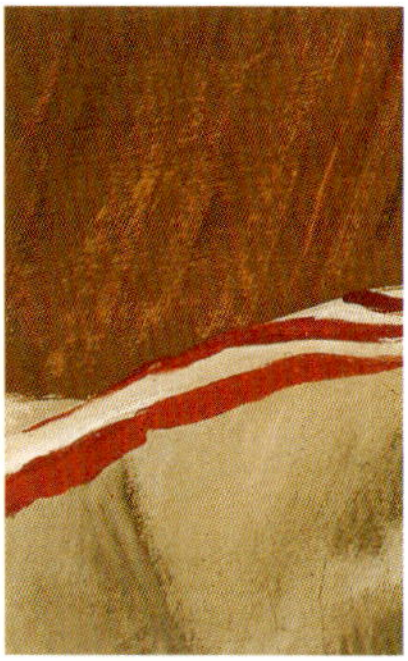

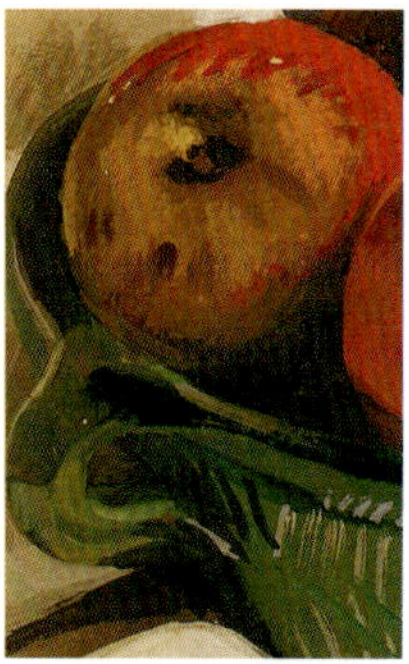

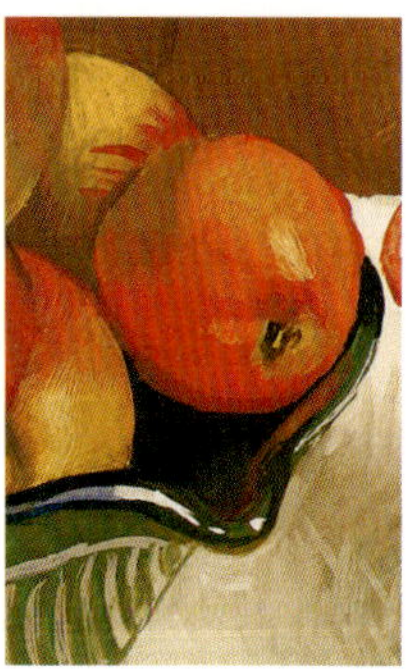

These were followed by the brilliantly coloured semi-abstract still lifes, such as Larionov's *Rayonist Sausage and Mackerel*, typical of their Rayonist period. Finally, after Larionov suffered shell shock in 1914, they moved to Paris, where they worked as designers for Diaghilev's Ballets Russes.

Still Life, Apples

Félix Vallotton, 1923
Oil on canvas
Kunstmuseum, Winterthur

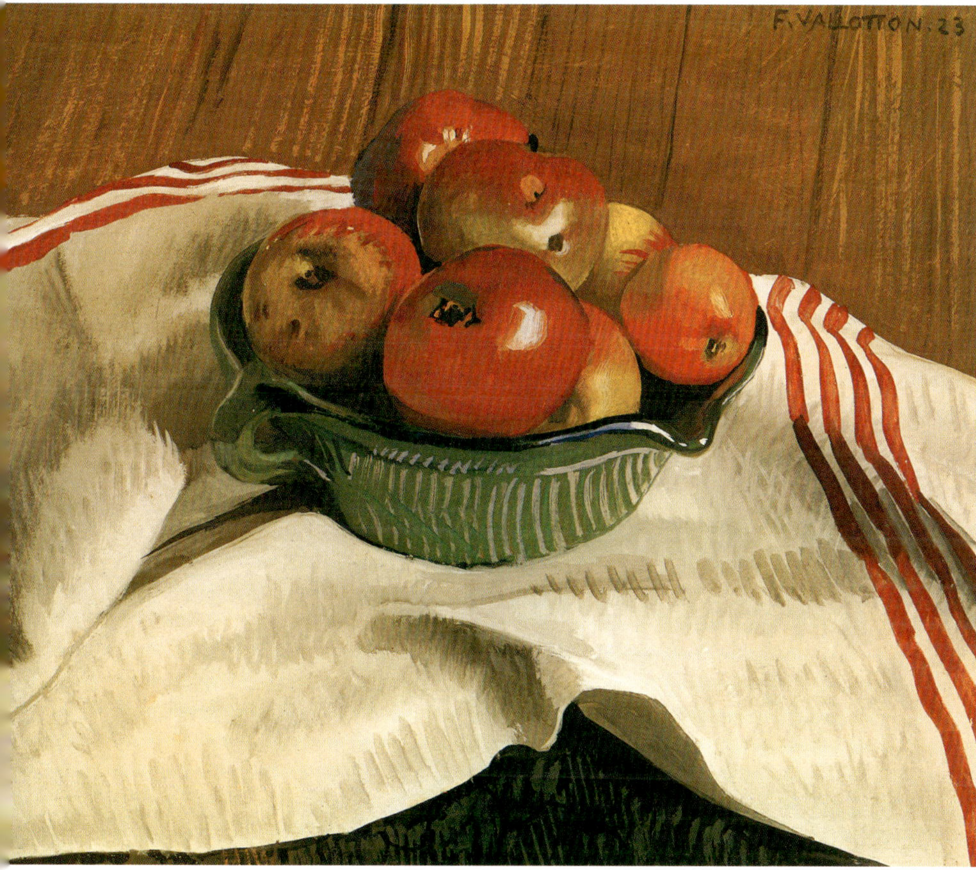
F. VALLOTTON. 23

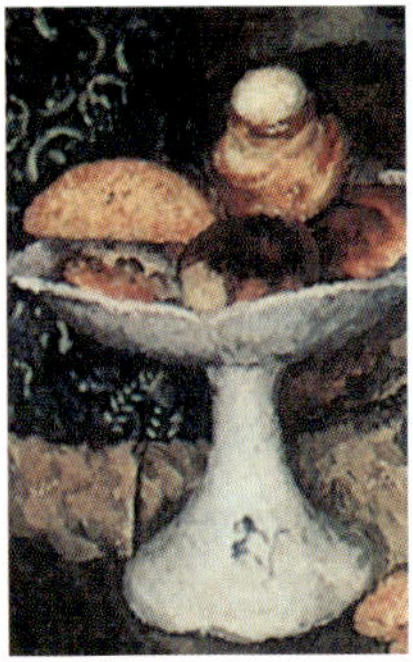

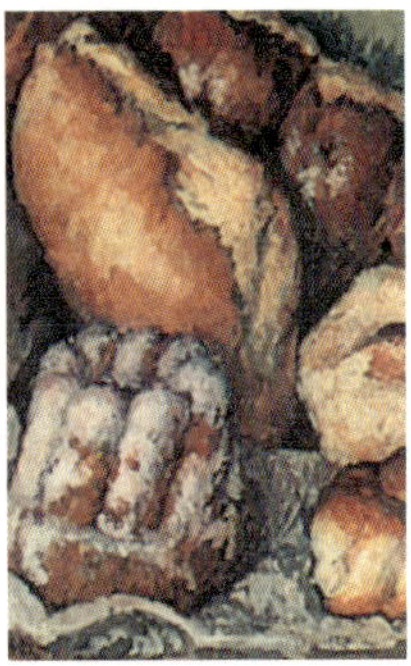

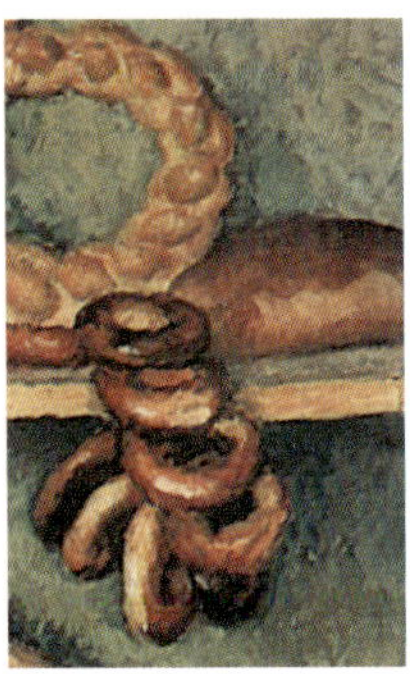

Pablo Picasso (1881-1973)

Pablo Picasso was born in 1881 in Malaga, Spain and was indisputably one of the greatest painters of the 20th century. Many modern artists painted still lifes. But it was Picasso who most exploited the genre, twisting it into previously inconceivable forms, using a wide variety

Muscovite Still Life, Breads

Ilya Mashkov, 1924
Oil on canvas, 128 x 145 cm
Tretyakov Gallery, Moscow

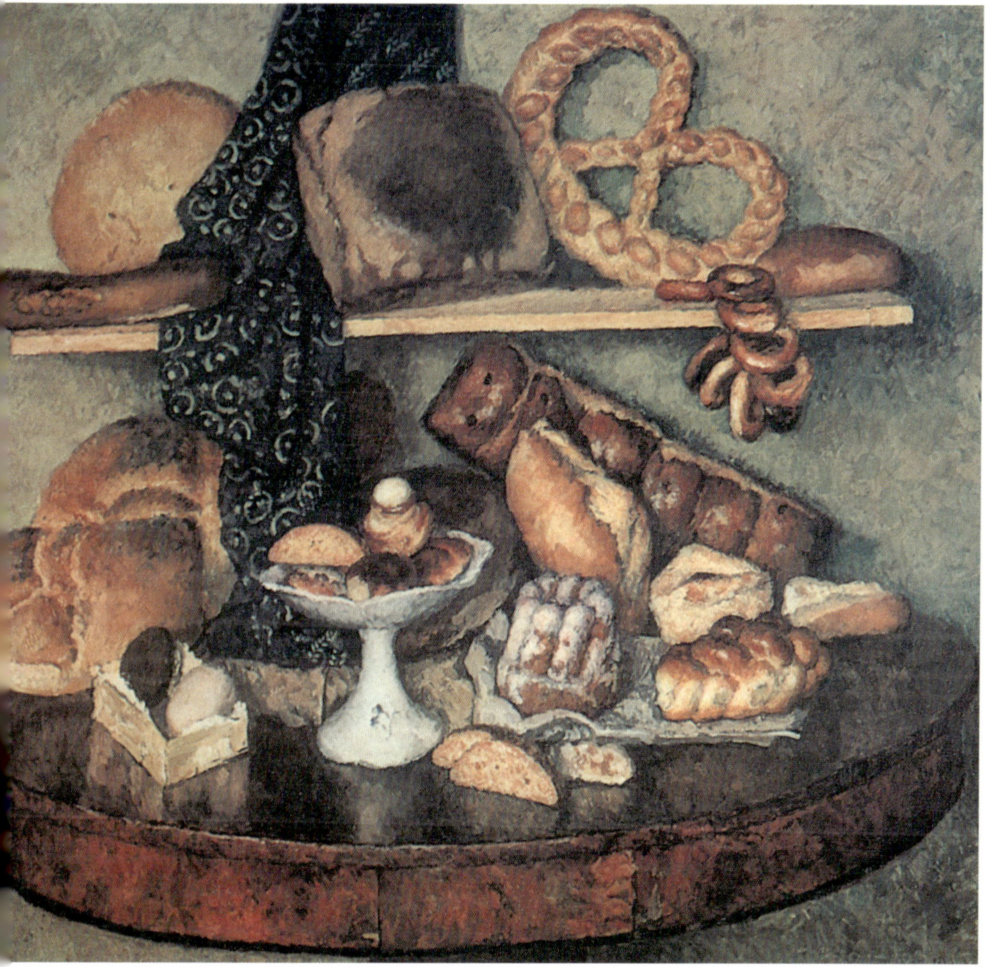

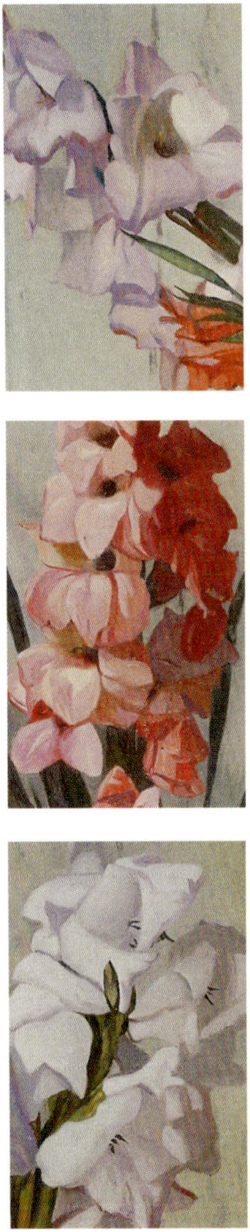

of stylistic permutations throughout his long career. On the subject of Picasso's still lifes, Jean Cocteau observed: "Picasso does not make trompe l'oeil, he makes thick spirit." Picasso's still life paintings are full of skulls that remind us of our mortality and overt images of sexuality.

Still Life with Gladioli

Félix Vallotton, 1924
Oil on canvas, 86 x 82 cm
M.C.B.A., Lausanne

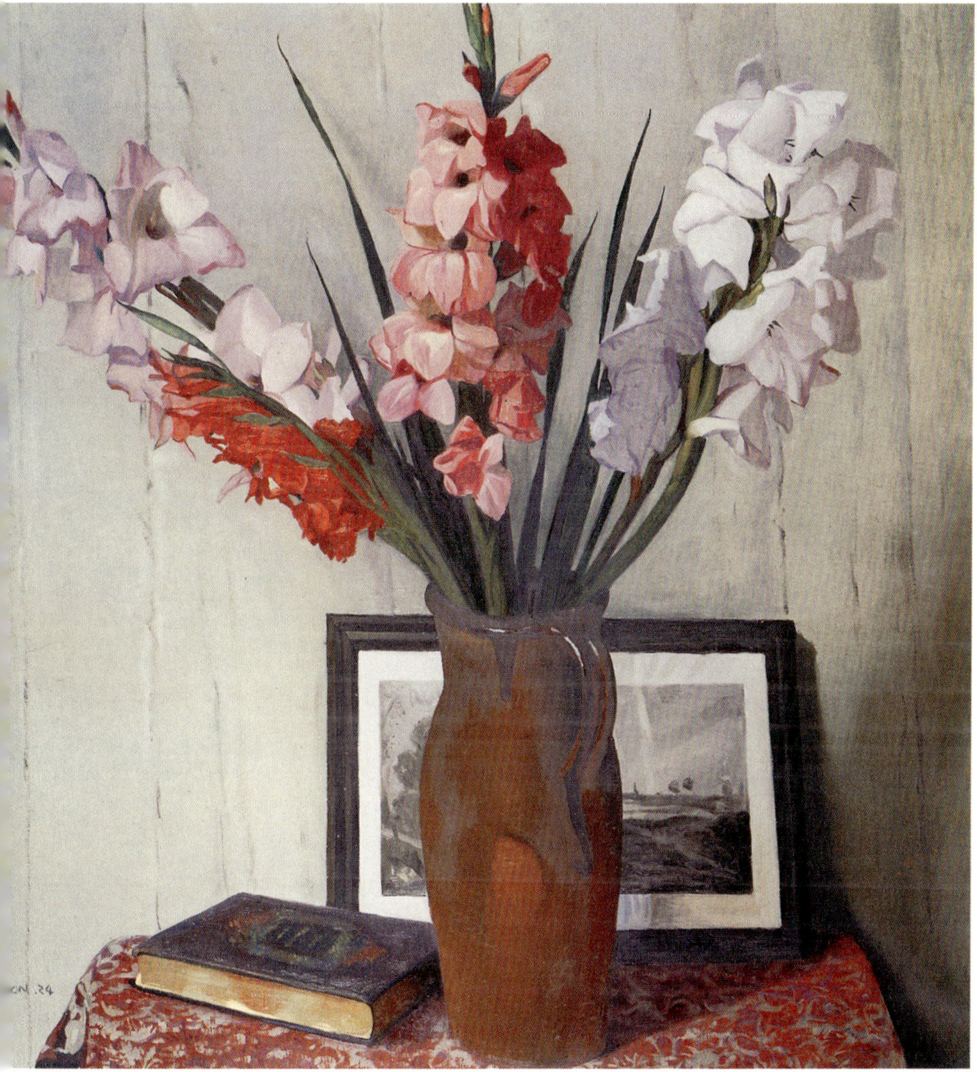

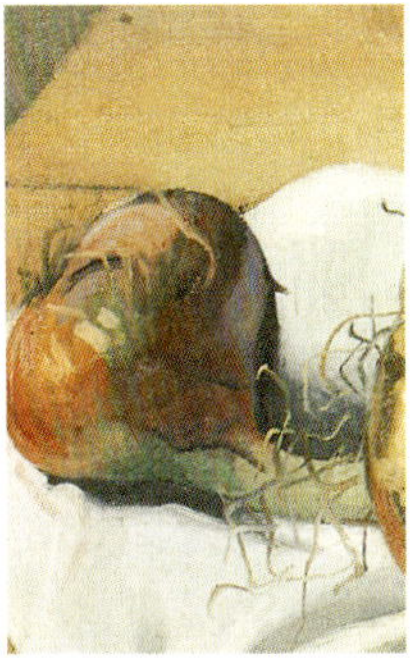

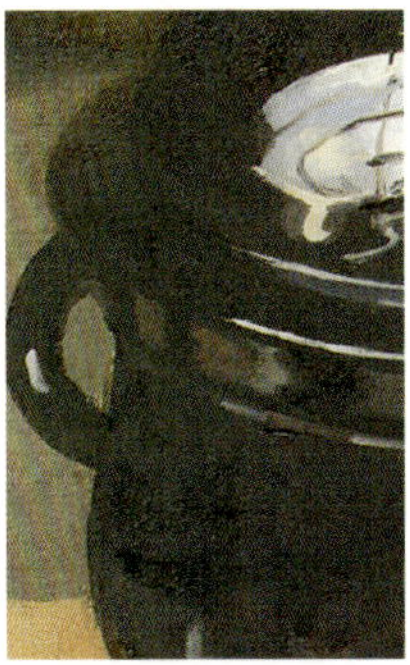

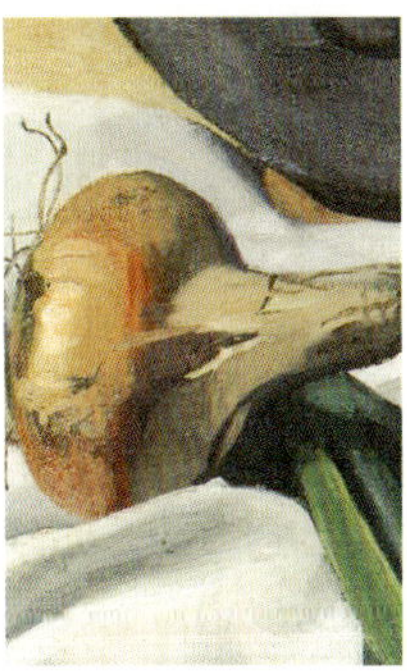

They tell you about the artist, his state of mind, his desires. One extraordinary painting called "Still Life on a Pedestal Table" is full of erotic curves and phallic shapes. His Cubist still lifes have dislocated forms, angles, many super positioned planes, references to reality, such as newspaper headlines or isolated texts.

Still Life with Onions and Soup Tureen

Félix Vallotton, 1925
Oil on canvas, 60 x 73 cm
Private collection

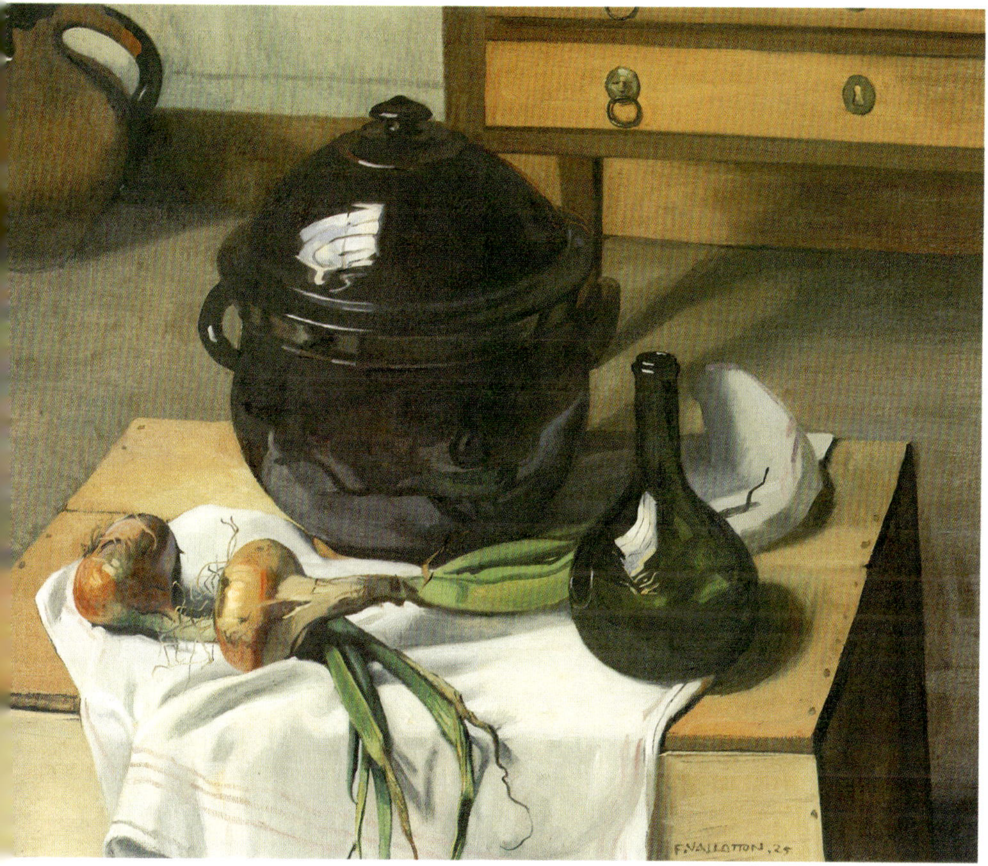
F.VALLOTTON. 25

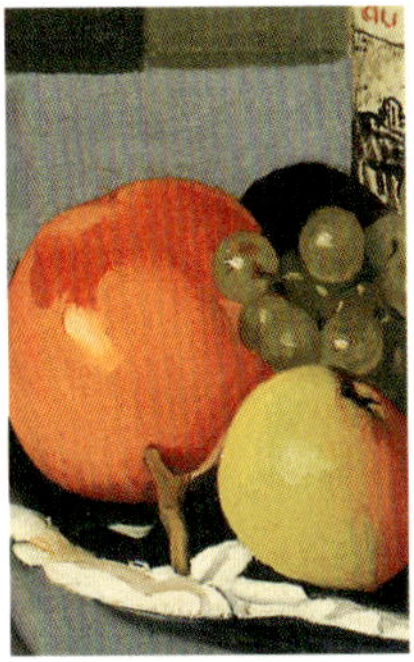

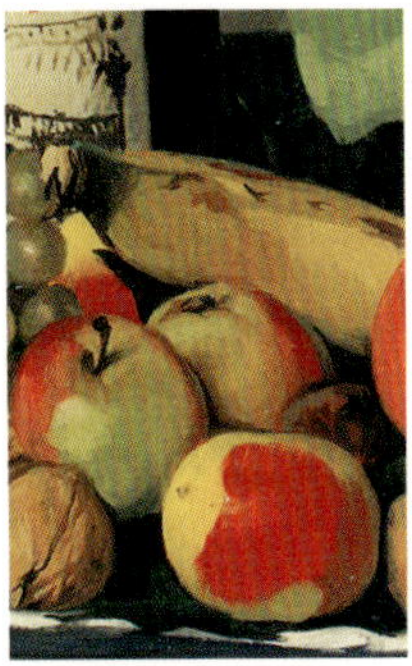

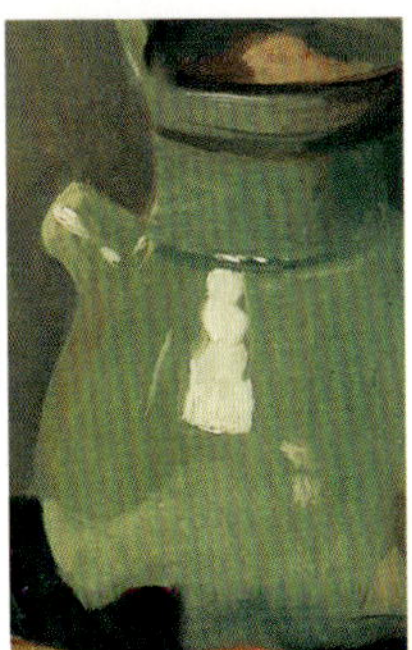

Picasso painted many still life compositions, often including musical instruments, as well as collage works. In Picasso's hands, the "Vanitas" still life painting tradition, with its ruminations on human vanity and mortality, took on a contemporary urgency.

Still Life with Bottle of Châteauneuf

Félix Vallotton, 1925
Oil on canvas, 60 x 73 cm
Kunstmuseum, Bern

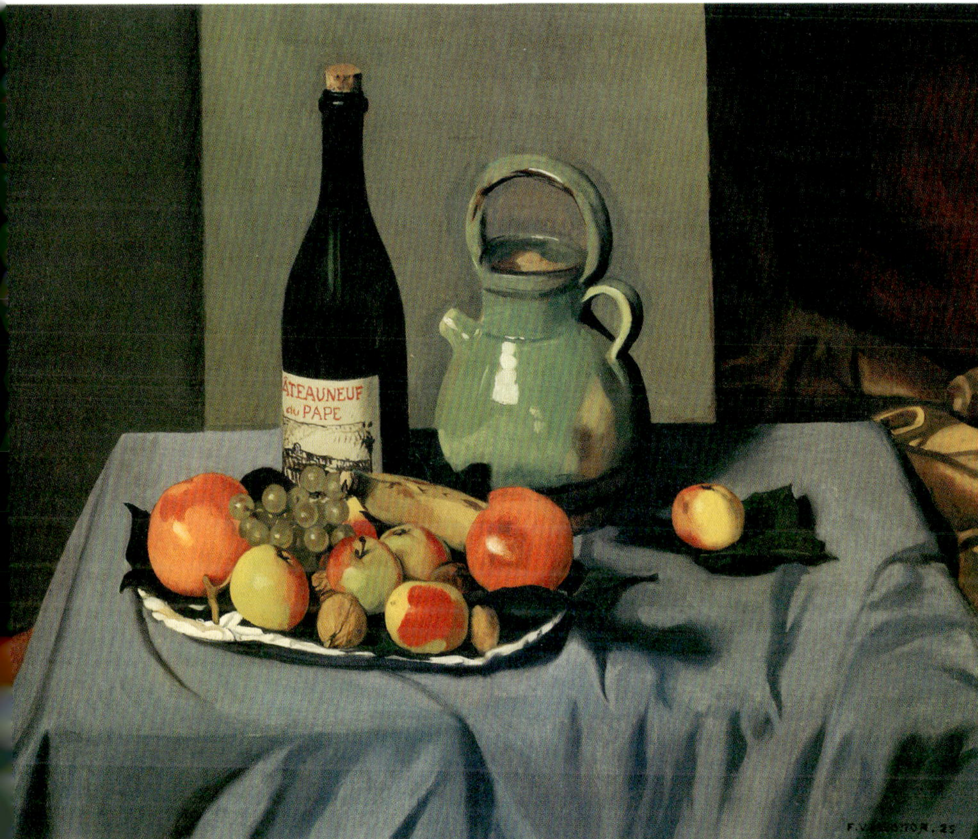
ÂTEAUNEUF
du PAPE

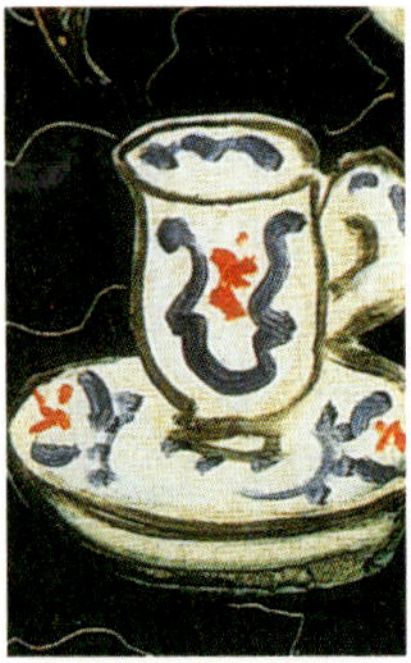

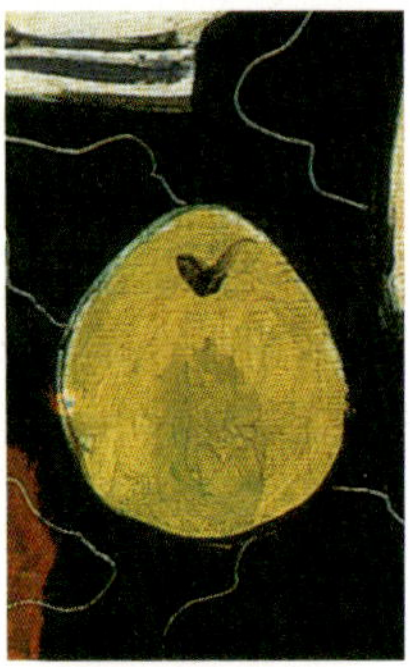

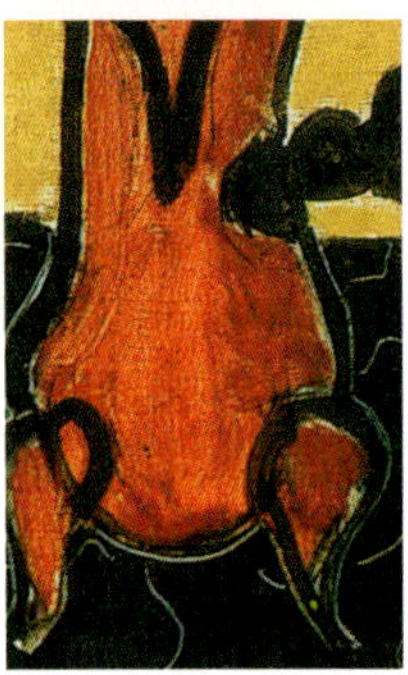

Within Picasso's framework, "pans too can scream" and his still life paintings draw upon a repertoire of skulls, candles, and flowers creating an allegory of the war years. At the time of his death in 1973, he was universally recognized as the leading artist of his era. Pablo Picasso died in 1973, having been the instigator of revolutions in artistic imagery in the 20th century.

Still Life with a Seashell on Black Marble

Henri Matisse, 1940
Oil on canvas, 54 x 81 cm
Pushkin Museum of Fine Arts, Moscow

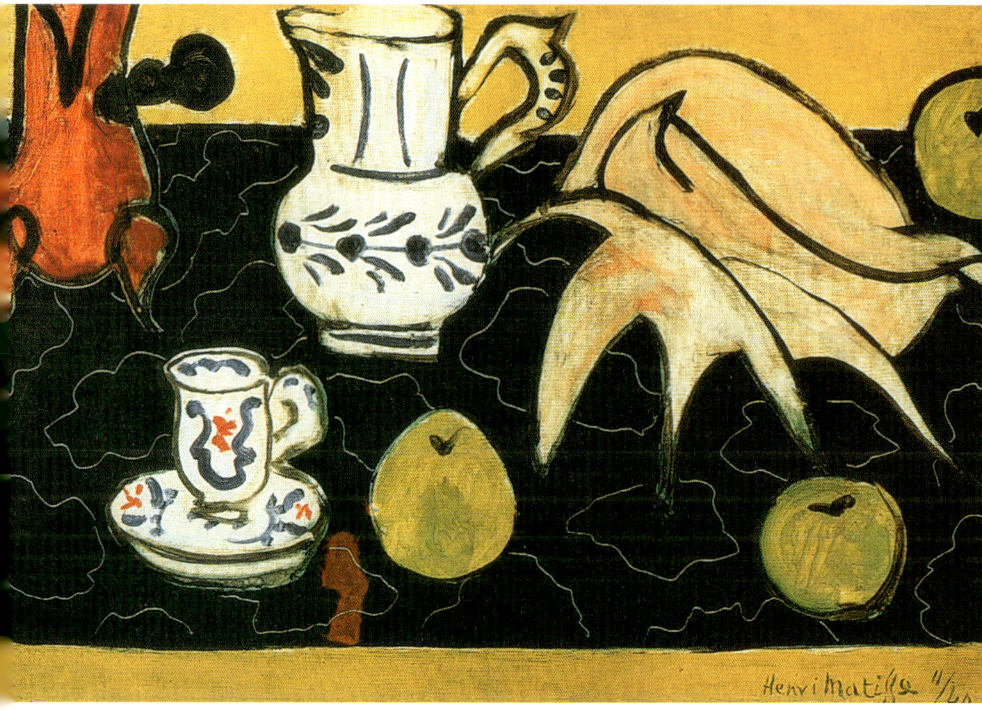
Henri Matisse 11/40

Index